TWO YEARS IN A
GULAG

TWO YEARS IN A GULAG

THE TRUE WARTIME STORY OF A POLISH PEASANT EXILED TO SIBERIA

FRANK PLESZAK

AMBERLEY

Dedicated to the Pleszak family

especially my children Oscar, Henry, and Rose

but particularly to my son Owain, who was never to see the completed work

Front cover: Photograph of a mountain gulag camp in winter by Sergey Melnikoff.

First published 2013

Amberley Publishing
The Hill, Stroud
Gloucestershire, GL5 4EP

www.amberley-books.com

British Library Cataloguing in Publication Data.
A catalogue record for this book is available from the British Library.

ISBN 978 1 4456 0177 9

Typeset in 10pt on 12pt Celeste Pro.
Typesetting and Origination by Amberley Publishing.
Printed in the UK.

CONTENTS

ACKNOWLEDGEMENTS

I would like to make special acknowledgements to:

The MOD Polish Enquiries section for providing all my father's military records, unclaimed medals, and especially his original gulag release document.

The Polish Institute and Sikorski Museum in London, the Hoover Institution Archives at Stanford University in California, and Memorial in Russia for all their assistance and information.

The internet and the hundreds of fantastic relevant websites.

But I would especially like to thank the members of the Kresy-Siberia group, without whose discussion, suggestions and help this book could never have been attempted and the following for permission to use extracts of their own works:

Azerbaijan International Magazine
The Kowalski family
Romuald Lipinski
Ministry for Culture and Heritage, New Zealand
The Rossi family
The Skulski family
The keepers of the Swirsky family archives
The Topolski family

FOREWORD

From Vilnius to Manchester via Siberia, Italy, and the Second World War

18 May marks the anniversary of the victory of the famous battle at the monastery of Monte Cassino in Southern Italy in 1944. This highly significant battle, one of the most important Allied victories of the war, had by then been raging for nearly six months. Its capture from the German Army had required four separate bloody battles involving Allied soldiers from Britain, America, Poland, France, New Zealand and India. Sadly however, its success and significance were largely overshadowed early the following month by the D-Day landings in Normandy, which signalled the beginning of the end of the Second World War.

For the Poles, members of the celebrated Polish 2nd Corps having led the final successful assault and capture of Monte Cassino, it represented the pinnacle of their wartime achievements. How proud it was for them in the eyes of the world to raise the red-and-white Polish flag above the ruins of the captured monastery. For most of the Polish soldiers who participated there it was their first combat involvement since their homeland was invaded by Germany nearly five years earlier on the first day of September in 1939.

But who were these Polish soldiers at Monte Cassino, why were they there in Southern Italy, where had they come from, how had they arrived there, and why could they even be bothered fighting at all? One of them, Mikołaj Pleszak, was my father.

Even before the victory at Monte Cassino, the Allies who had gone to war in Poland's defence had abandoned it to the desires and demands of the Soviet Union. For most of the disillusioned Polish soldiers there was no recognisable country of their own left that they felt able to accept. They knew that they could never return to their homes, and so it was for my father – he was never to see the family he left behind ever again.

For him the Battle of Monte Cassino was just the next phase in a long battle that had started in late 1939 at the start of the war when he was arrested and deported, not by German but advancing Russian troops. His was a battle just to stay alive, first in prisons, then in cramped cattle trucks, then in 'slave ships', then in hard labour gulags, and then in a desperate attempt to find a Polish Army he knew was being formed, but didn't know where. He survived all this to eventually take part in the Battle of Monte Cassino and several other battles against the German Army. Though he lived to the age of seventy-four he never saw a truly free Poland, nor was he ever able to return to his homeland.

My father, together with nearly 50,000 other poles, was decorated for his part in this famous battle. He had told me that he had been there, but little else of his early life. I could barely imagine the enormity of the journey, the horrors, or the personal sacrifices he had to make in order just to be a part of it. It was only with the advent of the internet and the thawing of relationships with Eastern Europe as the old Soviet Empire finally came to an end that details of what he and millions like him had been made to endure began to emerge.

Since his death in 1994, I have been tracing his background and have uncovered a story of a forced journey in hell in cattle trucks, slave ships, and on foot of over 40,000 km from his family home in a small village near modern-day Vilnius to a Russian gulag in Arctic Siberia, only eventually escaping Russia in a frantic mass-exodus across the Caspian Sea to Iran. So harrowing were some of the accounts I read during my research that I had nightmares which severely affected my sleep.

My father's story is just one of millions of similar but personal experiences, all individual, unique, and tragic. These occurred during a largely unknown and poorly documented period of modern history that has been denied by successive Russian governments and largely ignored by Western governments and media. With continued global interest in the Second World War this is, I believe, an interesting, informative, entertaining, and enlightening story of modern history.

He, along with more than 2 million Poles, had been deported by the Soviet Union at the start of the Second World War to labour camps across Russia. He was sent from his home in north-east Poland, near to the modern city of Vilnius, to a hard labour gulag in the far east of Siberia almost 15,000 km away, a sentence that usually meant death. He received an amnesty when Germany invaded Russia and on his release he travelled back to near Moscow in an attempt to join the Polish Army. He then moved on through Kazakhstan, Uzbekistan, Turkmenistan, Iran, Iraq, Jordan, Palestine, Egypt, and eventually to Italy, where he fought in battles against the German Army before finally settling for the rest of his life in Manchester, England.

He was never able to return to his home in Poland and was forbidden to have any contact with his relatives. He was just one of hundreds of thousands of Poles 'lucky' enough to complete this enforced journey; millions more never made it, either dying en route or remaining in the Soviet Union.

I attempt to recreate his journey, one which he couldn't even contemplate appreciating; one that only meant misery and suffering of the highest order. But it took him across three continents and back, through more than twelve time-zones, through magnificent scenery, fantastic cities, towns, and villages, through cultures so wide and varied, from climates of extreme cold to unbelievable heat, through forests and steppes, along lakes and rivers, across seas and mountains, through taiga and tundra, and from frozen seas to deserts.

So this is my father's story, which I describe in words and pictures, one that he never told me in full, one of which I was only allowed scraps of information, at times when he felt he could bear the sad and painful memories and bring himself to remember. I have used his memories, and with testimonies of others who similarly suffered, together with information gained from years of painstaking, slow research to paint a graphic picture of his unspeakable epic and added to it a personal view of some of the places he passed through, many of which most of us would never even have had heard of, in order to show the diversity of culture, climate and geography of the ever-changing places along the way.

In order to achieve the aims of this book, I have – hopefully not too dispassionately – described his journey and the hardships he had to endure in a purely documentary fashion. There is no way that I, brought up in a society where the worst horror we face on a regular basis is a trip to the dentist, can describe, understand, or even begin to appreciate the horrors that my father and his fellow deportees suffered on a daily basis for more than six long years, let alone try to describe his thoughts and feelings.

It is not my intention to be judgemental, to debate the politics of the whys and wherefores, or to apportion any blame or guilt to any individuals or regimes. I know the whole subject surrounding these Polish deportations is invidious and it still sets off highly charged emotions, but I have set out from the beginning to describe his journey in the context of that time and contrast his bleak, miserable time with the reality of the splendour, colour, and variety of all the places he passed through but could never enjoy.

So on 18 May I'm sure that across the world, as well as in the huge Polish cemetery at Monte Cassino that dominates the landscape, many a tear will be shed in remembrance of the gallantry and bravery that the Battle of Monte Cassino signifies. But for those Poles still surviving this period and their relatives, the Battle of Monte Cassino, however important and significant, is but a small piece of a very large jigsaw that is the Polish diaspora.

For my father, like General Anders – arguably the saviour of the exiled Poles – and millions of other Poles worldwide, the fight to see a free Poland has never been won. Both Anders and my father died in exile in England, never returning to see the country of their birth. The Poland that they knew and fought so long and hard for would never return. Even now, with Poland fully integrated into the European Union, the pre-war Polish Kresy region, the place of my father's birth, lost to the Russians in September 1939, remains part of Belarus and Ukraine.

MIKOŁAJ WINCENTY PLESZAK

My father Mikołaj ('Michael') Wincenty Pleszak was a quiet and unassuming man. He could be stern, sometimes comical, and I'm told he spoke with a thick Polish accent; I didn't notice it, to me it was normal. He was never outspoken or confrontational. I never really heard him say a bad word about anybody.

He wasn't particularly dynamic, or ever a high-flyer in any way. He was always employed in fairly low-paid manual jobs, an archetypal blue-collar worker.

Though I lived with him for a good proportion of the thirty-six years we spent on this earth together, I realise now that that I didn't really know much about him, or really how he came to be in England.

Being raised in England in a typical northern suburban environment with a Polish father, I was aware of the Polish community in Britain, but never really thought about it or why it was so big. I knew that there had been some immigration of Poles to England prior to the war, and a large resettlement of Poles after the war, but didn't really know why.

In researching and writing this book I've discovered an almost unknown forced mass-movement of a nation of almost biblical proportions. My dad was a small part of it, and I owe my comfortable upbringing and lifestyle to it.

Mikołaj Wincenty Pleszak
Born Petrograd (St Petersburg), Russia, 1920
Died Glossop, Derbyshire, England, 1994

1

EARLY DAYS

A Short History of Poland and the Pleszaks

Although the history of Poland is well documented, I think it's worth reminding ourselves of a few very brief facts in order to begin my father's story.

Poland (Polska)

Poland is situated between the Baltic Sea and the Carpathian Mountains in the plains of Central Europe. Its central location, situated between the great powers of the East and West, has directly contributed to its turbulent history.

Though there are records of pre-Slavonic and Slavonic tribes dating back to the fifteenth century BC, the documented history of Poland really begins in the tenth century AD with the Piast dynasty of a pagan tribe called the Palonie (from where the name Poland originates). The Palonie unified the surrounding tribes in the region that is now Poznan in Central Europe. They were, however, under constant threat of incursion from the Christian Germans to the west. In order to appease them, the Palonie relinquished their pagan beliefs and successfully converted to Christianity.

This conversion was achieved with the help of the Czechs, whose religious beliefs were derived, like that of the Germans, from the head of the Catholic Church in Rome – the Pope – and thus aligned theologically with Western Europe. In contrast, their neighbour and contemporary Vladimir the Great of Kiev, being impressed by the Byzantine Church, accepted Christianity from those acting under the authority of the Patriarch of Constantinople, the Eastern Orthodox Church, whose image of the Virgin Mary, like that given as a present to Vladimir himself, is still today a very powerful image in all forms of the Eastern Orthodox Church.

The consequences of this theological divide between the ecclesiastical allegiances of Poland and the countries to its east have continued to be a factor in Polish history ever since.

This Piast dynasty was to rule over Poland for more than three centuries, during which time the Palonie offered sanctuary to the Jews, who were being persecuted across Europe. So many accepted that at one point three quarters of all the Jews in the world were living peacefully in Poland.

From the eleventh century to the fifteenth, though there were periods of uncertainty and minor conflicts, Poland prospered into a significant European power. In the eleventh century Poland became a kingdom centred on the capital of Krakow.

The sixteenth century is generally considered to be a time of greatness for Poland, but it saw the last of its hereditary kings, with the nobility essentially deciding who should rule. The seventeenth century saw Poland in almost constant conflict with wars against Ukraine, Russia, and Sweden. A war with Russia left Poland devastated, with a large proportion of the population killed.

The eighteenth century brought about a period of decline both militarily and politically for Poland, largely due to a continuing threat from Russia to the east. Eventually, Poland suffered invasion from Prussia, Austria, and Russia. It was partitioned in 1772, again in 1793, and was permanently partitioned in the Third Partition of 1795. Throughout the nineteenth century Poland ceased to exist as a sovereign country, though Napoleon Bonaparte briefly reinstated Poland as the Duchy of Warsaw in 1813.

The First World War at the beginning of the twentieth century turned out to be a disaster for the empires that had divided Poland. Germany conquered the Russian-held parts of Poland and to court the favour of the Poles promised to form a Polish kingdom after the war. When the war ended in 1918, the Poles took charge of their country and expelled the defeated Germans. After 123 years the Polish nation was again reinstated.

The successful Allies decided that the new Polish Second Republic should have its own access to the Baltic Sea and so allocated a strip of land known as the Polish Corridor, which cut through Germany, severing the German lands of East Prussia off from the rest of Germany. This was to leave Poland in a vulnerable position with Germany, who were not only sore at losing this land, but had also become separated from one of their own significant power bases.

The new Polish Republic was soon in conflict, having bloody border disputes with Czechoslovakia in 1919 and Russia from 1919–21. The old adversaries of both Germany and Russia continued to be a threat throughout the 1930s.

At the same time, following the collapse of the Russian Empire, a Belarusian democratic republic was proclaimed in March of 1918, in the northern region of Poland. This republic was soon crushed by the Russian Bolsheviks, who proclaimed it a Soviet republic in January of 1919. Poland, determined to re-establish its historical boundaries, also invaded the country. The result of this clash was that Poland received the western part of Belarus under the terms of the Treaty of Riga, signed in 1921, and the remaining land became a constituent republic of the USSR in 1922.

Kresy Wschodnie, the eastern borderlands of Poland, is where my ancestors originated from. The area was to the east of the Curzon Line, a demarcation line proposed in 1920 by British Foreign Secretary Lord Curzon of Kedleston as a possible armistice line between Poland to the west and the Russian Soviet Federative Socialist Republic (Russian SFSR) to the east.

Because the Russian Empire had collapsed into a state of civil war following the Russian Revolution of 1917, there was no recognised Russian government with whom the eastern border of Poland could be negotiated. However, one of the first acts of the new Russian government was to publicly denounce the treaties which had partitioned Poland, leaving Poland in legal possession of the territories that it (Poland) had held before the Partitions of Poland in 1772.

These were lands settled by the ex-servicemen who had fought for Poland during the First World War and against the Bolshevik armies. They were given the land by the newly established Polish state, and they settled those areas and made a life for themselves and their families. Their initial years were hard, as the land that most of them received was scarred with shell-holes, trenches and other reminders of war. As time went on, life became more stable and seemed considerably easier.

It was during this turbulent period of Polish history that my ancestors lived. I know very little of my ancestors. The oldest relative I have any knowledge of is my grandfather Wincenty Pleszak, and I know too little about him. I do know he was born in 1890, in the village of Szwakszty like his father before him, which was about 500 km north-east of Warsaw, and about 50 km north-east of the major Polish town in the region Wilno (now known as Vilnius and the capital city of Lithuania).

Szwakszty

During their time there had been no Poland; Szwakszty was part of Tsarist-controlled Russia. It was (and still is) a very small rural farming village comprised of a few simple wooden houses. It is located between the three large lakes of Narocz, Miadziol, and Great Szwakszta. It is closest to Great Szwakszta, from where the village gets its name. The nearest town, Kobylnik, was 3 km away, about half-way to the huge Lake Narocz. At that time Kobylnik, though small relatively speaking, was the most significant town in the area.

Szwakszty is located in a low-lying, heavily wooded area surrounded by the forests of Terazdwor, Uzlo, the ancient woodlands of Dunilowicze, and the marshes of Czysciec. The area supported lots of farmsteads and subsistence agricultural villages that made their living from the poor pastures of Syrm.

Despite being located in the area of the short-lived Belarusian Democratic Republic, and having been a part of the Tsarist Russian Empire, Szwakszty was totally Polish in ethnicity. Here, unlike in some of the local villages and towns, there were no Byelorussians, Lithuanians, Ukrainians, or Tatars. Though in the local towns and villages there were at that time significant numbers of both Jews and Orthodox Christians, the Pleszak family were, as were the majority of the village of Szwakszty, Roman Catholics.

Nearly all the inhabitants in Szwakszty lived from the land, cultivating food crops and flax, raising cows, sheep, chickens, and pigs, collecting fruit, berries, and mushrooms from the surrounding dense forests and fishing in the numerous nearby lakes and rivers.

My grandfather Wincenty Pleszak lived with his parents in a typical village house, single-story, with a larder, cooking area and a large room used for everything else. Even though there was lots of water around, they were lucky enough to have a well next to the house. He had helped his father build the house and it was completed around about 1900.

Kobylnik

Kobylnik, like nearby Szwakszty, lies on a hilly neck of land between the three lakes of Great Szwakszta, Narocz, and Miadziol. It was first recorded in 1434 and was originally known as Minori Medalo (Little Myadel) after the nearby town of Myadel (it was separated into the

Old 'Stary' and New 'Nowy'). By the late nineteenth century it had developed into one of the most significant small towns of the region. At this time it had a population of around 1,200 people of which about half were Jews. It was a multicultural town, being the home to Poles, Belarussians, Ukrainians, some Tatars, and Russians. It supported Roman Catholics, Orthodox Christians, and Jews. Sadly, like in most of Russia, Jews were victimised and by the first part of the twentieth century many Jewish families had emigrated away from the *shtetl* of Kobylnik, mainly to America.

Despite being what could be described as a poor peasant community, as the community of Kobylnik grew, the number of houses and enterprises also grew and developed. People made their living from farming and fishing, shops opened, with shoemakers, tailors, blacksmiths, tinsmiths and there were stores that sold fish, furs, and agricultural products. There was also a small village Peoples' College, post office, and a silver fox-fur farm. Even a contemporary home for the elderly was created by the local residents. The local community bathhouses (*banya*) were attended on Fridays.

Most of the inhabitants were relatively poor; the town had neither electricity nor a central water supply system. Water was obtained from nearby wells, and the sanitary conditions were primitive. Though many families lived below the poverty line, most were able to own a horse and a few families managed to own a cow.

In the town centre was a market square and every Tuesday there was a small-scale market where traders from around the region traded their goods like furs, livestock, eggs, poultry, mushrooms and berries, and sold hides, tar for carriages, haberdasheries, footwear and fabrics, etc.

Kobylnik, being near to the richly stocked Lake Naroch, was also a centre of fish production. Fish caught there, apart from being sold locally, were also sold as far afield as Wilno, Warsaw, and Lodz.

Wilno (Vilnius), the main city of the region, was connected with the large town of Postavy by a stone-covered road which passed through Kobylnik. Initially it took five days by cart or sled to travel to Wilno and back from Kobylnik, but in the 1930s a motor bus service became available, travelling the route once a day.

All children from the nearby villages attended Polish schools but there was also a Jewish school, where children learned the ancient Jewish language, Hebrew, and the Bible. A primitive library was also created in the town. Kobylnik boasted three churches. In the centre of town was the Andreevsky Catholic church. It was a huge, red-brick neo-Gothic structure built in 1904 on the site of an earlier wooden church that had been built in 1463 but destroyed by fire in 1897.

The original bell tower, the central section of the original church, was saved and used as the entry portal to the grounds of the newer church.

Bordering the marketplace was the Russian Orthodox church of Ilinskaya, a stone construction built in the 1850s. There was also a synagogue near to the Catholic church.

Lake Narocz (Naroch in Russian)

Lake Naroch is the largest lake in what is now land-locked Belarus, a country with over 10,000 lakes. It belongs to the system of the River Wilija, a tributary of the River Neman, which flows to the Baltic Sea. It is in fact the largest of three nearly connected lakes. Narocz has a surface area of about 40 square km. Lake Miastro is smaller, only 10 square km, and Batoryno, at 8 square km, is the smallest of the three.

Lake Naroch itself measures about 11 km by 9 km at its longest and widest points. It drains at the south-eastern end into the small River Naroch (Naroczanka), which flows south, receiving water from another stream from Lake Viszniev at a village also named Naroch, then flows west to join the River Wilija east of the town of Smorgon near the border with Lithuania. River Naroch is significant in itself; it was the boundary between Russia and the Polish Republic following the Second Partition of Poland.

The lake basin originates from the glacial action of the last Ice Age, and is bordered by the low slopes of the Sventsyanskaya range on its north and north-east sides and Narochano-Vilenskaya lowland on the southern side.

The shores of the lake are mostly of sand or shingle, the water unpolluted, especially clear and of excellent quality. It supports an abundance of wildlife, with more than twenty-five species of fish and rich diversity of bird life such as osprey (*Pandion haliaetus*), little tern (*Sterna albifrons*), little grebe (*Podiceps ruficollis*), and white stork (*Ciconia ciconia*).

The land surrounding the lake is heavily forested and rich in mushrooms (when in season their collection becomes a national pastime) and a variety of berries such as bilberry, wild strawberry, blueberry, cranberry, and cowberry. Though the forest is mostly of pine, oak, birch, spruce and juniper, other tree and bush species can also be seen. The forest is home to hedgehogs, hares, foxes, wild boar, roe deer and elk.

During the winter months the lake freezes solid, making the fleets of fishing boats and nets redundant. Fishing can only be achieved by cutting holes in the ice, but for the tough local fishermen it's considered a great sport, still greatly enjoyed to this day.

From a young age Wincenty, together with his father, worked on the land but in the summer of 1914 world events were to intervene. On 28 June the heir to the Austrian throne, Archduke Franz Ferdinand, was assassinated in the Serbian city of Sarajevo. The powerful Austro-Hungarian Empire wanted the killer extradited, but Serbia refused.

Even though the age of imperialism was coming to end, nationalism was running high and complex alliances had been created in order to maintain peace. Germany, Austria-Hungary and Italy collaborated to form the Triple Alliance whilst Britain, France, and Russia created their own alliance known as the Triple Entente.

Russia declared support for Serbia and ordered a mobilisation of its army; the Austrian, French and German mobilisation orders followed in quick succession, each triggered by the other in a domino effect. On 28 July Austria declared war on Serbia, Germany declared war on Russia on 1 August, followed by France on the 3rd. A day later, on 4 August, Britain declared war on Germany. The First World War had begun. By late summer of 1914 the war was raging in both the east and the west of Europe.

It wasn't long before Wincenty, like most of the young men in the area, was called into the service of the Tsarist Russian Army to fight against the Kaiser's German Army on the Russian Western Front.

I'm not sure of his movements with the Russian Army, or the role he played. I don't believe he took part in the initial battles for East Prussia, but what is known is that after some training he was allocated to General Alexei Kuropatkin's Northern Army Group. He was eventually involved in the Riga Offensive, where the Russian Army was advancing on Riga and the German Eighth Army.

At the same time, about 150 kilometres further south, his hometown of Kobylnik was still occupied by the German Tenth Army.

The Battle of Lake Narocz, 1916

Following the Russian Army's initial success as they pushed westward towards Germany, they soon found themselves pinned back and retreating in front of a much more efficient and well-equipped German Army. By 1916 the battlefront had become established just to the east of Vilnius and the advancing German Army moved on towards Kobylnik.

It is known that there was some fighting and artillery action around the town, but there are no records of any damage either to the town or to the civilians that lived there. What is known is that during several of the skirmishes around Kobylnik, there were concerned reports from Kobylnik residents that the German Army had used gas. While it's not believed there were too many civilian casualties at Kobylnik, we know that in March 1916 the German Army occupied the town and, because of its developed amenities, established their regional headquarters there.

The most senior officer, who was to stay there until the end of the war in 1918, was Rittmeister Johannes Colsman of the Royal Prussian Ulanen-Regiment Großherzog Friedrich von Baden No. 7 unit of the German Army. During the German occupation his official title was Ortskommandant of the Staffelbezirk (military district) of Kobylnik in the Province of Wilna. He was an educated and respectful commander with a keen interest in social and cultural anthropology who showed a great interest in the local area and people. In the great tradition of the German Army he documented in letters and photographs his stay in Kobylnik.

Kobylnik was immediately turned into a garrison town. A town generator was installed, a soldiers' home was set up opposite the Catholic Church, and a cinema was even constructed in the marketplace. Some of the streets were renamed in German and they even constructed a narrow gauge railway from Wilno in order to bring munitions and German personnel to the front.

It's known that some of the male Kobylnik residents were used as labour for the German Army, but the Germans largely seemed to be respectful of the local inhabitants as they set up schools for the children of Kobylnik and at Christmas provided them with presents regardless of their religion. During the summer of 1917 there appears to have been an outbreak of typhus in one of the surrounding villages, which the German doctors were successful in suppressing.

The battles to the south and west of Kobylnik were fierce, and despite being better equipped, trained and more efficient than the Russian Army, the German Army still suffered many losses and injuries. Those that had been killed were buried in the Catholic graveyard on the outskirts of Kobylnik on the road towards Szwakszty, and several impressive gravestones, though largely neglected, remain to this day. Some of the wounded were treated in the Ilinskaya Orthodox church which had been pressed into service as a makeshift field hospital.

The local manor house became the place of residence for all senior officers. General Oskar von Hutier stayed there, as did Prince Leopold of Bavaria (Leopold Maximilian Joseph Maria Arnulf, Prinz von Bayern), the Supreme Commander of the German forces on the Eastern Front (Oberbefehlshaber Ost), and perhaps more interestingly so had his predecessor General Paul von Hindenburg (Paul Ludwig Hans Anton von Beneckendorff und von Hindenburg).

Hindenburg was later to become more important in Germany than the Kaiser himself, and eventually in 1925 became the second President of Germany. He was also the only candidate in the 1932 German election considered capable of defeating the upcoming Adolf Hitler. He narrowly won the election in a run-off but eventually, as we all know, ceded more and more political power to Hitler's Nazi Party.

Shortly after the German occupation of Kobylnik and at the height of the First World War, with French forces under heavy attack at the fortress town of Verdun, the French Commander-in-Chief Joseph Joffre appealed to his allies in early 1916 to launch offensive operations of their own in order to divert German resources and ease pressure on Verdun.

Russia responded quickly and identified an area of perceived weakness in the German line to the east of Vilnius. The plan was to assault it with a much larger force in the hope that they could break through and cause the Germans to relocate troops and resources from Verdun. Tsar Nicholas II and the Russian Chief of Staff, General Mikhail Alekseyev, planned an offensive at Lake Naroch itself, where 1.5 million Russian soldiers would face just 1 million combined German and Austro-Hungarian troops under the command of General Eichhorn and his German Tenth Army.

The Russian offensive, led by General Ragoza, temporary commander Second Army (part of General Alexei Evert's Western Army Group), started on 18 March 1916. It began with a two-day-long artillery bombardment (the longest yet seen on the Eastern Front) against the Germans, which for the most part failed to do the planned damage due to inaccuracy. Russian infantry troops from the northern and southern sectors then moved forward across no man's land in groups rather than spreading out against a heavily fortified German defence, suffering heavy casualties.

Due to the spring thaw, the ice on the lake was thin and it is believed thousands of men perished falling through the ice. In addition, many of the approaching infantrymen became bogged down in the thick mud, slowing the offensive. The lack of an effective supply system also hampered the Russians, and the battle raged on for almost a month. The foundering attack gained several kilometres of land in some places but made little impact on the overall German defences, or their troop allocations.

By the time artillery attacks were shut down on 14 April, the Germans had recovered the entirety of what little ground they had lost. Russian casualties numbered 110,000, while the Germans lost only 20,000. Both armies' casualty rates were increased by deaths due to exposure to the harsh northern weather; an estimated further 12,000 Russian soldiers alone died from frostbite.

Several huge war graves surround the lake itself, the largest being at Pronki on the western shore. The area around Lake Narocz still bears the scars of the terrible battles, though these are mostly now overgrown. Mieczyslaw Lisiewicz, in his book *Chronicles of Lake Narocz*, describes that when visiting the lake for a fishing trip just before the outbreak of the Second World War in late August 1939, 'his guide relates how skulls are drawn from the deeps by the nets – of the German or Russian dead from the war' and he 'tells of yachtsmen hearing the groans of the drowned Russians who fell through the ice on the lake in the 1916 Battle of Lake Narocz'.

The remnants of war have a more poignant memory for me though. One of my cousins, Alexei Ustinovich, the son of Maria, was killed as a young boy (in the 1960s) while playing with a grenade he found in the forest. It was clearly unstable and detonated, killing him instantly. Though it was more than likely a device from the Second World War, it may have originated from the Great War!

Following the Russian debacle at the Battle of Lake Naroch, and before its ultimate deadly conclusion, Kuropatkin's Northern Army Group were pressed into taking Riga from the Germans. This, too, sadly turned out to be a disaster and they were beaten back within a day, with the loss of 10,000 men and many more injured.

One of the casualties of the fighting during this campaign on the River Dvina near to the city of Dvinsk (now known as Daugavpils in Latvia) was my grandfather Wincenty Pleszak. He received a single gunshot wound to the throat. It must have been considered to be serious but recoverable, as he was evacuated eventually to St Petersburg, then called Petrograd, at that time the capital of Russia. We believe he was in hospital for some time and he was to spend the rest of his life breathing by means of a silver tube grafted onto his throat.

After his active army days were over he found work in Petrograd on the railways. It was here that he met my grandmother Aleksandra Palinowska, a Lithuanian, born in the city of Radviliškis. She had arrived in Petrograd some time earlier to work as a nanny for wealthy relatives who were resident there.

The period 1917 to 1920, however, was not for most people the best time to be in Petrograd, because of the start of the Russian Civil War, and for Poles in particular (like my grandparents), as the newly formed Polish Republic was in conflict with its previous occupiers, the Russians.

The Bolshevik Revolution, also known as the October Revolution, is traditionally dated to 24 October 1917. The October Revolution however, was the second phase of the overall Russian Revolution of 1917, after the February Revolution of the same year. The October Revolution overthrew the Russian provisional government and gave the power to Bolsheviks. It was followed by the Russian Civil War (1917–22) and by the creation of the Soviet Union in 1922.

As the Germans advanced on Petrograd (St Petersburg) in 1918, the new Russian leader Vladimir Ilyich Ulyanov (Влади́мир Ильи́ч Улья́нов), better known as Lenin (Ле́нин), reinstated Moscow as to the capital city for the first time since 1712 in order to prevent the capital city falling into German hands.

Historical note about the name St Petersburg
Founded by Tsar Peter the Great in 1703, it succeeded Moscow as the capital of the Russian Empire. It was renamed Petrograd in 1914 during the First World War because it was

decided that St Petersburg sounded too Germanic. It was then renamed Leningrad in 1924 following the death of Lenin but returned to the name of St Petersburg by a popular vote in 1991 following the collapse of the Soviet Union

Following the start of the Russian Civil War and despite the First World War having ended, not surprisingly life became harder and harder for my grandparents in Petrograd. By late 1919 Aleksandra was also pregnant.

Their first born, my father Mikołaj (Nicholas in English), was born in Petrograd on 15 April 1920. But their stay there was nearly over. I don't know by what route or by which means, but by late 1920 or early 1921, Wincenty, Aleksandra and Mikołaj Pleszak had arrived back in the village of my grandfather's birth, Szwakszty, living in the house that he had lived in with his father and tending the same 5 hectares of land he had before the war.

Mikołaj was soon joined by brothers Bolesław (William), known as Bolek, Franciszek (Frank), and sisters Honorata, Małgorzata (Margaret) and Maria. To his family my father was known as Kolya (the Russian diminutive of Nicholai).

Life in the 1920s and 1930s, like for all poor peasant communities, was hard. Sadly Malgorzata was to die before she was ten years old in a tragic accident involving a fire, and several children from Szwakszty and the surrounding villages died from whooping cough. But when my father did speak of his time in Szwakszty, he did so with affection and never grumbled or complained about it.

He talked of long, hot summers and bitterly cold winters which lasted from November to March. February he remembered as being typically very stormy with many blizzards. The local farmers would take it in turn to transport people around in a horse-drawn sled, while the children had to clear snow. During the winters, sheepskin or wool/felt coats and boots or overshoes were worn.

His childhood was of a strict Roman Catholic upbringing. The Polish school that he attended in Kobylnik was religion-based and all traditional Catholic religious festivals were respected. There were, however, no presents at Christmas or birthdays and no chocolate eggs for Easter, but food and drink, particularly vodka, was always plentiful. During Lent no meat was eaten, and during the service for Ash Wednesday the priest sprinkled ash on everybody's heads.

He also celebrated what he described as the 'Festival of the Thunderstorm' on 2 February. During this festival, holy water was taken home from the church and sprinkled around the houses to protect them from thunderstorms. I suspect this was a local interpretation of Candlemas, traditionally the mid-point of winter, on which the weather was supposed to act inversely as an indicator for the remainder of the winter. So, good weather at Candlemas was supposed to indicate more bad weather to come, whilst bad weather at Candlemas indicated that the worst of the winter weather was over. Maybe my father got it wrong; the sprinkling of the holy water might have been to attract thunderstorms and bad weather for the day rather than protecting from them?

On Saturdays there was usually a village party known locally as a Sobotka and Sundays were always celebrated by an eleven o'clock mass at Andreevsky Church, followed by merrymaking, card playing, sport, dancing, and drinking until about midnight. Music was supplied by those villagers that could play instruments like the clarinet, accordion, and fiddle. None of the Pleszaks played any (a legacy that exists today). Vacations and days out were unheard of.

My father attended school until he was fourteen years old. When not at school he would work on the land, helping with his bothers to cultivate the smallholding of oats, wheat, barley, flax and potatoes and tend the few sheep and cows they could afford. As the family grew in number and age Wincenty, with the help of a small army pension, rented a further 5 hectares of land together with 10 hectares of woodland, which was used for timber and firewood and for collecting mushrooms, wild pork and berries. In the winter, during snowy periods, despite the region being uniformly flat the children would travel around (including going to school) on hand-made wooden skis.

As my father was the eldest he helped his mother with the cooking. Despite being poor, food was plentiful, their small holding providing them enough for their needs. Potatoes were cooked into a wide variety of tasty dishes, gherkins and cabbage were pickled, and fish (my father especially talked about catching pike) caught in the nearby lakes and rivers were smoked or pickled.

The Pleszak home was a typical small, single-story wooden house, the one main room being separated by curtains. All the children slept in a single room. Nobody knew anybody that had their own bedroom. There was no electricity, and water came from a well in the garden.

My grandmother would weave wool from the sheep and also use the wool to produce felt. In addition to the food crops, flax was also cultivated. This would be used to create linen, which was laid out in the fields and (in a primitive form of retting) covered with water. The linen would be left to dry in the sun for about four days until bleached white and ready for weaving into linen, which was done on the village communal loom and spinning wheel.

Flax

Flax (*Linum usitatissimum*), also known as linseed, is a cool temperate annual herb plant. It has erect slender stems branching only at the apex. It is an attractive plant with greyish-green leaves and bright-blue (sometimes white) flowers. It grows to around 80–120 cm tall.

It is cultivated for fibre production from the stalks and for a vegetable oil known as linseed oil or flaxseed oil from its seeds.

It is one of the oldest commercial oils and solvent-processed flax seed oil has been used for centuries as a drying oil in painting and varnishing.

Flax fibre is extracted from the bast or skin of the stem of flax plant. It is soft, lustrous and flexible. It is stronger than cotton fibre but less elastic. The best grades are used for linen fabrics such as damasks, lace and sheeting. Coarser grades are used for the manufacturing of twine and rope. Flax fibre is also a raw material for the high-quality paper industry for the use of printed banknotes and rolling paper for cigarettes.

Before the flax fibres can be spun into linen, they must be separated from the rest of the stalk. The first step in this process is called 'retting', which is the process of rotting away the inner stalk, leaving the outer fibres intact. At this point there is still straw, or coarse fibres, remaining. To remove these the flax is 'broken' into small, short bits, while the actual fibre is left unharmed, then 'scutched', where the straw is scraped away from the fibre and then pulled through 'hackles', which act like combs and comb the straw out of the fibre.

There are several methods of retting flax. It can be retted in a pond, stream, field or a container. When the retting is complete the bundles of flax feel soft and slimy, and quite a few fibres are standing out from the stalks. When wrapped around a finger, the inner woody part springs away from the fibres.

Pond retting is the fastest. It consists of placing the flax in a pool of water which will not evaporate. It generally takes place in a shallow pool, which will warm up dramatically in the sun; the process may take from only a couple days to a couple weeks. Pond-retted flax is traditionally considered lower quality, possibly because the product can become dirty, and easily over-retts, damaging the fibre. This form of retting also produces quite an odour.

When there was time, children of Szwakszty played sports and enjoyed the forests and lakes. Having said that, my father, who lived near two huge lakes that he regularly visited, never learnt to swim. He also told me that as a child he had climbed a tall tree and fell from near to the top, which was to make him fearful of heights for the rest of his life.

Following local traditions Wincenty chose the profession that my father was to follow. It was decided that he was to be a tailor, and so he was apprenticed to a local tailor in nearby Kobylnik for which Wincenty had to pay for the privilege. As his tailoring abilities developed he was obliged to move in with his mentor, but he still received food and clothing from his own family. My auntie Maria was usually sent to deliver his food. She recalled (crying as she told me) that when she used to arrive the other apprentices would taunt her and make fun of her, but my father was very kind and supportive of her, protecting her and ensuring she was always safe. During his apprenticeship as a tailor he may have also spent some time in the nearby city of Postavy.

So that was my father's early days; not idyllic, quite harsh, and probably very strict but I suspect typical of north-eastern Poland before the Second World War.

2

1939: TWO INVASIONS

The Start of the Second World War

Poland, though having only just regained its independence after nearly 125 years of Russian rule, must have watched nervously over its borders to the west throughout the 1920s and 30s. The post-First World War new world order in Europe was developing and must have looked ominous.

The First World War had ended on 11 November 1918. Though this allowed the re-emergence of Poland as a sovereign state for the first time since the Third Partition of 1795, many of the disputes that had led to the war remained unsettled.

Germany, bloodied and defeated, hadn't actually surrendered. The start of American involvement in 1917 on the side of the Allies had tipped the balance of power against Germany and the German High Command realised that a victory was not possible and sought a mutual end to the fighting – an armistice. So at 11 a.m. on 11 November 1918 – the eleventh hour of the eleventh day of the eleventh month – a ceasefire came into effect, signed in a rail road carriage in the forest at Compiègne near Paris. Germany's fate was finally decided six months later with the Treaty of Versailles. Representing the new Polish state was Józef Piłsudski.

Józef Klemens Piłsudski

Piłsudski was born in the village of Zalavas to the north of Wilno in Russia in 1867. While studying medicine at the University of Kharkov he became a socialist and joined the People's Will organisation. In 1887 he was arrested and exiled to Siberia by the Tsarist authorities on a false charge of plotting with Wilno socialists to assassinate the Russian Tsar Alexander III.

On his release in 1892 he joined the Polish Socialist Party (Polska Partia Socjalistyczna – PPS) and edited the left-wing, underground newspaper called *Robotnik* (The Worker), which promoted socialism and Polish nationalism. The paper was suppressed in 1900 and Piłsudski was again arrested.

After escaping he formed a PPS military unit that carried out bank raids and assassinated members of the Tsarist police. In 1908, his gang stole 200,000 roubles from a mail train and used the money to build up a new revolutionary army which he hoped would enable Poland to fight for its independence from Russia.

During the First World War Piłsudski and about 10,000 of his men fought with the Austrians against the Russian Army. After the Russian Revolution and Russia's withdrawal from the war (the Treaty of Brest-Litovsk) his loyalty was brought into question and he was arrested and imprisoned in Magdeburg in Germany in 1917.

He was released on 8 November 1918 and upon the Armistice of 11 November he was appointed Commander-in-Chief of Polish Forces by the Regency Council (a temporary body established during the First World War as the highest Polish political authority on Polish-occupied land) and entrusted with creating a national government for the newly independent country. On that date, now known as Poland's Independence Day, he proclaimed an independent Polish state for the first time since 1795.

The new Polish nation was soon in conflict and Piłsudski presided over military actions against the Ukraine in 1918 and successfully defended Poland against the Russian Army between 1919 and 1920. During the Russian Civil War his army made considerable gains and the Soviet-Polish Treaty of Riga (1921) left Poland in control of substantial areas of Lithuania, Byelorussia and the Ukraine.

Piłsudski remained in charge of the army until 1923 when he retired. It wasn't to last long; in May 1926 he staged a military coup and for the next nine years he was virtually the dictator of Poland. Though leading the reborn Poland, he remained aloof and isolated, even to the point of eating alone in inexpensive restaurants. He died a Polish hero in 1935.

At the end of the First World War, the Allies agreed that an independent Polish state should be created from those territories that had been previously part of the Russian Empire, the Austro-Hungarian Empire, and Germany. The eastern border region (Kresy Wschodnie or known as just Kresy), would be available to a mixed population of Poles, Lithuanians, Ukrainians and Belarussians, with no group being in a majority.

The Eastern demarcation of Poland was drawn up by British Foreign Secretary Lord Curzon of Kedleston, and hence known as the Curzon Line. He suggested a border to the east of Warsaw running from Hrodna in the north through Brest-Litovsk to Lwów (Lviv) in the south. Initially the Curzon Line included Lwów with Poland, but a later version (Curzon 'B') showed Lwów outside Poland, and this confusion was to be a matter of some debate after the Second World War when the spoils of war were being carved up.

After the successful Polish border conflict with Russia (1919–20) a large part of the land that had been under Russian control situated to the east of the Curzon Line was incorporated into Poland. But as the Russian Empire had collapsed into civil war following the Russian Revolution of 1917, there was no recognised Russian government with whom the eastern border of Poland could be negotiated. It is significant and not surprising then that one of the first acts of the new Russian government was to denounce publicly the treaties which had allowed for the creation of Poland. The loss of this land must have been a bitter pill to swallow.

The Kresy region was also settled by the ex-servicemen who had fought for Poland during the First World War and against the Bolshevik armies in 1920. They were given land, known as Osady, by the newly established Polish state, with the intention they could be quickly redeployed into military service in the event of invasion from the east. Though their initial years were hard, the land that most of them received being scarred with shell-holes, trenches, and other debris of war, they soon turned their battle-weary land to good use and an uneasy peace ensued.

Having said that, the potential threat from Russia was never underestimated. In 1924 the Korpus Ochrony Pogranicza, KOP (Border Protection Corps) was created. This was a Polish military unit created specifically for defence of the eastern border against armed Soviet raids and local bandits. Although the unit was part of the Polish Army, it was commanded directly by the Ministry of Internal Affairs rather than the Ministry of National Defence. It was composed of elite soldiers from all parts of the country. Initially the KOP consisted of six brigades and five regiments, each of them guarding part of the eastern border with Soviet Russia in order to combat any threats to national security.

Although a peace treaty with Russia had been signed, the Kresy region of Poland was considered to be insecure. Armed bands of saboteurs crossed the border from the east on a daily basis and the police forces in the area were having trouble coping with the problem. In 1924, for example, the town of Stolpce, located 20 km from the border was seized by Soviet saboteurs and pillaged. Though the First World War was over, the peace seemed, for Poland at least, uncertain.

Following the Treaty of Versailles, the German people harboured significant resentment for the other countries that had been deemed to have won the war. In the first instance they (the Germans) hadn't been invited to attend and therefore had no part in the discussion of the direction the new Europe would take. Furthermore, Germany was forced to agree to the terms of the treaty regardless of whether its people liked them or not.

Of the 440 provisions in the treaty, the most important and controversial required Germany and its allies to accept full responsibility for causing the war, and under the terms of articles 231–248 disarm, make substantial territorial concessions, and pay reparations (essentially a fine) to the countries that had formed the Allies for the damage inflicted across Europe.

It also led to the formalisation of the League of Nations, which it was hoped would act as a multinational world policing body achieved through collective security. It was, however, limited from the outset because its membership initially neither included America nor the USSR, who were already at that time world superpowers.

Even before meeting in Versailles, the leaders of Britain, France, and the United States had made clear their differing expectations of the peace conference. Britain wanted a relatively strong, economically viable Germany to act as a counterweight to French and Russian dominance in Central Europe, France had wanted Germany to be punished, and the United States wanted a European peace as quickly as possible, with financial compensation for its military expenditures.

So when the treaty was implemented, it was done with a certain amount of reticence, and it didn't take long before it became obvious that the terms of the treaty were too harsh on Germany. The demilitarisation of the Rhineland (Germany's borders with France and Belgium) left Germany feeling vulnerable and defenceless, the concessions of land caused feelings of separation, anguish and disunity of the German speaking peoples, and the reparations were clearly untenable as Germany's own economy had also been severely damaged during the war, leaving them in a position of being unable to pay.

Before the First World War Germany had been a prosperous country, with a gold-backed currency, expanding industry, and world leadership in optics, chemicals, and machinery. By 1923 it was struggling with the burdens placed upon it by the victorious Allies. In a short-sighted and perhaps misguided move they decided to produce more money in order to meet the reparation payments demanded of them. Hyperinflation ensued, which saw the German mark increase from about 4 to the US dollar in 1914 to over 80 billion in 1923. It came as little surprise that they were unable to meet their second reparation payment required by the Treaty of Versailles.

In response, France, under their Prime Minister Raymond Poincaré, occupied the German Ruhr area on 11 January 1923. This region had coal mines and was the centre of steel production for the Germans, and as such was a major economic source for the fragile German economy. This occupation, fraught with strikes and public disorder, increased the burden on the German nation. It also cost the French the goodwill of the United States and the occupation helped to boost international sympathy for Germany.

Seeing a European catastrophe looming, a multinational commission led by the Americans was established to try and resolve the problems of Germany's inability to keep up with its reparation payments, headed by the American banker and politician (later to be the thirtieth Vice President of the United States), Charles Gates Dawes. The result of the commission was the 'Dawes Plan', for which Dawes himself was a co-recipient of the 1925 Nobel Peace Prize.

In simple terms the 'Dawes Plan' (which eventually evolved into the Young Plan) contained two main points. The first demanded that the Ruhr to be vacated by the French occupying forces, and the second point allowed foreign loans, mainly from America, to be available to Germany. The French, with their own domestic economic problems, eventually accepted the Dawes Plan and withdrew completely from the occupied areas by August 1925. America loaned money to Germany, Germany used it to pay for its war reparations to France, France used it to pay Britain the money they owed, and Britain used it to pay America the money they owed. This seemed to be the perfect solution to everybody's problems and world harmony seemed to have been restored. Investment in Germany was stimulated and it initially seemed to solve many of the world's money problems.

Unfortunately, in October 1929 the American stock market suffered a rapid drop. Investors lost huge amounts of money and this stock market crash led to the Great Depression, a period regarded as the longest and worst period of high unemployment and low business activity in modern times. Banks, stores, and factories were closed, leaving millions of Americans jobless, homeless, and penniless. Many people came to depend on the government or charity to provide them with food and necessities.

The Depression became the worldwide business slump of the 1930s, affecting most nations around the globe. America could no longer loan Germany money for reparations, and they even wanted the money back. It led to a sharp decrease in world trade as each country tried to protect its own industries and products by raising tariffs on imported goods. Distrust started to re-emerge between nations. Unemployment increased to high levels and countries tried to solve the problem by increasing the size of their armies.

In 1923 Italy invaded the Greek island of Corfu in a minor border dispute, while over in the east in 1931 Japan invaded China, creating industries and opening mines in the Manchuria region claiming this economic growth would relieve the depression back in Japan.

By 1935 the dictator of Italy, Benito Mussolini, was also in a position to flex his international muscles and launched a full-scale invasion of Abyssinia (now know as Ethiopia). Italy had attempted this before in 1896, but had been humiliated by a poorly equipped army of Abyssinian tribesmen. Mussolini wanted not only revenge but also the fertile land and mineral wealth of Abyssinia. His intention was to (re)establish Italy as world power.

Over in the east, Japan, though having been in conflict with China since the invasion of Manchuria in 1931, embarked on a full-scale invasion of China in 1937. Starting in July with the invasion of mainland China, it began with the bombing of Shanghai and Guangzhou, followed by the Nanking massacre in December.

Unfortunately, the League of Nations proved toothless. Protracted negotiations with Italy almost seemed more damaging to Italy's trading partners than Italy itself, and since Japan was a significant member of the League of Nations, nobody wanted to upset them. Appeasement was their only solution, which solved nobody's problems.

The ensuing world turmoil created the ideal environment for the development of a visionary. Germany found one in Adolf Hitler. Though an Austrian by birth, he had served in the German Army in the First World War and like many disillusioned Germans considered that the German politicians had let the German people down at the end of the war. By 1933 he was Chancellor and the *de facto* ruler of Germany. For some in Poland it seemed that their short-lived independence was already under threat. On 25 July 1932 Poland signed a non-aggression pact with their old but continuing adversary to the east – the Soviet Union – and on 26 January 1934, a non-aggression pact to their west with Germany.

Hitler took advantage of his adopted country's hatred of the Treaty of Versailles. He was also aware that a majority of Europeans agreed that the treaty was too harshly implemented and used this to his advantage. So when he began to break the terms of the treaty, he was allowed to do so by the League of Nations, who were effectively paralysed with guilt over the handling of Germany's situation.

Hitler had a clear vision for Germany. He wanted

Germany to be a dominant power in Europe again. To do this he needed to re-arm. He was given an excuse he needed in the early 1930s when there was high unemployment. He provided the nation's youth with military training, reducing unemployment and providing the country with pride in itself.

To unite all German-speaking people into one country (Grossdeutschland). In accordance with the Treaty of Versailles the land conceded by Germany meant that German-speakers existed all over Europe. To bring them back together as one country would restore his nation's pride.

To create living space (*Lebensraum*) for Germany. But the only way that Hitler could do this was to take control of the countries around Germany, despite this being considered expansionist.

To racially cleanse the Reich. Hitler promoted the notion that the German (Aryan or Noble) race was the most pure and perfect, and that other races were below it. If Hitler were to cleanse the Reich, then he would have to remove elements that would denigrate his racial ideals.

To destroy communism. Hitler considered that communist politicians had contributed to the defeat in 1918 and blamed communism for many of Germany's misfortunes. But since Britain and France had also shown opposition to the ideals of communism, he believed they also could potentially support Germany taking a stance against the USSR. Russia must have felt concerned as they joined (albeit temporarily) the League of Nations in 1934.

In 1936, in contravention of the Treaty of Versailles, Hitler moved troops back into the Rhineland. Many British people felt that Hitler had a right to do this and although the French voiced concern they had been tarred by their difficult occupation of the Ruhr and weren't prepared to act alone. As Hitler continued to flout the terms of the treaty the world adopted a stance of appeasement. In so doing, it enabled Hitler to increase his power and allowed Germany to re-establish itself as a major European presence. The same year saw the start of the Spanish Civil War, with significant participation from both Italy and Germany.

By 1938, Hitler was in a position to demand the integration of German-speaking Austria into Grossdeutschland. He had earlier infiltrated Austrian politics with his own national socialist doctrine, and once the Austrian National Socialist Party came to power on 11 March he was able to move. The following day the *Anschluss* (annexation) of Austria was announced. In a bloodless operation, Austria had become part of Germany. International concern was voiced with England, France, and Italy making the strongest condemnation. Sadly, the League of Nations, in particular England and France, were powerless to act and Italy was heavily committed in the Spanish Civil War and was easily appeased by Hitler.

The next step of Hitler's expansionist dream was Czechoslovakia. Fall Grün ('Case Green') was his pretext for the re-unification of the ethnic German populations living in Czechoslovakia's northern and western mountainous border regions, the Sudetenland, with his Grossdeutschland. Their incorporation into Germany would leave the rest of Czechoslovakia powerless to resist subsequent occupation.

In England, Prime Minister Neville Chamberlain was struggling with the politics of the now volatile Europe. He flew to Munich on 29 September 1938 to discuss the Czechoslovakian crisis with Hitler, Mussolini, and French Premier Édouard Daladier. There was no Czech representative present.

Sadly, the option of appeasement was employed again. The Sudentenland would be returned to Germany, with the German guarantee to observe the new Czech borders. A document to this effect was signed by both Hitler and Chamberlain.

Chamberlain returned to England on 30 September 1938, arriving at Heston Aerodrome in London and, holding the infamous document aloft, addressed the gathered crowds:

The settlement of the Czechoslovakian problem, which has now been achieved is, in my view, only the prelude to a larger settlement in which all Europe may find peace. This morning I had another talk with the German Chancellor, Herr Hitler, and here is the paper which bears his name upon it as well as mine. Some of you, perhaps, have already heard what it contains but I would just like to read it to you ... My good friends, for the second time in our history, a British Prime Minister has returned from Germany bringing peace with honour. I believe it is peace for our time.

Chamberlain may have believed it, he desperately wanted to believe it, but sadly everybody else had a deep feeling of foreboding and impending doom.

Things continued to look bleak. Hitler himself travelled to Prague in October 1938, crossing the German/Czech border at Wildenau to a huge fanfare and much adulation. Hindsight is a wonderful thing; all the cues were there, but the politicians still held out for a peaceful and diplomatic end to the crisis. Everybody else could see what was coming.

They didn't have long to wait. On 15 March 1939, under plan Fall Grün German troops entered Prague and Czechoslovakia ceased to exist. Within three short weeks Mussolini's Italy had also invaded Albania.

By August 1939, the world was a world that held its breath. Poland could foresee what was about to happen as it watched the bubbling war clouds over its western borders. What was less clear was what was happening to its east, and with all the turmoil following the First World War in Western Europe it may have even taken its eye off the ball beyond its eastern borders.

Russia too had been in turmoil. The withdrawal from the First World War, the Revolution, and Civil War had all taken their toll. It had also meant that Russia or more specifically the Soviet Union had seemed comparatively quiet on the world stage, but internally Russia had been going through a massive metamorphosis.

Lenin had died in 1924 and had been replaced by the spectre of a man, an ogre of such proportion and significance that his like has thankfully rarely been seen. This person is unarguably the most significant name in my father's story; without his influence, there would be no story to relate and I wouldn't be here writing this now.

His name, though I don't need to write it, was Josef (Koba) Vissarionovich Dzhugashvili (Иосиф (Коба) Виссарионович Джугашвили). We know him better by his pseudonym of Josef Stalin (his surname, Сталин, meant man of steel, an indication of his own opinion of himself). He hadn't been one of the key players in the Bolshevik seizure of power in 1917, but he soon rose through the ranks of the Communist Party. By 1922 he had become the General Secretary of the Party, and following the death of Lenin in 1924 he was successful in a power struggle over Leon Trotsky, gradually outmanoeuvring all other rivals. By the late 1920s, Stalin was the unopposed dictator of the Soviet Union.

He was born on 18 December 1879 in Gori, Georgia. His father was a cobbler and Stalin grew up in humble circumstances. He studied at a theological seminary where he first read Marxist literature. He never graduated, instead devoting his time to the revolutionary movement against the Russian monarchy. He spent the next fifteen years as an activist and on a number of occasions was arrested and exiled to Siberia.

His forced collectivisation of agriculture cost millions of lives, while his programme of rapid industrialisation achieved huge increases in Soviet productivity and economic growth but at great cost. Moreover, the population of the Soviet Union suffered immensely during the Great Terror of the 1930s, during which Stalin purged the party of 'enemies of the people', resulting in the execution of thousands and the exile of millions into the Gulag system of corrective labour camps.

By 1939 he was in total control of all aspects of the Soviet Union, and as Hitler over in the west was engaged in border disputes, so too was Stalin, but over in the Far East. The summer of 1939 saw the Nomonhan Incident in Manchuria (Eastern China). Though described as 'a strange war' in the 20 July 1939 *New York Times* editorial, this forgotten conflict had several relevant consequences.

In Russia this conflict is better known as the Battle of Khalkhin Gol. At that time, Manchuria was still a puppet state of Japan, known as Manchukuo. The Japanese maintained that the border between the two states was the Halha River (or in Russian the Khalkhin Gol), while the Mongolians and their Russian allies maintained that it ran about 16 km east of the river, just east of Nomonhan village, and so a bitter border dispute followed.

The Russians, under the command of General Georgy Konstantinovich Zhukov, quickly gained a stranglehold on the Japanese forces, who were vastly inferior to their Russian counterparts. Zhukov, a military genius, using pioneering but unproven military tactics eventually routed the Japanese Army, causing horrendous losses to an army that had hitherto only known victory against the militarily inferior Chinese.

Khalkhin Gol should have ended the military aspirations of the Japanese military. They should have taken this brutal lesson to heart, but unfortunately the only thing they learned was that they should not try a full-scale invasion of Russia (perhaps the reason why they did not help Hitler in 1941 when he advanced into Russia). Defeat, though, persuaded the Japanese to expand into the Pacific, where they considered the United States a weaker opponent than the Soviet Union. If the Japanese had not lost at Khalkhin Gol, perhaps they would never have attacked Pearl Harbour and brought America into the war.

Russia gained a hero from this conflict – Zhukov, who was awarded the official Soviet title of Hero of the Soviet Union in recognition of his feats. The pioneering tactics included the grouping of armour which he would later use to great effect against the Germans. Zhukov went on to have a glittering Soviet military career but significantly, the name of Zhukov will re-emerge later, as it appears several times in the story of my father.

Georgy Konstantinovich Zhukov

Гео́ргий Константи́нович Жу́ков was born into a poverty-stricken peasant family in Strelkovka, near to Moscow. He was initially an apprentice furrier in Moscow, but in 1915 was conscripted into the army of the Russian Empire.

After the October Revolution he joined the Bolshevik Party, where his background of poverty was seen as an asset. After recovering from typhus he fought in the Russian Civil

War from 1918 to 1921, by 1923 he was commander of a regiment, and by 1930 of a brigade. He was a keen proponent of the new theory of armoured warfare and was noted for his detailed planning, tough discipline, strictness, and a never-give-up attitude. He survived Joseph Stalin's Great Purge of the Red Army command in the late 1930s, some believe merely by a clerical oversight.

In 1938 Zhukov was directed to command the First Soviet Mongolian Army Group and as we saw earlier, successfully defeated the Japanese at the Battle of Khalkhin Gol. Following the German invasion of Russia in 1941, he directed the transfer of troops from the Far East, where a large part of Soviet ground forces had been stationed prior to Hitler's invasion of Russia. The successful Soviet counter-offensive in December 1941 saved Moscow and drove the Germans back, out of reach of the Soviet capital. Zhukov's feat of logistics in saving Moscow is considered by some to be his greatest achievement.

He went onto have further successes in the Battles of Stalingrad, Leningrad, and eventually Berlin, where as commander of the 1st Byelorussian Front of the Red Army he stormed and defeated the remnants of the German Army.

By 1938 Germany was increasing its demands on Poland. In particular the demand for the return of the predominantly German Baltic port city of Danzig (Gdansk), and for the construction of a roadway to connect East Prussia with the rest of Germany. As such a road would run through the Polish Corridor, the proposal was rejected. Poland feared that if these demands were accepted, it would become increasingly subject to the will of Germany and eventually lose independence just as had happened to the Czechs a short while earlier.

The 'gathering storm' in Europe predicted by Winston Churchill was clearly gathering pace. Hitler issued orders to prepare for a possible 'solution of the Polish problem by military means', and by July, under the pretext of conducting summer manoeuvres, strong German forces were moved into assembly areas near the Polish frontier. Other forces were dispatched to East Prussia, ostensibly to participate in the twenty-fifth anniversary of the Battle of Tannenburg.

The Soviet Union, seemingly fearing Hitler's anti-communist rhetoric, claimed to have requested an alliance with the United Kingdom, France, Poland, and Romania. This was rejected, principally as Poland and Romania refused to allow Soviet troops onto their territories. The Soviets however, didn't trust Britain or France to honour any collective security, as they had failed to assist Spain against the Fascists or to protect Austria or Czechoslovakia from Germany. They also suspected that the Western Allies would prefer the Soviet Union to fight Germany by itself, and avoid any military conflict themselves. In view of these concerns, the Soviet Union abandoned the talks and despite obvious ideological differences, turned instead to negotiations with Germany. The Soviets accused the Western powers of reluctance to take the Soviet Union's military assistance seriously while emphasising the Soviet right to cross Poland and Romania if necessary.

Poland, fearing the inevitable, entered into a treaty with Britain and France hoping that if any foreign army invaded Poland, Britain and France would automatically come to their aid as an ally.

In July 1939 open Soviet-German trade negotiations were underway, and on 19 August a trade agreement was reached. Four days later on 23 August, a German delegation headed by Foreign Minister Joachim von Ribbentrop arrived in Moscow. In the early hours of the following morning the 'Treaty of Non-Aggression Between Germany and the Union of Soviet Socialist Republics' was signed together with the Russian Foreign Minister Vyacheslav Molotov in the presence of Soviet leader Joseph Stalin. The fate of Europe had effectively been sealed.

The ten-year pact of non-aggression, better known as the 'Molotov-Ribbentrop Pact', was supplemented by a secret protocol, which divided Eastern Europe into German and Soviet zones of influence. Poland was to be carved into two, roughly along the lines of the Curzon Line. Germany had effectively neutralised the possibility of any Soviet opposition in a potential campaign against Poland.

It seems the Poles and the British had a change of heart and appeared willing to negotiate with Hitler, but it was too late. Fighting had ended in Spain, and the war in China had stagnated, but few people believed war would be avoided. Exactly a week after signing the 'Molotov-Ribbentrop Pact' Hitler, as if needing one, created his own excuse to invade Poland.

The Gleiwitz Incident

Today Gleiwitz (Gliwice in Polish) is an industrial city in Upper Silesia, south-western Poland on the Kłodnica River, about 20 km to the west of Katowice. In 1939 it was a German town close to the Polish border.

Situated on Tarnogórska road is the Gliwice Radio Tower, an 118-metre-high construction of larch wood, possibly the tallest wooden structure in the world. Though having few similarities it is sometimes known as 'the Silesian Eiffel Tower'. It was originally designed to carry aerials for medium-wave broadcasting and was commissioned in 1935. Today it is only used for mobile phone services and a low-power FM transmitter, and is the home of a museum of broadcasting.

On the night of 31 August 1939, under orders from the chief of the Gestapo Heinrich Müller, a small group of German operatives, dressed in Polish uniforms and led by Alfred Naujocks, seized the Gleiwitz station and broadcast a short anti-German message in Polish. The objective was to make the attack and the broadcast look like the work of anti-German Polish saboteurs.

In order to make the attack scene more convincing, the Germans brought in a local German Silesian, Franciszek Honiok, a known Polish sympathiser, who had been arrested the previous day. Honiok was dressed to look like a saboteur, killed by a lethal injection, shot several times, and left dead at the scene so that he appeared to have been killed while attacking the station. His corpse was subsequently presented as proof of the attack to the police and press.

It is now known that the attack, though used as justification for the start of the invasion of Poland, actually failed miserably, a fact that only came to light post-war when Allied investigators began researching captured German documents. The radio was merely a low-power relay station for Radio Breslau, whose stronger signal drowned out the fake 'Polish propaganda' emanating from Gleiwitz. It didn't matter anyway; Germany had made up its mind.

The Gleiwitz incident, however, was only a part of a larger operation carried out by German forces that night. At the same time as the Gleiwitz attack there were several other incidents orchestrated by Germany along the Polish–German border. The entire project, called Operation Himmler, comprised of more than twenty separate incidents with the intention of giving the appearance of Polish aggression against Germany.

Poland's fate seemed inescapable. The Polish Navy sent three of its destroyers – *Burza* ('Storm'), *Błyskawica* ('lightning'), and *Grom* ('Thunder') – to Britain and away from the powerful German Navy in Operation Peking.

On the same day, Marshal of Poland Edward Rydz-Śmigły announced the mobilisation of his troops but was pressured into revoking the order by the French, who apparently still hoped for a diplomatic settlement, failing to realise that the Germans were fully mobilised and concentrated at the Polish border.

This meant that Poland's military were not in a state of readiness to defend Poland. In some quarters there is resentment for these actions, believing that Poland would have been in a better position if Poland's military had been ready to face the German Army.

The following day, 1 September 1939, Germany launched the Fall Weiss operation ('Case White'). The first invasion of Poland had started. Later that day in a speech in the Reichstag, Adolf Hitler cited twenty-one border incidents, three of them serious, as his justification for his subsequent actions.

Anti-Polish propaganda had been continuous for months, and Polish reconnaissance missions along the border with Germany had reported the massive build-up of German forces along the common border, but France and Britain, in the deluded hope of German appeasement, had prevented a full Polish mobilisation for war. Suitable defences were only begun on 28 August, just three days before the invasion began and Poland managed to mobilise only 70 per cent of its planned forces; many units were still forming or in transit to their designated front-line positions.

At 4.40 a.m. the German Luftwaffe began bombing the Polish town of Wieluń in central Poland. The reason Wieluń was chosen is to this day unclear, as it had no military or industrial targets of note. The attack continued until 2.00 p.m., by which time the bombing had destroyed over 75 per cent of the town, including the historic Gothic church, killing more than 1,200 civilians.

Five minutes after the air raid on Wieluń started the old German naval training ship *Schleswig Holstein* began bombardment of the Polish naval base at Westerplatte, a small forested island separated from Gdansk by a harbour channel and located on Baltic Sea coast at the mouth of River Dead Vistula (one of the Vistula delta estuaries). This picturesque peninsula, though in fact the second casualty of the war, has the unhappy distinction of being the site of the official start of the Second World War. The ruins of the battle are preserved as a museum to this day, and the event is commemorated by an impressive monument.

The initial attack was followed up by an unsuccessful attack by German naval infantry. A further two assaults that day were also repelled. Over the coming days, the Germans repeatedly bombarded Westerplatte with naval and heavy field artillery, along with dive-bombing raids by Junkers Ju 87 Stukas (Sturzkampfflugzeug). Repeated attacks were repelled by the Poles for a week. However, on 7 September, after running out of ammunition, the commander Major Henryk Sucharski was forced to surrender.

At 8.00 a.m. the German Army (Wehrmacht) attacked near the Polish border town of Mokra, north-west of Częstochowa. The Volhynian Cavalry Brigade (Wołyńska Brygada Kawalerii) were quick to react, initially repelling the Germans and recording one of the few Polish victories of the war.

The fighting was fierce, with heavy casualties on both sides. Sadly, the initial Polish success didn't halt the German advance for very long and the German Army pressed on towards Warsaw. An ill-prepared though brave and determined horse-mounted Polish Cavalry were no match for the German Army geared up for modern warfare. An impressive monument now celebrates the site of the short-lived Polish victory.

At 9.00 a.m. England and France issued an ultimatum to Germany. It went unheeded and later that day, as German aircraft bombed Polish cities, further German fronts were created along Poland's northern, western, and southern borders.

The main route of attack, eastwards from Germany across the western Polish border, was led by the Army Group South, commanded by General Karl Rudolf Gerd von Rundstedt. This Prussian aristocrat and career soldier had initially been out of favour with Hitler but had been reinstated to lead the attack on Poland.

A second route in the north carried supporting attacks from East Prussia, commanded by General Fedor von Bock's Army Group North, and a co-operative German-Slovak tertiary attack by units of the Field Army Bernolák (Slovenská Poľná Armáda Skupina), from the territory of German-allied Slovakia in the south. Their goal was to converge on and crush the Polish capital of Warsaw.

In order to achieve their goals Germany employed a new warfare strategy of 'Blitzkrieg' (Lightning War), which pioneered massive use of tanks, motorised infantry, and air power to create spearheads for quick penetration into enemy territory. German forces were numerically and technologically superior to the Polish armed forces. It's believed that the Germans used about 85 per cent of their armed forces against Poland, and not surprisingly, the Polish forces found themselves severely outnumbered and outclassed.

Two days after the German invasion, on 3 September, England and France declared war on Germany but failed to provide any military assistance. The Second World War had officially begun. By then, German units had already penetrated deep into Polish territory. In the face of the onslaught the Polish Army fragmented; some units were retreating while others delivered disjointed attacks wherever they could.

On 10 September, the Polish Commander-in-Chief, Marshal Edward Rydz-Śmigły, ordered a general retreat to the south-east, towards Polish-friendly Romania. Meanwhile, the Germans pressed on towards Warsaw, and by the 13th Poland's capital was under siege. In the south, German forces had also reached the city of Lwów.

By Sunday 17 September, the Polish defence was completely broken, with all units in retreat and disarray, and heading south for Romania. However, a new and perhaps more sinister and unforeseen obstacle was put in their way – a full-scale invasion from Poland's long-standing nemesis – Russia.

Starting at 4.00 a.m., about 1 million Soviet Union Red Army soldiers crossed into Poland from the east. The attack was deployed on two fronts: the northern Belarusian Front under Mikhail Kovalyov, and the southern Ukrainian Front under former Red Army commander in Belarus Semyon Timoshenko. Timoshenko, like Zhukov, had joined the army from a peasant background and risen rapidly through the ranks. He was a close personal friend of Stalin, and became a member of the Communist Party's Central Committee. He survived Stalin's Great Purge, to be left as the Red Army's most senior professional soldier.

Poland's second invasion had begun, and for my father, his fate was about to be sealed. It was as a direct consequence of this invasion that his, and I suppose my life was mapped out in the way that it was.

The Polish Army were clearly unprepared to face two invasions at once. Most units had been deployed to the west in anticipation and the east was left protected by only twenty under-strength battalions of about 20,000 troops of the Border Defence Corps (Korpus Ochrony Pogranicza), under the command of General Wilhelm Orlik-Rueckemann. When the Soviet Army invaded, the Polish High Command were based in Kolomyja, south-east of Lwów, near to the Romanian border. Initially their orders were to resist the Soviet Army, but it was very soon decided to save as many Polish troops as possible and escape to France via Romania and Hungary. As a result, there was never actually a state of war between Poland and the Soviet Union, or for that matter between Poland and Germany.

Russia had invaded partly in response to German requests for it to honour its part of their 'Moltotov-Ribbentrop Pact' but also the Soviet government alleged that it was acting to protect the pro-Soviet Ukrainians and Byelarussians who lived in the eastern parts of Poland. Russia may have also feared that Germany might take more territory than had been agreed when they had carved Poland up between themselves the previous August.

This, the so called 'Liberation Campaign', as named by the Soviet leadership, was in violation of the Soviet-Polish Non-Aggression Pact and though denounced by Britain and France, they yet again didn't intervene, leaving the Soviet Union with a free reign over eastern Poland. And so, the advancing Soviet Army were confronted with a weakened Polish Army, mainly in retreat and trying to escape south.

The Red Army quickly achieved its targets, meeting only light Polish resistance as most of the Polish Army had been deployed in the west, and in fact had launched a major counter-offensive against the Germans in the Battle of the Bzura. This was the largest battle during this campaign, taking place near the River Bzura, west of Warsaw, and raging from 9 to 19 September.

By the 22nd, Germany had captured more territory than had been outlined in the 'Moltotov-Ribbentrop Pact'. To correct this oversight there was an exchange of captured Polish territories in compliance with the terms of the protocol. In a near-farcical ceremony the Red Army and the Wehrmacht held a joint military parade in Brześć (Brest), at which those Polish areas captured in excess of the August pact were transferred from German to the Soviet authorities.

Despite the Russian intervention, the German Army didn't have it all its own way. Polish resistance was fierce and the Polish Army did have some notable, but almost irrelevant success. Any Polish–Soviet battles were hopelessly one-sided, the Soviet Army generally having to deal with already mauled and depleted Polish Army regiments. Some of the final skirmishes took place around the town of Sambor. Despite several Soviet tanks being destroyed, most of the surviving soldiers, significantly including their commander General Władysław Anders, were taken prisoner.

With the sheer might of the well-prepared and equipped German onslaught and the Russian involvement, the inevitable was just a matter of time away. And so it was that on 27 September Poland was forced to capitulate. A ceasefire was signed at 12.00 a.m. However, the Polish government refused to surrender or negotiate a peace with Germany and ordered all units to evacuate Poland and reorganise in France. Poland's Fourth Partition had begun.

It's estimated that over 60,000 Polish troops were killed in the fighting, with over 400,000 others being captured by the Germans and another 250,000 more captured by the Soviets. About 120,000 Polish troops escaped to Romania and Hungary and another 20,000 escaped to Latvia and Lithuania. The majority eventually made their way to France, then onto Britain where they were to form the First Polish Army Division. These men fought at the Battles of Narvik in Norway, Falaise Gap in Normandy, and at Arnheim in Holland. Polish naval elements took part in the sinking of the *Bismarck*, and Polish pilots proved to be excellent during the Battle of Britain. Those that were not to escape, particularly the officers, were not so lucky, as we shall see later.

So that was the start of the Second World War. It's considered by some historians that there weren't two separate World Wars at all, just the one that started in 1914 and ended in 1945, with a break of about twenty years in the middle while the main protagonists regrouped. I realise that my summary here is a very simplistic view of a very, very complex issue, but it gives an indication of the state of Europe as prelude to the start of my father's story, and for which it was the single most influencing contributory factor.

3

ARREST

The Odyssey Begins

Coordinated Polish resistance ended on 6 October. On the 19th western Poland was officially incorporated into the German Reich, and Hitler installed former Stormtrooper Hans Michael Frank as the Gauleiter (Governor General) of the German portion of Poland, and as we know under his direction over 6 million Poles died. He was caught by the Americans at the end of the war, convicted, and hanged for his war crimes in October 1946.

A month later, on 29 November the whole of the Kresy (eastern Poland) region, with more than 13 million people, was incorporated into the Soviet Union. Of these less than 40 per cent were Poles, the rest were mainly Byelorussians, Ukrainian, and Jews. The Fourth Partition of Poland had begun and sovereign Poland ceased to exist after less than twenty years of independence. My father's home was now officially in Western Byelorussia.

For the Poles, historical adversaries of Russia, their conversion to Soviet citizenship was only met with trepidation; they were only too aware that their annexation by the Soviets would leave them susceptible to Russian methods of repression that had been honed since the Revolution in 1917, but in reality had been operation long before under Tsarist rule.

Germany, having conquered Poland, turned its attentions to the West. By the spring of 1940 Denmark and Norway had been captured, and in the early summer France, Belgium, and Holland also fell. Italy declared war in support of Germany in June 1940, and the Italian Army attacked France just before its surrender. The United Kingdom was then targeted by Germany, who attempted to deprive the island of vitally needed supplies and obtain air superiority in order to make a seaborne invasion possible. The Second World War was in full swing.

The Soviet Union directed some of its attention to the north. Stalin demanded that Finland agree to move their border 25 km back from Leningrad. He also demanded that Finland lease the Hanko Peninsula to the USSR for thirty years for the creation of a Soviet naval base.

Finland were not forthcoming, and so on 30 November the Red Army attacked. The Soviet-Finnish War, known by some as 'The Winter War', had begun. Because the attack was judged to be illegal, and following the invasion of Poland, the Soviet Union was expelled from the League of Nations on 14 December.

Stalin had expected to conquer the whole of Finland by the end of 1939, but under the disastrous command of Kliment Voroshilov, whose Soviet forces massively outnumbered the Finns in both men and equipment, they met with fierce resistance and were frustrated by the Finnish Army.

In January 1940, Semyon Timoshenko was moved from southern Poland and took charge of the Soviet Army fighting in Finland. Under his leadership, the Soviets succeeded in breaking through the Finnish Mannerheim Line on the Karelian Isthmus. This prompted Finland to sue for peace in March, and in doing so they ceded about 10 per cent of Finland's territory and 20 per cent of its industrial capacity to the Soviet Union.

Though Timoshenko's personal reputation increased and he was made the People's Commissar for Defence and a Marshal of the Soviet Union, the overall results of this short war were mixed. Soviet losses on the front were massive, and some of the soldiers that were to survive were punished with imprisonment or exile to Siberia. Aleksander Topolski in his book *Without Vodka* describes sharing a cell with one of these unfortunates. In addition, Russia's international standing suffered, particularly following its earlier attack on Poland. Even worse, the military organisation and fighting ability of the Red Army was brought into question, a fact that didn't go unnoticed by Germany and which may have contributed to Germany's decision to launch the invasion of Russia in 1941. The Finns, though, retained their sovereignty, and gained considerable international goodwill.

This 'minor' Soviet distraction, however, didn't take away the focus of the Soviet activities in the Kresy region. Even before the Russian invasion of 17 September Soviet subversion in Eastern Poland had been increasing. Once the Soviet Army took control, the whole region became gripped with terror. The ethnic tension which had been suppressed and largely ignored before the invasion now reared its ugly head. The ethnic Poles were confronted and harassed and in some cases met with violence by pro-Russian Byelorussians in the north and Ukrainians in the south. Local administrations composed of People's Committees in conjunction with the dreaded NKVD sprung up everywhere.

ЧК	ГПУ	ОГПУ	НКВД	МГб	КГБ	ФСБ
Cheka	GPU	OGPU	NKVD	MGB	KGB	FSB

The changing name of the Russian State Security service:
An evolution of terror!

Russia and the Soviet Union have always employed a state security service. We have all heard of, and are familiar with at least one of the many acronyms that have been used. All, without exception, have struck fear to those coming into contact with them. It seems that once the old name became discredited, it was re-branded and relaunched. For me, growing up in the post-war era, KGB is the name I am most familiar with, but since the Bolsheviks came to power several names have been used. In the late 1930s and throughout the Second World War the Soviet secret police service was the NKVD, a name to this day synonymous with hatred and terror.

Cheka, ЧК, 1917–1922

чрезвычайная комиссия. The full name of the agency was the All-Russian Extraordinary Commission for Combating Counter-Revolution, Speculation, and Sabotage (Всероссийская чрезвычайная комиссия по борьбе с контрреволюцией и саботажем). This was the first of a succession of Soviet state security organisations that became notorious for large-scale human rights abuses including torture, mass- and summary executions and civilian repression. It was founded by Lenin in 1917 and created by Polish communist revolutionary Felix Edmundovich Dzerzhinsky (Polish: Feliks Dzierżyński, Russian: Феликс Эдмундович Дзержинский). Dzerzhinsky was born in the Polish town of Kojdanava, now in Belarus, and not only home to the Belarusian State Archives of Films, Photographs and Sound Recordings, but the highest point in low-lying Belarus at 346 m above sea level. He was one of the few high-ranking Soviet officials to escape persecution by his own organisation, dying of a heart attack in 1926.

GPU, ГПУ, 1922–1923

Государственное Политическое Управление. State Political Directorate – Gosudarstvennoye Politicheskoye Upravlenie. Secret police of the Soviet Union. Formed from the Cheka in 1922.

OGPU, ОГПУ, 1923–1934

Объединённое государственное политическое управление. Joint State Political Directorate – Ob'edinennoe Gosudarstvennoe Politicheskoe Upravlenie. Created in 1923 from the GPU. Responsible for the creation of the gulag system and persecution of the Russian Orthodox Church and other religious organisations.

NKVD, НКВД, 1934–1946

Народный комиссариат внутренних дел. People's Commissariat for Internal Affairs – Narodny Komissariat Vnutrennikh Del. This was the leading secret police organisation of the Soviet Union. Created in 1934 from the OGPU. Often referred to as 'Organy' or 'The Organ'.

MGB, МГб, 1946–1953

Министерство государственной безопасности. The Ministry of State Security and Soviet Secret Police Agency (Ministerstvo Gosudarstvennoi Bezopasnosti). Created from the NKVD in 1946.

KGB, КГБ, 1953–1991

Комите́т Госуда́рственной Безопа́сности. Committee for State Security. Formed from the MGB in 1953 and generally regarded as the supreme Soviet state security organisation.

FSB, ФСБ, 1991–

Федера́льная слу́жба безопа́сности. Federal Security Service – Federalnaya Sluzhba Bezopasnosti. The domestic state security agency of the Russian Federation, created from the KGB on the dissolution of the Soviet Union in 1991, and still in place today.

The modern-day Belarussian state security service is still known as the KGB.

It was directly through NKVD intervention that my father's story takes a dramatic switch. As early as 17 September, the first day of the Soviet invasion, the Red Army had reached Kobylnik. Blue-capped, khaki-uniformed Russian soldiers began distributing leaflets to the frightened population. They simply read, 'We have come to liberate the population from the Polish yoke.'

In some areas Soviet aircraft dropped leaflets proclaiming that landlords and settlers were to be crushed, and that Polish soldiers should turn their weapons against their officers. There was going to be no ambiguity in the Russian intentions towards the Poles.

By the Byelorussians and to a certain extent the Jews the Soviet Army was met with open arms, and regarded as a liberating or rescue force. The residents of Kresy, and particularly those around Kobylnik in the north, had often had an uneasy relationship in particular with the pro-Russian Byelorussians.

Even though the new Soviet regime immediately imposed many changes, the Byelorussians and Jews held out hope for better times ahead. The Poles, however, didn't share this optimism and were immediately wary; there had been too much Polish –Russian history and recent rhetoric to be complacent. There were also widespread concerns over how the Polish–Byelorussian/Ukrainian relationship, fraught at times, would be affected.

It wasn't long before the tentacles of the NKVD reached out and touched my father's village of Szwakszty. As was happening across the whole of Soviet-occupied eastern Poland, the NKVD followed immediately behind the Red Army and began the introduction of Soviet administration. Committees were formed with local Byelorussians (and in the south Ukrainians) as members. They were infiltrating, surveying, and documenting every village and its inhabitants. The local NKVD people's committee was created in the nearby town of Kobylnik and was soon making its presence felt in Szwakszty.

On 22 October 'elections' were held for the People's Assembly of Western Belarus. These were organised on the Soviet pattern; candidates were selected by the Soviet government, no other candidates were allowed to stand and so there were no alternatives for the 'voters'. The representative for Szwakszty will have been appointed by the head of Postavy county, at that time one Captain Brykov. The election is described below for the village of Szwakszty in a handwritten attestation of the NKVD process (see image 2).

Julian Kisty was chosen as the village representative, he used to be the village chief. The Russians wanted somebody else in this position but the people did not agree, because our village is totally Polish and we had no police. Julian Kisty was warning everybody, and was helping us, that's why at the beginning there were no searches or arrests.

Russian propaganda meetings took place every day with officials from Kobylnik, often the meetings were held by local communists and two brothers Szuszkiewicz from the village of Czuczelice and police chief from Kobylnik called Choruzy who originated from the village Pleciesze. These meetings were voluntary, in principle, but the leader/ spokesman had to inform everyone by himself. As well as this, all political speakers threatened us if we did not attend.

About the political matters, spoke soviet political spokesman Trzeciak who said that Russia plays a waiting game and when England 'The Prostitute', 'War Monger', 'Cause of all the Evil in the World', will completely stick with the Germans in the war, then the almighty Red Army will go across Europe, will take over England, crush the capitalistic, rotten ideology of America, and set a new way in the world.

During these meetings when people asked for the children to be taught in Polish at the local school, and not in Byelorussian, they were told not to think about Poland, there is no Poland, and there will be no Poland and wherever the Red Army walked into, there will be nothing else but communism.

During those meetings they proposed a female candidate, a midwife from Kobylnik into the so called 'Assembly of Western Byelorussia' and we were told that she would be our representative and stand for us and our interests in Moscow. Then the officials walked around the village to document all people for the election of the representative (all ages).

The voting took place in October. Everybody had to vote. When voting, our names were checked, we were given a paper with name of the one candidate and we had to vote behind a screen.

We either had to cross her name out or leave it as if we agreed. There were armed policemen around and NKVD representatives. After voting Julian Kisty told me personally that 75 per cent of votes were crossed out. After counting the Russians put away the crossed out votes and replaced them with the votes for the candidate, then sent it away to Kobylnik.

In the end we found that our village very happily chose our midwife as the candidate with a 90 per cent majority!

Those who did not want to vote were brought over forcefully and the sick were brought on carts. I swear that in our village no one knew that these elections were part of some sort of plebiscite.

Pleszak family document

By the end of October, following the election of the delegates there were meetings of the Supreme National Assemblies, which addressed the government of the USSR with a request to join the Byelorussian Soviet Socialist Republic (Eastern Belarus). All resolutions were passed and Western Belarus was duly incorporated into the USSR. Wilno (Vilnius) itself was handed over into the jurisdiction of the Republic of Lithuania, and the southern part of Kresy was incorporated into the Soviet Republic of the Ukraine. Chillingly, at the same time a resolution was also announced to confiscate 'landowners' land' without recompense.

On 31 October Vyacheslav Molotov boasted, 'One swift blow to Poland, first by the German Army and then by the Red Army, and nothing was left of this ugly offspring of the Versailles Treaty!' The following day, 1 November, the Supreme Council of the USSR declared that all Polish citizens who found themselves on land taken over by the USSR were now Soviet citizens.

Very rapidly the administration of the annexed land was transformed along the lines of the Soviet model. This was undertaken by the army, the NKVD, and by the newly arrived Soviet Party activists appointed to the higher administrative posts. Polish education and language were phased out, libraries closed, and books burned. Churches were destroyed, priests arrested, and the wearing of crosses was forbidden. Owning a typewriter became a crime. Properties were confiscated, bank accounts closed, and the Russian Rouble replaced the Polish Zloty. Poles were fired from their jobs, and seemingly random arrests became more frequent.

In some areas Byelorussian and Ukrainian gangs attacked the military settlers in their *osadas*, which involved looting and even killing. Some of the assailants, armed with knives and axes, were so threatening and prevalent that the settlers' families went to bed fully dressed, and the men slept alongside their own weapons. It seems that retribution was carried out on the *osadas* and their military settlers for their involvement in the Polish–Bolshevik war. Hell had arrived across the whole of Poland.

Communist propaganda was also being distributed in villages, towns and cities. The more the Poles saw of it, the more they hated it. The NKVD and their supporters made it clear that Poland was to be removed from the map; even the Polish language was forbidden.

It became clear that the Soviet authorities wanted to remove from Western Belarus any potential enemies and resistance to their regime. The constant NKVD-controlled surveys, the regular, almost daily checking of lists of family members and possessions continued throughout the Kresy lands.

My father, aged nineteen, was two years too young to be conscripted into the Polish Army. He described himself to me as an anti-communist partisan. I know he had an absolute hatred and loathing of the Soviet Union and Russians but I'm not sure whether this had already formed before the invasion, or whether it developed because of his treatment following his arrest. Maybe it was some of both, but I'm convinced he didn't actually take part in any anti-Soviet activities. Perhaps he referred to himself as a partisan as a convenient way of explaining his arrest. Having said that, it is clear that following the Russian occupation, and as early as October 1939, Polish partisan groups were forming all across the Kresy region, some of which were in direct confrontation with the Red Army and in some cases with pro-Soviet Belarusian nationalist activists. I wished I'd pressed him on this subject, but his past was always a touchy subject.

Young, single Polish adult men were targeted very quickly as 'enemies of the state'. They were considered likely to pose the biggest resistance and trouble to the new Soviet regime. Arrests increased, and people were imprisoned for any reason, however trivial or even imagined. Offences as innocuous as telling 'inappropriate' jokes, suspicious behaviour, and ethnic origin all became reasons for arrest. Invisible boundary lines guarded by Soviet soldiers were created overnight, and anybody 'illegally' crossing (violating) these were immediately taken into custody. It may have been one of these seemingly insignificant violations that signalled my father's downfall.

What we know happened is that in late 1939 he had some confrontation with either the NKVD or a local pro-Soviet militia gang. At the time this wouldn't have been so unusual, as detentions, beatings, and imprisonment were becoming ominously more frequent. At the same time bands of armed Byelorussians were also being more threatening and violent towards the ethnic Poles. Whatever happened was so worrying to him that it caused him (and it seems others as well) to flee and hide in the local forest.

These forests were so dense and impenetrable that hiding and remaining undetected would have been relatively easy. The well-organised local partisans did it throughout the war after Germany had invaded, but for young, frightened, and confused young men it must have been, despite the dangers of venturing out, very difficult to remain there. It seems that my father often returned to his home, frequently staying overnight.

By that time arrests, interrogations, and horrifically torture had become the norm. Techniques used by Russia during the 'Great Terror' during the 1930s were now being employed throughout the Kresy region. Those arrested were interrogated, sometimes beaten, sometimes tortured and were often forced to admit to crimes that they hadn't committed, and even worse were forced to implicate and accuse others. So bad was their treatment that they would often just give the name of somebody known to them in order to reduce their own suffering. It wasn't long before most Polish civilians had been 'shopped' by somebody else in the custody of the NKVD. As more and more people were arrested, those still free became fewer in number, with the realisation that their time would surely come!

And so it was for my father in October 1939 (I've based the date on facts that will appear later in this narrative). He never knew who it was, it may have been a friend, or a neighbour, a work colleague, or just somebody who knew the name of someone not yet arrested. It was irrelevant; his name had been given to the NKVD. The dreaded knock came, as was usual, in the middle of the night at 3 a.m. Two uniformed NKVD officials and six armed militia, together with a *ponyatoy* (Понятой), a civilian who was required by law to assist with arrests (to legitimise the activities of the NKVD) banged on the door.

After pushing their way in they held his father Wincenty, his pregnant mother Aleksandra and two sisters Maria and Honorata at gunpoint while his two younger brothers Boleslaw and Franciszek had to lie, terrified, face-down with their hands clasped behind their heads as the NKVD apprehended my father. The two NKVD intruders then proceeded to search the small house in a very rough but meticulous manner while a militia henchman documented the search. As happened all over the region, nothing was found incriminating to either my father or his family. He was told to take food for two days and then he was dragged away without any belongings or possessions, just the clothes he was dressed in. His family were told rather sternly that he would be back home in two days after the 'investigation into his crimes'.

It was the last time Mikołaj Pleszak was to see his parents, his brothers and his sisters or his childhood home ever again. He was never to meet his unborn brother, and he was never known as Kolya again!

We believe he was immediately taken through his local town of Kobylnik south, along the shores of Lake Naroch, directly to the city of Vileyka, the regional NKVD administrative centre. He was probably transported along with others detained that night in a 'Black Raven' (черный ворон, better known in the west as a Black Mariah), the infamous vehicle synonymous with NKVD repression in the thirties. The vehicle may even have been marked, as was a common NKVD practice, as a bread (хлеб) van in order to disguise its true sinister identity.

City/town	Local name	Location	Approx. distance	Country
Stara Wilejka	Вилейка	50 km south of Kobylnik	55 km	Poland (Polska)

Modern-day Vileyka, originally known to the Poles as Stara Wilejka (not to be confused with Nova Wilejka, which is on the eastern outskirts of Vilnius) is now the Vileyka district centre of the Minsk *voblast* of the of the Republic of Belarus. It is situated on the River Viliya, about 100 km north-west of Minsk.

Though it was first mentioned in 1599, there is little documentary reference to it prior to then, the area it is built on being described as 'nothing but a stretch of forest'. The inception of the town was around 1766, when it officially became a village, the centre of a rural district, which formed part of the district of Oszmiana.

In 1793 during the Second Partition of Poland it was annexed to Russia, and after the Third Partition of Poland in 1795, when the province of Minsk came into being, Queen Catherine II of Russia promoted Wilejka to the rank of a district town in the newly formed province of Minsk. The inhabitants of the village were granted urban rights, and the houses of the village, the estate of the local landlord, and the inn formed the nucleus of the old town. The first session of the first district of the old town took place in 1797 in the inn owned by a David Kopelowitz.

The first settlers were mainly Jews who had lived in nearby villages and farms. At the same time more villages were added to the district of Wilejka, which in 1842 was transferred to the province of Vilna (Vilnius). By 1904 Wilejka was also serviced by a railway station, which connected Wilejka to Polotsk in the north and Molodechno to the south.

During the First World War, the Russian Revolution and the wars that ensued, the town changed hands several times between the Germans and Russians. Following a brief spell in independent Belarus following the First World War it became part of Poland after the Polish military victories against Russia in 1919–21.

After the wars a sort of stability ensued whereby the economic situation and the inhabitants' well-being improved, but as it was a predominantly Jewish town the anti-Semitic movement in Poland that increased in the 1930s led to the situation of the Jews in the town deteriorating, so much so that many Jews emigrated to America or moved further east into Russia.

On 17 September 1939 Wilejka, like Kobylnik was occupied by Russian forces. The situation in the town immediately changed for the worse as the process of russification was executed. One of the leading enterprises, the sawmill owned by Yeshaya Edelman, was taken into Russian ownership and Edelman himself arrested. He was the first Jew to be detained on a charge of being 'an enemy of the new regime'. Sadly, he was never heard of again.

During the Russian invasion of Poland in September 1939 it was incorporated as part of the BSSR into the Soviet Union, but from June 1941 to July 1944 the German Army occupied the town as they advanced eastwards in Operation Barbarossa. It returned into Russian hands in 1944. Wilejka suffered serious damage during the war and the administrative district voblast moved south to the town of Molodechno.

Belarus became independent from the Soviet Union in 1991 and the modern town is located on the banks of the River Viliya. The town's main industries are the Zenith Optical plant, wood-processing enterprises, motor-repair facilities, building materials plants, and food enterprises. It is also home to Belarus' largest artificial reservoir, which was built in 1974 with a total area of 63.3 square km. It is surrounded by farmland and supports both collective farms (*kolkhoz*) and state farms (*sovkhoz*). About 6,000 people are employed in agriculture. The total territory of agricultural land is 110,000 hectares, of which about half is arable land.

Vileyka's centre, high on the banks of the River Viliya, is dominated by Lenin Square, which like many cities in Belarus still to this day maintains its Soviet-era statues. Just in front of local government buildings, a huge concrete Lenin looks out over the town centre, flanked by the Catholic church of the Exaltation of the Holy Cross, built between 1906 and 1913, and the Russian Orthodox church of the Holy Mary Egyptian, which was constructed in 1865.

The surrounding area of Vileyka is very heavily forested, accounting for over 40 per cent of the territory, with the majority of the district situated on the borders of the Naroch-Vileyka lowland. These forests are so dense and impenetrable that partisans were able to hold out without capture throughout the German occupation of the Second World War.

Just off the main road between Vileyka and Naroch down narrow winding tracks is a memorial to the partisans of the Vileyka forest. If it wasn't for the small but frequent direction arrows it would be impossible to find.

Pyotr Mironovich Masherov

Alongside the Russian-built memorial are the restored forest dwellings built by the partisans in 1942–4. They include the forest headquarters of Pyotr Mironovich Masherov (Пётр Миро́нович Машёров), the former maths and physics teacher who was to become the popular leader of the local partisans.

As he was so successful against the occupying Germans he was also held in high regard by the Russians and was awarded the title Hero of the Soviet Union in August of 1944 upon liberation of Belarus by the Russian Army. After the war he embarked on a political career holding several key positions in the Belarusian government and in 1965 became the first Secretary of the Communist Party of Belarus. He was thus the *de facto* president of Belarusian Soviet Socialist Republic.

He continued to be a very popular and highly regarded figure, advocating an early form of glasnost. He was considered by many to be the likely successor of Leonid Brezhnev, the ageing General Secretary of the Communist Party of the Soviet Union. Sadly he died prematurely in a car accident when his vehicle, escorted by police, collided with a truck carrying potatoes in Minsk (the capital of Belarus).

It was declared an accident, but some think that it was staged by the KGB to eliminate a strong potential candidate for the leadership of the USSR. In his honour one of the major streets in Minsk was named 'Masherov Avenue', though this was renamed to 'Victory Avenue' in 2005.

My father arrived at the town Wilejka and was taken directly to the heavily guarded local prison (*tiurma*/тюрьма), which was, and (though now a specialist cancer hospital) still is, located next to the police station on one of the main streets of Wilejka, Ulitsa 1 May (улица 1 мая). He wasn't expecting it, but he was to remain here for several months.

On arrival he was frisked and even his boots were closely examined. He was taken to an admission room where there was already a group of similar unfortunates, all no doubt with gravely concerned faces, and some looking close to a nervous breakdown. Two NKVD bureaucrats completed the process of booking the prisoners in while an armed guard watched the proceedings from inside the room. He was relieved of his belt and shoelaces and assigned to a cell.

My Auntie Maria told me very (very) tearfully that initially their father Wincenty would attend the prison every day, taking food and water for his eldest son, but the Russian authorities would neither let Wincenty see him, or pass on the food parcels. He was now a '*zek*', the term for prisoners, derived from the Russian word заключённый (з/к), meaning incarcerated!

Within the prison there were ten small cells, each about 5 m by 6 m, containing nearly 126 packed detainees. The cells were designed to house no more than forty! The cell my father was kept in had concrete floors, a little window, the 'Judas hole' in the door covered with a leather cloth through which food could be passed and from where they could be observed, and a dim light bulb hung from the ceiling which was never switched off. Everybody had to sleep facing it with their arms exposed from under any blankets they may have had. The small cell windows, approximately 30 cm by 40 cm, opened onto a courtyard.

Rooms on the second floor had barred windows and were completely covered with metallic louvres, which restricted the daylight. 'It was impossible to see even a small patch of sky.' These rooms, which were bare except for a small table and chair, were used as offices for the interrogators. He never mentioned it but there may have been a portrait of Stalin and the flag of the Soviet Union on the wall. The conditions in the prison were indescribably awful, as outlined in a handwritten testimony:

Prison conditions, Hygiene, Buildings
In prison the conditions were awful, in ten cells in Stara Wilejka, 5x6 there were 126 prisoners. We could not layout to sleep as there was no space. At night we slept sitting up, leaning against each other. They would take us to bathe once a month. There was no change of clothes, so the clothes were sweaty, smelly, and dirty, and there were fleas everywhere. Twice a day we would take our shirts off to chase the fleas.

Pleszak family document

No class of person had avoided arrest; the cells contained farmers like my father, doctors, lawyers, teachers, labourers, and shop workers – the NKVD had been indiscriminate in their approach.

The squalor in the prison cells was appalling. Though there was a barrel, which acted as a latrine (known as a *parasha*), floors were covered with a disgusting melange of excrement, urine, blood, vomit, and food. The smell by all accounts was appalling, and though the detainees soon became accustomed to it in some published descriptions I have read, guards when entering the cell recoiled at the stench. One memoirist recalls that during his fifteen years in Soviet internment he was never given any toilet paper, and that the 'distinctive smell' associated with those incarcerated was noticeable even after their release.

The *parashas* were emptied regularly by the detainees, which by some was regarded as a relief from the boredom and squalor of the cell, but the sheer number of detainees meant that they were more often than not overflowing. Food was supplied each day, and usually consisted of a warm watery soup made from rotten cabbages and/or fish entrails, with some poorly made bread, and occasionally some sugar.

It almost defies description, but it was nothing to compare with the hell that was to come! His nightmare had started and it wasn't going to end for some time. In fact it was going to get a whole lot worse and he didn't know it.

While held in the prison, every night was interrupted with some of the detainees being removed for 'questioning'. It seems that the NKVD required a confession from each detainee to legitimise their arrest. Nobody knew whose turn it was going to be, and seemingly at random, detainees were jerked from their sleep and removed. Guards would arrive, always in the middle of the night, and escort or drag the reluctant away to their fate. Nobody young or old, professional or peasant would escape it, and eventually it was my father's turn.

The interrogator sat behind his desk. He would neither introduce himself nor have his nameplate on the desk. The questions were generally the same, deliberately boring and repetitive. Occasionally, to make accusations seem to be as true as possible, the interrogator would introduce new 'facts'. They would either scream or calmly and deliberately repeat the same questions over and over again, often for hours. They seemed capable of repeating exactly the same question for hours on end without the slightest variation and without showing any signs of fatigue.

The accused's past was meticulously examined in infuriatingly minute detail in order to find 'pressure points'. It seemed the more confused they became the more confident the torturer(s) became. Long questionnaires were completed only to be torn up and the whole process repeated again. Sessions usually began with the time-honoured formula, 'Why do you think you've been brought here? What crimes have you committed? If you were innocent you wouldn't be here!' These typical NKVD sensory deprivation tactics sometimes developed into a beating.

This was typical of the *Yezhovshchina* ('Yezhov era') of interrogation, named after the notorious former NKVD chief Nikolai Yezhov (Николай Ежов). This diminutive but ruthless character was dubbed the 'poison dwarf' and was famously removed from photographs with Stalin after he was relieved from power in 1939 and executed. This type of interrogation involved repeated questioning, and as the detainees became more confused, they became more open to suggestion, which essentially led them into constructing their own 'confession'.

Individual interrogations went on night after night, consisting of continual questioning by relays of interrogators, sometimes for days on end. This was known as the 'conveyor', and some who had experienced it claimed that it was as painful after three days as any physical torture, and that a week of it would break anyone.

From reading other testimonies it seems that 'simple' interrogation became increasingly not enough, and other more sadistic methods were employed to extract confessions. I have no knowledge that my father suffered any of these, but apart from general beatings with fists and/or feet or the use of wooden clubs, the dreaded '*stoika*' method was frequently used, which had the detainee leaning against a wall on tiptoes and supported only by the fingertips for hours on end. It's claimed that sustained use of this method could break even the most resilient of people. There was also the 'swallow', where the victim had their hands and feet tied together behind the back and was then hoisted up into the air by their hands. I don't even want to imagine what this horror must have been like.

Refusing to confess was not an option. Everybody, it seems, had been detained 'legitimately', and sooner or later they would sign the confession placed before them. Some signed quickly, others signed reluctantly but once signed, they came off the conveyor, and were ready for sentencing.

Each day several of the prisoners who had confessed would be called from the cell during the day and taken for trial, and on 18 February 1940 it was my father's turn. He was led from the Wilejka prison to the building next door, now a police and administrative building but in 1940 the local courts. The session itself was farcical, held behind closed doors by an NKVD troika (тройка) chaired by the local NKVD chief, together with a local prosecutor, and the Wilejka Communist Party secretary. In the briefest of sessions he was presented before them and immediately found guilty and sentenced to eight years' hard labour for anti-Russian activities. There was no defence, no option for appeal. It was all over in a few minutes. He was returned to his cell to await his fate.

I have recently received the details of his sentence from the Office of Internal Affairs in Magadan Region, which confirmed that he was sentenced in accordance with Articles 64 and 76 of the Criminal Code of the Belarusian Federation (BSSR). These articles are directly comparable with Articles 58/2 and 58/11 (see the table below) of the Russian Federation (RSFSR), meaning that he was found guilty of armed revolt and counter-revolutionary activity!

Article 58 (Статьи 58)

In order to justify and legitimise mass control, the Soviet Union used a series of criminal codes as the 'legal' basis for much of their political repression. It was especially prevalent under Stalin, when the criminal code did not limit the discretion of prosecutors. For example, if police decided that a prescribed six-month sentence was inadequate for a suspect possessing anti-Soviet literature in peacetime, they could always beat and torture him till he 'confessed' to a more serious offence. In effect Article 58 was a carte blanche for the secret police to arrest and imprison anyone deemed undesirable or even suspicious, making its use their foremost political weapon.

It was first developed after the Revolution, though it had been in development for some time before. It was revised in 1934 as the criminal code of the RSFSR – Russian Soviet Federated Socialist Republic (уголовный кодекс РСФСР). This version was divided into two parts, a 'General Part' comprising of Articles 1 to 57 and a 'Specific Part' comprising of Articles 58 to 205. The 'Specific Part' outlined specific crimes and associated penalties for violations. Most NKVD officials and interrogators carried a small paperback version of the criminal codebook at all times.

The most notorious of the codes was Article 58, which had been created in February 1927 for use on those suspected of counter-revolutionary activities. This article introduced the formal notion of the 'enemy of workers', referring to political or class opponents of the Soviet Union. Its usage was derogatory, and meant to imply that the 'enemies' had conspired against the Soviet society as a whole. Those convicted under Article 58 were condescendingly known as 'politicals', and were considered to be the lowest of the low!

Article 58 led to the imprisonment of many prominent people together with multitudes of innocent civilians from all walks of life. Sentences could be very long, some extending as long as twenty-five years, and they could be extended indefinitely without trial or consultation. Inmates under Article 58 were known as '*politichesky*' (полити́ческий), whereas common criminals were called '*ugolovnik*' (уголо́вник). After release prisoners were often forbidden to live within 100 km of large cities.

Article 58 was a complex criminal code, with many subdivisions as per the simplified table below:

Article   Description

58-1   Counter-revolutionary activity. A counter-revolutionary action is any action aimed at overthrowing, undermining or weakening of the power of workers, peasants, Soviets (council), and governments of the USSR and Soviet and autonomous republics, or at the undermining or weakening of the external security of the USSR and main economical, political and national achievements of the proletarian revolution.

58-1a   Treason. Traitors to the motherland (including defectors).

58-1b   Treason by military personnel. Treason to the motherland, including defection. Stalin applied this charge to Soviet POWs returning to the Soviet Union after the Second World War. Often carried a death sentence and property confiscation. Relatives were subject to five to ten years of imprisonment and property confiscation or five years of Siberia exile, depending on the circumstances. The relatives were considered to have either helped, known of and not reported, or simply lived with the offender.

58-1g   Non-reporting of treason by military personnel.

58-2   Bourgeois nationalists and separatists. Armed uprising or intervention with the object of seizing power.

58-3   Abettors of the enemy. Contact with foreigners. Anyone who was considered to have helped or had contact with an enemy of the state.

58-4   Agents of the international bourgeoisie (e.g. émigrés). Any kind of help to those not recognizing the equality of communist political system, or striving to overthrow it.

58-5   Inciting a foreign state to declare war on USSR. Urging any foreign entity to declaration of war, military intervention, blockade, capture of state property, breaking diplomatic relations, breaking international treaties, and other aggressive actions against USSR.

58-6   Espionage, spies. Includes 'suspicion of espionage', 'unproven espionage', and 'contacts leading to suspicion of espionage'.

58-7   Subversives. Undermining of state industry, transport, monetary circulation or credit system, as well as of co-operative societies and organisations, with counter-revolutionary purpose (as defined by 58-1) by means of the corresponding usage of the state institutions, as well as by opposing their normal functioning. The offence according to this article was known as wrecking and the offenders were called 'wreckers'.

58-8   Terrorism. Attacks on Soviet officials were punishable by the 'supreme measure of social protection' (shooting) but murders of ordinary citizens only rated a ten-year prison sentence. This also included 'terrorist intent' which could be as trivial as speaking rudely to an official.

58-9   Sabotage. Damage of transport, communication, water supply, warehouses and other buildings or state and communal property with counter-revolutionary purposes.

58-10   Anti-Soviet agitation and propaganda. Carried at least six months of imprisonment, but in times of unrest or war carried a death penalty and property confiscation.

58-11   Membership of a counter-revolutionary organisation or hostile group.

58-12   Non-informers. Carried at least six months of imprisonment.

58-13   Being on the losing side in the former Civil War, service to former (Tsarist) government.

58-14   Counter-revolutionary sabotage. Any failure to perform a task, conscious non-execution or deliberately careless execution of 'defined duties', aimed at the weakening of the power of the government and of the functioning of the state apparatus is subject to at least one year of freedom deprivation, and under especially aggravating circumstances, up to the highest measure of 'supreme measure of social protection'.

The sentence for the above crimes was either the death sentence or up to ten years' imprisonment (or exile), which in both cases was usually accompanied with property confiscation and the formal recognition as 'enemy of workers'.

Criminal codes of other Soviet republics also had analogous articles that could be directly related to that of the RSFSR, as below.

	RSFSR	Ukrainian SSR	Belarusian SSR	Azerbaijani SSR
Treason by military personnel	58/1B	54/1B	63/2	63/2
Military recruitment abroad	58/1V	54/1V	63/3	63/3
Non-reporting of treason	58/1G	54/1G	63/4	63/4
Armed insurrection	58/2	54/2	64	64
Counter-revolutionary activities	58/11	54/11	76	73

These criminal codes remained in use until 1958, when they were abandoned by the then First Secretary of the Communist Party of the Soviet Union Nikita Khrushchev, and replaced with a law code more aligned to Western norms.

Within days of receiving his sentence, my father was called for '*etap*', a term used in the Soviet prison system for transport. He was taken from his cell, given a cursory medical check, and together with other convicts was loaded onto the back of an open-top truck guarded by armed Soviet soldiers and driven the short distance south to the town of Maladzyechna.

City/town	Local name	Location	Approx. distance	Country
Maladzyechna (Molodechno)	Молодéчно	25 km south of Stara Wilejka	80 km	Poland (Polska)

Now called Molodechno, it was known to the Polish as Maladzyechna and was originally a fortification on the right bank of the River Usha. At the end of the nineteenth century it (significantly) became an important railway transit station on the route from Vilnius (and cities in the west) to Minsk and on to Moscow.

Following the Partitions of Poland, the area was annexed by Imperial Russia and its palace and castle were abandoned. During the final stages of Napoleon's invasion of Russia it was here that his Grande Armee made its last stand in the former Grand Duchy of Lithuania. In early November of 1812 Napoleon Bonaparte gave his last orders to his marshals here, after which he left for Vilnius. On 21 November of that year the Polish-born Russian general Yefim Chaplits arrived and defeated the already-routed French forces led by Marshal Victor. As a result of the battles the town was completely destroyed and the monastery and the castle laid to ruin. However, the ruined ramparts of the castle, built in 1388 and allegedly used by Napoleon, can still be seen just outside of the town, alongside the road to Vileyka.

At the beginning of the the Second World War it was annexed to the Byelorussian SSR, where it became part of the Vileyka voblast on 4 December 1939. After the German invasion of the USSR the new German authorities set up the infamous Stalag 342 for the Soviet prisoners of war there.

On 5 June 1944 the advancing Red Army, in fierce fighting, liberated the city from the Germans. Unfortunately historical monuments like the spectacular Triumphal Arch, built in 1920, were destroyed and sadly never rebuilt.

The heavy damage that Vileyka suffered during the war made it unsuitable to perform the role of the administrative centre, and so Molodechno became the new administrative centre when civilian control was restored in the BSSR on 20 September 1944. This Molodechno *voblast* also survived the 1954 reform that halved the amount of *voblasts* in the BSSR, but on 20 January 1960 the *voblast* was disestablished and it became part of the modern Minsk *voblast*, in which it remains today as part of the Republic of Belarus.

It's likely that my father and his fellow convicts were taken either to the Maladzyechna teaching school or to one of two large warehouses near the train station, which had been converted into makeshift but notorious prisons. Though he had received his sentence and presumably signed a confession of guilt, his questioning didn't stop. Regular interrogation continued, usually every other night, and if the interrogators were unhappy with a response or didn't get the answer they wanted he would receive a beating or, as happened too frequently, was made to spend the night standing in a cell with freezing water up to his ankles. Bearing in mind that the winter of 1939/40 was one of the coldest on record, this must have been an awful torture. Unhappily, this particular torture was to return to blight his life again later on.

7. Treatment of Poles by NKVD, Check ups, Tortures, Punishment, Propaganda, Communist Information about Poland.

Check-ups were inhuman. If you could not answer a question you were flogged. You would be put in a cell with water up to your ankles. This check was done every other night.

Pleszak family document

4

DEPORTATION

The Trans-Siberian Experience

While my father was being held in detention, the whole of Eastern Poland continued in its state of turmoil. The Soviet authorities, since their invasion of 17 September, had been busy collating the information collected during the surveys that had been conducted prior to the elections in October. Detailed lists were compiled for all cities, towns, and villages of families and their belongings. These lists had been completed by 5 January 1940, but even by 5 December 1939, just over a month after the enforced elections, resolution number 2001-558, calling for the forcible deportation of Polish nationals, had been presented to the Council of People's Commissars of the USSR by Lavrentiy Beria.

Lavrentiy Beria

I include a brief description of Beria not only because he presided over possibly the darkest incident affecting all the Kresy Poles, and as such the significant part he played in my father's story, but also because there are two other very similarly named protagonists that are also relevant to this story (Berzin and Berling) and I want to avoid confusion between the three.

Lavrentiy Pavlovich Beria (Лаврентий Павлович Берия) was born in 1899 in Merkheuli, in the Abkhazian region of Georgia, which was then part of Imperial Russia. His early aspirations were of becoming an architect, and he initially worked as a building inspector in Azerbaijan after graduating from college. He joined the Bolsheviks in 1917 and was active in Georgia during the October Revolution, after which he joined the Cheka. He was a ruthless and willing tool of the Soviet state, even leading the repression of a Georgian Nationalist uprising, in which 10,000 people were allegedly executed. He was quickly promoted through the ranks, eventually becoming the head of the NKVD in Georgia.

In 1938, fellow Georgian Stalin brought Beria to Moscow and appointed him deputy to Nikolai Ivanovich Yezhov (Николай Иванович Ежов), the diminutive but callous and brutal head of the NKVD. Within a short time Yezhov had been arrested and replaced by Beria, whose reputation for getting things done at any cost had not gone unnoticed. Stalin used Beria to stage his purges, and under Beria the NKVD was responsible for the deaths of millions of Russians. Even the Soviet armed forces suffered, with estimates of up to a third of all officers being arrested, three out of five marshals and fourteen out of sixteen Army commanders being executed.

He is remembered as one of the cruellest leaders of a regime known for its brutality, but perhaps more significantly in the context of this story, was responsible for the restructuring of the Soviet labour camp system. These camps had been in existence for some time, even before the Revolution, but under Beria's jurisdiction they were to be used not only as punishment but also, ominously in a land rich in resources but short of manpower, to fuel the Soviet economy!

With the murder of revolutionary Marxist theorist Leon Trotsky in the Mexican town of Coyoacán in August 1940, all the leading figures involved in the Russian Revolution were now dead, apart from Stalin himself. Of the fifteen original members of the Bolshevik government, ten had been executed and four had died in dubious circumstances. Beria prospered under Stalin and he became a member of the Central Committee of the Communist Party. In February 1941 he became Deputy Prime Minister and in 1946 joined the Politburo.

Stalin died on 5 March 1953, a few days after collapsing in the night following a dinner with Beria and other Soviet leaders. Some consider Beria himself directly responsible for Stalin's death. A power struggle broke out in Moscow and Beria attempted to succeed Stalin as the head of the Soviet Union, but was defeated by a group led by Nikita Khrushchev, Vyacheslav Molotov, and Georgy Malenkov. Beria was arrested and accused of conducting 'anti-state activities', including spying for Britain. He was found guilty and was executed on 23 December 1953.

By 25 December 1939 Stalin had sanctioned resolution 2001-558, and four days later it was already being executed when Soviet Rail and Camp commanders, under the guidance of the NKVD, developed a logistical plan to deport the 'undesirables' from the Kresy region to work in labour camps across the Soviet Union.

Trains specially converted were distributed to railway sidings throughout Soviet-controlled Kresy (with the exception of Wilno, which had been handed over into Lithuanian control). According to the ruling of 29 December one transport (echelon) was to consist of fifty-five trucks, with a passenger coach reserved for a military escort, and one for first-aid, which was supposed to have comprised one medical orderly and two nurses.

Each truck, which in most cases was a crudely converted cattle truck, typically red in colour, bolted from the outside, was supposed to accommodate twenty-five people, but from most written testimonies and recently published documents it can be seen that the number was much higher, often exceeding fifty, sometimes up to ninety people per truck. Some trucks were designated as *shizo* (шизо штрафа изолятор – penalty isolator) to accommodate trouble causers, and the final truck was often fitted with a 'cat' – a row of metal spikes that pointed down to the tracks and were designed to mutilate any would-be escapees making their getaway through the floor.

Mass Deportations

The deportation of whole groups of civilians from their homes to different regions was a well-used policy in Russia and the Soviet Union. It was a method by which the ruling party retained its power and controlled its subjects. Russia used it on its own citizens and it was used by the Soviet Union on any of the states with which it was associated. It was used in the first wave of mass terror in the early thirties when farmers and rural communities were targeted and again in the late thirties in what is known as 'The Great Terror', when cities and towns were targeted.

Deportation across Russia, and later the Soviet Union, had regularly been inflicted on the Poles during the last few hundred years. Reports of visitors to Siberia tell of Polish villages there inhabited by the descendants of nineteenth-century deportees. During the partitions of Poland, Poles who rose in armed rebellion against Russian rule in the uprisings of April 1794, November 1831 and January 1863 were normally sent to Siberia, as were those whom secret service police agents deemed too patriotic to Poland or not deferential enough to the Tsar.

Nor did deportations end with the re-establishment of a sovereign and independent Polish Republic in 1918. Poland's eastern border, as described by the Treaty of Riga which brought closure to the Polish–Bolshevik War of 1920, left substantial Polish minorities on the Soviet side of the border. In 1934–5, by order of Stalin, all Poles that lived near the Polish border were deported to Kazakhstan, and once Poland had collapsed in the autumn of 1939 Stalin was in a position to use his deportation option again.

Detailed instructions defined that the deportees could only take clothing, underwear, shoes, bedding, kitchen and dining utensils, one month's supply of food for all the family, small agricultural and domestic implements, and some personal valuables and money. The total weight of luggage was not to exceed 500 kg per family. Those with property were forced to turn over their homes and farms, together with land and equipment, to the local authorities.

People to be deported were awakened in the night and given less than one hour to prepare for the journey. They were then herded into the already prepared cattle rail road cars, in which they spent weeks and sometimes months, until they reached their final destination.

Soviet Resolution 2001-558 ultimately led to four mass deportations of Polish citizens. The first occurred during the night of 9/10 February 1940. About 220,000 civil servants, government officials, police, small farmers, and forest workers were targeted.

The second was during the night of 12/13 April when around 230,000 civilians, including members of families of people previously arrested, families of those who had escaped from Poland, together with tradesmen and farmers were deported.

The third took place between 25 and 30 June. A further 240,000 citizens were targeted, comprising those who fled the German onslaught, small merchants, doctors, teachers, and journalists.

The fourth mass deportation was a year later, during the week of 14–21 June 1941, which for the first time included Wilno, which had by then returned to Soviet control. In total, estimates of between 1 and 2 million Poles were forcibly removed from their homes and deported. The numbers may in reality have been considerably higher.

The act of evicting the citizens of any particular district, typically consisting of 250–300 families, was supervised by a troika of officials led by the district head of the NKVD, aided by Communist Party members, militia and local activists. In Byelorussia there were 4,005 troikas in thirty-seven operational territorial divisions, employing 16,279 people of whom 11,674 had been brought over from the East Byelorussian region of the USSR. The overall supervision of the first deportation in February 1940 was performed by Beria's deputy, V. V. Chernyshev, aided in Byelorussia by L. F. Tsanava, and the Ukraine by I. A. Serov and M. Merkulov.

Punishment Camps in the Soviet Union

The deported Poles were sent to a variety of detention camps across the Soviet Union where they worked on forestry, agriculture, mining, or industrial projects. I don't intend to give a detailed description of each of these camps (except in a later chapter for *lagiers*, which was where my father was sent), but I will give a small description of the various types for completeness. There are many published works describing these Polish deportations, but excellent and harrowing accounts of both deportation and life in these camps can be read in *Stalin's Ethnic Cleansing in Eastern Poland: Tales of the Deported, 1940-1946* from the Veritas foundation, London.

Posiolki

Work camps or settlements for families, simply to isolate them from community as a whole, usually located deep in the taiga forest or the steppes of Uzbekistan.

Osadnicy

Camps for teachers, forest rangers, land managers, some doctors, and intellectuals.

Specposiolki

Similar to the previous, but mainly for those who escaped the advancing German Army and were caught by the Russians. These were camps with medium restrictive regimes; generally no watch towers or fences; security was virtually assured by their remote location in tundra, taiga or steppe. Included Jewish families and some wealthy families from western Poland.

Tiurmy

These jails were medium- to short-term detention centres, used for individuals awaiting trial and/or deportation. Often used for executions.

Kolchoz

A term used for a collective farm in Russia. Some deportees were sent to these, but these were generally a small minority.

Sharashki

This was an informal name for a special type of detention camp used for secret research and development under the auspices of the Soviet labour camp administration. These were set up in realisation that during the Soviet purges many eminent academics, scientists, and engineers who had been exiled and used for hard manual labour could be better utilised in their own field of expertise. Those identified in camps were removed to a *sharashka*, where they were given better treatment, better food, and were encouraged to continue in their own field of work. Some of the most notable *sharashka* inmates were writers Aleksandr Solzhenitsyn and Lev Kopelev; rocket engineers Sergey Korolyov (designer of the *Sputnik* space rockets), Valentin Glushko, and Yuri Kondratyuk; aircraft engineers Andrei Tupolev, Vladimir Petlyakov, Vladimir Myasishchev, and Nikolai Polikarpov. Initially *sharashki* were known as 'Special Construction Bureaus', and were collectively known as the 'Fourth Special Department'.

All the above camps were labour camps, which were very harsh and brutal. Everybody including children had to work, but some of the deportees could earn a small payment, providing they had completed their allocated work assignment (known in camp parlance as a *norm*). The meagre food allocations were also dependant on *norms* being completed.

Lagiers/Hard Labour Camps

These were camps for corrective purposes used as punishment for real criminals, such as those deemed to be hooligans, trespassers, thieves, those convicted of any misbehaviour or even religious offences, criticism of the authorities or similar offences, and those considered to have transgressed an often unwritten and misleading Soviet edict. Those like my father convicted under Article 58 were all sentenced to a *lagier*. Normally only single people and military commanders and soldiers were banished there. These were restricted camps, typically with towers, guards, dogs and barbed wire, usually in a far remote and isolated location where they had to work hard, and a harsh and unforgiving regime ensued. For many sentenced here it was a horrible, slow death sentence.

All the Poles deported by the Soviet authorities, whether convicted like my father or deported *en masse*, were sent to one (and sometimes more than one) type of the punishment camps described above. They were all labour camps; what they were not was either concentration or internment camps, which were used for confining groups people together in a single place because of who they were and not for what they had done.

The former were typically camps for collecting large groups of people considered to be undesirable. The term 'concentration camp' was used to signify the 'concentration' of a large number of people in a single place. It's origin comes from the Spanish *'reconcentration'* which was used to describe the camps established by the Spanish to support an anti-insurgency campaign in Cuba in the late 1890s. It was adopted by the British to describe the camps operated in South Africa during the Second Boer War of 1899–1902.

The term concentration camp lost some of its original meaning after Nazi death camps were discovered, after which the term became 'generally' synonymous with the worst excesses of man's treatment to his fellow man. It has been used ever since to refer to a place of mistreatment, starvation, forced labour and genocide. The term 'concentration camp' is now only used in this extremely pejorative sense.

I used the word 'generally' in the previous paragraph because Nazi concentration camps are known about globally, and considered by most as some of the worst examples of human brutality. But, it has to be said that the Nazi Germans kept lots of documentary evidence, including much photographic and film footage of their treatment of their undesirables. In addition to this, many of their camps were liberated by Allied forces who brought their existence to the attention of the world media. However, there were far more of the Russian camps described above and though not designed for eradication purposes along the lines of the Nazi extermination camps, they were considered to be much harsher environments, and no less brutal to those incarcerated in them. Their existence was kept secret, and was only really known by those sentenced to them or those working in them, and little information ever reached the West through the firmly closed doors of the Soviet Empire.

The Soviet authorities, unlike their German counterparts, didn't film or photograph themselves or their actions so much, so comparatively little evidence ever emerged. But since the disillusionment of the Soviet Union in 1990 and the emergence of the internet as a truly world-wide medium for research and disseminating information, much more information has come to light, with researchers, historians, archivists and families putting information and images on the internet for all to see.

Gulag (ГУЛАГ)

For most people the above paragraph on *lagiers* would accurately describe a gulag, whilst for others any of the Soviet camp types could be described as a gulag. In reality the term Gulag was originally an acronym for the name of the Soviet government agency responsible for managing and administering the labour camps – the NKVD's Главное Управление Исправительно-Трудовых Лагерей и колоний (or transliterated into English Glavnoye Upravleniye Ispravitel-Trudovykh Lagerey i Koloniy – the Chief Administration of Corrective Labour Camps and Colonies). The term quickly developed into a more general meaning of the whole system of Soviet penal labour and is now widely used to describe any camp used in the Soviet repressive system.

The gulag system had been in existence for quite some time, used as inefficiently managed prison camps where people died through illness or accident. It's not too clear how they developed, either through the process of collectivisation (which started in 1929) or through meticulous planning by Stalin and his cronies. It was probably some of both but once started they seemed almost self-perpetuating with camps erupting like a rash across the whole of the Soviet Union, however inhospitable their location.

In their early days they were considered to be less brutal and food rations, treatment, and clothing were better than they were to become in later years. Escapes during this time, though not common, were much more easily achieved than in later years. Stalin himself was exiled to 'the Katorga', the forerunner of the gulag and allegedly escaped four times. Some believe that he introduced the cruel oppressive system of the gulags after his own experiences.

According to Anne Applebaum, by 1937 the gulags had become labour camps where prisoners were considered expendable and could be worked to death. Around this same time terms used for prisoners became far more derogatory and prisoners were often considered as vermin, or worse! The term *zek* (as described earlier) was always associated with somebody not considered a citizen of the Soviet Union.

Every prisoner, young or old, had to work. It was an 'eat as you work system', with food rations being allocated for tasks completed (known in gulag terms as a *norm*). These norms were carefully calculated (by a *normirovshchik*) and special camp *norm* administrators (*naryadchik*). In the early days of the gulag a food allowance of 1 kg of bread was given to those completing their *norm*. For exceptional workers, 'shock workers' or *stakhanovites* (named after Aleksei Grigorievich Stakhanov who, allegedly, had mined 102 tons of coal in less than six hours; fourteen times his quota) there was an extra kilogram, whilst for those unfortunates unable to complete their *norm* there was a reduced allowance.

In 1938 Beria took over as the head of the NKVD and, though he soon realised prisoner labour could never be as productive as free labour, he was determined to make gulag labour profitable. Initially food rations improved in an attempt to curb the high death and sickness rates which were affecting production quotas. By 1940 conditions had deteriorated drastically and food allowances had dropped to 400–450 grams a day for those completing their *norms*, with *stakhanovites* getting an extra 200 grams and those on punishment rations a mere 300 grams or less!

It is believed that there were nearly 500 separate camp complexes, each one comprising hundreds, and in some cases even thousands of individual camps. There are estimates that there may have been up to 7 million prisoners in these camps at any one time. Before they were discontinued in 1953 it is suggested that more than 20 million people had passed through the gulag system, and this doesn't include the camps set up by the NKVD in 1944 specifically for the large numbers of prisoners of war captured in Red Army's advance west, known as the GUPVI – Main Administration of War Prisoners and Internees.

Even though my father spent time in the gulags it's not a term that he ever used; if he ever spoke about them he just referred to them as prison camps. I first learned of the term in the early 1980s when I became aware of Aleksandr Solzhenitsyn's book *The Gulag Archipelago* in which he compared the system of labour camps dotted across the Soviet Union with a vast 'chain of islands'. I have to confess that I didn't, until researching my father's past, associate the camps my father was in with gulags.

The freezing cold, snowy evening of 9/10 February 1940 saw the first wave of mass deportations of the Poles. My father was still in detention and was spared from it. His family were also not included in this or the subsequent mass deportations. I've no idea why, as other families from Szwakszty were. Maybe it was because my grandfather Wincenty had served in the Russian Army. I suspect I'll never get to know.

Ominously, by 1 April 1940 special trains had moved, out of sight of public view, into railway sidings in most of the cities in the Kresy region. Maladzyechna was no exception, and a train in sinister secrecy was being prepared with twenty-three of the dreaded cattle trucks. The start of the second wave of mass deportations was about to begin.

A few days later, in the dead of the night, my father and all the other convicted Poles were ordered without warning from their cells. They had been called for *etap* by armed Soviet guards. There were lined up five abreast in a single column and before setting it off it was made very clear to them that talking was forbidden, they were to look straight ahead at the person in front of them and anybody walking too slow, too fast, stopping, wandering to the right or to the left would be considered as making an attempt to escape and would be shot. The message was unambiguous. After a meticulous counting session which had to be repeated several times and documented, they set off to what was for them an unknown destination.

After a relatively short journey they arrived at the railway siding to be greeted by the waiting trains with their long lines of red cattle trucks. Though it was the early hours of the morning, the siding was a hive of activity with NKVD officials, administrators, railway personnel, civilian workers, and Red Army soldiers. The trains looked outwardly like normal rail cars, but the activity and the increased protection around them made them stand out from normal trains.

They were then treated to the same routine of meticulous checking and counting, repeated several times to ensure the arrival numbers tallied with those departing the prison. It was the escort guards' worst fear, allowing any of their detail to escape; it could immediately place them in the same position as those they were guarding!

The prisoners were ushered to the open doors and forced to climb into the high, empty cattle trucks. There were no steps or ladders; even for fit, healthy men it would have been a struggle but for weak, hungry, and confused prisoners pressured by the screaming, agitated guards and the push from those behind it was a huge task. Those that struggled were given no help or consideration from their fellow prisoners and especially from the guards and NKVD officials. Once loaded the doors were slammed shut and bolted, but the train didn't set off. My father with his fellow prisoners sat in the dark, pondering their fate.

Leading up to the night of 12/13 April a huge commotion surrounded the waiting train. The NKVD had rounded up the second batch of civilians, who without trial had now been brought in family groups to the waiting train. Just as my father's group were shown no mercy and forced to climb into the high cattle trucks, so were the arriving group, which included young and old men, women and children, pregnant women, the infirm and the disabled.

In total 551 deportees were loaded into the twenty-three carriages at Maladzyechna and once loading had been completed and all the paperwork completed, the train, escorted by the 15th Brigade Guards of the Red Army, very slowly edged away from the railway siding and onto the main railway line heading south-east towards the then Russian town of Minsk and away from Poland. In Moscow, Beria was being kept abreast of the situation across the whole of the Kresy by his vast network of NKVD officials.

The cattle truck in which my father was to spend the next couple of months had been very crudely converted for the carriage of what was essentially human cargo, not a group of passengers. It would have had two or three wooden shelves installed at each end to serve as beds, but with no bedding provided. The shelves were totally insufficient for the numbers of people in the carriage. Those unlucky not to get a space on one of these bunks had to spend their entire journey sitting and sleeping on the filthy floor and beneath the bed boards, and even for those on a bunk their headroom was restricted so that they had to sit or lie uncomfortably or bent over and hunched up.

Some but not all carriages had a rudimentary stove made from a simple metal barrel fitted in the middle of the floor. There was never enough coal or wood for burning, and when lit the stove worked inefficiently. There was no flue, so smoke would billow about the carriage and suffocate everybody, so much so that it was generally never used, but when it was lit those near to it almost fried whilst those further away continued to freeze – literally. Those unfortunates who slept with their backs against the moist walls of the cattle truck woke up in the morning with clothes frozen to the walls; in some accounts of family deportations there are reports of girls and women having their hair frozen to the carriage walls!

There were no proper windows as such, so they would never have been able to properly see out. There were two small, heavily barred window openings very near to the ceiling of the carriage that let in a little light, but generally the inside of the carriage was dark, even during the day. The only view of the outside world was through small cracks in the wooden carriage walls. Some of the families in other carriages brought candles but these were very soon used up.

Toilet facilities were crude; simply a narrow hole in the floor, which for the family carriages sometimes had a privacy curtain installed. In most carriages these holes had been edged with iron to prevent them being widened and used to escape through. In some accounts trading went on through these holes when the train had stopped at a station, whereby the carriage inhabitants would barter some item of their belongings (family deportees had been allowed to bring some personal items) through the hole in exchange for items like bread, water, medicine, tobacco, or candles. But for its primary use as a toilet it was used almost constantly, and the smell can only be imagined. Sometimes in the winter it would totally freeze up. There was no toilet paper or washing facilities.

The deportees were packed inside the trucks like sardines, and for prisoners convicted like my father they only had the clothes in which they were arrested. There was no allowance for the changing weather. At first it was too cold and they had insufficient clothes, and had to resort to herding themselves together to keep warm. In spring and summer the temperature rose, so prisoners spent all day and night in their underwear because the heat in the carriage was so intense.

There were no washing facilities, but some memoirists mention that occasionally on very long journeys the trains stopped and the prisoners were allowed to use bathhouses, but these seem to have been in exceptional circumstances and not the norm.

Food rations, like in the prisons, were irregular and totally inadequate and prisoners were continually hungry. They were supposed to have received hot soup, known as *balanda* (баландан) and 800 grams of bread, *paika* (пайка) for each person every day. This was of course only ever loosely adhered to. To make matters worse, each truck became dominated by real criminals, known as *urkas* (whom, as we shall see later dominated the daily routine and were used by the escort guards as a brutal policing service to keep the inhabitants subdued and submissive). It was generally the *urkas* who took it on themselves to organise the food in the carriage, ensuring they got the most before distributing the rest.

It wasn't unusual for there to be no food for days, and the *balanda* often substituted by *kipiatok* (warm water). Sometimes they received salted fish which caused a severe thirst, and which for most memoirists seems to have been more of a torment to them than their hunger. There are accounts of prisoners being so desperate for water during their train journey that they were forced to lick the condensation from the rusty nails of the carriage or the frozen wooden sides of the compartment walls.

The *balanda* (soup) when it did arrive was a watery melange containing fish heads, bones, eyes, animal entrails, and rotten vegetables or vegetable stalks. Having a bowl or cup in which to put it was a high priority and for those lucky enough to own one it became a highly prized and fiercely guarded possession. The *paika* was always of dubious composition, usually insufficiently baked and often described as being like clay. There are reports that it would sometimes have sawdust added to the ingredients to 'bulk it up'! Some of the trains had a metal cup chained to the carriage wall for the prisoners to share for water when they were lucky enough to have some supplied. I can't even begin to think about or really imagine the absolute horrors my father and his fellow deportees were to suffer. I can only get an idea from the written literature of books such as Janusz Bardach's *Man is Wolf to Man*, Aleksander Topolski's *Without Vodka* and others. It's too distressing to imagine, I don't know how words could ever describe their misery. I won't even begin to try.

And so in these indescribably awful conditions the train made its slow way east from Maladzyechna towards the nearby Russian border. I'm not sure how, maybe it was through gaps in the carriage wall, or through a crack in the door but within a short time the occupants of the train realised that they had passed over the border out of what was for them Poland and into Russia. For most it was heartbreaking realisation. It was a very emotional and tearful experience for all the ethnic Poles and, as seems common with most accounts, spontaneous singing of patriotic and religious songs such as 'We Will Not Forsake Our Land' and 'Into Thy Care' immediately started throughout the length of the train.

Within a short space of time after crossing the border the train passed by the Russian city of Minsk and was into the RSFSR, travelling east through the European plain towards Moscow. My father wouldn't have seen the beautiful and historic cities or the countryside along the way, and all I have of his record of this journey is a faded, red-pencilled line he drew on an old atlas showing the route that he took, but his incarceration had moved into the next phase, and the world outside was passing him by. My father, and most of those on his and all the other trains, had left Poland behind. They were not to know it then, but most would never return.

Russia (Россия)

Russia, the Russian Federation (Российская Федерация), or the RSFSR (РСФСР) – Russian Soviet Federated Socialist Republic (Российская Советская Федеративная Социалистическая Республика) – is a huge, transcontinental country extending over much of northern Eurasia (Europe and Asia). It covers an area of 17,075,400 square km, making it the largest country in the world. It covers almost twice the total area of the next-largest country, Canada.

Russia was also the largest member of the Soviet Union (Сове́тский Сою́з) or more fully the Union of Soviet Socialist Republics, the USSR (Сою́з Сове́тских Социалисти́ческих Респу́блик – CCCP), which was a constitutionally Marxist socialist state that was created following the Russian Revolution in 1922 and lasted until 1991. As Russia was the primary member of the Soviet Union, hosting the capital city of Moscow, the terms 'Russia', 'USSR', and the 'Soviet Union' were often used interchangeably. It became the *de facto* model for all future communist states.

It was formed as a federal union of the RSFSR and those neighbouring areas under its military occupation or ruled by branches of the communist movement. Initially established as a union of four Soviet Socialist Republics, the USSR grew to envelop sixteen constituent or 'union republics' which by 1956 included the Armenian SSR, Azerbaijan SSR, Byelorussian SSR, Estonian SSR, Georgian SSR, Karelian ASSR, Kazakh SSR, Kyrgyz SSR, Latvian SSR, Lithuanian SSR, Moldavian SSR, Russian SFSR, Tajik SSR, Turkmen SSR, Ukrainian SSR, and Uzbek SSR.

The boundaries of the USSR approximately corresponded to those of late Imperial Russia, with the significant exceptions of Poland, most of Finland, and Alaska.

The USSR lasted until 8 December 1991, when it was dissolved and replaced by the Commonwealth of Independent States (CIS), which was an unsuccessful effort by Russia to keep the USSR together in an economic alliance. In recent years the representative countries have operated in complete independence from Russia itself, which at times has led to severe mistrust and on occasion military conflict.

Russia is located on the eastern part of Europe and northern part of Asia, and is covered by eleven time-zones. The East European Plain occupies the west of Russia, with the Ural mountain chain forming the approximate border with Asia. It has borders with North Korea, the People's Republic of China, Mongolia, Kazakhstan, Azerbaijan, Georgia, Ukraine, Belarus, Lithuania, Poland, Latvia, Estonia, Finland and Norway.

Russia is home to the highest mountain in Europe, Mount Elbrus (Эльбрус) with its distinctive twin peaks at 5,642 and 5,621 m. It is located in the western Caucasus Mountains, near to the border with Georgia.

Most Russian territory lies in the temperate climatic zone; the islands of the Arctic Ocean and northern continental areas lie in arctic and subarctic zones; the Black Sea coast of the Caucasus is located in the subtropical zone. The climate is almost everywhere continental, with cold winters and hot summers.

Siberia (Сиби́рь)

The Asian part of Russia (east of the Ural Mountains) is infamously, even invidiously known as Siberia (Сиби́рь). The international benchmark of cold, isolation and deprivation, the name itself is synonymous with repression, brutality and horror. But it belies a vast expanse of incredible, spectacular and mainly untouched natural beauty, which is bestowed with an abundance of natural wealth in flora, fauna, and minerals. The latter of these involves ores of almost all economically valuable metals and some of the world's largest deposits of nickel, gold, lead, molybdenum, diamonds, silver and zinc, as well as extensive unexploited resources of oil and natural gas. Siberia, though sparsely populated, has been occupied by differing groups of indigenous nomads such as the Yenets, the Nenets, the Huns, and the Uyghurs.

Siberia is usually sub-divided into three distinct regions: the West Siberian Plain, eastern Siberia, and the Russian Far East. All but the extreme south-western area of Siberia lies in Russia, and it makes up about 77 per cent of Russia's territory (13.1 million square km), but only 27 per cent of Russia's population.

City/town	Local name	Location	Approx. distance	Country
Minsk	Минск	65 km south of Maladzyechna	145 km	Russia (Россия)

The first truly Russian city he passed through after leaving Polish territory was Minsk, now the capital and largest city of Belarus. It is situated on the Svislach and Niamiha Rivers and is the headquarters of the Commonwealth of Independent States (CIS).

The earliest references to Minsk are in 1067 and in 1242 Minsk became a part of the Grand Duchy of Lithuania. It received its town privileges in 1499. From 1569, it was a capital of the Minsk voivodeship in the Polish–Lithuanian Commonwealth. It was annexed by Russia in 1793, as a consequence of the Second Partition of Poland. In 1919 it was briefly capital of Belarus before becoming part of the Byelorussian SSR in 1921. It became capital of independent Belarus in 1991.

The city, levelled twice during the Second World War, was rapidly built in typical Stalinist architectural splendour, but sadly due to the total devastation inflicted on it, little of the old town now remains. The pride of Minsk is the recently reconstructed main railway station, which is overlooked by the impressive Gates of Minsk. Because it was a major centre of partisan resistance during the Second World War it was awarded the title Hero City in 1974.

Minsk is located on the south-eastern slope of the Minsk Hills, a region of low, rolling hills running from the south-west (upper reaches of the River Nioman) to the north-east. The River Svislach, which flows across the city from the north-west to the south-east, is located in the *Urstromtal*, an ancient river valley formed by water flowing from melting ice sheets at the end of the last Ice Age. Early Minsk was initially founded on the hills along the river. However, in the twentieth century, it grew to include the relatively flat plains in the south-east.

The city is surrounded by the mixed forests typical of most of Belarus, though pine is the most predominant tree species. It has a moderate climate, owing to its location between the strong influence of the moist air of the Atlantic Ocean and the dry air of the Eurasian landmass. Its weather is, however, unstable and tends to be changeable.

In the early 1960s Lee Harvey Oswald, infamous as the alleged assassin of President John F. Kennedy, spent nearly three years living and working in Minsk. He worked as a metal lathe operator at the Gorizont Electronics Factory, which produced radios and televisions along with military and space components. He lived in an apartment overlooking the River Svislach and in 1961 met and married Marina Prusakova, who was originally from Saint Petersburg. Following his return to America in June 1962, he eventually ended up in Dallas, and the rest, as they say, 'is history'.

From Minsk the train containing my father continued east towards Smolensk and would have passed near to, possibly even through the small town of Gnezdovo (Гнёздово), about 20 km to the west of Smolensk. The name won't mean much to most people until it is linked to the nearby Katyn (Катынь) Forest where, around the time my father's train passed through, a despicable act was being perpetrated at the hands of the NKVD. This 'act' was being 'executed' in strict secrecy and was to remain hidden from the world for nearly three years, and when discovered became a key moment in my father's journey, and a significant factor in the plight of the Polish nation right up to the present day.

City/town	Local name	Location	Approx. distance	Country
Smolensk	Смоленск	350 km north-east of Minsk	495 km	Russia (Россия)

The city of Smolensk itself is located on both banks of Dnieper River, about 350 km south-west of Moscow. Its name comes from the resin (*smola*) extracted from pine trees that are common in the area.

Though an ancient city, and indeed one of the oldest in Russia, it has suffered tragically because of its location – being directly between Western Europe and Moscow – so much so that it has the dubious distinction of seemingly getting razed in every major conflict involving the forces of East and West. Despite this, it remains an impressive city with many outstanding churches and other architectural monuments dating back through the nineteenth to the twelfth century.

This once walled city has been almost completely destroyed several times throughout its long history, most notably by the Mongol armies in 1238, then by Napoleon in August 1812 when two of the largest armies ever assembled clashed there. During the hard-fought battle, described by Leo Tolstoy in *War and Peace*, Napoleon was victorious over General Kutuzov's army and entered the city, only to be driven out in December of the same year by poor weather. In 1941, when Germany invaded Russia nearly 95 per cent of the city was destroyed, only to suffer more damage in 1943 when the Germans were routed by the advancing Russian armies.

Among the many military monuments in Smolensk is the Eagles monument, unveiled in 1912 to mark the centenary of Napoleon's Russian campaign. In celebration of its heroics in the Second World War it was another city bestowed with the honour of Hero City status. After the Second World War Smolensk was rebuilt with its original pattern largely preserved, and today Smolensk is noted for electronics, textiles, food and flax processing.

My dad's train may have stopped at Smolensk; if it did it wasn't for long. It would have soon been back on the tracks heading ever eastwards and now towards Moscow.

City/town	Local name	Location	Approx. distance	Country
Moscow	Москва	350 km north-east of Smolensk	845 km	Russia (Россия)

Moscow, the capital city of Russia, is now the most populous city in Europe with nearly 13 million inhabitants, almost 7 per cent of the total Russian population. Like any other great city it has many negative aspects, but these do not diminish the splendour and magnificence of this huge city. Like most Russian cities it has a hugely elaborate main railway station, as is befitting the starting point of the famous Trans-Siberian Railway, which my father was now travelling along 'courtesy' of Stalin and his Soviet administration.

Moscow is famous not only for its performing arts culture but also its spectacular architecture. Saint Basil's Cathedral, with its elegant domes, is perhaps the most photographed cathedral in the world. But the Kremlin, Red Square and the White House are equally impressive.

Historically it was the capital of the former Soviet Union and the Grand Duchy of Moscow, the pre-Imperial Russian state. It is named after the river upon which it is built, and its name means 'the city by the Moskva River'. The origin of the name is unknown. Although several theories exist, the most reliable theory is that the name is derived from the Mongolian Moshkha, who sacked the city in 1237. It did, however, spend a time from 1712 to 1918 as the second city of Russia while Saint Petersburg acted as the capital.

Moscow is a major economic centre, the home to huge commerce, industrial, and financial institutions. It possesses a complex transport system that includes the world's busiest metro system.

In November 1941, the German Army was stopped at the outskirts of the city and then driven back during the Battle of Moscow. Many factories had been evacuated, together with much of the government, and the city was declared to be under siege. In recognition of the siege Moscow was one of twelve Soviet cities awarded the title of the Hero City. Moscow is exposed to cold winters, warm and mild summers, and very brief spring and autumn seasons.

City/town	Local name	Location	Approx. distance	Country
Nizhny Novgorod (Gorkiy)	Нижний Новгород (Го́рький)	550 km north-east of Moscow	1,395 km	Russia (Росси́я)

Nizhny Novgorod, colloquially shortened as Nizhny, is the fourth-largest city in Russia and was founded by Grand Duke Yuri II of Russia in 1221 at the confluence of the two most important rivers of his principality, the Volga and the Oka. Its name literally means 'Newtown the Lower', to distinguish it from the older Novgorod. A major stronghold for border protection, Nizhny Novgorod fortress took advantage of a natural moat formed by the two rivers.

In 1817, the Makaryev Fair, one of the most celebrated in the world, was transferred to Nizhny Novgorod and attracted millions of annual visitors. By the mid-nineteenth century it was established as the trade capital of the Russian Empire.

Henry Ford helped build the large car, truck and tractor plant GAZ (Gorkovsky Avtomobilny Zavod – ГаЗ Горьковский автомобильный Завод) in the late 1920s, which is still producing vehicles to this day.

There are more than 600 unique historic, architectural, and cultural monuments in the city. The Kremlin, Spassky (Staroyarmarochny) Cathedral, the Monastery of the Caves, and the Chkalov Staircase are especially noteworthy. UNESCO has included Nizhny Novgorod in the list of 100 cities of the world which are of great historical and cultural value.

Maxim Gorkiy

Nizhny Novgorod only regained its original name in 1990, having been known as Gorkiy from 1932 in honour of the celebrated author and poet Maxim Gorkiy (Максим Горький), who was born there.

Gorkiy, born as Aleksey Maksimovich Peshkov (Алексей Максимович Пешков) in 1868, had a troubled and often violent childhood, so much so that he later adopted the name Maxim Gorkiy, which roughly translates as 'the bitter one'. Moving through several jobs in his youth, he ended up as a dishwasher on a Volga River steamer, where he was befriended by a cook who taught him how to read, and so began his passion for literature.

He eventually found work as a reporter, and using his own harsh experiences of life became a founder of the socialist realism literary method and a political activist. From 1906 to 1913 and from 1921 to 1929 he lived outside of Russia, mostly in what was then fascist Italy. His much-lauded return by the Soviet authorities saw him decorated with the Order of Lenin and given a mansion (previously owned by the millionaire Ryabushinsky, and now the Gorkiy Museum) in Moscow and a dacha in the suburbs. One of the main streets of Moscow, Tverskaya Ulitsa, was renamed in his honour, as was the city of his birth. Though his celebrated return was treated as a Soviet fillip of communism over capitalism, the real reason for his return may have been his lack of money and the fact that he hadn't achieved the literary acclaim in the West he had been expecting.

Significantly though, in 1929 he was used publicly by Stalin to try to justify and promote the gulag system, which had come to the attention of the world's media. He visited the infamous Solovestsky camp system and wrote a positive article justifying the gulag system, which by then had already gained some notoriety in the West. He was later to say everything he had written was under the control of the Soviet censors. He died in 1936.

The train continued ever eastwards through the vast Soviet European Plain. Most accounts describe the trains as proceeding slowly, often being shunted into sidings, or stopping in deserted areas and remaining motionless for hours and sometimes days.

Every day there would be an inspection; sometimes there were several inspections a day. Usually the train would come to a halt out of sight of railway stations or villages, and if it was during the day the prisoners would have to get off the train and line up five abreast and kneel or sit, guarded by armed escorts with savage dogs while they endured the usual ritual of being counted, recounted, and then counted again.

When inspections were carried out at night the prisoners would be herded to one end of the carriage and then counted as they were forced back to the other end. Accounts describing this process always include the brutality of the guards, who used hammers to hit the legs and heads of the prisoners as they passed by to be counted.

The inspections also included using the hammers to check the carriages for the soundness of the wooden floors and walls and for any signs of attempted breakouts. Escape attempts were very rare, but Janusz Bardach in his book *Man is Wolf to Man* describes his successful escape from a train, only to be very rapidly caught, returned to the train and severely beaten in punishment.

It's no surprise that many soon fell ill and many died in transit. Those that died on the journey, and there were significant numbers, were removed in an undignified fashion, often described as being like the moving of meat carcasses into special wagons attached to the end of the train. The poor food they received soon led to the development of diseases like scurvy (lack of vitamin C) due to the lack of fresh vegetables in their meals, and night blindness (nyctalopia – lack of vitamin A) because of the lack of dairy products. On the trains used for the mass deportations of families there were young and old, nursing mothers, together with the sick and infirm. Children were even born into these dreadful conditions, but sadly they don't appear to have been afforded any preferential treatment, consideration, or allowances.

It's more than likely that the train carrying my father had stopped along the way. From memoirists it is recorded that when trains stopped at stations, those deportees exiled *en masse* who had been allowed to take some belongings and some money with them were able to buy or barter goods with locals at the station. This luxury was not available to the convicted deportees like my father; they were totally dependant on their captors.

Gorkiy was to be the first real stop that my father had since leaving Maladzyechna. Around about June the train pulled into Suchobezwodn station on the outskirts of the city. All the 'political' prisoners like my father were transferred from the cattle trucks and delivered to a huge transit prison nearby. These prisons were similar to the prisons he had been detained in in Wilejka and Maladzyechna. However, they contained a higher proportion of *urkas* (common/career criminals and thugs), and since the prison administrators only held all prisoners for a short time they seemed less interested in the welfare of their 'guests', and so the time in these prisons was fraught, hard and often brutal.

On arrival they were shaved all over, made to shower using 'a cup of hot water, a cup of cold water, and a small piece of black, evil smelling soap' (Anne Applebaum, *Gulag*), and then had their clothes steamed to de-louse them.

In the cramped cells there was a constant struggle for space on the insufficient bunks and even floor space. When food was given out, it was typically bowls of poor-quality soup (*balanda*) for dinner, hot water (*kipiatok*) and bread (*paika*) in the mornings. The whole proceedings were dominated by the *urkas*, and despite the utter confusion and pandemonium that usually ensued the guards didn't get involved at all, leaving the mayhem to sort itself out 'however' that might be achieved. It doesn't need saying but the *urkas* got the best of the food while the weak, old and defenceless had to rely on the leftovers.

Generally the time in these transit prisons was boring; apart from the melee that ensued at meal times, there was a roll call twice a day where everybody had to line up and be counted. Escape was impossible but the guards had to ensure that the headcount was always correct. The rest of the time was typically spent talking, playing cards or trying to catch and kill the lice that still covered their bodies.

These transit prisons were also used like a cattle market for the selection of workers who were thought able to perform certain jobs. As stated earlier the gulag system was expected to support the Soviet economy, and for those roles like mining and forestry only the 'fit and able' would be suitable. No camp commander wanted to carry dead weight, feeding and guarding unproductive workers would be economically untenable. So gulag medical staff were sent to try and get the most able prisoners to support their production quotas. A brief assessment was conducted of the prisoners' overall well-being – a quick check of the teeth and muscle tone was all that was needed.

My dad was still only twenty. He would have been in comparatively good health – ideal for heavy manual labour! It's not surprising then, that he was soon called for *etap* and was on his way again – moving ever eastwards.

City/town	Local name	Location	Approx. distance	Country
Kazan	Казáнь	450 km south-east of Nizhny Novgorod	1,845 km	Tatarstan (Татарстан)

Kazan, initially a small frontier town, was transformed into a powerful citadel and world-famous trading capital on the Volga. In 1922 it became the capital of Tatar Autonomous Soviet Republic, and now is the capital city of the Republic of Tatarstan. Like Rome it stands on seven hills.

Tatarstan is located in the centre of the East European Plain, about 800 km east of Moscow. It lies between the Volga and the Kama rivers, and extends east to the Ural Mountains. The major part of Tatarstan lies in the forest zone with only its south regions located in the forest-plain zone, though today only a small part of the Tatarstan forest remains. The climate is moderate continental and despite its location summer droughts are often experienced.

Kazan is the capital of a multinational republic which has its own language, culture, age-old traditions, festivals, and faith. But their past has been and remains intertwined with the history of Russia in the most dramatic and sometimes fateful way. It is a place where two worlds meet, with origins in both the West and the East. It is home to Europe's biggest mosque, the Kul-Shariff Mosque.

In the late 1980s and in the 1990s, after the dissolution of the USSR, Kazan again became the centre of Tatar culture, and since 2000 the city has been undergoing a total modernisation and renovation. In its millennium year of 2005 it opened its first ever metro system.

At Kazan's railway station a minaret-like tower, adorned by flashing lights of green and red, proudly highlights the colours of the Tatarstan flag. On passing through Kazan my father, travelling east, was now heading for the mighty Urals, the mountain range that divides Europe from Asia.

City/town	Local name	Location	Approx. distance	Country
Yekaterinburg (Sverdlovsk)	Екатеринбýрг (Свердловск)	800 km north-east of Kazan	2,645 km	Russia (Россúя)

After passing over the Urals and about 40 km to the west of Yekaterinburg my father will have passed over an imaginary border from Europe into Asia. He won't have seen it but there was (and still is) a granite obelisk indicating the exact spot of the boundary. It was constructed in 1926 and replaced an earlier marble pyramid adorned with a two-headed gilded Imperial Russian eagle, which was erected in 1837 but destroyed after the Russian Revolution.

In 2004 a new obelisk was unveiled about 20 km west of Yekaterinburg. It is constructed of two huge stones, one taken from the furthest point of the Russian European continent, Cape Rock, and the other from the furthest point of the Russian Asian continent, Cape of Deghnev. These two stones are meant to symbolise the union of two parts of the Russian world and tourists can visit this and the older obelisk and stand with one foot in Asia and another foot in Europe.

Yekaterinburg was originally named Sverdlovsk after Lenin's right-hand man, Bolshevik party leader and official of pre-Soviet Union Russia Yakov Mikhaylovich Sverdlov (Яков Михайлович Свердлов). It is situated on the eastern side of the Ural Mountains along the River Iset. It is surrounded by forests, taiga, and small lakes. The winter lasts for about five months and summer snow is not unusual.

The city was already a base of heavy engineering; Uralmash, the world's largest machinery manufacturer, and producer of the famous T-34 tank, had been established there since the 1920s. During the Second World War, as Germany conquered more and more of Western Russia, many government technical institutions and manufacturing facilities were relocated to Yekaterinburg. Many of them stayed after the victory, so Yekaterinburg is now a hub of commerce, manufacturing, industry and research positioned in Central Russia.

Dominating the skyline of central Yekaterinburg can be seen the Yekaterinburg TV Tower, which is the world's tallest incomplete architectural structure. Construction started in the late 1980s, but at the beginning of the 1990s and with its shaft at a height of 220 m, work was stopped. It had been planned for it to be over 400 m, with a restaurant at its summit. Following the cessation of work it was illegally used for climbing, bungee jumping, and base-jumping, but after several fatal accidents it was closed off completely. Sadly, as it is now at a slight incline it is unlikely ever to be completed.

In May 1960 Francis Gary Powers, in an American U-2 spy plane, was shot down near to Yekaterinburg. The wreckage of the aircraft was triumphantly put on public display, Powers was captured, put on trial, and found guilty of espionage. Although sentenced to ten years, of which seven were to be hard labour, he was swapped after nearly two years for a Soviet spy, the English-born KGB Colonel Vilyam Fisher (Vilyam 'Willie' Genrikhovich Fisher, Вильям Генрихович Фишер) who was held by the Americans.

Yekaterinburg however is most famous for the events following the Russian Revolution in 1918 when Tsar Nicholas II, his wife Alexandra and their children Grand Duchesses Olga, Tatiana, Maria, Anastasia and Tsarevich Alexei were executed by Bolsheviks in the Ipatiev House.

The soldiers who performed the execution were Hungarian prisoners of war and allegedly spoke no Russian. They were chosen because the local Cheka (state security organisation – predecessor of the KGB) feared that Russian soldiers would not shoot the Tsar and his family, particularly his daughters. One of the executioners was Imre Nagy, who later became Prime Minister of Hungary but was executed after the crushing of the anti-Soviet revolution of 1956 by the Red Army.

Ipatiev House survived until 1977 when it was destroyed by order of the then local Communist Party leader and graduate of civil engineering who was to become the first President of the independent Russia – Boris Nikolayevich Yeltsin (Борис Николаевич Ельцин), who feared it would become a shrine to Tsarist sympathisers and activists.

The location of Ipatiev House was declared sacred by the Russian Orthodox Church and on the exact location the hugely impressive, gold-pinnacled Church on Blood was constructed and opened in July 2003.

City/town	Local name	Location	Approx. distance	Country
Omsk	Омск	800 km east of Yekaterinburg	3,445 km	Russia (Россия)

Omsk is situated in southern Siberia on the banks of the north-flowing River Irtysh, at its confluence with the River Om. The climate is dry and continental, and characterised by dramatic swings of weather.

In the 1800s and the early 1900s, Omsk was a Cossack outpost, the administrative centre of Western Siberia and the steppes. It was the seat of the anti-Bolshevik government until 1919, when it was overrun by the Red Army following the start of the Revolution.

Although part of today's Omsk is typified by industrial suburbs, it boasts a quaint but compact centre with parks, museums, interesting architecture and an excellent selection of public street sculptures. Most of these are to be found along the main street Leninskaya Ulitsa.

City/town	Local name	Location	Approx. distance	Country
Novosibirsk	Новосибирск	700 km east of Omsk	4,145 km	Russia (Россия)

Novosibirsk is Russia's third-largest city after Moscow and Saint Petersburg, and is also the largest city in Siberia. It was founded in 1893 as the future site of the Trans-Siberian Railway bridge crossing the great Siberian River Ob. It was originally known as Novonikolaevsk after the last Russian Tsar, only having its name changed in 1925.

The city lies in the southern part of the West Siberian Plain along the River Ob. To the south is the Ukok Plateau, part of the UNESCO World Heritage Site entitled Golden Mountains of Altai. The climate is sharply continental, with severely cold and snowy winters and hot and dry summers.

Novosibirsk Zoo has an international recognition for its thirty-two different societies for preserving endangered species. Though a large, modern town Novosibirsk is lacking in typical Russian architectural splendour, but the Ballet and Opera Theatre are spectacular and for this the inhabitants of Novosibirsk are quite rightly very proud.

The Novosibirsk region is well known for many different industries (heavy machines, textiles, chemicals and many others). The people of Novosibirsk generally live in typical Soviet-era apartment blocks; private houses are rare.

City/town	Local name	Location	Approx. distance	Country
Krasnoyarsk	Красноярск	800 km north-east of Novosibirsk	4,945 km	Russia (Россия)

Krasnoyarsk, one of the oldest cities of Siberia, was originally founded in 1628 as a Russian border fort. During the nineteenth century it became the centre of the Siberian Cossack movement when it comprised a wooden fortress and wall. It remained an advanced border post for over a century and was never conquered. During the Cold War it was home to a huge air base, which has since been converted into apartment blocks.

The River Yenisei flows from west to east through the centre of the city; due to the Krasnoyarsk hydroelectric dam 32 km upstream, it never freezes in winter or exceeds 14 Celsius in summer through the city.

The Krasnoyarsk region includes several geographic zones including tundra, taiga and Arctic desert. To the south Krasnoyarsk is surrounded by forested hills, including the spectacular and huge Stolby Nature Reserve.

Stolby is Russian for 'pillars' and the area has numerous granite rock formations up to 100 m high, many with unusual shapes. It is a major rock-climbing location and many local climbers intentionally do not use any belaying equipment, calling their extreme rock climbing *stolbizm*, which is known around the world as solo climbing.

To the west the hills form the Gremyachinskaya Griva crest, notable for its ski-jumping tracks, but the area to the north of the city is rather plain, with forests to the north-west and agricultural fields to the north and east.

City/town	Local name	Location	Approx. distance	Country
Irkutsk	ркутск	1,100 km south-east of Krasnoyarsk	6,045 km	Russia (Россия)

Irkutsk lies on the River Angara, a tributary of the Yenisei, which flows from Lake Baikal 70 km upstream. It takes its name from the smaller River Irkut, which joins the Angara at that point. It is a truly magnificent Siberian city, so much so that 'to miss seeing Irkutsk is to miss Siberia' according to a local writer.

It is situated close to the breathtaking Lake Baikal in a landscape of rolling hills within the thick taiga typical of eastern Siberia, and in stark contrast to the flat, open steppe of western Siberia. It has a subarctic climate, characterised by an extreme variation of temperatures between seasons. Temperatures can be very warm in the summer and brutally cold in the winter.

Irkutsk grew out of the winter quarters established for gold-trading and the collection of the fur taxes from the indigenous people, the Buryats. From then it gained a reputation as the place for exile. In Genghis Khan's army, punishment was usually either death or exile to Siberia via Irkutsk. In the early nineteenth century many Russian artists, officers and nobles were sent into exile to Irkutsk for their part in the Decembrist revolt against Tsar Nicholas I. From that time it evolved into a major centre of intellectual and social life for these exiles, and much of the city's cultural heritage is because of them.

Marshall Piłsudski himself was exiled to Siberia and spent some time in a prison in Irkutsk in 1887. While imprisoned here he took part in a prisoners' 'revolt', caused after one of the prisoners had insulted a guard and refused to apologise. Piłsudski and other political prisoners were brutally beaten by the guards for their defiance. He then took part in a subsequent hunger strike until the authorities reinstated political prisoners' privileges, which had been suspended following the 'revolt'. During the fight Piłsudski lost two teeth, which is thought to have caused him later to cultivate his prominent moustache and, while speaking before groups, to hold his head in a characteristically bowed position. For his involvement Piłsudski was sentenced to six months' imprisonment.

From Irkutsk Piłsudski was sent further north to spend some of his exile near to Russia's longest river – the River Lena, over 4,320 km long. It was here, just a few short years later in 1896 that one Vladimir Ilyich Ulyanov was also exiled. It is thought that he took his more popular and infamous name from this river and the whole world came to know him by his name of Lenin. On his way into exile Lenin travelled by standard passenger train with his guards and even complained about the overcrowded carriages he had to endure! The names of (in)famous exiles doesn't stop there; Vyacheslav Mikhailovich Molotov (Вячесла́в Миха́йлович Мо́лотов), second only to Stalin and signatory to the 'Molotov-Ribbentrop Pact' that effectively allowed the start of the Second World War, was held here for two years from 1913.

Lake Baikal (о́зеро Байка́л)

Beautiful Lake Baikal, known as the 'blue eye of Siberia' due to its fantastic clarity and turquoise colour is the oldest, deepest and most voluminous lake in the world. It holds more than a fifth of the world's – and over 90 per cent of Russia's – (liquid) freshwater. Though it has about 350 rivers feeding it, it only has a single river, the Angara, flowing out and has the world's second-largest lake-bound island, Olkhon.

It lies in a rift or gorge in an area where the earth's crust is moving apart. It has been calculated that it is about 25 million years old. Though not the largest lake in the world by surface area it is the deepest at 1,640 m, and below this is about 7 km of sediment, which means the rift floor is nearly 9 km below the surface of the lake. The whole area, typical with continental shelves, experiences frequent seismic activity. The lake widens every year and has many hot springs surrounding it.

Until the Trans-Siberian Railway was built, little was known about it and very few visitors had ever seen it. Its age and isolation have produced some of the world's richest and most unusual freshwater fauna, so much so that the extent of biodiversity present in Lake Baikal is equalled by few other lakes.

It's difficult to believe that there's no mythical Lake Baikal monster, like there supposedly is in Loch Ness in Scotland. I've never read of any sightings of such, but of particular note is the Baikal seal (*Phoca sibirica*), known locally as the *nerpa*, the only mammal living in the lake, which is found throughout the whole area of the lake but nowhere else. Like the Caspian seal, they are thought to be related to the ringed seal of the Arctic and are the longest-lived of seals (up to fifty-six years in females) and unusual in that they feed their young on milk twice as long as other seals. It remains a scientific mystery as to how the seals originally came to Lake

Baikal, as it is hundreds of kilometres from any ocean, although it is speculated that they may have come at a time when a sea-passage linked the lake with the Arctic Ocean.

Another animal of note in Lake Baikal is the trout-like Omul fish (Coregonus autumnalis migratorius). It is fished, smoked, and sold in markets around the lake. For many travellers on the Trans-Siberian railway, purchasing smoked omul is one of the highlights on the long journey. Bear and deer both live and are hunted along the shores of Lake Baikal.

City/town	Local name	Location	Approx. distance	Country
Skovorodino	Сковородино	2,150 km north-east of Irkutsk	8,195 km	Russia (Россúя)

Skovorodino is a town in Amur Oblast. It is located to the east of the Yablonovy Mountains and south of the Stanovoy Mountains in a permafrost region of the upper stream of the Bolshoy Never River. It is about 7,300 km to the east of Moscow and is less than 70 km north of the Chinese border.

Skovorodino was founded in 1908 as a settlement of Zmeiny (Змейный) during the construction of the Trans-Siberian Railway. It was then renamed Never-I (Невер-I) after the nearby river. In 1911, it was once again renamed, this time to Rukhlovo (Рухлово). In 1938, it was again renamed Skovorodino in honour of a chairman of a local Soviet (A. N. Skovorodin) who had been killed there.

The town itself is split along the lines of the railway itself, with the old town being on one side and the new town on the other side of the line. Neither appears to be particularly new or prosperous but the old part of town though slightly less well-off does contain beautiful Siberian wooden houses.

City/town	Local name	Location	Approx. distance	Country
Khabarovsk	Хабáровск	1,200 km south-east of Skovorodino	9,395 km	Russia (Россúя)

Khabarovsk is only about 30 km from the Chinese border on the mighty River Amur at its confluence with the River Ussuri. It is the second-largest city in the Russian Far East, after Vladivostok. The area was originally part of Imperial China and was called Boli, only finally ceding to Russia in 1858 when the Russians founded the military outpost of Khabarovka (Хабáровка), named after the Russian explorer Yerofei Khabarov.

It lies in a mountainous territory encompassing several climatic zones. The northern part is scarcely populated permafrost tundra. The indigenous nomadic people, the Evenk, are reindeer breeders. Climate in the Amur River valley is sharply continental, with cold and windy winters and hot, sunny and humid summers. From the end of June to the middle of September, there like the rest of Siberia, is an awful plague of mosquitoes.

Among the local wildlife can be found brown bears (*Ursus arctos*), leopards, reindeer, tigers, the famous Chinese 'root of life' – ginseng, northern larch trees, and wild grapes.

The city itself has recently undergone renovation and been restored and in parts rebuilt. The Khabarovsk Bridge (built in 1916) used to be the longest in the Russian

Empire. Unlike Vladivostok, the city has never been closed to foreigners, despite it being the headquarters of the Far East Military District. It is truly a city of the Russian Far East (the Russian territories along the Pacific seaboard), retaining its historically international flavour.

Lenin Square leads onto the main street of Khabarovsk, the beautiful, tree-lined Ulitsa Muravyova-Amurskogo, which is usually filled with crowds from across Asia, but it exudes an atmosphere characteristic of great European cities. Its proximity to the River Amur together with its nineteenth-century architecture has led to its comparison to a European coastal resort.

All the major cities he would have passed through would have had similar transit prisons to that he spent time in in Gorkiy. I don't know for sure if my dad spent any time in any of them, I remember him mentioning the names of Novosibirsk, Irkutsk, and Khabarovsk, but I can't recall in what context he mentioned them. Maybe he spent time in transit prisons there or maybe he just remembered passing through them.

At some point after leaving Gorkiy the train carriages he was being transported in changed from converted cattle trucks to *Stolypinka* carriages. Some memoirists describe these as slightly better than the cattle trucks, and they may have been connected to normal scheduled trains as opposed to special prisoner train convoys.

Pyotr Stolypin

Stolypinka carriages were named after Pyotr (Peter) Arkadyevich Stolypin (Пётр Аркáдьевич Столы́пин) who has often been described as the last major statesman of Imperial Russia. As the effective Prime Minister of Russia he is remembered for his attempts to repress anti-Tsarist revolutionary groups and introduce reforms in landownership that were hoped would quell peasant unrest and provide support to the Tsar and the royal family.

He was also responsible for the introduction a new penal system that made it easier to arrest, convict, and sentence suspected anti-Tsarist factions. Under this legislation, between 1906 and 1909 over 3,000 political revolutionaries were convicted and executed, the hangman's noose became known to the Russians as 'Stolypin's necktie'. In addition to these thousands more were exiled in specially converted train coaches which became know as *Stolypinkas*.

Stolypin was assassinated in Kiev in 1911 by the revolutionary Dmitry Grigoriyevich Bogrov (Дмитрий Григорьевич Богров) whilst attending an opera performance with the Tsar. Because of his closeness to the Russian imperial family, the Romanovs, and his political power he is considered by most historians as the person having the ability to protect and save the Russian royal family. His untimely death probably sealed the fate of the Romanovs a few short years later in Yekaterinburg.

Whereas the cattle trucks had been predominantly red in colour *Stolypinkas* were typically dark green in colour with thick iron doors coming together in the middle of the cars secured by huge iron bars. The carriages contained wire enclosures, allegedly designed to hold sixteen prisoners but it seems there were often up to twenty-five people or more crammed into one enclosure. These were typically arranged in three tiers of sleeping shelves on either side which were joined to make a continuous platform. These prevented prisoners from straightening up or relaxing. There was a toilet to which the guards would accompany everybody and at other times the guards would patrol the carriages banging the walls to ensure that there were no attempted escapes.

Alexandr Topolski describes the *Stolypinka* he travelled in as not too overcrowded and he was able to lie on his bunk and see through windows which had had their lower half painted so they couldn't be seen into by people when the train was standing at station platforms.

As the train travelled on eastwards my father probably didn't know his ultimate destination, though the further east he went, I'm sure it became apparent to him that the more likely it would be that he was going to Kolyma!!

Now, to you and me this name probably means very little. It probably didn't mean much to my father and the other Poles still travelling east. But to most Russians, especially the *urkas*, and those already with knowledge of it, Kolyma is a name synonymous with hell, or worse. For those in the know, given a choice between death or Kolyma there was usually ever one answer – death! Though for most going there there wouldn't be a choice; Kolyma typically meant death anyway.

Around about the end of September or beginning of October 1940, with the war already entering into its second year my father eventually reached the end of his rail journey from hell.

It wasn't, however, the usual terminus of the Trans-Siberian Express at Vladivostok, but even further east on the Pacific coast. The train eventually came to its final stop and disgorged its human cargo at Nakhodka, a town that had developed into a huge transit camp and port staging post for the gulags of Kolyma. My father's youth and probably his strength had sealed his fate to what was for him the unknowns of Kolyma.

But what or where was this legendary, almost mythical Kolyma? It wasn't here at Nakhodka. Kolyma, often referred to by such superlatives as the 'Black Planet', 'Devil's Hell', the 'Cauldron within a Cauldron' (Ayyub Baghirov), and even the 'White Desert' was still some way off even though my dad was on his way there for sure, but it his train journey into exile had now come to an end!

City/town	Local name	Location	Approx. distance	Country
Nakhodka	Нахо́дка	750 km south-west of Khabarovsk	10,145 km	Russia (Росси́я)

The city is built along Nakhodka Bay which was discovered almost by accident in 1859 by the Russian Naval corvette *Amerika*, which sought shelter in the bay during a fierce storm. Hence Nakhodka's name, which in Russian means 'a lucky find' or 'discovery'.

Originally Nakhodka was a small fishing village, but its fortunes changed for the better in 1950 when the Soviet authorities closed Vladivostok to foreign shipping, leaving Nakhodka as the primary deep-water port of the Russian Far East. Its economy and well-being are purely based around the massive port area which dominates the coastline throughout the city.

Nakhodka's fairly large population works, and the city's economy is based, mostly around the huge port and port-related activities such as fish processing and canning, ship repair, transport and timber industries. Unfortunately, these have suffered since 1991 when Vladivostok was reopened to foreign shipping.

The coastline outside of the main city is spectacular with dramatic coastal rock formations. The most impressive of these lie just a few kilometres north of the city, at the mouth of the River Partizanskay. Here can be found the mysterious twin 'pyramid-like mountains' known as Brother and Sister (брат и сестра).

It's not clear whether they are natural or man-made structures, but the area surrounding them is steeped in ancient history and it is known that they had been a holy place for he ancient settlers; people had come from as far as China and Korea to pray here when they were known as Da-nai-shan (Sister) and Er-nai-shan (Brother).

Recent research suggests that despite their isolation from any other hills in a flat plain, their very similar height, and the fact they are roughly lined up to cardinal compass points like all great pyramids, they are in fact natural structures. Having said that it is clear the side of Sister which faces Brother has been enhanced at some time in prehistory and Brother itself had been reshaped into a pyramid.

Sister is 319 m high and Brother about 4 km away was originally 320 m. Sadly in the 1960s the top of Brother was blasted away and turned into a quarry, and now stands at only 242 m. Though it is still used as a quarry many people believe the original blasting was in an attempt to discover huge statues and treasures that many locals believed Brother to be hiding. Very sad.

The climate of Nakhodka is monsoonal and the prevailing wind directions are northern in winter and south-eastern in summer. Though a period a poor weather that affected Nakhodka in the early 1960s was attributed by the locals to the desecration of Brother!

The city itself is bordered on west by taiga (deep, often impenetrable forest) where the world famous wild Siberian (Manchurian) tigers (*Panthera tigris altaica*) can still be found. The eastern side of the city is the waters of Peter the Great Bay, and the Sea of Japan. It stretches 20 km along the coast of the Nakhodka Bay. The main street of the city is the Nakhodkinsky Avenue and almost all city bus routes run along this main thoroughfare.

5

SHINING PATH

Slave Ship from Mainland Russia to 'Mainland Russia'

Nakhodka is today the second-largest city in Primorsky Krai (region) of the Russian Far East after Vladivostok, but when my dad was there it was still a small, insignificant fishing village. It had recently been developed into the main staging post for the camps of Kolyma and huge transit camps had sprung up by the railway tracks along the Bay of Nakhodka (Bukhta Nakhodka).

It's believed that 12–15,000 Poles arrived there following the Russian invasion of Poland, but in addition to these there were many other nationalities and not least of all the Russian common criminal fraternity, the nasty and dreaded *urkas*. My father and his fellow prisoners were unloaded straight from the trains, surrounded by aggressive guards and vicious dogs while their documentation was checked, and then escorted to one of these huge transit camps, overlooking the Bay of Nakhoda out to the Sea of Japan. It would have been my father's first ever view of any sea and ominously, just below the camps were piers and probably huge freighters that were destined to carry my father on the next phase of his journey.

But why Nakhodka – a seaport at the easternmost extremity of the Soviet Union? This wasn't the final destination, which by then they knew would be Kolyma. The reason was, that Kolyma was (and still is) so remote, prisoners and people living or working there referred to the rest of the Soviet Union as the mainland even though they were physically connected to the same land mass. So remote in fact that some even referred to Kolyma as a planet!

The only means of getting there was an arduous sea journey of about eight days; road and air transport wasn't an option. Even now the Kolyma region remains isolated. Dalstroy had started construction of a road to it in the early 1930s, but because of the harsh conditions it is today in a poor state and often impassable. Bizarrely it is more accessible during the long winter when rivers freeze. Now known as the M56 Kolyma Highway, the 'Federal Automobile Highway Kolyma' (Федеральная автомобильная дорога Колыма), it was an attempt to make a land connection from Kolyma to the main Russian road network near Irkutsk. It is over 2,000 km and because it is the only road in some areas is locally referred to simply as 'The Route' (Трасса).

The section between the regional main cities of Magadan and Yakutsk is chillingly known as 'The Road of Bones'. So high was the death rate of the prisoners working on its construction that their bodies were either left at the side of the road or even incorporated into the road itself! It is said that for each metre of the road constructed one prisoner lost his life and was incarcerated into the road. Given that the road is over 2,000 km, there would be over 2 million prisoners entombed in the road!

The camp at Nakhodka was, like all the Pacific coast transit camps it seems, always overcrowded. According to Robert Conquest there were often over 100,000 prisoners and it has been reported that at times there were so many prisoners awaiting deportation that up to 20,000 prisoners who couldn't be accommodated in the seemingly endless array of huts had to sleep within the confines of the barbed wire fences, an area known as the *zona*, in the open air, and with no protection from the harsh elements. The Poles were assigned to a segregated area of the camp only for Poles, enclosed by further barbed wire fences, a *zona* within a *zona*, and hence a prison within a prison.

The weakened, emaciated, and distraught prisoners were in a wretched condition. Body lice, the permanent companion of all prisoners though a nuisance, also caused plagues of typhus, and despite a regime of de-lousing, illness and death rates were high.

The prisoners were here for a reason, and despite their poor condition were assessed for their working potential. The Soviet economy depended on the gold from the mines of Kolyma, and the mines had a requirement for huge numbers of labourers, and so a regular 'slave market' was in operation. Officials from the gold-mining authorities together with their medical staff would come and examine everybody recently arrived to determine whether they were fit for hard labour by feeling their muscles, inspecting their heads and shoulders and checking their mouths, teeth and eyes. My dad, like most of those assessed, was categorised as suitable for hard labour. His case history notes would have been clearly stamped with this assessment and then he just had to wait for his call for the ship.

Those deportees arriving in Nakhodka between December and April are often considered to be 'lucky' because the next phase of their journey out into the Sea of Japan and onto the Sea of Othotsk is not navigable. Thus they were spared from the rigours of their ultimate destination, as they waited for the spring thaw. While their life in Nakhodka was harsh, brutal and unrelenting, it was nothing compared to the ultimate hell that would surely come.

My father was not to be so lucky! Within a short period of time after arriving in Nakhodka he was called for *etap*. He was awakened at the first light of dawn and in the now familiar five-abreast column, was marched out of the transit camp to join a seemingly endless caterpillar-like queue of prisoners slowly making their way, under the control of armed guards, towards the crude piers, and the waiting cargo ships in the bay. The march from the camp to the ships took hours to complete, and for most prisoners, my father included, it was to be their first experience of the sea and sea journeys.

The ship that he was about to embark on was more than likely the infamous, even notorious *Dzhurma* (Джурма). The name means 'shining path' in the language of the local indigenous Evenki (Эвэнки) people, but its quaint, interesting name belies an awful story that lasted almost twenty years!

The scene must have been awful and was depicted by the artist Nikolai Getman who created a self-portrait of his own embarkation to Kolyma from the port of Vanino, which was created further up the coast and a short time later than Nakhodka, but like Nakhodka, a final transit terminal for the prison camps of Kolyma.

Stalin's Slave Ships

Dzhurma was originally built by the Dutch shipbuilders Koninklijke Maatschappij in Vlissingen (Flushing) in 1921. It was a merchantman cargo ship of about 7,000 tonnes and measured almost 125 m. It was originally known as *Brielle*, and by the time it was laid up during the Great Depression of the early thirties it had circumnavigated the globe on several occasions.

It was purchased by the Soviet authorities specifically for the Kolyma gulag operations, arriving for duty in 1935, registered as M-28643, and renamed *Dzhurma*. It was used throughout the gulag period until 1953 when it transferred to normal shipping operations. It is believed to have been scrapped in about 1968.

Whilst in gulag transport employ it was also used to transport Lend-Lease equipment supplied by the United States of America to support the Soviet war effort. There are at least twelve reports of the *Dzhurma* visiting the American western seaboard ports of San Francisco, Seattle, and Portland.

The core of the gulag fleet consisted of the ships *Dalsroy*, *Dzhurma*, *Felix Dzerzhinsky*, *Indigirka*, *Kulu*, and the *Sovietskya Latvia*, but there were at least another twenty-eight ships of varying sizes that were used either infrequently or regularly to transport prisoners to Kolyma. All were ex-cargo ships crudely converted for the bulk transport of prisoners.

The ships themselves were operated in a complex arrangement through the Soviet agencies; 'The Main Administration of the Northern Sea Route' (Главная Управления Северной Морской, Пути, ГлавсевМорПут or ГУСМР – Glavnaya Upravlenie Severnoi Morskoi Puti, Glavsevmorput or GUSMP) and 'The Peoples Commissariat for Water Transport' (Нароный Комиссарнит Водного Транспорта, НарКомВодТранс or НКТР – Narodnyi Komissariat Vodnogo Transporta, NarkomVodTrans or NKTP) on behalf of Dalstroy (Дальстрой). In simple terms NarkomVodTrans owned the ships, but they were operated by Glavsevmorput to supply the needs of Dalstroy. NarkomVodTrans and Glavsevmorput went through many reorganisations during the 1930s but ultimately all these agencies were under the direct control of the omnipotent NKVD.

Dalstroy (Дальстрой)

Dalstroy was an organisation originally set up in 1931 by the OGPU (predecessor of the NKVD) to manage road construction, mining, and all projects involving forced labour in the Soviet Far East. Its full name was the 'State Trust for Road and Industrial Construction it the Upper Kolyma Area' (Государственный трест по дорожному и промышленному строительству в районе Верхней Колымы – Дальстрой).

It was responsible for, and oversaw the development of gold-mining of the Kolyma area using forced labour. It ultimately created over eighty gulag camp complexes across the Kolyma region, utilising estimates of over 20 million forced labourers. By 1939, the gulag system was the largest – and I'm trying not to use the word 'employer' here – utiliser of manpower in the whole of Europe. A large proportion of these worked for Dalstroy. Eventually by Stalin's death in 1953, the total area covered by Dalstroy had grown to over 3 million square km.

While Dalstroy managed the production of gold and construction of roads, the actual labour was supplied by yet another NKVD organisation with yet another forgettable acronym, SEVVOSTLAG (СЕВВОСТЛАГ) which was the North-Eastern Corrective Labour Camps – SVITL (Северо-восточные исправительно-трудовые лагеря – СВИТЛ). The differentiation between the two came from the fact that Dalstroy acted as an economic enterprise and wanted to attract skilled labour and marriageable women to the Far East, and in fact advertised throughout Russia for such, but they didn't want to be associated with the stigma of a gulag organisation. Though there was a clear demarcation between the two, in reality the two organisations can be considered as a single entity; the head of Dalstroy was the *de facto* head of both, and had complete control over both.

As I've previously said these slave ships were crudely converted cargo ships, their vast holds used as huge prison cells having few amenities. They were crammed, in truly appalling conditions, full of prisoners as described by Stanislaw Kowalski:

> The cargo ship itself, carrying in her holds up to eight thousand prisoners, was hell on earth. Packed like sardines in five tiered bunks, our movements were limited to the space occupied by our bodies; stinking latrines, set in the corners, continuously spread odour around; fresh air supplied by an opening to the hold was far below what humans needed to exist; and food rations, cut to the bare minimum of bread, sauerkraut, and a measure of water was merely another miserable torture. The elements of nature like the weather and the waves acted only to aggravate matters.

And so in these conditions, with my father deep in the hold the *Dzhurma* unmoored and slipped her berth in Buhkta Nakhodka and set off in a north-easterly direction through the Sea of Japan into what Robert Conquest, ironically but purposely, describes as 'The Kolyma Middle Passage'. A poignant comparison to the brutal transport of Africans across the Atlantic Ocean to the slave markets of the Caribbean and North America. It was by that time a journey the *Dzhurma* had been making regularly, fully laden, for over fve years.

Sea of Japan

The Sea of Japan is almost totally enclosed, bound by the Russian mainland and Sakhalin Island to the north, North Korea and South Korea to the west, and the Japanese islands of Hokkaidō, Honshū, and Kyūshū to the east. Because it is almost totally enclosed it has a negligible tidal flow.

It is connected to the Pacific Ocean (including the Sea of Okhotsk) by five shallow straits. The Strait of Tatary between the Asian mainland and Sakhalin in the north, La

Pérouse Strait between the islands of Sakhalin and Hokkaidō, the Tsugaru Strait between the islands of Hokkaidō and Honshū, the Kanmon Straits between the islands of Honshū and Kyūshū, and the Korea Strait (Genkainada) between the Korean Peninsula and the island of Kyūshū. The Korea Strait itself is composed of the Western Channel and the Tsushima Strait, on either side of Tsushima Island.

The name of this sea though is the subject of some dispute; the Koreans believe its name should return to its original name of East Sea. The warm 'Japan Current' flowing northeast through the southern channel through the sea maintains Vladivostok as the only year-round ice-free port of eastern Russia making it an ideal location for Russia's eastern sea trading, fishing, and naval bases.

La Pérouse Strait (Пролив Лаперуза)

This narrow, shallow channel separates the Russian island of Sakhalin and the Japanese island of Hokkaidō. It is the main shipping route between the Sea of Japan and the Sea of Okhotsk. It was for Stalin's slave ships the route from Nakhodka to Kolyma. It was named after Jean François de Galaup, Comte de La Pérouse, the famous French explorer who navigated the channel in 1787. At its narrowest point between Cape Krilon on Sakhalin and Cape Soya on Hokkaidō it is only 40 km; the depth along the strait varies from about 20 to 40 m.

It has notoriously strong currents, dangerous rip tides, is prone to fog, and together with a rocky island known as Nidzhe-gun (the Rock of Danger) makes navigation extremely hazardous. Apparently in the early days, navigation through the strait in foggy conditions was achieved by the use of 'listeners' on deck who detected the rocks in foggy conditions by listening for the roar of sealions living on the small rocky outcrops.

To help navigation several lighthouses were contructed. The first, in 1896 was the Cape Krilon lighthouse, built at the western point of the strait on Sakhalin Island. In 1906 a bell buoy was installed by the Japanese on the Rock of Danger, but because its position was frequently moved by the strong currents, it was replaced on the rock itself by a concrete tower with an autonomic beacon and fog bell in 1913. At the eastern entry to the strait the Aniva lighthouse was constructed in 1939 on a rock outcrop called Sivuchya, not far from the treacherous Cape Aniva.

It's no surprise then that many a ship came to grief while passing through this difficult passage. Significantly, in December 1939 the ship *Indigirka* (Индиги́рка) after poorly navigating the channel ran aground on Todo Reef off the northern tip of Hokkaidō south of Cape Krilon. It eventually capsized but the Soviet crew were reluctant to accept aid from the nearby Japanese mainland.

The *Indigirka* was one of the dreaded slave ship fleet; it had sailed from Kolyma bound for Vladivostok with a cargo of eminent engineers and scientists crammed into its hold. They had initially been sent to the hard labour camps of Kolyma, but were being transferred to Sharashki in order to better use their expertise rather than for manual labour. Nearly 750 of the 1,200 being transported were to lose their lives, most trapped inside the hold and prevented from leaving to protect the sinister nature of the transport. Unimaginable as it may seem this is just one of many unbelievable stories of catastrophes associated with 'Stalin's slave ships'.

La Pérouse Strait was also the scene of some fierce battles at the height of the naval battles between the USA and Japan. Arguably the most famous American submarine of the Pacific fleet, the USS *Wahoo* (SS 238) which had amassed an incredible twenty-one kills and had been the first submarine to wipe out an entire enemy convoy single-handedly also met her fate here, sunk not by the channel but by Japanese naval bombers on 11 October 1943 as she was returning home from patrolling in the Sea of Japan. The actual location was to remain a mystery until the wreck was located by Russian divers in 2006, still upright and largely intact on the sea floor.

Sea of Okhotsk

The Sea of Okhotsk was named after the first Russian settlement in the Russian Far East, now the town of Okhotsk. In reality both the Sea of Japan and the Sea of Okhotsk are part of the western Pacific Ocean. The Sea of Okhotsk lies between the Kamchatka Peninsula in the east, the Kuril Islands in the south-east, the island of Hokkaido to the far south, the island of Sakhalin along the west, and a long stretch of eastern Siberian coast. It is connected to the Sea of Japan on either side of Sakhalin, on the west through the Sakhalin Gulf and the Gulf of Tatary and on the south through the La Pérouse Strait.

It is the coldest sea in East Asia, its winter climate being similar to that of the Arctic where extreme severe weather conditions are normal. The sea plays a significant role in determining weather patterns of the region and during winter its navigation is often impossible. Formation of large unpredictable ice floes is common because the large amount of freshwater flowing from the River Amur lowers the salinity and raises the freezing point of the sea.

I've no real idea what my father had to endure on his voyage to Kolyma. Like so much of his journey it was to stay private to him until his dying day. I know it must have been unspeakably awful, and by the time he was to suffer it he had already endured the terror of arrest, prison, sentencing, and the hell of being transported in a cattle car. But in all the research I have done in preparing this book, this single event, which for my father probably took just over a week in time, caused me the most personal distress. I found the accounts and stories more horrific and disturbing than any other of the parts of his story, even more so than the accounts of the terrible cattle trucks and the brutally harsh gulags to which he was now bound. In fact so disturbing were some of the accounts I read that I started having nightmares and severely disrupted sleeping, so much so that I had to take a long break from researching this particular aspect.

The following descriptions from Stanislaw Kowalski illustrate the horrors of the conditions that the Poles and other deportees were transported in:

Each of the ships of the fleet, like the *Dzhurma, Sovlatvia (Sovietskya Latvia), Dalstroy, Decabrist* and many others, carried within its hold many thousands of the persecuted people, destined for extinction. All of these vessels, though of cargo design, were fitted with elaborate internal arrangements to enable the carrying of the maximum load of prisoners. And this arrangement was of a kind that no other slave ship in the history of mankind was equipped with, not even the slave ship that carried African slaves to America.

A typical slave ship was *Dzhurma*. Its internal structure illustrates best how the human cargo was transported northwards within its holds. A wooden structure had been erected around the walls of its cargo holds, and comprised of four-tiered bunks, with the floor serving as the fifth. Each of the bunks was divided into sections to accommodate five men in lying position. To take their places the prisoners had to slide in legs first with their heads facing the passages to avoid suffocation. If there were not enough places to accommodate prisoners, men had to use the passage-way as they're put up for a sea voyage lasting six to eleven days.

The sanitary arrangements consisted of two 50-gallon barrels, called 'parashas', which were emptied periodically into the sea. It was quite common for these barrels to spill over, causing the inside of the holds to smell with the odour of human waste. An outside latrine was also available, but only a few prisoners at a time were allowed to use it. Therefore the queues were always long and moved slowly. This outside arrangement was fenced with barbed wire to prevent prisoners from jumping into the sea, especially when the ship was in Japanese territorial waters.

In this crowded ship, like in the entire prison system in the Soviet Union, food was always a commodity in short supply. At the time, the whole country went hungry and slaves were at the bottom of the list when it came to allocation of food. In the ship the rations were even far below the general prison standards. The daily meal of the prisoner during the journey consisted of reduced ration of bread, a portion of sauerkraut and a bucket of fresh water for each group of fifty men. This provision of food followed the maxim practised within the system that 'men who don't work don't need food'.

Ventilation of the interior of the holds was another problem for the prisoners. Fresh air was delivered through the overhead opening of the hold. However, even when fully opened the amount of air let in was barely sufficient to keep the prisoners away from suffocation. Then, the openings and the main door were always closed when the vessel passed the Japanese waters. For this, and other, reasons every journey took its toll in human life. Often there were additional fatalities caused by unforeseen and unexpected maritime perils.

Right from the time I left Buhkta Nakhodka everything worked the wrong way for me. The cargo ship itself, carrying in her holds up to eight thousand prisoners, was hell on earth. Packed like sardines in five-tiered bunks, our movements were limited to the space occupied by our bodies; stinking latrines, set in the corners, continuously spread odour around; fresh air supplied by an opening to the hold was far below what humans needed to exist; and food rations, cut to the bare minimum of bread, sauerkraut, and a measure of water was merely another miserable torture. The elements of nature like the weather and the waves acted only to aggravate matters.

While in the middle of Japan Sea we met with a violent typhoon, which made the ship rock, swing, and sway like a little toy. Hammered by the fury of waves the vessel went up and down, rolled from one side to another, and when facing a gorge of water, would plunge into its depth as if in a suicidal attempt to bring an end to herself and her human cargo. We, the system's prisoners, fared no better. Soon the sickly smell of vomit added its odour to the stench of the latrine spills, making a sickening mess of the entire hold's interior.

Sick like a dog I laid on the floor paying no attention to anything but my nauseating sickness. Suddenly I heard a sound of cracking wood above me. I jumped to my feet to watch helplessly the flying debris falling down upon my friends and colleagues. Where the centre bunk had stood, there was a huge heap of moving and listless bodies mixed with the pile of splintered lumber.

I hardly got to my feet when a sudden stream of people picked me up and carried towards the exit of the hold. Half naked I was pushed up the broken steps and thrown outside into the merciless hands of the raging storm. Instantly I went into a spin, doing a crazy dance like a man beat on all sides by the raging power of the sea. The blowing wind and waters rushing over the deck had no mercy on my fellow-prisoners and me. In between of nature's fury I saw some screaming men washed down to the edge of the ship and then disappear over the side in a flood of surging water. These were the fortunate ones – nature had spared them from a more painful and slow death in the terrible land of Kolyma.

I held on for life to hanging ropes not to follow these victims into the dark churning sea. While fighting surges of salty seawater, I was completely helpless against the fury of the cold wind. Its gusts blowing savagely made me shiver and tremble like a leaf subjected to a sudden blast of a squall. I cursed the whole ugly world around me to get the anguish out of my system. In one of the sporadic breaks of the nature's fury, I made my way towards the entrance of the hold. At a convenient moment, when the guards pushed others away, I jumped down to the slimy floor down under. Falling into the dirt, protected from the fury of the weather, I felt like I had reached the safety of heaven.

The centre bunks already stood up. In semi-darkness I found my friend Ted, who came out intact and unscarred from the incident, and who as a good soul took care of my personal belongings. He did even better – he reserved for me a tiny bit of space on the top layer of bunks right under the opening of the hold. I climbed as fast as I could to immediately take the possession of this priceless piece of ship's space for the remainder of the insane journey.

Every story adds to the impression of how horrific these voyages were. In Robert Conquest's *Kolyma – The Arctic Death Camps* there is a vivid description of a hold packed full of women, half naked because of the heat, their bodies covered in boils and spots because of the filthy conditions. They had been completely stripped of their dignity and there was no longer any shame – they crouched near the giant cask used as a latrine in full view of the soldiers.

All the accounts, harrowing as they are, describe the experiences of prisoners who lived to tell their stories. As I said earlier some of the accounts I came across during the course of my research belie belief, and while I won't describe them in any detail, I will mention a few examples to underlie the fact that I'm so lucky that my father survived, and I'm here describing the events.

Janusz Bardach, himself a Polish deportee en-route to Kolyma, describes a brutal mass-rape that occurred during the voyage when the *urkas* discovered women in an adjacent hold. The scene is too horrific to contemplate but, the mass-rape and murder of the women deportees was often followed by the rape of the younger male prisoners in a sexual frenzy by the criminal *urkas*, and appears to have been a regular occurrence throughout the life of these slave ships. Political prisoners generally were powerless to help and had to watch in horror. Even the guards generally turned a blind eye. These gang rapes came to be known as 'The Kolyma Tram' or 'The Kolyma Streetcar' and Martin Bollinger in his book *Stalin's Slave Ships* quotes another witness, Elena Glinka: 'If Hell exists, the Kolyma Streetcar must have been its earthy manifestation.' The awful scene is illustrated by Danzig Baldaev in his book *Drawings from the Gulag* which also goes on, in many truly alarming images, to depict the disturbing brutal reality of 'life' in the gulag system.

Other accounts describe fires being started in the hold during the voyage. Because the guards feared rebellion they locked the holds; thousands of prisoners suffocated or were boiled to death, trapped with no means of exit. Still other accounts describe water cannon being used to suppress rioting prisoners in temperatures that dropped below -40°c; the frozen corpses were unloaded when the ship docked in port, or as some reports state, were just dumped overboard into the sea! The stories of slave ship horror go on and on.

Whatever my father had to endure on this voyage I'll never know, and I don't really want to even think about it. But after about eight days at sea *Dzhurma* was nearing the fabled Kolyma. The mighty cargo ship, with what for me was a precious cargo, entered the Gulf of Tauyskaya (Тауйская Губа) and once again approached land.

Dzhurma changed her course from a northerly direction and steered east parallel to the coast, passing by the small island of Spafaryeva and into the sheltered Nagayevo Bay. As she did so she passed beneath Kamenny Venets (Каменй Венец) a distinctive rocky outcrop, which early seafarers thought were the ruins of an ancient castle guarding the entrance to the bay.

These ancient weather-beaten rocks, where even today very few visitors have ever ventured, enjoy a magnificent panoramic view from out the Gulf of Tauyskaya to the Sea of Okhotsk and up the enclosed bay to what was to be the final destination of the *Dzhurma*.

And so my father's first ever sea voyage was coming to an end. For him and his fellow prisoners, the astounding beauty that they were travelling through was completely invisible. The end was signalled by the sudden quietness as the engines, which had thundered constantly for over a week as the *Dzhurma* ploughed through the Sea of Japan and then the Sea of Okhotsk, idled as the ship entered the port of Nagayevo.

Almost immediately after the ship came to a halt, the commotion as the wretched prisoners still alive were escorted from the ship began. My father waited in the eerie hold with trepidation, listening to the distant muffled sounds of the activities outside. He had finally arrived at Kolyma; what must have been his thoughts as he waited for his exit?

City/town	Local name	Location	Approx. distance	Country
Nagayevo	Нагаево	3,100 km north-east of Nakhodka	13,245 km	Russia (Россия)

Nagayevo, though having been continuously inhabited for nearly 400 years, still has a sparse population. It is renowned for its harshness, even in a region notorious for its severe weather conditions. The port had originally been built to support a small seafaring community but despite Soviet, and even modern investment it is still relatively underdeveloped.

What it does have though is a perfect natural harbour, protected from the cruel waves of the unrelenting Sea of Okhotsk by the massive Poluostrov Staritskogo peninsula. For much of the year the sea remains frozen solid with ice, often up to 500 km from shore, but even when not frozen, the imposing dark-grey sea, almost totally enclosed by steep barren cliffs and a rocky shore line, remains inhospitable despite its haunting natural beauty.

The ship will have moored at a primitive pier; there may have been other of the slave ships there too. When Vladimir Petrov arrived on the *Dzhurma*, the *Dalstroy* was also moored in the harbour. It was probably several hours before it was my father's turn to leave the ship. The hatch eventually flew open, sending a chill wind through the hold.

From the usual heavily armed and agitated guards came the command to 'hurry up and get your belongings and make ready for disembarkation'. Eventually, my father squeezed his way out of the hold and onto the deck, his eyes temporarily blinded by the daylight after over a week in almost total darkness.

On the quay all the prisoners who had already disembarked were being mustered by the guards with their fierce dogs. Those that sadly hadn't survived the journey were removed by teams of prisoners and laid in a pile at one end of the quay for counting; apparently the dead still had to be accounted for.

'Encouraged' by guards who freely used their rifle butts, the steady stream of prisoners moved along to a small gangplank that led from the ship to the pier (the remains of which can still be seen to this day) and onto the quay. My father had arrived in Kolyma!

Once all the prisoners had been corralled on shore, a camp official began a roll call, shouting each name in turn. Eventually it would have been my fathers; 'Pleszak, Nikolai'. To which the reply was 'here', followed by the article of his conviction; '58 – 2, 11'. After each prisoner had confirmed his name he made his way to the far end of the port where further officials and guards checked each prisoner's name with their records and once satisfied were assigned to the ever growing columns of prisoners waiting impatiently.

There were probably over 2,000 prisoners arriving with my father and the roll call probably took several hours to complete. They were arranged in columns of several hundred, and typically five abreast. The Soviet system was meticulous in its record keeping.

Once the records had been updated the huge column of prisoners under heavy escort were given the usual threats about how to march in a column and led out of the port, which at the time only had a single unpaved road from the port of Nagayevo towards the town of Magadan. It's likely that at that time their route would have been covered with placards and huge posters of Stalin and Soviet propaganda, some of which can still be found to this day. It probably made the Polish prisoners choke; it was adding insult to injury.

Ahead of the column in the distance would have been the stark beauty of the mountain ranges, valleys, forests, and rivers of Kolyma, but even if they could have seen any of it they would have all been blind and impervious to it. The weather was probably blowing a gale, it could have been pouring with rain, possibly even snowing; the Kolyma weather is notoriously harsh and unrelenting.

There's an oft-quoted rhyme about Kolyma, but it's worth repeating:

Колыма, Колыма	*Kolyma, Kolyma*	Kolyma, Kolyma
чудная планета	*Chudnaya planeta*	Wonderful planet
десять месяцев зима	*Dvenadsat mesyatsov zima*	Twelve months winter
остальное – лето	*Ostalnoye – leto*	the rest – summer

6

KOLYMA

Wonderful Planet

So this was Kolyma, the name that wrought fear in the hearts of most Russians. I can only imagine what my father's thoughts must have been. Just as the term gulag is synonymous with the worst excesses of repression of the Soviet penal system, then Kolyma is synonymous with the worst excesses of the gulag system.

But what was Kolyma in reality?

Kolyma (Колыма)
Kolyma is actually a vast, isolated, mountainous arctic wilderness of striking natural beauty, largely unspoiled by man and bestowed with a wealth of natural exploitable resources. At its easternmost point it is separated by a mere 80 km across the Bering Sea from Alaska. When not used in terms of gulags, Kolyma specifically refers to a geographical region consisting of the River Kolyma basin together with the coastal region south of the Kolyma mountain range to the shores of the Sea of Okhotsk. It includes the regional capital Magadan.

The River Kolyma itself rises in the Kolyma mountain range of the Anadyr Plateau whose highest peak at 3,000 m is Mount Chen in the Cherskii chain (coincidentally named after the Polish explorer Jan Stanisław Franciszek Czerski). It flows in a northerly direction for almost 2,500 km to its mouths in the East Siberian Sea. It has nearly 300 tributaries, and drains a huge basin of nearly 700,000 square km which covers parts of the Sakha Republic, Chukotka Autonomous Okrug, and Magadan Oblast.

In parts the river is very wide, up 170 m, has an average depth of about 6 m, a discharge of 4,000 cubic metres a second, and an average flow of around 10 km an hour. It's considered to be Russia's sixth-most important river after the Ob, Yenisey, Lena, Amur, and the Volga.

It is a very clear but cold river, only being completely free of ice for about 100 days each year during the brief Kolyma summer from June to October. In the upper course of the river it flows rapidly, cutting through steep gorges, but as the river widens as it enters the Kolyma plain it slows considerably. For the last 75 km it divides into two large branches with numerous islands and flows into the East Siberian Sea (part of the Arctic Ocean) near the coastal town of Ambarchik where the sea is covered with an ice crust of up to 2 m for ten months of the year.

The mountains of the Kolyma basin support a huge mineral wealth, especially gold, silver, tin, tungsten, mercury, copper, antimony, coal, oil, peat, and uranium. The river basin ecosystems, consisting of lowland tundra and mountain taiga interspersed with forested river valleys, support a fantastic diversity of wildlife.

There are nine distinct natural ecosystems or biomes in Kolyma, but these are generally combined into three main groups: alpine desert, tundra, and taiga.

The rocky alpine desert is characteristically sparse in vegetation, consisting of little more than lichens and mosses. This is replaced by the low bush tundra, home to osier (small willow) and elfin cedar woods. The severe weather exerts a strong effect on the tundra plant life. The strong winds in the mountainous areas force plants to be low-growing and almost stunted in growth. Herbaceous plants include reed, cotton, quack, and bluegrass, arctic poppy, fireweed, the ubiquitous rhododendron, sedges, and wild leek. The forest tundra flora consists of dwarf plants, such as stunted dahurian larch, thickets of dwarf birch, willow, and elfin cedar. Due to the harsh subarctic climate with its long cold winters Kolyma is covered with permafrost over large expanses of its area. Of all the trees the larch is the most prevalent, and in the winter turns from green to beautiful red and orange, so much so that the region is often referred to as the 'Golden Taiga'.

The entire Kolyma watershed, the valleys of the Kolyma River system, together with several other river basins of the Sea of Okhotsk coast, are all in the taiga zone. This ecosystem consists of pine, spruce, larch, Siberian cedar, aspen, dahurian larch, sweet poplar, birch, chosenia (a species of willow), willow, alder, dwarf birch, labrador tea, bilberry, elfin cedar, reed grass, hellebores, bluegrass, knotgrass, wild geranium, tansy, sedge, Siberian broome, and fireweed. Medicinal plants include valerian, ferns, juniper, lingonberry, dandelion, wild rose, mountain ash, and honeysuckle. The berries which are found in abundance throughout the area are typically rich in taste.

The elfin or dwarf cedar (*Pinus pumila pallas*) seems to have made a special impression on the Kolyma prisoners; many accounts include reference to it. It is a truly evergreen shrub, maintaining its iridescent green foliage throughout the year. As well as the nuts for food, its pine needles were also collected and boiled down to make to a thick, yellowy-coloured, foul-tasting potion called *khvoya*. This was given to all prisoners in order to combat scurvy. I don't believe that it worked but it seems that it was usually mandatory to drink it in many camps in Kolyma before meals. Varlam Shalamov in his book *Kolyma Tales* tells how collecting the pine needles was considered by the prisoners as 'a pushover job', infinitely preferable to their normal hard labour. He also describes how they were able to forecast winter weather through the behaviour of the trees as they would lie prone a few days before the start of any snow but in the spring they would rise up just before the onset of the thaw.

Harsh as the Kolyma environment is, consisting of the lowland tundra and mountain taiga interspersed with forested river valleys, it supports a fantastic diversity of wildlife. The River Kolyma itself provides habitat for a multitude of fish species including pike, perch, grayling, omul, chir, muksun, white salmon (nelma), sturgeon, taimen, and karas.

Along the banks and in the surrounding areas can be found moose (elk), sable (related to martens), wolverines (large weasels), brown bears, Manchurian, morthern, and musk deer, bighorn, and snow sheep, wild reindeer, arctic and red foxes, wolves, lynx, hares, ground squirrels, marmots, pikas (related to rabbits and hares) and lemmings, with polar bears and walruses inhabiting the northernmost regions.

Though Kolyma supports about 250 bird species, notably the sterkh (Siberian white crane), sandhill crane, loon (diver), Ross's Goose, snowy owl, golden and white-tailed eagle, ptarmigan and nutcrackers, many are only summer visitors such as the black-billed capercaillie, hazel grouse, chiffchaff, nuthatch, cuckoo, black woodpecker, waxwing, various wagtails, thrush, crossbill and other perching birds. Migratory waterfowl, mainly ducks, nest on the lakes and in marshy river valleys, and a wide variety of sea birds nest along the rocky coastline before migrating before the onset of the Kolyma winter. The only birds left on the tundra in winter are snowy owls and the hardy ptarmigan.

The seas around Magadan, which can be frozen for up to five months of the year, are the habitat of many large animals such as whales and seals, as well as many species of commercial fish. The thriving Magadan fishing industry is only able to continue working the whole year round by using a fleet of icebreakers.

So abundant and widespread is the wildlife that it's no surprise that hunting for sport is threatening the indigenous wildlife, as are illegal logging, poaching, and habitat destruction, significantly from gold-mining, which I will come to a little later.

The Magadan region has a subarctic climate with long, very cold winters lasting up to six months of the year. Though the weather is notoriously harsh, the southern coastal region around the city of Magadan, offered some protection from the sea by its coastal cliffs to the south and the mountain ranges to the north, though less extreme than the interior, is still for most of the year very cold and uninviting. winter temperatures of -50°c are not unusual!

Inland the climate in the taiga of Kolyma can drop to a frightening -70°c and the coldest permanently inhabited place on earth, Oymyakon (Оймякóн), with the lowest-ever recorded temperature of -71.2°c, can be found in the Kolyma mountain range. Varlam Shalamov described in his short story 'Carpenters' how long-term prisoners even without thermometers were able to determine the temperature. Frosty fog meant -40°c, exhaling easily but with a rasping in the throat was -50°c, but exhaling with difficulty and with a rasping in the throat was -60°c and lower than -60°c spit froze in mid-air.

Permafrost covers most of the Kolyma region. In some areas along the banks of the River Kolyma it is up to 2 km deep. Over the years preserved remains of prehistoric animals and in particular mammoths have been found, some dating back over 10,000 years. The baby mammoth Dima, a unique whole animal, is perhaps the most famous.

The indigenous Yukaghirs who inhabit the area constitute one of the smallest ethnic groups in Russia. Their local name for themselves is Odul, and their language is classified as genetically isolated. They survive like the local Chukchi and Yakuts by hunting and herding reindeer, and are perfectly adapted to survive under these extreme conditions.

During the Kolyma summer, the temperature can rise to 30°c, the rivers thaw, the ground warms up (but not to more than a depth of 2 m) and the frozen ground gives way to shallow and treacherous swamps. The sticky, waterlogged grey or blue clay characteristic of Magadan region is known as *gley*, and provides an ideal habitat for the large numbers of bloodsucking insects that blight the region. These insects, like mosquitoes, horseflies, gadflies and midges, swarm on the tundra and the taiga in summer. Though they are a source of food for many forest birds, they are more than just a nuisance to people and livestock; they can at times be a complete hazard.

But why was my father, with millions of other prisoners, here in this harsh, remote, isolated, extreme, and difficult-to-reach wilderness of natural beauty? I alluded to it earlier; Kolyma has vast deposits of minerals, in particular gold.

Gold was first thought to have been mined in about 1910, but not really in commercial quantities until about 1927. These first significant mining operations used free labour, but in the inhospitable, underpopulated region it was clearly unsustainable for the quantities demanded by the Soviet government. By 1930 Russia and the Soviet Union had turned on the *kulaks*, the rich peasants. This period of collectivisation and forced labour projects produced a ready supply of workers, a good proportion of whom were sent to Kolyma and used for gold-mining operations.

As described in chapter 5, Dalstroy (State Trust for Road and Industrial Construction in the Upper Kolyma Area) was created in 1931 to administer all forced labour projects in the north-east of Siberia. Gold production came under the responsibility of Dalstroy and its first head, Eduard Berzin.

Eduard Petrovich Berzin (Эдуард Петрович Берзин)

Berzin was born in 1894 in the Latvian capital of Riga. Like his contemporaries he came from a poor, peasant background, but unlike most of them he was he was well-educated, academic, and had a passion for culture. He eventually studied art in Germany at Berlin's Academy of Fine Arts, where he met his wife Elza Mittenberg (Элза Митэнбупг), also an artist, and also from Riga.

The First World War saw him fighting for the Imperial Russian Army. By 1918 he had been promoted to commander of the First Latvian Fusiliers, where he helped crush socialist and revolutionary opposition opposed to Lenin, for which he was awarded with special responsibilities including the protection of Lenin himself. Having earned the trust of Feliks Dzerzhinsky, the head of the Cheka, he soon became a member of the Russian secret police himself.

By 1926 he was tasked by Stalin with the setting up of a cellulose and paper production plant at the Vishera complex of labour camps in the Ural Mountains (sometimes known as Vishlag). His enthusiasm and even-handed approach, whereby he valued the effort of his prisoner labour force, saw the project become an overwhelming success. Under his authority his prisoners were treated surprisingly well, receiving wages, and benefited from cinemas, theatres, libraries, discussion clubs, shops, reasonable living conditions, food and proper dining facilities.

In 1931 Stalin rewarded him by appointing him as the first head of Dalstroy, giving him the opportunity to turn the gold production of Kolyma into a profit in order to finance the rapid industrialisation taking place across Russia. He arrived in Nagayevo Bay on the very first of the 'slave ships', *Sakhalin*, in early 1932 together with some engineers, the first prisoners, and their guards.

Initially, the priorities of Dalstroy were preparation for gold excavation. The first work centred on creating the port of Nagayevo to allow the expected influx of workers, supplies, and prisoners. Even this, possibly the simplest of their immediate priorities, proved difficult in the harsh environment and steep coastline without any modern heavy-lifting and construction equipment; everything had to be unloaded by wooden barges.

Establishing Nagayevo as the regional centre was clearly untenable. A more sheltered location, a few kilometres inland along the Magadanka River, was selected and so the city of Magadan was born. All the early buildings were constructed of local timber from the surrounding forests, but the prisoners were to spend several years living in tents.

Top of the list of priorities, however, was the building of roads into the taiga to establish the lifeline required to support the goldfields. The initial plan for the first year was to establish a main artery going north to what is now the town of Seimchan, some 900 km away. Unfortunately, the difficulty of the terrain, the harsh conditions, the lack of tools and manpower meant that this goal was only eventually achieved in 1937!

The main reason for the slow pace of the construction was the difficulty of the terrain; forests, mountain, rivers, valleys, boulders and particularly the swamps. These swamps arise because most of the land is permafrost, which prevents any groundwater from escaping and in the summer thaws near the surface, creating vast swamps, the ideal breeding ground for the multitude of biting insects, but offering no support to roads, which sink into it.

In order to navigate the region special road construction techniques for the swamps were developed whereby the path of the road would be cut and the top layer of the ground removed. A lattice of tree trunks and logs would be laid out along the route of the road and then the removed topsoil and turf together with gravel was used to cover the construction.

So hard were the working conditions in the first year of 1932–3 that it's been said that more than half of the prisoners working on road construction died. But, primitive as these roads may have been, they were to be invaluable in the early years and several can still be seen in Kolyma today.

In the first year of operations about 10,000 prisoners were brought to Kolyma and Berzin had total control of all aspects of the operations of Dalstroy; he was considered almost as a Tsar. His autonomy from the Soviet authorities was almost total but in return he was expected to deliver ever-increasing quantities of gold.

Because of the massive infrastructure efforts in the early years, the first gold-production season yielded only 500 kg of gold, but with the increasing numbers of prisoners arriving and under Berzin's management, three years later this had risen to 14 tonnes. Berzin was astute and his experience made him realise that to maximise the efforts of his workforce for gold production they should be relatively well fed, appropriately clothed and housed, and have realistic and achievable production goals (*norms*). In the early days the prisoners even received an actual payment for their efforts. Exceptional workers, the *stakhanovites*, were sometimes rewarded with shortened sentences.

Initially prisoners were expected to excavate 1 cubic metre a day, but increasing demands from Moscow for gold saw this increasing to 2 cubic metres a day in 1934, and by 1936 to 4–6 cubic metres, all for the same quantity of food rations. Berzin's efforts didn't go unnoticed and he was awarded the 'Order of Lenin' for 'surpassing the mining Plan'. But the achievement wasn't obtained without cost, pressure from Moscow demanding more and more gold led to greater numbers of prisoners arriving at Nagayevo with bigger and bigger expectations on the workforce and at the same time with reducing daily food rations.

Berzin himself was a workaholic and devoted Party activist. Apparently, he spent every day touring the mines and construction sites of Kolyma clad in his trademark bearskin overcoat and being chauffer-driven in a Rolls-Royce that had been supplied from Moscow. It had previously belonged to Nadezhda Konstantinovna Krupskaya (Надежда Константиновна Крупская), the widow of Lenin. It is said that his wife Elza, and their children, son Petia and daughter Mirza, saw very little of him apart from family holidays.

While Berzin was consolidating and increasing gold production in Kolyma, back in Moscow political turmoil had set in. The rapid Soviet industrialisation had by the early 1930s turned into a massive collectivisation campaign. Agricultural output was increased by removing the smaller subsistence farms, often run by the richer peasants, the *kulaks*, and replacing them with large-scale collective mechanised farms. This brought peasants under direct political control and enabled them to be taxed more efficiently. This led to a massive redistribution of people and a drastic reduction in the standard of living for most of the *kulaks*, so it is no surprise that it was met with widespread unrest and violent reactions among much of the rural population.

In December 1934 the prominent and popular Bolshevik leader Sergei Kirov was assassinated in Leningrad. This gave Stalin the excuse to clamp down on all opposition, and so began the dark period of the Stalinist purges. Following the appointment of the dreaded Yezhov as head of the NKVD in December 1936, the Soviet Union entered into a period known to most as 'the Great Terror'. The whole nation was to endure a period of total repression, persecution, and state-sponsored violence as had never before been seen. Nobody was safe.

High-profile arrests, show trials, deportations and executions ensured that Stalin retained his absolute power and tightened his stranglehold on his shocked and terrified nation. Much of the military leadership was decimated together with high-profile Party officials, academics, engineers, artists and scientists. Prisoners in ever-increasing numbers began arriving in Kolyma.

During this period, Berzin and the Dalstroy hierarchy at the extremity of the Soviet empire seemed largely untouched by the machinations emanating from Moscow. Berzin himself openly condemned some of the brutal treatment of prisoners, dire living conditions in the camps, unjustified extension of their conviction terms and other irregularities as 'directly jeopardising the implementation of the production output and political objectives' of Dalstroy. However, unsurprisingly, the Dalstroy autonomy wasn't to last.

In 1937 Berzin and his family returned to Magadan from a family holiday in Italy, France, and Germany. By this time prisoner numbers in Kolyma had risen to 70,000 and they were mining over 50 tonnes of gold. Despite this, Stalin made clear to the Dalstroy management his unhappiness with the 'almost sympathetic' and lenient treatment of the prisoners, who amounted to about 90 per cent of the total Dalstroy workforce.

In December of that year the ominously named ship SS *Yezhov* arrived in Nagayevo with several high-ranking Party officials, including Berzin's replacement. It left a week later with Berzin himself onboard, summoned to Moscow. He never made it; he was removed from the train he was travelling on at the town of Aleksandrov about 70 km from Moscow and driven in secrecy the rest of the way to Moscow.

He was eventually executed in Moscow's notorious Lubyanka prison in August 1938. His crime: spying for Germany and England and 'creating a Trotskyite espionage and sabotage organisation with the intention of giving Japan control of the gold-rich deposits of Kolyma'. His wife Elza was destined to spend ten years in the gulags, his son Petia was sent to an orphanage (and was later to die as a Red Army soldier in the Siege of Stalingrad) and his daughter Mirza was brought up by her grandparents.

I suppose in many ways, and unusually, his legacy is of a staunch Bolshevik, an efficient stalwart of the Party line, but he is considered by some more favourably in a regime where all his contemporaries are only remembered for their total brutality. In 1989, on the fifty-eighth anniversary of the municipal charter of Magadan, a huge bust of Berzin was unveiled in the centre of Magadan. The guest of honour was Asia Odinets, the daughter of Mirza, Berzin's granddaughter. The town itself still retains his name at one of the main schools, and Berzin Street (улица Берзина) can still be found to this day.

The demise of Berzin brought to an end the period known as the 'golden years of Kolyma'. The whole of the Dalstroy hierarchy was affected. Notables like his deputy, Ivan Filoppov (И.Г. Филиппов), the head of USVITL, were either incarcerated in the despicable system they had previously managed or 'committed suicide', probably in Magadan's stone-built central prison. This prison was, ironically, from the onset of Dalstroy known as 'Vaskov's House', after the initial head of USVITL from 1932 to 1934, Rodion Ivanovich Vaskov (Р.И. Васьков). The name has persisted to the present day despite the fact that Vaskov, like Berzin, presided over a regime far less brutal than those that were to follow.

The new head of Dalstroy was the Yezhov-appointed, high-profile NKVD Colonel-General Karp Alksandrovich Pavlov (Карп Александрович Павлов). A ruthless Party functionary, he had a simple, brief and clear objective. In short he was to convert the camps of Kolyma to harsh corrective penal intuitions even at the expense of commercial output. The gulag prisoners were to become a truly expendable unit of labour. Immediately work days were increased from six to eight hours in the winter and ten in the summer to a minimum of twelve hours and often more. *Norms* were recalculated with almost unachievable limits. Food rations, already minimal, were reduced and appropriate clothing was no longer considered a necessity. Annual productions quotas were revised upwards, which led to prisoners in ever-increasing numbers being required, and treatment of the prisoners became evermore harsh and uncompromising.

The news of the appointment of Pavlov reverberated throughout the whole of Dalstroy, from senior camp official down to the prisoners themselves. Vladimir Petrov, a prisoner himself at the time, describes in his book *Soviet Gold* the arrival of Pavlov. He was aware of any remnants of liberalism vanishing and the camp becoming an even harsher environment. Pavlov had absolute control. Pavlov, like Berzin, was often seen around the whole of Kolyma.

Petrov remembers seeing him when he was struggling to stem a leak from a drainage ditch during heavy rain.

The arrival of Pavlov initiated a period of terror as never before seen in Kolyma. The year 1938 is generally accepted to be the worst in the Kolyma gulag history, but it's considered that Pavlov himself wasn't the main instigator. That dubious distinction fell to his deputy, the new head of USVITL, the dreaded Colonel Stepan Nikolaivich Garanin (Степан Николаевич Гаранин). From all accounts he was a sadistic, murderous bully who treated prisoners with no less than complete disdain. Just as Yezhovshchina had gripped the Soviet Union during the Great Terror, so Garaninshchina gripped Kolyma.

Garanin's brutality was legendary. All accounts of the period contain awful stories of the personal violence and sadism meted out by him personally. Robert Conquest explains, at evening roll call, after the prisoners returned from the mines, Garanin would call out those who had not met their quota and they would be driven from the camp and shot under his personal supervision.

The personal horror stories go on. But even more sinister, under the auspices of Garanin the NKVD created a purpose-built death camp, solely for the purpose of mass-extermination. Its name was Serpantinka (Серпантинка), sometimes called Serpantinnaya. It was created in the dark valley of the River Khatenakh (Хатынах) about 400 km north of Magadan, converted from the barracks of a road-building unit and heavily fortified. It had a huge garage that for a time housed two tractors whose engines were allegedly used to mask the noise of the shootings and screams of the prisoners within! It's said that in 1938 alone there were 26,000 deaths in the Serpantinka, and that most of the bodies were crudely buried in the surrounding valley.

Mercifully Garanin lasted only a year. He was arrested in 1939 and like Berzin accused of spying for Japan and shot. His official arrest mugshot photo clearly shows the fear on his face; he must have seen similar fear on the faces of those that suffered his brutality during his reign.

After his demise the whole of the Serpantinka camp structure was razed to the ground and all the personnel involved were executed, from the senior commanders down to the lowly drivers and executioners themselves. It seemed as though Dalstroy wanted to rid itself of all traces of this particular piece of its unsavoury history. In reality though, there is so little known about the Serpantinka operations because so few of its inmates and operatives ever survived to tell of the gruesome details.

It is said that despite the Khatenakh valley surrounding Serpantinka having vast deposits of gold, it wasn't actually mined until many years later because of all the corpses buried in shallow graves. In 1991 a memorial was unveiled on the site of the original camp to commemorate all those that had lost their lives there.

Garanin was initially replaced as head of USVITL by a major of state security, Yegorov (Егóров), of whom I can find very little information. He was replaced in early 1940 by the ill-fated Colonel Vishnevetsky (Вишневецкий). Vishnevetsky was sentenced to fifteen years in the gulags following his disastrous attempt to start mining operations in the Pestraya Dresva region, about 500 km up the coast west of Magadan, towards Kamchatka. Petrov describes in his book a conversation with a fellow prisoner who was part of the team led by Vishnevetsky that sailed to Pestraya Dresva. The weather was extremely bad and they encountered severe difficulties when they came into the bay, but the authorities ordered them to begin unloading at once. The story goes on to describe how the barges were buffeted into the ship, killing horses and making the unloading of the cargo deadly. When it was time for the prisoners to be lowered for disembarkation, they refused: 'the sea was too wild. Vishnevetsky came back on deck with his revolver and ordered them down at once. He even started to make a speech about how we – Bolsheviks – are afraid of nothing.'

Eventually both barges, battered by the gale, broke free and sank together with the men, equipment, and provisions that they contained. Many of the men had also been lost overboard from the ship itself. Eventually Vishnevetsky faced reality and issued orders to cease loading and turn back to Magadan.

Vishnevetsky's demise must have happened while my father was in Kolyma, and from May 1941 colonel of state security Evekl Idelevich Drabkin (Драбкин, Евекль Иделевич) reigned supreme as head of USVITL.

Pavlov himself lasted as head of Dalstroy until 1940, departing Kolyma after apparently falling out with Beria. He went on to hold several senior NKVD posts, retired in 1948, but committed suicide in 1957.

A new chief of Dalstroy appeared in Kolyma. He was Ivan Fedorovich Nikishov, member of the supreme Soviet of the USSR and commissar of state security, 3rd Grade – a rank equivalent to that of lieutenant-general in the army. Soon the 'line' of the new chief became evident, a 'line' that was, of course in consonance with both Beria and Stalin's policies.

So during the whole of my dad's time in Kolyma, Ivan Fedorovich Nikishov (Иван ФеДорович Никишов) was head of Dalstroy. The general impression of Nikishov is of a hard and ruthless administrator, but he was well aware of the previous failings of the Dalstroy hierarchy, and keen to conform to the demands of Moscow.

While in Magadan he divorced his wife and married a young communist activist almost half his age called Gridassova. who was described as a 'crude and avaricious creature'. She was head of Magadan's women's prison and eventually elevated to the head of MagLag, responsible for all prisoners in the camp district of Magadan and the surrounding districts.

While Berzin had lived in a primitive wooden house between Nagayevo and Magadan, the Nikishov's lived in a luxurious 'modern' villa 75 km from Magadan which boasted, among other luxuries, its own hunting reserve. He was to remain chief of Dalstroy until he retired in 1948.

My dad was marched from the slave ship out of the port of Nagyevo to Magadan's transit camp and truly into the clutches of the Dalstroy system. The steep route would have taken him close to the wooden house that Berzin had lived in. A church has since been built on this spot. The march to the transit camp would have been along the only major road in Kolyma, the infamous Kolyma Highway (Kolyma Trasse). Along its route there were many camps, hospitals and other Dalstroy installations. Rather than name them individually, the administration merely used the distance from Magadan along the Kolyma Highway as their name. The transit camp was known as 'Kilometre 4'.

Most memoirists describe this particular march in stark contrast to previous marches to and from prisons in that most of the civilians in Magadan that they encountered barely raised their heads to even notice them. They had seen so many prisoners that they were almost oblivious to them. Magadan had been founded on prisoners whereas on 'mainland' Russia most civilians, predominantly the women, had been openly aggressive and abusive to the prison guards, often throwing items of clothing and food to the prisoners. Most perhaps had lost husbands, sons, or daughters to the 'Organy' (NKVD).

All of the prisoners had already endured months in detention with little food or water, often enduring beatings and having had no exercise. They were in a terrible physical condition and found the short journey uphill to the transit camp arduous. In *Man is Wolf to Man*, Bardach explains that after eight days in the ship his muscles were badly weakened and that the majority of his fellow prisoners couldn't walk upright. Vladimir Petrov found himself among the stragglers at the back of his group on the march up the hill. They were closely followed by guards leading growling sheep dogs. 'The guards, increasing their pace somewhat, came nearer until they were almost on top of us, and began to sick their dogs, which eagerly attacked the last stragglers. There was a fearful noise of clothing being torn to shreds, frightened screams of the attacked, and the snarling of the dogs. Gathering all my strength I increased my speed, fighting off the pain in my legs. Taking a quick glance to the rear, I saw an old man fall. Then another tripped and fell. A half a minute later I heard two shots and looking back again I noticed one of the guards catching up with his comrades on the run.' Eventually the procession reached the high fence, turned left, and struggled through the gate under the Magadan Transit Camp illuminated sign. Once everyone had made it into the yard, the gates were closed behind them.

The Transit Camp at 'Kilometre 4' was my father's, and millions of other prisoners', first experience of life in Kolyma. The camp was primitive and brutal, but secure, heavily guarded, and managed with ruthless efficiency. The camp itself was in use throughout the Kolyma gulag years, and like so much of the Kolyma gulag infrastructure some traces of the transit camp at 'Kilometre 4' can still be found to this day, though it's now much less imposing and less likely to wreak the fear into people that it once did.

In its early days the transit prison contained simple military tents for barracks, but by the time my dad arrived these had been replaced more substantial, but no more inviting wooden huts. On arrival, the Poles remained segregated from all other prisoners, and were made to wait outside until they were called in groups for 'cleansing'. This consisted of a visit to the barber to have their heads shaved, followed by a march to the *banya* (баня) for a shower, which would normally be expected to make them feel better but as we will see a little later became yet another ordeal that they had to endure. The final stage of the cleansing was the de-lousing, whereby they were treated with an anti-louse powder and their clothes disinfected with chemicals and heat, the latter of which would often destroy those items of clothing worn out from continual wear. When this happened 'new' items of clothing would be grudgingly replaced by the *predurok* (high-'ranking' *urka*) overseeing the cleansing. These would inevitably be hardly better than the items lost and invariably completely the wrong size.

Once allocated to a barrack, life in the Kolyma transit camp was initially not much different than in all the previous transit camps and prisons. There were the frequent roll calls (*poverka* – поверка), sitting around, chatting, playing cards, removing lice: all pretty boring, but overshadowed by an air of impending doom.

7

GULAG

Soviet Corrective Labour Camp

Eventually, everyone was called for a medical. My father probably got the call towards the end of November or even early December. The routine was always along similar lines to that described by Janusz Bardach. He describes the clean white walls and wooden floor of the examining room, in which a doctor reviewed his file and a female doctor inspected his eyes, ears, teeth, tongue and throat. He had to breathe deeply, cough, exhale loudly, and cough again. She listened to his heart and pressed on his liver, intestines and kidneys. He flexed his muscles, did twenty-five sit-ups and push-ups, and ran on the spot for five minutes. The examination finished with an anal inspection. The doctor declared Bardach healthy and said to the NKVD officer, 'First Labour category. No restrictions.' His file was clearly marked with 'TFT', which stood for trudna fizichesky trud (трудно физический труд – тфт), or 'hard physical labour'. This was true for my father. It seems that none of the Polish prisoners arriving, regardless of age, health, or physical condition were allocated to the lesser categories of light or medium physical labour. In fact it appears from most accounts that the Poles were usually maintained segregated from most of the other Kolyma prisoners and usually sent to the worst working areas of the region!

Since the gold-mining season was over and the harsh Kolyma winter had set it my father was allocated to work parties operating in the environs of Magadan. This entailed clearing ditches and particularly clearing roads of the deep snow to enable trucks to drive into the interior with supplies and equipment for the many camps.

This type of work continued for my father until around June 1941. He mentioned that he had also worked in agriculture, so may have also have spent some time on one of the several farms that surrounded Magadan. What I do know is that towards the end of June he was called for *etap*. His time had come.

Unceremoniously, he and his comrades were awoken in the early hours, told to collect any belongings they had, and ordered outside for *poverka*. After the rigours of the all-too-familiar formalities they were marched out of the transit camp and loaded onto the back of open-top trucks, probably the ubiquitous double-axled GAZ AA, or triple-axled GAZ AAA, and departed the transit camp northbound heading towards the dreaded taiga of Kolyma.

Initially the road was substantial; after all, it was the famous Kolyma Highway, now known as the P-480; it was the lifeline of Dalstroy. On leaving Magadan (Магадан) the road crossed the Magadanka River and climbed steeply towards the north. They will have passed by the old airport, several Dalstroy installations, and then into the mountainous region of smallish hills known as Sopki (сопки). After about 40 km they passed the camp at Uptar (Уптар), and a short distance further they passed through the settlement of Sokol (Сокол), now the home of the modern-day Magadan International Airport.

As they continued northbound on the Kolyma Highway they came to the town and regional gulag administration centre of Palatka (Палатка), situated about 65 km north of Magadan. They may have stopped there for food (unlikely), formalities and/or refuelling. Nobody will ever know; it's irrelevant anyway, because at this point the trucks pulled off the Kolyma Highway, turning left off the paved road onto mainly unprepared and treacherous mountain tracks. They were heading deeper into the Taiga towards the Western Mining Administration regional headquarters at Ust-Omchug (Усть-Омчуг) and the dreaded mining complex at Butugychag (Бутугычаг) some 150 km distant.

Ayyub Baghirov, an Azerbaijani prisoner, describes his journey along the very same road in his essay 'Kolyma – Off to the Unknown: Stalin's Notorious Prison Camps in Siberia'.

Convoy to Butugychag: One gloomy morning at dawn, we were transported in open trucks from Magadan. Our route took us through some of Kolyma's uninhabited virgin territory. We drove for a while, leaving behind the fog-enshrouded Nagayev pier. The weather became colder; though it was dry. When the convoy stopped, the guards would get out and take a rest, and we would go in search of some 'gift of nature', such as cedar nuts. It kept us from becoming weak from hunger.

We were surprised when the guards didn't pay much attention to us prisoners when we jumped out of the trucks. Obviously, they already knew that it was impossible for us to escape anywhere.

They had the right to shoot us any time 'for attempting to escape'. Where could one escape in the wild wilderness of the taiga? If you died, the wild animals would devour you. If you succeeded in managing to reach civilization, you would be reported and receive an extended sentence that was even harsher. In reality, it was practically impossible to escape from the camps of Kolyma, although such attempts were made, especially in the spring and summer.

The sites for these camps, which were located out in the middle of uninhabited taiga forests, had been very carefully selected. They were situated in sheltered areas between boulders and hills. With the help of a large staff of armed camp security, thousands of sheepdogs, Chekists and Army frontier guards, it was so easy to catch anyone trying to escape.

Besides, there was an enormous network of informers among the prisoners – secret agents appointed by camp administration who also helped to prevent the prisoners from escaping. En route, we saw that on the edge of the road near the ditch, some places already were covered with gravel.

We headed up into the Kolyma Mountains, travelling such a long way, passing through forests. There were no inhabitants. We bumped and swayed from side to side in the truck.

Despite how exhausted we were, the trucks continued moving forward, day and night. The drivers constantly had to use their brakes. Actually, despite our own pathetic situation, we felt sorry for the drivers who had to navigate such dangerous passes through the mountains and taiga.

During the short breaks, the drivers wouldn't even get out of the trucks to stretch their legs. They would just fall asleep right there on the seat.

They were so tired that we would have to wake them up to start moving again. Especially when we passed close to the rivers where the road was so icy and slippery, the drivers had to be so alert and cautious. They would get out of their trucks, search for the right place to drive in order to avoid any surprises or accidents. Sometimes the snow would drift across the road, and the trucks would get stuck. We would get out and push the trucks out of the snow with our bare hands. But all in all, the drivers in Kolyma were very courageous and skilful.

Petrov too was impressed with the drivers' skills on the demanding roads, commenting on their abilities on narrow winding and treacherous precipices often for long hours without sleep. Not all journeys were without mishap though; Petrov describes a truck he was being transported in sinking through the ice when crossing a frozen river with the driver still onboard, and Bardach was lucky to escape alive after being thrown from the back of a truck as it careered over a precipice and was completely destroyed as it crashed down the valley with most of the passengers, guards, and the driver losing their lives.

The arduous 150-km drive to Ust-Omchug must have taken hours. When they eventually arrived, it was clear that Butugychag wasn't to be their destination. The trucks passed through Ust-Omchug and my father's and his fellow passengers' hearts must have dropped further as they continued along the road deeper and deeper into the Tenkinski region (Тенькинский район), moving ever closer to the gold-mines of Khatenakh (Хатынах) and the unthinkable possibility that they were bound for the dreaded Serpantinka!

Mercifully they were to be spared this fate; about 55 km out of Ust-Omchug and travelling in a westerly direction, the trucks arrived at the village of Nelikoba (Нелькоба), turned right and drove northwards down the valley of the River Tenika (Тенька). It was the very next valley to Khatenakh and Serpantinka. The rough road continued for a bumpy 40 km along the River Tenika, passing below the highest peak in the region, Tenkenskaya (Тэнкєнская) at 1,654 m, until the river neared its confluence with the mighty Kolyma; the river that gave its name both to the whole region and to the harshest penal regime of the Soviet Union.

The River Kolyma at this point turns from flowing south to flow north, creating a natural flood plain. It is an incredibly picturesque region of high, snow-capped mountains, deep valleys and lakes. Not far to the north, a short distance up the River Kolyma is the famous and beautiful but improbably named Jack London Lake (озеру Джека Лондона). This large lake, at the foot of the Anagag (Анагаг) mountain, was named by one of the early discoverers of gold in Kolyma, Y. A. Bilibin, a reader of the works of the American writer Jack London; the author of tales of the Klondike gold rush and classics such as *The Call of the Wild* and *White Fang*.

City/town	Local name	Location	Approx. distance	Country
Duskanya	Дусканья	405 km north-west of Nagayevo	13,650 km	Russia (Россия)

The trucks travelled down the Tenika to just before it flows into the Kolyma, where it is joined by a small tributary flowing into it from the right called the Duskan (Дускан). At this point the trucks came to a final stop and the party of prisoners unloaded. They were then herded up the imposing, steep-sided river valley of the Duskan for about 5 km until they finally came to their destination; the gold-mining complex of Duskanya (Дусканья). The almost 400-km journey from Magadan had probably taken two days or more to complete and this, the very last stage, the trek on foot up the valley, was the most arduous.

The Duskan was the same valley that Varlam Shalamov used in his short story 'Dry Rations' from his book *Kolyma Tales*.

Like the majority of gulag camps in Kolyma, Duskanya was laid out in a rectangular format for better surveillance; in fact no irregular-shaped camps were allowed by law. It was comprised of high barbed-wire fencing with tall wooden watch-towers enclosing a *zona* of simple wooden barracks, some wooden administrative buildings, perhaps a kitchen/dining area, and a punishment isolator (штрафне изолятор). Outside the wire fence would have been commander's quarters, the guards' facilities (*vakhta*), and the food and equipment stores. The whole complex would have been built by previous prisoners who would not only have created the route up the valley from the road, but also sourced the timber from the surrounding area for all the structures.

More than likely the entrance to the camp would have been emblazoned with a slogan extolling Soviet virtues, with words to the effect of 'work in the Soviet Union is glorious, honourable, valiant, and heroic' or simply 'the country needs metal (gold)'.

It seems the Poles arrested following the Soviet invasion of Poland were in most cases kept separate from the normal Soviet criminals and sent to camps throughout Kolyma. Petrov, who was at Khatenakh around this time, remembers the arrival of the Poles in the upper Kolyma area and heard rumours that the conditions they were kept in were far worse than the other camp inmates. They may possibly have been my dad's group at Duskanya.

On arrival to the camp the transit guards would have handed the prisoners over to the authority of the camp commander at the camp allocation office. Once he had checked the paperwork and signed for them he would have dismissed the transit guards and put the prisoners under his own guard. He will then have probably given – or arranged for a *politruk* (Soviet political officer) to give – a lengthy speech in accordance with the 'Party line'.

He would then have allocated the prisoners to barracks, where they would have been received, depending on the time of day, by the elder or most senior prisoner of the barracks, known as a *starosta*. He would have been blunt and unambiguous about what was expected of them; 'you work – you eat, you stop working – you die'.

The *starosta* will have split the new arrivals into workgroups or gangs (often referred to as a brigade), with a foreman (gang leader/brigadier) who was responsible for the brigade fulfilling its daily *norm*. The arrival in camp is described in a handwritten Pleszak attestation:

6. Life in the camp, average day, Quotas, Remuneration, Food, Clothes, life
After arrival we got a group of Poles together with a foreman. We chose Zyligowski as the foreman; however we worked like that for a few days only. After a few days they divided us among the Russians full of thieves, bullies, and bandits. The conditions of work were very bad. We worked night shift from 7 p.m. to 7 a.m. in the gold-mine and two more hours from 7 a.m. to 9 a.m. From 9 a.m. we would start going back.

At 10 a.m. breakfast consisted of 0.5 litre of Barley soup with fish, 600g of bread which was wet and felt like clay. At 11 a.m. we could go to sleep to 5 p.m., from 5 p.m. to 6 p.m. dinner which was the above mentioned soup and half a spoon of Barley. At 6.30 p.m. we had to go to roll call – still hungry. We worked like this until midnight when we get half a litre of soup and back to work with no rest until 9 a.m. 80 per cent of us were sick with different sicknesses. You would only get help from a doctor if you collapsed and could not get up. The dead were buried like animals, no coffin, just straight into the mud.

There would have been no settling in; all the newcomers would have been put to work on the next available shift. Zyligowski, typically for a gang leader, would be keen to maintain his own rations and wouldn't want them jeopardised by his new team members' ineptness. My father and the new team members would have initially been allocated the 'easier' roles within the brigade.

Following their pitiful first meal in camp, they would have been assembled outside for the usual roll call, the *poverka*. Once this had been successfully completed they would have been given a piece of work (known as a *razvod*) by the allocation officer and marched off to their assignment for the day. On arrival they will have been recounted, to ensure the numbers tallied with those taken at the *poverka*. Work at the gold-mines didn't just entail digging for gold. There were a multitude of jobs that needed doing, all back-breaking, heavy manual jobs, which had to be performed with mostly inappropriate tools, by undernourished men in a poor physical and mental condition.

New prisoners were usually started on the wheelbarrows. These were crudely made wooden constructions with an inefficient wheel. They were often overloaded and very difficult to manoeuvre. They were hard enough to use on the surface but as excavations got deeper and deeper towards the gold seams, they had to be manhandled up a wooden gangplank structure that zigzagged from the excavation to the surface; they were often so heavy when pushed up the steep inclines that it took prisoners working in pairs to move them. Work at the gold-mines ranged from clearing an area of boulders, stones, and shrubs in preparation for digging to begin, to actually digging an area for gold, and wheelbarrowing to the gold-washing facilities.

Janusz Bardach describes his time pushing wheelbarrows at the gold-mines as simple at first, but as his brigade cleared ground further from his dumping area, he had greater distances to travel over the uneven boards. Going uphill, the metal wheel could stick or the load tip over. Going downhill, the wheelbarrow would run away from him. It was more than his muscles could endure.

Stanislaw Kowalski, a Pole and about the same age as my father, found the work particularly hard:

> I was still a slave compelled to work at the gold face, to dig and to cart 5 cubic meters of clay to the gold-washing arrangement, called '*butara*'. For a group of undernourished and often sick men such a menial goal was almost an unattainable task. There were few men in the working teams that ever reached such a work tally. For their superhuman effort they received somewhat better rations. However, in most cases the strenuous labour resulted in premature and sudden death to the heroes of the slaving class. The only consolation to it was that death saved them from the dehumanising status of a goner, which came to everybody who reached the end of his physical strength. These prison conditions caused a slow process of body deterioration ending with the man's demise.
>
> I was one who was ill suited for hard labour. Whenever I saw the glitter of gold its shine quickly tarnished when I touched the dirt with the shovel, pick and wheelbarrow. It acquired a morose view when my stomach turned upside down with hunger, when pestilent flies invaded my swollen eyes, and when the shouts of guards forced me to do the job for which I was physically unfit and mentally unprepared.

The work may have appeared haphazard and frantic, but like everything in the gulag world it was carefully calculated, monitored, and recorded. Each day's work will have been distributed to the work gangs by the assignment man, who was usually also responsible for such trivialities as allocating where prisoners could sleep within the barracks. The area to be worked would have been marked out and assessed throughout the day, it was in everybody's interest to complete their *norm*, nobody wanted a reduction in their already meagre rations. The amount of work was decided by the *norm*-setter (*normirovshchik*) and progress was carefully monitored and recorded by the *norm* assessor. There were of course ways of falsifying a *norm*, this was known as *tufta* and typically involved collusion with the *norm* assessor and/or brigadier. This often involved the use of deception, bribery, sexual favours, or in some (rare) instances, good relations. But, as is life, brigadiers and *norm* assessors were of varying reputation, some helpful and sympathetic, others harsh and uncaring.

Digging in Kolyma was always hard regardless of the season. Apart from the top layer, the ground was permafrost and always difficult to dig. A feature of the Kolyma region was that rich deposits of gold lay near to the surface, making manual digging the easy option. Where deposits were deeper, the first team on site was often the blasting team, typically managed by the assignment man, who would use dynamite to break the ground up for the subsequent work gangs. In other areas huge pits and conventional underground mines were created. All these operations were referred to as mines in Kolyma parlance.

The wheelbarrows with their loads would be laboriously pushed to the dumping ground for 'empty' soil or, if a gold seam had been reached, to the gold-washing/panning facilities called *butara* (Бутара). A typical daily *norm* would be 125 full barrows, which often had to be pushed 300–400 m to the dumping ground or *butara*.

Butaras were large, in some instances huge, wooden structures into which water was diverted from a stream. The spoil was deposited into receiving troughs and then transported via a conveyor system to a washing facility to extract the gold. In some areas a steam-driven mechanical washing facility was in place with crude heaters to thaw the gold-rich spoil.

Work continued everyday, week after week, regardless of the weather. Occasionally a Sunday was given as a rest day, but these were seldom. Anatol Krakowiecki in his book *Książka o Kołymie* (Book of Kolyma) tells of how digging for gold was considered to be the hardest of work assignments, describing how prisoners traipsed back from the mines 'like a procession of human phantoms' after completing days of work. He goes on to say that 'only prisoners could have endured the continual hard work, animals would have refused or died!'

During the summer months, work during the day was hot and sweaty and the incessant flies, particularly the huge Siberian mosquitoes, were a continual nuisance, their bites causing terrible itching and welts. Work was never allowed to slacken; foremen and overseers hustled around, cajoling, shouting to ensure that everybody, even the weakest and most exhausted men gave their maximum effort. There were few let-ups during the day, but smoke breaks known as *perekur* were allowed, where local poor-quality tobacco known as *makhorka* was rolled into cigarettes and smoked, but the time taken had to be made up at the end of the shift. Those who couldn't manage the work in the mines were given the slightly less demanding job of digging ditches, but their food allocation was reduced accordingly. It wasn't long before even strong, healthy men were turned into emaciated shadows of their former selves. It's not difficult when looking at the pictures to see why the death and suicide rate was so high.

After long, hard days (or nights), and even on the rare days off, the barracks were of little comfort. They were crudely constructed wooden structures, often with moss or straw pressed between the timbers and in holes to prevent draughts. They contained row after row of four-tiered bunks, usually referred to as cots in gulag terminology, made from whole pieces of the local larch trees.

Located in the central passageway of the barracks, a stove converted from a petrol barrel was used to inefficiently heat the barracks. Wood was used as fuel, and by all accounts, if you could get near to them they were red hot, but just a few paces away the temperature was freezing.

The best bunks were considered to be those on the upper tiers closest to the stove. These though were always occupied by the high-ranking prisoners and the dreaded *urkas*. Low-ranking 'political prisoners' and foreigners like my dad would have had to make do with whatever was left; it was first come, first served. The worst beds were those on the lower tiers furthest from the stoves. Prisoners slept directly on the wooden planks, and though they did have blankets, these were dirty and smelly. Prisoners, it is said, always slept with their clothes on, and always on their backs, though I can find no explanation of this phenomenon anywhere. Friendships were never made in the barracks; it was too dangerous. There were too many informers waiting to report you to the authorities, and because of the varying job allocations and packed and squalid conditions, you could never depend on staying close to anyone for any length of time.

Lighting, if they were lucky, was supplied by an electric light bulb. Most descriptions I've read about electricity in camps say that it was erratic, fluctuating between extremes of voltage which caused the bulbs to vary constantly between a dim flicker and very bright, usually accompanied by an annoying hum. Duskanya was so remote that electricity wasn't even an option in 1941. Light was supplied by home-made gas lanterns; named after the region, they were called *kolymkas* and used hot coals in a tin can with copper tubes attached. Life in the barracks must have been truly miserable.

I've referred to food several times; this was always of poor quality and in totally inadequate quantities. The enduring impression I've got from all the accounts I've read is that the prisoners lived in a permanent state of chronic hunger, not the hunger we feel when we've missed a meal or been ill for a few days and start to recover, but the absolute gnawing desperate pain of too little and inappropriate food for an extended period of time. It's unimaginable, and I don't want to even try. Farcically though, food allowances were actually carefully worked out by scientists in Moscow, whole teams of dieticians carefully calculating the minimum food that each prisoner would need for any particular job type.

Typically prisoners working in gold-mines would receive between 600 g and 800 g of poor-quality bread (*paika* – пайка) each day; it was given in the morning with some warm water or, if they were lucky, *kasha*, a sort of porridge. The bread had to last the whole day. Its allocation was always a serious affair and elaborate procedures for distributing it were devised so that prisoners didn't feel cheated by receiving smaller quantities. Nikolai Getman explained that the distribution of food was a source of tension and described one system of food distribution that involved one prisoner sat facing away from the day's rations who would call out a prisoner's name at random whilst another prisoner held up a portion behind him.

Stealing in the gulag system was always considered a primary virtue; anything that could be stolen would be stolen, and if not used by the perpetrator would be bartered for items that could. Bread, however, was the exception; it was too important. Usually nobody stole bread, it was the worst possible crime. The only exception to this was when a prisoner died in the night; if the person sleeping next to them was able to conceal the death then he was able to receive the dead man's bread allocation for a short period of time.

The prisoners had varying methods of getting the maximum out of their bread ration. 'Old-timers' familiar with the conditions and with experience would savour their bread, eating only small quantities at a time, often rolling it around their mouth to ensure the maximum sensation from eating it. Newcomers would typically devour the bread ration in one go, hungrily swallowing it, leaving none for later. Nobody shared their *paika*, nobody asked, and nobody expected to get; it was an unwritten law.

Other meal times consisted of *balanda*, a thin, watery soup often made from the tops of vegetables or rotten vegetables. Sometimes it contained fish, or at least fish bones, and occasionally traces of meat could be detected in it, but this was usually after one of the mine horses had died! The *balanda* was always described as a tasteless gruel, its chief virtue being that it was at least served warm, but having said that it was always necessary to eat it as soon as possible as it would soon cool off, particularly in the long winter months.

When the meals were served in the camp, if you were lucky you could sit and eat your soup sat at a table, but like everything else in the gulag world it was survival of the toughest. Space was at a premium and the most senior prisoners and the *urkas* were first in. Solzhenitsyn describes in his magnificent book *One Day in the Life of Ivan Denisovich* work gangs almost racing back from their work assignments to get to the kitchen before rival work gangs. Most memoirists tell how never a drop of soup was spilled, and of how some prisoners managed to acquire or make their own spoon, which always became their most prized possession. Often though, during work times, *balanda* was served at the work site. A barrel of soup would be delivered and distributed out in the cold. The prisoners would have to stand around, even in the freezing weather, and try to keep warm while eating their *balanda*. A usual working day was twelve to fourteen hours, whether worked through the day or the night, but in reality a working day didn't finish until *norms* had been fulfilled. For those that didn't make their *norms*, the bread ration was reduced to 400 g or in worst cases 200 g, together with fewer helpings of *balanda* or *kasha*.

The poor and inadequate food together with the harsh working conditions left men physically scarred. Even those that hadn't been injured at work stooped with back problems, and many had lasting problems with their hands, which became permanently formed to the shape of the shovel or pick. Prisoners devised a multitude of techniques to avoid doing the heavy work. There were high incidences of prisoner self-mutilation. This was called *samorub*; prisoners would literally chop off their own fingers, hands, or even feet. Others would keep open wounds infected by rubbing all sorts of unsavoury items into them. The list of techniques goes on and on. Others would fake illness, a technique known as *mastyrka*, often using elaborate almost ingenious techniques to give the impression of illness. All this being in aid of trying to get few days' respite from work. It rarely worked however, and punishment was harsh; extended prison sentences, reduced rations, and for the self-mutilators they were crudely bandaged up and sent back to work, even those with quite serious injuries. If on return they were a burden to their normal work gang then they were allocated a different assignment, or worse. Anne Applebaum describes one incident where a thief cut off four fingers on one hand but, instead of being sent to an invalid camp, had to sit in the snow and watch the workers. He soon requested a shovel and used his surviving hand to continue digging. Nevertheless, many prisoners thought the potential benefits made the risk worth taking.

My father wouldn't have been at Duskanya long before the short Kolyma summer began to turn into the 'fabled' Kolyma winter. Already by mid-September the first intermittent flurries of snow would have started falling, and the air would have turned decidedly chilly. September also brought the start of the miserable Kolyma 'rainy season' with days of unpleasant, cold drizzle, sleet or driving rain. Clothes and footwear had no time to dry on the crude barrack stoves, so prisoners would usually choose to sleep in them without even trying. Whatever the weather, work continued unabated as gold production was the priority; Petrov notes this time of the year as being particularly high in suicides.

October saw the start of winter proper. Deep snow and blizzards that lasted days engulfed the workplaces and camps. So dense were the snowstorms that there were frequently periods of complete 'white out'. Those camps like Duskanya, high in the mountains, were particularly susceptible to the snow.

The reports I've read describe the visibility down to zero, and ropes having to be installed between huts in order to get safely from one to another. Other reports tell of work gangs only finding their way back to the camp by using the guards' dogs, which could smell their way home. Still other stories, including Janusz Bardach's, tell of prisoners getting lost on the way back from an assignment and the bodies not being found until the thaw in spring, and only a short distance from the camp itself.

The first indication that winter had arrived was not usually the heavy snow and frozen streams but the allocation of winter clothes. These were clean but all had been used before. You were lucky if the ones you received were only second-hand.

The winter clothing was distributed by the *starosta* but there was no process to it; after he and any of the senior *urkas* had taken their pick, the rest were handed out at random. It was each man for himself and his own responsibility to get an appropriate size. Typically all clothing would have been ill-fitting and there would have been a bazaar scenario of swapping and bartering with fellow prisoners to try and get better-fitting garments.

The winter clothing, though more suited for the cold than their normal summer attire, was still fundamentally inappropriate to the extreme Kolyma winter conditions. A typical winter clothing allocation would have comprised long cotton underwear, quilted pants, and a quilted over-jacket called a *fufaika* (sometimes referred to as a *kufajka* by the Poles) filled with kapok or felt, tied around the middle with some piece of old rope as a makeshift belt. In addition felt hats with ear flaps were allocated, but any old rags had to be used as scarves. If they were lucky they received leather gloves (*perchatki*), but if not at least they were issued with gloves made of wool or cloth. The prisoner's identification was attached to the front and back of the jacket and often to the hat as well.

Footwear was a continual problem. Most prisoners wore *laptys*, hand-made shoes from any available material, leather boots that they arrived with or pilfered from other prisoners, or hand-made boots known as *ch-te-zed* (ChTZ – ЧТЗ). These rudimentary shoes were made from old rubber vehicle tyres and named after the Chelyabisnk Tractor Factory (Челябинский тракторный завод – *Chelyabinskiy traktornyy zavod*). The winter footwear allowance was the issue of loose-fitting *valenki* (валенки) – felt boots. Though providing some warmth, they were not water resistant, and should have been worn with rubber over-shoes or galoshes, which were seldom available. Many accounts of prisoners describe their wet *valenkis* never drying out, and especially on long hikes becoming so sodden they became very heavy, making even simple walking an effort. Some prisoners describe a method of stuffing the *valenkis* with paper in order to insulate them. Socks were only a luxury to be dreamed of; old rags were used to wrap around the feet and ankles. I believe that at one period during the war American rubber army boots were distributed in Kolyma; these had been supplied under the Lend-Lease arrangements. The fact they had been issued to the slave labour force caused the authorities some concern, and so they were not used on a wide scale. The Lend-Lease arrangements though are an interesting subject regarding Kolyma, and I'll come back to them a little later in the story.

Clothes were treasured items and were often stolen, bartered, or gambled for. If a prisoner died they would immediately be stripped of all their clothing, with the lucky recipients gaining from their demise. Bardach describes a scene where one unfortunate collapsed, presumed dead; he was immediately relieved of all his items of clothing and left in the snow. Barely had he been stripped to his last item when he mumbled something to the surrounding vultures. It mattered not though, he was left there naked without assistance, and the vultures profited from his sad passing.

As I've previously stated, the daily work assignments continued regardless of the weather. Although there was supposed to be no work when the outside temperature was extremely low, this was rarely observed; quotas had to be filled and in any case very few camps had the luxury of a thermometer.

During winter work involved clearing snow and keeping roads open where possible, clearing ditches, tree felling and wood collection. In some instances the mining continued throughout the winter. The blasting team would blast an area and the work gangs would rake the sands into huge piles. Crudely heated steam hoses would then be used to inefficiently thaw the sand which would then be barrowed to the *butar*. The water for the *butar* would normally have been fed from a diverted stream but when frozen steam hoses were used to melt the ice, which would quickly refreeze and then be used again.

The equipment used was never the best quality; the wheelbarrows were made in the local carpentry works and were uncomfortable, inefficient, and had a metal wheel which made moving them, particularly in soft ground, very difficult. The picks and shovels too were unsuitable for the type work for which they were used. Even when more efficient American shovels with work-saving handles were supplied under the Lend-Lease agreement, but these were instantly modified by the attachment of the Russian-style long handles and by beating the raised edges so as to be able to move a larger amount of earth but less efficiently.

The Soviet Union received much equipment from America under the Lend-Lease agreement, with many supplies finding their way to Kolyma. Rubber Wellington boots, navy-style pea jackets, tools (like the previously mentioned spades), some canned food, and heavy machine equipment like bulldozers. In some reports it is said that the bulldozers were primarily used for digging graves for the dead prisoners rather than mining operations. Other reports describe prisoners stealing the grease intended for lubrication for use as food.

The most stunning fact about the Lend-Lease agreement that found its way to Kolyma was the fact that they were delivered to Magadan via the very same ships that transported the prisoners. Marty Bollinger describes how many of the slave ships made sailed to America to collect the Lend-Lease goods. Even the dreaded *Dzhurma* made several trips to the West Coast of America during the war.

Perhaps the biggest and most unusual piece of equipment to arrive under Lend-Lease was a mechanical floating gold-dredge. This huge piece of equipment was in effect a floating, mobile gold-extracting factory. It was delivered in wooden crates and apparently with only English assembly instructions. The authorities had to scour the camps of Kolyma to find an English-speaking prisoner. A Greek engineer, Sergei Yanonnaki, an acquaintance of the artist Nikolai Getman, was discovered and given over 100 staff and the task of its assembly.

Though it was the only gold-mining dredge of its type in use in the whole of the Soviet Union, it was given the number 183-A in order to create the impression that it was one of hundreds in operation. It turned out to be a great success, with many copies being produced locally. At the peak of gold-mining operations there were over fifty identical dredges in operation gouging the river beds in search of gold.

Even today there are about eight still left working in Kolyma, including the one originally delivered from America and painted by Getman, operating nearly seventy years after its original delivery, upstream from my father's camp, near to the town of Susuman (Сусуман), which proudly wears an image of the dredge on its city coat of arms.

I mentioned the clothes above, and it's not surprising that these soon got dirty, smelly and infested with lice. In fact the lice were so prevalent that it almost became a pastime or ritual locating and removing them. Apart from their nuisance factor they were harbingers of disease and skin infections. So much a problem were the lice that the authorities, even in depths of winter, were forced to have regular de-lousing sessions where all prisoners were made to remove their clothing for de-lousing and then shower themselves. I would have thought that this would have been a positive, possibly even pleasurable event for the prisoners. But I'm wrong. It wasn't a typical relaxing, invigorating Russian-type *banya* (баня): in Russia there is and expression to the effect of 'as happy as a man coming from the banya'. It seems that it was a dreadful experience, so much so that all the books I've read about the gulags of Kolyma mentioned the hardship, loathing and even terror of the bathhouse.

Varlam Shalamov dedicates a whole short story to it entitled 'In the Bathhouse'. The problem was that while in theory the process should be beneficial, the reality was that it placed an additional heavy burden on those already struggling under the weight of their miserable gulag existence.

The reasons are multiple, but to list a few: the bathhouse and de-lousing occurred at the end of a long day, and everybody had to endure it on the same day. Each brigade were led into the cold, dingy and usually draughty bathhouse in turn, where they had to strip naked and hand over their belongings for de-lousing. Often when it was particularly cold fully clothed brigades would be allowed inside while other brigades were showering with their restricted allocation of warm water and miniscule ration of soap. While showering the clothing was de-loused and hung to dry in a totally unsuitable drying room, so much so that when they collected their clothes, they were usually still wet and very cold. But, often worse things occurred, usually, but not exclusively at the hands of the *urkas*; these included lots of theft, which as I've said before was a primary virtue amongst prisoners, and the bathhouse was a place where prisoners could vent their pent up sexual frustration, often with unwilling participants.

I've repeatedly referred to the *urkas* (Урка) throughout this narrative, so I suppose I should explain in a little more detail who (or what) they were, particularly since they played such a significant, if not 'important' role in gulag society. Martin Amis in his novel *House of Meetings* describes them succinctly: 'On the outside, the *urkas* were a spectral underclass. In the camps, of course, they formed a conspicuous and vociferous elite.' This almost oxymoron in terms is very accurate, the *urki* (*urkas*) were convicted career criminals who on sentencing formed a subculture that predated the labour and prison camps, but which exerted great power within them over the other inmates. In Soviet times, as petty thieves and criminals, they were considered above the political prisoners and enemies of the people imprisoned in the camps.

They had developed over a long period of time, starting perhaps as far back as the beginning of the seventeenth century. By the time my dad was imprisoned, they had achieved the status of prison and camp trusties, almost a self-managing security service within the Soviet penal system. According to Solzhenitsyn, except for the so-called 'new privilegentsia' and a few 'hereditary proletarians', the *urkas* were the only class to benefit from Bolshevik policies following the Revolution.

And so developed a multi-tiered prisoner caste system with a strict, unviable pecking order. In real terms the *urkas* held complete power over the politicals, the so-called counterrevolutionaries, the 'enemies of the people' like my dad, sentenced under Article 58, and convicted of some undefined, even unknown crime. The *urkas* on the other hand, having committed mere 'trivial' crimes against real individuals, were found guilty to a lesser extent and even considered a kind of 'class ally' to the Bolsheviks. In a stark contrast, politicals were considered the most dangerous to the state, and treated most harshly. They were the underclass, the lowest of the low, completely dominated by and regularly assaulted by the *urka* fraternity who grouped together in gangs (maybe packs would be a more befitting word). They would steal food, warm clothing and blankets, and sexually assault and treat other prisoners with complete indifference. All this went on under the eyes of the Soviet guards, who looked on and did nothing.

Of course membership of a criminal gang wasn't a guarantee of any sort of safety. They operated with their own internal code of conduct, and if violated retribution and punishment was swift, brutal, and often lethal. Lives could be, and often were, lost over a seeming triviality such as a game of cards, which was the *urkas'* usual pastime.

Urkas were instantly recognisable by their tattoos, which played an integral role in their life. These tattoos comprised (and still do for modern-day Russian criminals) a complex system of symbols which described detailed information about the wearer, their crimes, their allegiances and even their protests against the state itself. The tattoos were characteristically bluish in colour, and more often than not blurred because of the lack of suitable tattoo instruments. If no ink was available a substitute ink was crudely created from burning shoe leather and mixing the burnt remnants with urine, or by mixing candle soot with sugar and water. It was then applied with some sharp object, such as broken glass or nails! It seems that if a prisoner, even if a lowly political, had artistic tendencies they could be better accepted by the *urkas* by doing tattoo artwork for them. Aleksander Topolski describes in his book *Without Vodka* his time tattooing *urkas*.

My first tattoo project was for my tall captor – changing the anemic butterfly on his forearm into a rose. He was tattooed all over and there was little space left on his body for a new design. Only then did their attitude towards me change.

From that time on, our compartment became a tattoo atelier and pictures of hearts aflame, anchors and crosses were covering more and more square inches of the gang's swollen and painful skin.

The hierarchy of the camps was such that the camp was administered by the senior commander and his detachment of guards, but the internal policing was performed, unhindered by the authorities, by the *urkas*. They were in effect almost an extension of the terror that the NKVD had been on the outside. It seems that all the senior positions and best jobs were managed by *urkas*, and it was they that were responsible for all aspects of life in the gulags. Without any responsibility they supervised all work allocation, they managed the kitchens, they controlled life in the barracks, they managed the stores, they raised workers from their beds in the morning, and they meted out summary punishment – even killings – without any fear of retribution or reprisal from the authorities. They routinely stole from the camp stockpiles for personal gain, and to curry favour with any superiors. As a result, the other lowly prisoners were often forced to work even harder to make up the difference.

It's not surprising then that the politicals, terrorised from within, many suffering terrible frostbite, overworked in inhumane conditions, underfed, and inadequately clothed, soon became weak and ill. Diseases like scurvy, pellagra, typhoid, and night blindness, all familiar since the time of their arrest, took a massive toll. Countless numbers died. Others at the end of their endurance, destroyed mentally and physically and unfit for work, led an appalling existence, unsupported by anyone by scavenging the dumps and rubbish piles. Those that lived in this manner had almost reached their unfortunate end. In gulag slang individuals in this condition were known as a *dokhodyaga* (доходяга), roughly translated it means a goner. An apt term; nobody lasted long in this condition, and I haven't read that anyone ever recovered from it!

I don't know what condition and state of mind my dad was in when he was there. I remember, when I was very young, seeing with my dad a news clip of emaciated prisoners being released from Auschwitz, and he said that he had been like that when he was in prison! Just surviving the gulag required everybody to compete with fellow inmates for food, living space, clothing and medical care. I can't imagine what coping strategies my dad and his fellow prisoners used; strong willpower, mental toughness, skill, ruthlessness and massive amounts of luck. Some prisoners clearly retreated into religious or intellectual contemplation to maintain some semblance of sanity. Making acquaintances was not an option; you could trust nobody. Any friendships that developed were normally short-lived and very superficial. There was also the threat of the *stukach*, the informer, ready to shop anybody for the slightest thing. It must have been a nightmare of a nightmare. I suspect the main attribute of my father's survival was his age, as a young, fit twenty-one-year-old.

One of the questions I did ask my dad, rather naively, with almost romantic visions of Steve McQueen in the film *The Great Escape*, was 'Did you ever try to escape?' I can remember his look now, one of incredulity and amazement. I realised I'd asked a stupid question even before his curt reply. 'No, there was nowhere to go to, and they used to make you spend the night standing in freezing water.'

The dreaded nights in freezing water; the isolator. It seems this was a common technique of punishing, demoralising and controlling prisoners. It is referred to in most accounts of Kolyma; Bardach and Petrov both describe their times in the isolator. Though common to, it wasn't exclusive to Kolyma. My father suffered it earlier in his detention, first in Poland and then possibly in transit camps along the way too. On a recent visit to the Museum of

Genocide Victims in Vilnius, a former KGB (previously NKVD and Gestapo) building, there was a preserved cell used solely for the purpose of making inmates stand in freezing water for extended periods of time. My dad suffered from very painful in-growing toenails throughout his life, and attributed this to frostbite from these punishment cells.

All camps in the gulags had their isolator. It was usually a grim, separate, miserable construction on the edge of the camp. I don't know what my father had done to have had the 'pleasure' of experiencing time in his. It seems that for politicals any insignificant act of disobedience, rebellion or action could end with a spell in the isolator. Prisoners sent here had to serve their time in their underclothes, often only getting a plank to sleep on. Food rations were reduced to 300 g of bread and a cup of hot water. If they were really lucky they might get a small bowl of *balanda* every three days. There are accounts of additional cruelty while interned in the isolator, such as regular beatings or being doused with cold water.

Janusz Bardach dedicates a whole chapter to the five days that he spent in an isolator, in which he mentions prisoners being made to stand all night; it could quite possibly be the one my father had referred to! He describes a windowless concrete building with a flat roof surrounded by barbed wire. Inside, a vestibule contained hooks for the prisoners' clothes. A corridor led to a number of small rooms with icy water on the floors. Stripped to his underwear the water was so cold that it forced Bardach to huddle on the wooden bench at the far end of the dark room for the duration of his isolation, but despite this he considered those with no benches forcing prisoners to stand for the duration of their stay as the most torturous.

Another author who endured time in the isolator was Jacques Rossi, and he described how to try and get some sort of comfort from the wooden bench:

A lesson to learn: How to distribute your body on the planks trying to avoid excessive suffering? A position on your back means all your bones are in direct painful contact with wood ... To sleep on your belly is equally uncomfortable. Until you sleep on your right side with your left knee pushed against your chest, you counterbalance the weight of your left hip and relieve the right side of your rib cage. You leave your right arm along the body, and put your right cheekbone against the back of your left hand.

But having said that my dad never considered escaping, there were in reality lots of attempted escapes. Shalamov describes some in his book *Kolyma Tales*, and Petrov made an escape attempt himself, but then thought better of it, returning back to the camp. The remoteness, desolation, and harshness of the Kolyma environment were the biggest barriers to escape. I've never read anywhere that there were successful escapes and to me it looks totally impossible that anybody ever could. For those that made an attempt there were whole teams of horse-mounted guards with fierce dogs ready to track them down and (sometimes) bring them back.

Retribution for those caught alive was swift. Execution, extension to their sentence, time in the isolator and perhaps one of the more grisly punishments meted out was 'punishment by mosquitoes'. This punishment, common in Soviet prison camps throughout Siberia and Russia, relied on the indigenous blood-sucking insects around the camps. Kolyma in particular is notorious for the massive mosquitoes (комар – *komar*) thriving in the summer months. In

Kolyma this punishment was known as *komariki* (little mosquitoes), and was also frequently used for minor indiscretions against the camp authorities. It entailed the unfortunate prisoner being stripped naked, and then hung crucifixion-style to a nearby pine tree whereupon he was left at the mercy of the masses of blood-sucking mosquitoes and gadflies. Although the punishment only lasted between thirty minutes to an hour it was usually enough, since they would have lost so much blood that a slow and painful death was almost inevitable. Such executions were normally carried out beyond the barbed wire of the *zona*, but in full view of the other prisoners, to purposely act as a deterrent.

Escapees that were killed while escaping, or executed before they were returned to camp, were often left where they died, and to satisfy the bookkeeping of the camp authorities their hands would be severed and brought back to camp as proof of their capture.

For those prisoners that died in the camps, there was a crude burial of sorts, providing that the ground was soft enough to dig, otherwise the naked corpses were 'stacked' up waiting for the spring thaw. Special assignments were detailed the burial task, and one of the camp orderlies or *starostas* would make a crude grave marker from an old tin can with the deceased's camp number marked on it.

So within this awful nightmare, as 1941 moved into 1942, my father, still a mere twenty-one years old, passed his third winter of captivity deep in the heart of the Kolyma hinterland. In the outside world things were moving on, but I suspect my father, in the isolation of his gulag nightmare and the Soviet penal system, was oblivious to any global developments.

Interestingly, Vladimir Petrov comments in his book that he, a Russian national, lived from day to day working through each hour of his sentence towards the day of his freedom; he had no expectation of any early release. But he got the impression from those Poles that he came into contact with that they were expecting some sort of divine intervention that would release them from their unjust confinement. It appeared to him they were living in the hopes that something would happen to free them from the Soviet grasp and allow them to return home. Robert Conquest also quotes a similar sentiment from an anonymous Soviet prisoner who believed that the Poles had hope and belief in a liberation while he and his fellow Soviet prisoners hoped for nothing and had faith in nothing!

Maybe it was because religion had been suppressed in Soviet Russia, but the Poles still had their faith – I know my father, like many of the Poles imprisoned, was a fairly devout Catholic at the time of his arrest. But as 1941 moved into 1942, any end to his incarceration probably seemed no nearer.

8

AMNESTY AND ANDERS

Freedom? Almost!

In the outside world, far away from the gold-mines of Kolyma, world events had taken a dramatic change of course. The war in Europe had moved on apace. Following the invasion of Poland, Denmark and Norway (April 1940), Belgium, Holland, Luxembourg and France (May 1940) had all been easily conquered and were under German administration. Romania (October 1940), Yugoslavia and Greece (April 1941) followed, with Slovakia, Hungary, and Bulgaria allying themselves to Germany.

Hitler and the might of his sophisticated German military had marched across Western Europe to the shores of the English Channel. They now stood less than 35 km from the English mainland. Mussolini, Hitler's chief ally, was also bullish, invading British Somaliland in August, Egypt in September, and Greece in October. On 27 September a Tripartite Pact was signed in Berlin by Adolf Hitler of Germany, the Japanese Ambassador Saburō Kurusu and Italy's Foreign Minister Galeazzo Ciano, forming a military alliance and officially founding the Axis powers of the Second World War.

Russia too had been busy. Following on from the short 'Winter War' with Finland in November 1939, the Soviet Red Army had by June 1940 occupied the eastern parts of Romania and by the end of July the Baltic states of Lithuania, Latvia and Estonia.

During the summer and autumn of 1940 Germany attacked England with the might of its air force (Luftwaffe) in what we now all refer to as the Battle of Britain. It seems that this onslaught was a prelude for a German amphibious assault on England called Operation Sealion (Unternehmen Seelöwe). The fiercest battles took place between July and October, and as we know the Luftwaffe was unsuccessful in gaining air superiority over the British Royal Air Force and Operation Sealion was abandoned.

However, German bombing of Britain continued. November 1940 saw the worst of the aerial bombardments, which continued though until May 1941 when the Luftwaffe bomber units were suddenly withdrawn. They were moved east in preparation for what was to be a very significant event affecting the plight of my father.

Despite the fact that Hitler had failed to suppress Britain, he believed that by December 1940 England lay powerless before his German air power. Britain's major cities lay in ruins, and the fighting ability of the British forces had been severely dented, leading him to believe that Britain wouldn't have the ability to pose any significant threat to Germany.

In Poland the battered remnants of the Polish Army that had fought in vain against the well-equipped might of the German Army were also forced into trying to evade the Russian Army. Many, as we shall see later, were unfortunately unsuccessful and fell captive to the Russian Army. Others were lucky enough to escape through Romania and Hungary to France, where they regrouped and helped defend France. Eventually, most were evacuated to England when France capitulated to the Germans, where they established the Polish government-in-exile (which remained in place until the Polish independence from the Soviet Union in 1990). Their leader was Polish commander-in-chief and Prime Minister, General Władysław Sikorski. Others escaped France to French Lebanon, and when France fell crossed over into British Palestine. There they formed the Carpathian Rifle Brigade which, together with the British Army, participated in the Battle of Tobruk in Libya from August to December 1941.

Polish airmen that escaped Poland initially fought alongside the French Air Force, and eventually formed Polish squadrons within the Royal Air Force. By the time of the Battle of Britain four Polish squadrons had been formed, 300 and 301 bomber squadrons, and 302 and 303 fighter squadrons. The latter went on to achieve the highest number of 'kills' of any squadron during the fighting. Over 12 per cent of all the Allied success during the battle were attributable to Polish airmen.

Polish sailors, some of whom escaped Poland on the eve of the German invasion (Operation Peking), were to crew many ships supplied by the British government. The Polish Navy went on to achieve some great naval successes, not least of all its involvement in the operations against the German battleship *Bismarck*.

However, the uneasy German–Russian alliance (the Molotov-Ribbentrop Pact) established before the German invasion of Poland was proving to be more and more untenable. The ideological differences between the two great powers were becoming evermore apparent. Their tenuous relationship seemed to be wearing thin. Stalin for his part trusted nobody and was particularly wary of Hitler's ambitions. In November 1940, shocked at Hitler's rapid domination over mainland Europe, he sent Molotov to Berlin in an attempt to stall any possible aggression from Germany. The Russian delegation pressed Germany to honour their treaty obligations and distance themselves from Finland, who for their part had from May 1940 pursued a campaign to re-establish good relations with Germany.

The meeting only seemed to incite Hitler, who saw the Soviets as aggressive, accusatory and creating difficulties. He went further, dropping suggestions that the Soviet Union should concentrate its efforts towards Asia and not Europe for any expansion of Soviet interests and power. It may also have led Hitler to believe that the Soviets were even planning an attack on Germany itself. As the rapid Soviet militarisation was underway, an early pre-emptive attack on Russia would be strategically important, particularly since the Russian war with Finland had exposed a certain Soviet military frailty. Additionally, the rich oil fields in the Soviet territory of the Caucuses may have been seen as a solution to the dwindling oil supplies that Germany obtained from Romania.

German plans to invade Russia had been in preparation as far back as July 1940, just a month after the fall of France. Hitler had instructed his high command to draw up plans for the invasion of the Soviet Union. The initial plans devised by General Erich Marcks were codenamed 'Fritz' and involved a massive all-out assault on Moscow, with secondary attacks on Leningrad in the north and Kiev in the south.

The plans were revised by General Franz Ritter Halder in December 1940 and renamed 'Directive 21'. The new plans proposed three key thrusts into Soviet territory; major attacks against Moscow and Leningrad, and a smaller attack against Kiev, after which the plans included pushing on north-east to Archangel and south-east into the Don/Volga region.

Eventually, under Generalfeldmarschall Walther von Brauchitsch, who had previously overseen the plans for Operation Sealion, the plans to invade Russia were rationalised into a major thrust in the north with assaults on the cities of Moscow and Leningrad. Activities in the south were to be restricted to the occupation of the Ukraine to the west of Kiev. The new plans were renamed 'Operation Barbarossa' (Unternehmen Barbarossa) in honour of Frederick I, a twelfth-century Prussian king who was prophesied to rise from his grave and restore Germany to world power.

Operational orders were issued in January 1941 with the expectation that a ten-week campaign would start on 15 May. But like so many plans, events interceded, and delays were inevitable. The German Afrikakorps under General Erwin Johannes Eugen Rommel landed in North Africa in February, Yugoslavia, a supposed ally of Germany, withdrew the offer of German assistance, and Italy, having invaded Greece, began to struggle and required help from Germany.

The German High Command massed the greatest army ever assembled in history to invade the Soviet Union. It comprised of 148 army divisions, a total of over 3 million soldiers, 7,000 artillery pieces, 3,000 tanks, 3,000 aircraft, 600,000 vehicles, and 700,000 horses. They were arranged in three spearheads pointing at the Soviet Union.

The attack commenced at 3.00 a.m. on the Sunday morning of 22 June 1941 along a frontier nearly 3,000 km long. The northern group, led by Feldmarshal Wilhelm von Leeb's Army Group North, attacked through Finland and East Prussia, targeting the Baltic States and Leningrad. Generalfeldmarshall Fedor von Bock's Army Group Centre attacked from Poland and East Prussia, moving on towards Minsk and Smolensk. In the south Generalfeldmarshal Gerd von Rundstedt's Army Group South attacked from Czechoslovakia, heading towards Ukraine and the Caucasus Mountains.

Operation Barbarossa had commenced and Germany had begun its Eastern Front. The Soviet Union was now officially involved in the Second World War, and for them the 'Great Patriotic War' (Великая Отечественная война) had commenced. The Soviet Red Army was ill-prepared, and despite being well-equipped, was still suffering from the paralysis of Stalin's purges. When the opening German barrage started the Red Army units were taken by surprise, slow to react, and their command indecisive. German superior tactics, recent combat experience and high morale saw them advance quickly on all fronts, destroying huge numbers of Soviet tanks and artillery and rendering the Soviet air force largely ineffective.

Army Group North encountered little opposition and pushed south from Finland towards Leningrad and east as it quickly raced through the Baltic states where the advancing German Army were initially treated as a liberating force by the anti-Soviet residents.

To the south, Army Group South marched on relentlessly towards Kiev despite heavy rains.

Army Group Centre had the most direct route to Moscow. My father's village of Szwakszty, his local town of Kobylnik, and the city of Vileyka all lay along their path. Even as early as the first day, 22 June, the effects were being seen in Kobylnik. A young resident at the time, Meier Swirsky, (in an unpublished document) recalls,

Like thunder from the blue sky came the attack by Germany on the Soviet Union on 22 June 1941. The German Army moved eastward with unimaginable speed and ease. The streets of our town were full of soldiers of the retreating Red Army, and refugees. Autos, military units, loaded horse-drawn carriages, people, everything moved east.

According to information from refugees of Western occupied Poland, the 'special' treatment of Jews by Germans became known. It was necessary to escape. But, escape to where? How does one move with children and old people? People rationalised as follows: 'if it is meant to die, it is better to do so at home'. And therefore the Jews of Kobylnik, with sad and melancholy faces sank into wearisome anticipation.

To the south in the city of Stara Wilejka, the NKVD moved its remaining prisoners out of the jail where my father had been imprisoned and marched them east ahead of the oncoming German Army. The column of prisoners was attacked by German aircraft, but continued east. Sadly salvation was not at hand; a few days after leaving Stara Wilejka the NKVD guards slaughtered the remaining prisoners and fled east to the relative safety of Russia.

The German occupation of Poland and its treatment of Poles and Jews is well-documented, but Meier Swirsky gives a personal insight into life in Kobylnik following the German occupation.

With the prevailing mood Jews faced July 27th when the first German reconnaissance troops arrived. Within six days a significant number of German troops arrived in town.

At that time an organised police force consisting of local citizens came into being, who were ready to accept the new power and diminish the rights of Jewish citizens. Non-Jewish citizens met the Germans with joyous anticipation. Krugliak Avsiuk who knew a little German was the key welcomer. The Jews immediately felt the hostile attitude of the new power.

In the first days of the occupation Jews were prohibited from walking on sidewalks, visiting the marketplace, or leaving their houses in the evening. Every Jew was obligated to wear on their chest and their back a yellow Star of David in order to be easily identified from a distance. Everyone was obligated to work every day as directed by the local authority. Everyone was ridiculed physically and morally. There were local people who were deriving satisfaction from watching how the Jews were beaten, insulted and humiliated. Forced labour was imposed on adults as well as on youngsters (children). I was barely fourteen and I was forced to work every day on a variety of jobs. We sawed wood; built a road near the town of Sheremetovo (15 km), fixed a road at the village of Gluboky's Creek, picked potatoes, and executed any request by the Germans or local authorities. I especially remember the cleaning of snow from the road at the village of Vareniki (8 km from town). The winter was a cold and difficult one. We worked no less than fourteen hours a day, without warm clothing, food or rest, with ridicule and mockery by onlookers. We returned home at night, walking 8 km against the piercing cold wind. For our work we received neither pay nor food.

Jews stopped coming out of their homes, they stopped turning on lights at night to avoid attracting attention; they lived in total isolation. Only through gardens at night did they try to stay in touch with neighbours, and with those local residents who, despite the potential punishment for contact with Jews, continued to sympathise and help. So far as foodstuffs are concerned each person handled it in the best way they could. We stayed and lived in our house, near our garden, but without a cow that was taken away from us. In the basement we still stored vegetables, but good people provided other essentials at night. For this they usually received in exchange shoes or clothing.

At first nobody fully understood the German attitude toward Jews, and it was truly hard to comprehend why the local population offered the Germans such ready assistance. It is true that the people were completely impotent vs the arbitrary local authorities. Yet there was no response to the question 'for which sins are Jews being punished?' Jews lived in Kobylnik for centuries, with the belief in Moses and tradition of their ancestors. During all those years there was no record of Jewish community drunkenness, robbery, fights, divorces, not to mention murder. Jews lived an honest and generous life as taught by the Bible, and helped by their admirable nature. We knew, however, that over the millennia Jews experienced discrimination, insults and ridicule in many places.

Soon the first murders took place. On July 2nd fifteen communists were arrested and shot, four Jews among them. Shai Veksler – the tinsmith, Shimon Tsofras – the hairdresser, Boris Solomon – the teacher, Khaya-Rivka Gordon – the housewife. Ultimately they were brought and laid to rest on the Jewish cemetery.

Into our town came in, mostly at night, single refugees from Lithuania who succeeded in escaping during executions carried out by the Germans. They told us how Jews were mercilessly exterminated. It became clear what we could expect. It is worth noting that in Lithuania the local German collaborators were particularly cruel toward the Jews. At that time there was talk about the possible annexation of our area by Lithuania. This unsettled the Jews as well as many local residents who considered the Lithuanian authorities to be antagonistic and cruel. The attitude of the Germans became more hostile particularly after a German military official was killed, for which the Germans retaliated by killing hundreds of innocent farmers.

On 5 October 1941 a special German military outfit arrived in Kobylnik and began to arrest the town's Jews. Vantzekovich, the mayor of Kobylnik, prepared a list of Jews and identified them as communists. Fifty-one Jews were arrested. Another twelve were sent to excavate a pit near the Catholic cemetery, for an obvious purpose. The following statement was made by one of the twelve people who dug the pits, and who eventually became a resident of Israel. 'This happened at 3 o'clock in the daytime. Those rounded up were led on Vilenski Street to jail, where they were forced to take off their shoes and upper clothing. Khaika Botvinik with a nursing child implored the police to spare her child. In response the policeman grabbed the baby and smashed its head against a tree. The trembling body was thrown into a pit and Khaika, the mother, was shot dead. Shooting started ... People were falling dead, the wounded were shot again or buried alive ... Shlomo Yavnovich succeeded in crying out with pain in his voice to the twelve people: 'Jews avenge for our spilled blood'. Zelik Narotzky attempted to escape. He succeeded in running about 50 m when a bullet cut him down. Yankel-Beinish Greenberg who was among the twelve could not contain himself and began hysterically cursing the killers; for which he was shot and thrown into a pit.

On 21 September 1942 the last mass murder of Kobylnik's Jews took place. The same day the remaining Jews of Myadel were also killed. During the gathering of Kobylnik's Jews onto the market place, some succeeded in hiding or leaving town. All the rest were herded into a public house, which was close to the local church. The windows were boarded up, and the police and Germans surrounded the house. Tevia Feitelman attempted to escape but was shot at once. The same day a few families were released among whom were special workers that were needed by the Germans. Among the released was also our family. The released families were transferred to Myadel and settled in the ghetto. The remaining 120 people were executed at dawn of the following day. A witness was Leibel Solomon, the only one who succeeded in escaping (he lives in the USA). When the doomed were led to their execution, several people attempted to run to the bridge spanning the local river. German bullets met them all. Solomon was lucky. The people were brought to a prepared pit in the same area of the Catholic cemetery as in October 1941. All were extremely exhausted and worn out, without hope of rescue or will to live. Nevertheless, there were some who loudly condemned the killers and threw at them shoes and stones. All were killed ... Thrown into the pit and covered with earth.

Just over twenty years after the German occupation during the First World War Kobylnik was once again under the control of the Germans. It wasn't only the Jews of Kobylnik that felt the brutality and terror of the German occupation. My father's family were to endure even more heartache. In late 1941 my uncle and my father's younger brother Franciszek was arrested at home by the German military police. It wasn't the first time that the Germans had come to arrest him. I was shown by my auntie Maria, who in 2003 was still living in the same family home that my father was dragged from in 1939, a space behind the chimney of the kitchen stove a space where both Bolesław and Franciszek had to squeeze in to hide from the Germans who had to come to search for them. Unfortunately, not long after Franciszek was taken away, Bolesław too was caught. I now know that they were both eventually sent to Dachau, the notorious German concentration camp near Munich in southern Germany! My grandfather was now left at home with his two daughters Maria and Honorata, and a new brother my father was never to know, Valera.

For the local Jews, as can be seen from the testimony above, life got worse and worse. Some did escape to the surrounding forests, as I have indicated in an earlier chapter where as a partisan army harried the German occupying forces throughout the whole of the German occupation. Sadly the majority remained in Geman hands and many were sent to the ghettos that were established throughout the occupied Polish territory. Stara Wilejka itself had a massive ghetto, but sadly on 21 September the last remaining Jews still in Kobylnik were massacred. There were only 120 Jews remaining; in the evening of the 20th they were all rounded up to Kobylnik's market square from where they herded into the community hall (Dom Ludowy) that stood net to the Catholic church. The windows and doors of the community hall were boarded up, and for over twenty-four hours the Jews were kept holed up inside, crowded, hungry and afraid. The following day they were led to a previously dug pit and murdered.

Meier Swirsky was one of the Jews in the community hall, but had a miraculous escape and lived to tell us his story:

> Among the Jews, there was a popular seamstress who was forced to sew for the local government workers. Out of curiosity, one of her clients came to the community hall and remembered that the seamstress hadn't finished sewing her dress. She demanded that the seamstress be freed in order to finish sewing the dress. The seamstress refused to be released without her husband and children. The dress was so important for the client of influence that she got the seamstress and her family freed. The seamstress was my mother!

Events in Kobylnik, though significant to me, were minor to the objectives of Operation Barbarossa. The German Army was making huge advances across the whole of its Eastern Front, and by the second week had already reached Minsk. While Stalin remained shocked and paralysed in Moscow his soldiers were taking a pounding and being captured in large numbers. To the German High Command it seemed that the war would soon end in its favour.

On 30 June Stalin appointed himself the head of the State Defence Committee. He assumed total political, military, and economic power, and the Red Army began to reorganise in the face of the German onslaught. On 3 July Stalin addressed his entire nation in a radio broadcast proclaiming a scorched-earth policy and calling for the Russians already under occupation to fight hard against the invaders. He went on to appeal not only to communist ideals and to Russian nationalism but also, significantly, announcing that he would welcome help from those countries that opposed Germany!

Just two days later on 5 July talks began in London between the Polish government-in-exile and representatives of the Soviet government. British Foreign Secretary Anthony Eden hosted the negotiations with the Polish Prime Minister in exile Władysław Sikorski and Soviet Ambassador to London, Ivan Mayski, with a view to re-establishing diplomatic relations between Poland and the Soviet Union.

By 10 July General Zhukov had reorganised the Red Army into a three-group command structure. These were named the Northwest Direction, led by Marshal of the Soviet Union Kliment Efremovich Voroshilov, the West Direction under Marshal of the Soviet Union Semyon Konstantinovich Timoshenko, and the Southwest Direction under Marshal of the Soviet Union Semen Mikhailovich Budennyi. Each of the army groups comprised several army 'Fronts' which were the largest effective command the Russians could coordinate.

Diplomatic events were also moving fast. On 12 July Britain and the Soviet Union signed a treaty of mutual action against Germany, and just over two weeks later on 30 July, witnessed by Anthony Eden and Winston Churchill, the Sikorski–Mayski agreement was officially signed in London re-establishing the diplomatic relationship between Poland and the Soviet Union, broken since 17 September 1939. Significantly, it did not include the thorny issue of the Polish–Soviet border.

A further, and for the purpose of this narrative, much more significant event occurred two weeks later on 12 August when the Soviet Presidium of the Supreme Council issued a decree granting an amnesty 'for all Polish citizens in the Soviet Union deprived of their freedom'. Two days later a Polish-Soviet military agreement was signed enabling the formation of a Polish Army on Soviet territory subordinated to the Polish government-in-exile based in London. In the agreement Stalin agreed to declare all previous pacts he had with Germany null and void, invalidate the September 1939 Soviet–German partition of Poland, and release the Polish prisoners of war that were still held in Soviet camps.

(I feel that I need here to be careful and respectful of my usage of the word amnesty. I know for Poles, even now, it's an unfortunate, even highly invidious term, which tends to imply that Stalin had a legal right for the persecution of the Poles, and suggests forgiveness of a crime, or wrongdoing, which the Poles clearly had not committed. There's still much debate on the usage of the word, some prefer to see the word in quotes whilst others don't. In my usage of it I use it only to describe the notification of intended release of all Polish citizens, military and civilian, from their forced captivity in the Soviet Union.)

Away from the politics and machinations in London the war in the east was still in full swing. Throughout July and August, the Germans continued their merciless advance east. By 10 August Army Group North were planning to launch their final drive on Leningrad, and by the 20th had laid siege to the fabulous historic city of my father's birth. The Finnish Army, whose government had declared war on the Soviet Union on 24 June, reoccupied their 1940 border on 31 August and were a mere 50 km from Leningrad. The Leningrad Blockade (блокада Ленинграда) had begun, and Hitler transferred much of Army Group North's armour south to help the assault on Moscow.

Army Group Centre had also made huge advances into Soviet territory. On 28 June Minsk was captured, but their advance moved relentlessly on towards Moscow. They were so confident of victory that two of their armoured Panzer Divisions were taken out of action for a refit. On 8 September Hitler decided to concentrate his forces on Moscow. His generals believed the Soviets would bring together all their remaining forces to defend the capital, where the mighty German Army could deliver their knockout blow.

On 25 August, in the south, Soviet, British and Commonwealth forces had under the codename Operation Countenance invaded Persia (Iran). The purpose was to secure Iranian oil fields and ensure Allied supply lines for the Soviets fighting against Axis forces on the Eastern Front. Though Iran was officially neutral, its monarch, Reza Shah Pahlavi, was friendly toward the Axis Powers, and was subsequently deposed.

2 October saw the start of Operation Typhoon, the German advance on Moscow. Known as the Battle of Moscow, to the Russians Битва под Москвой and the Germans as Schlacht um Moskau, the attack started with some German success but the autumn rains made

the ground too muddy and it was impossible to continue the operation until the winter frost arrived. Stalin was in a panic. The people of Moscow were sent to the outskirts of the city to dig antitank ditches, and engineering, commercial and industrial production was relocated east; even the Soviet national treasure of Lenin's body was moved over 2,000 km east to the city of Tyumen (Тюмéнь).

To the south, Army Group South had encircled the Crimean port city of Sevastapol (Севастополь) at the end of October and occupied Rostov-on-Don (Ростóв-на-Донý) on 20 November. They looked set to advance ever-eastwards to the third trophy city and key to the oil-rich Caucasus, Stalingrad (Сталингрáд).

But, as my father was passing his winter of 1941/2 in far-off Kolyma with seemingly little hope of reprieve, events were about to change in Europe. In fact several significant events occurred that changed the course of history not only for my father but countless millions of people around the globe.

By late 1941, the German Army units were utterly exhausted and the Soviet defenders started to demonstrate an ever-increasing success in their resistance. A week after losing Rostov-on-Don, the Soviet Red Army counterattacked and successfully, albeit temporarily, retook the city. The distances that the German Army had to cover meant that supply lines were extended over huge and vulnerable distances. This enabled both partisan groups and units of the Red Army to harass and disrupt valuable and needed supplies to the front, which meant additional German effort was expended protecting the convoys and trains.

Importantly and significantly, as it had for Napoleon in 1812, the natural ally of Russia, its notorious winter weather, hindered both sides. Torrential rain leading to 'General Mud', followed by painfully low temperatures and 'General Frost' slowed the German advance to an almost total stop.

Stalin and his capital city were gripped with terror; armed Red Army troops tried to keep order and prevent a mass-evacuation, despite Stalin himself having temporarily left the city. Initially Stalin was reluctant to relocate snow-equipped, battle-experienced Siberian units of the Red Army from the east, as he feared a Japanese attack. Stalin dismissed both Budennyi and Voroshilov. On 7 December, the day after the Soviet Army launched a counterattack around Moscow, the Japanese bombed the American naval base at Pearl Harbour in Hawaii. The following day the United States and Britain declared war on Japan and America formally entered the Second World War. Hitler, unhappy at the reverse in developments in the east, disposed of some of his senior military tacticians and took complete command of the German Army. So for the first time since the start of the war, two totalitarian leaders, of seemingly opposing ideologies, dictated the war, each with the mission of the total destruction of the other with total disregard for humanity itself.

My father, far away, was, I assume, oblivious to these developments, and probably cared more about surviving the hunger and brutality of each day rather than global events taking place a lifetime away. But the Polish–Russian agreement of 14 August, mentioned earlier, was so hugely significant that it would not only change the course of his life forever, allowing me to write this narrative all these years later, but would also be hugely significant in world politics for years to come.

The agreement that had been signed by the Polish General Zygmunt Bohusz-Szyszko stipulated that a Polish Army was to be formed as quickly as possible in the USSR and would be part of armed forces of the Republic of Poland. It was expected that Polish units would be moved to the assist the Red Army front only when they achieved full operational readiness, though in reality Stalin wanted the Poles to bolster his own troops as early as possible.

All Polish military personnel captured by Soviets and Polish civilians currently interned were to be granted an immediate amnesty. However, many camps were not informed of the amnesty and huge numbers of the Poles only found out by chance. Other camps held up the release of their prisoners in order to complete their work quotas.

'Cometh the hour, cometh the man.' This oft-quoted and seemingly comedic epithet is, I believe, wholly appropriate for the person nominated by General Sikorski to take the role of Commander-in-Chief of the future Polish Army. For me he was arguably the saviour of a whole generation of Poles, who, without his courage, diplomacy and understanding, would surely have perished. His name, Władysław Anders.

Władysław Anders

Anders was born on 11 August 1892, to Baltic-German parents, in the Polish village of Krośniewice-Błonie, about 150 km west of Warsaw. After leaving school he studied mechanical engineering at Riga Technical University where he became a member of the famous Polish student organisation Arkonia. After his graduation he joined the Imperial Russian Army of Tsar Nicholas II, graduating from the St Petersburg military academy. He saw action as a young officer with the 1st Krechowiecki Lancers Regiment during the First World War, and by the time of the Russian withdrawal from the war, he had been wounded several times but had been promoted to commander of a cavalry squadron.

On returning to the newly independent Poland, he was a prominent supporter of Marshal Piłsudski, and became leader of the Polish Army's 15th Poznanski Lancers Regiment. During the Polish–Soviet war of 1919–20 he led his cavalry through a series of brilliant campaign victories against the Russians, which he achieved with the aid of French military advisers who had been sent by the French government. This was the start of a strong relationship between Poland and France. Anders himself benefitted directly by studying at the École Militaire Paris during 1922–4, an esteemed establishment whose previous students included such notables as Napoleon. Anders described his time there as 'two happy years'. On returning to Poland he continued his military career, bizarrely fighting against Piłsudski after Piłsudski's coup of 1926. By the mid-1930s Anders had risen to the rank of General.

In the late summer of 1939, the now Lieutenant-General was the commander of the Novogrodek Calvary Brigade stationed at Lidzbark in north-western Poland not far from Grunewald, the historical site of a famous Polish military victory in 1410. Sadly, there was to be no repeat in 1939. The East Prussian border and the massed German Army Group North were menacingly a mere 25 km to the north. When Germany invaded on 1 September Anders, with his cavalry, engaged the German Army but was unsurprisingly no match for the overwhelming German Army. Fighting a series of skirmishes, he withdrew south through Mlava (Mława) and Plock, where he was wounded, to the south of Warsaw (Warszawa). Realising defence was going to be useless and shocked on learning of the Russian advance from the east on the 17th, he pushed further south, heading for the Romanian/Hungarian border.

By the 27th he was in direct conflict with soldiers of the Red Army, who were preventing Polish military units escaping south. After unsuccessfully trying to negotiate a safe passage, he found himself in a fierce fight with the Red Army which further fragmented his already much-diminished forces. The night of the 29th saw the remnants of his proud cavalry brigade in hand-to-hand combat with Red Army soldiers and local Ukrainian partisans, in which Anders was quite badly wounded and left unconscious. It must have seemed to him that his time was up. When he awoke the following morning he was able to stagger to the nearest village, Jesionka Stasiowa, whereupon he was turned over by one of the villagers to the local Ukrainian militia and a Red Army detachment.

He was immediately escorted to the regional headquarters of the Red Army at Stary Sambor (now the Ukrainian town of Старий Самбір). After an initial interrogation, he was sent to the town of Stryj, where his wounds were dressed, before moving to a hospital in Lwów (Lviv) where he was again interrogated, and where he significantly refused the offer of a senior position in the Soviet Army. After some time in the hospital, he was able to negotiate, with the help of a bribe, a transfer from the Soviet to the German zone of occupation. By the beginning of December it looked hopeful as he boarded a train heading west for Przemyśl, but shortly after his departure the train was halted by the dreaded blue-capped NKVD and he was escorted back to Lwów. This time there was to be no hospital. Interrogations accompanied by beatings started immediately, first in an abandoned villa, and then continuing at the NKVD headquarters. He was held 'responsible for the casualties caused to the Soviet Army in September', accused of 'betraying the international proletariat by fighting against the Russian Army in 1918–20', and 'of being a spy as he had consented to the formation of a Polish government, and for repeatedly declining the offer to enlist in the Soviet Army'. He had also predicted that the liaison between Germany and the Soviet Union would end in acrimony, suggesting possible German routes of attack into Russia.

He was led away to the notorious Brigidki prison where he was to stay until the end of February 1940 when he was suddenly transferred by train to Moscow and the prison and headquarters of the NKVD, the dreaded Lubyanka (Лубянка). Interrogations and beatings continued for a short while and then he was transferred across Moscow to the Butyrki prison (Бутырская тюрьма). Though the interrogations ceased, his treatment remained harsh and he was to spend more than six months in solitary confinement, lasting until September, when he was returned to the Lubyanka.

During the winter and spring of 1940/1 he was once again in a cell shared with other prisoners, and because the prisoner turnover rate was high he was able to learn a little of world events. Some of the news caused him concern, especially reports of detention camps containing significant numbers of Polish Army officers. It was a concern that would return again and again! He remained, however, totally unaware of the German invasion of Russia. But when in mid-July he was rocked in his cell by explosions in Moscow, he knew that the course of the war had changed. It was, as he described in his book 'a moment of unconfined joy'.

Towards the end of July 1941, and after initially being accused of being a German spy (because he had predicted the German invasion of Russia) his treatment started to change for the better. He received better food and conditions, and was shaved and allowed to bathe regularly. After initially dismissing the explosions as exercises, the Russian authorities eventually admitted to him that the Germans had invaded Russia and were heading towards Moscow.

In the afternoon of 4 August (around about the time my dad was starting life in the gold-mining complex of Duskanya), Anders was taken from his cell for what he thought was his usual interrogation, but was led to a plush office, treated almost courteously, and presented before none other than the dreaded Lavrentiy Beria. This was to be no interrogation, and in a cordial discussion Anders was told that not only was he now a free man, but that the Poles and the Russians must put their differences aside and fight together against their common enemy, Germany. Beria went further and confirmed that following the Polish–Soviet treaty there would be an amnesty for all Poles and a Polish Army was to be formed. Beria informed Anders that he had been selected by the General Sikorski and the Polish authorities, with the approval of the Soviet government, to be the leader of this army! Under the terms of the Polish–Russian agreement the Soviets would equip the Polish force and grant credits to the Polish government, from which they would pay for food, transportation, arms, uniforms, ammunition, and medicine.

Early that evening, and after twenty-one months in prison, seven of which had been in solitary confinement, he departed the Lubyanka a free man. He was escorted to a special NKVD flat with the promise that the Soviet authorities would take care of all his needs. His Soviet liaison officer was a lieutenant-general of the NKVD, Georgii Sergeevich (Георгий Сергеевич Жуков), a famous name indeed, but not to be confused with the more famous Georgy Konstantinovich Zhukov. Within a short space of time other Polish officers were released, including Colonel Zygmunt Henryk Berling, a fellow Pole but with whom Anders felt uneasy on account of Berling's insistence on a closer co-operation with the Soviet Army. Though Anders kept him at arm's length he will reappear again later in this story.

For a short while Polish releases were nothing more than a trickle, and Anders was a general of a 'virtual Army' with no soldiers. As previously stated 14 August was the signing of the Polish–Russian Military Agreement, which stated, 'A Polish Army will be organised as soon as possible on the territory of the USSR and this Army will become part of the armed forces of the Sovereign Polish Republic.' Stalin expected there to be about 25,000 prisoners available to the army, and so agreed on two army divisions of 10,000 men and a reserve division. Following the agreement, release from prisons began in earnest and more and more Polish officers, though fewer than expected, began to report for duty in Moscow. Under the arrangement with Stalin, Polish military personnel were to be paid cash sums ranging from 500 roubles for NCOs and lower ranks to 10,000 roubles for generals. Civilians received a rail travel certificate (UDOSTOVERENYE – УДОСТОВЕРЕНИЕ) in lieu of a passport, supposedly valid to a specific destination of their choice, and a subsistence allowance of 5 roubles a day while en route.

1. A typical pose of my dad, aged about sixty-five. (Pleszak family collection)

Pleszak – rolnik –

Z niewoli bolszewickiej zostałem zwolniony w połowie października 1939 roku i powróciłem do wsi Szwakszty, gmina Kobylnik, pow. Postawy.

Po powrocie do wsi zostałem wybranym na „przedsiedatiela derewni" Kisły Juliana, który był poprzednio sołtysem. Władze powiatowe dążyły do wyboru innego, ale ludność nie zgadzała się na to. Ponieważ wieś nasza jest całkowicie polska, dlatego nie było milicji. Kisły pomagał i ostrzegał przed prowizem i niebezpieczeństwem, wskutek tego początkowo we wsi nie było ani rewizji ani aresztowań. Zebrania agitacyjne odbywały się niemal codziennie, prowadzili je politrucy z Kobylnika. Dość często zebrania prowadzili miejscowi komuniści: dwaj bracia Szuszkiewicze ze wsi Brzezelice, oraz komendant milicji z Kobylnika (którego imienia nie pamiętam), pochodzący z Pleciaszów. Zebrania te w zasadzie były dobrowolne, ale przedsiedatiel musiał osobiście zawiadamiać o nich, poza tym sami politrucy grozili karami za nieobecność. O sprawach politycznych informował politruk powiesci Brzeciak, który wypowiadał się w ten sposób, że Sowiety prowadzą politykę wyczekującą, a kiedy Anglia „prostytutka" „podżegaczka wojny", sprawczyni wszelkiego smutku w świecie, wstabi się kompletnie w wojnie z Niemcami, wówczas niezwyciężona i wszechpotężna czerwona Armia przejdzie przez całą Europę, zajmie Anglię, sięgnie zgniłego świata kapitalistów Amerykę i ustanowi nowy ład na świecie. Kiedy w czasie zebrań ludność polska żądała nauczania w miejscowej szkole w języku polskim a nie w białoruskim, wówczas oni odpowiadali, żeby o Polsce wogóle nie myśleć, że Polski nie było, nie ma i nie będzie, że tam gdzie raz

2. Handwritten account of the Szwakszty elections. (Pleszak family collection)

3. Władysław Anders. (Permission of Polish Institute and Sikorski Museum)

Above: 4. Harsh living conditions, Buzuluk, autumn 1941. (Permission of Polish Institute and Sikorski Museum)

Left: 5. Mikołaj Wincenty Pleszak, 9th Supply Company, 2nd Armoured Brigade, Polish 2nd Corps. (Pleszak family collection)

6. The first Polish arms. (Permission of Polish Institute and Sikorski Museum)

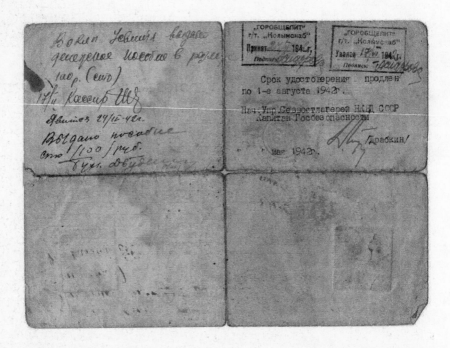

7. *Udostoverenye* for citizen Pleszak (гражданин Плешак) – Front, dated 17 February 1942, permitting travel to Akmolinsk in Kazakhstan. (Pleszak family collection)

8. *Udostoverenye* for citizen Pleszak (гражданин Плешак) – Reverse, showing allocation of two lots of 100 roubles, two stamps for the Kolymsnab store, and a document validity extension until 1 August 1942. (Pleszak family collection)

Above: 9. Cramped
oil tankers packed
with refugees
finally leave Russia
across the Caspian
Sea to freedom.
(Permission of
Polish Institute and
Sikorski Museum)

Right: 10. Churchill
and Anders at
Mondolfo, 26 August
1944. (Permission of
Polish Institute and
Sikorski Museum)

11. My dad's driving licence (outside). (Pleszak family collection)

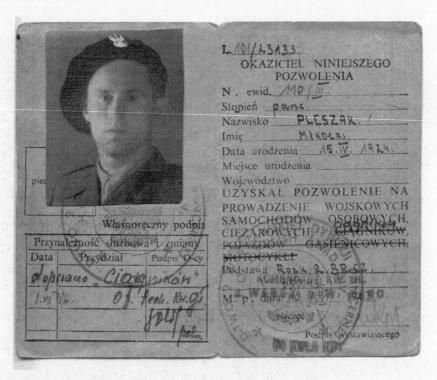

12. My dad's driving licence (inside). (Pleszak family collection)

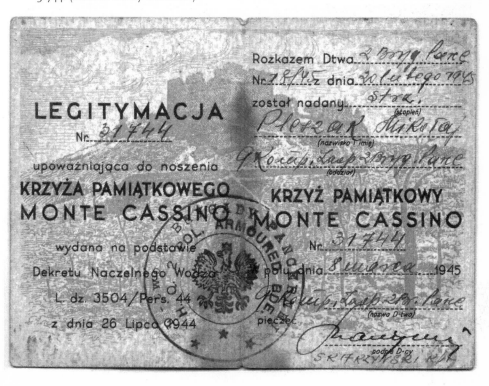

Above and below: 13 & 14. My father's Monte Cassino Cross and award certificate, numbered 31744. (Pleszak family collection)

DISCHARGE CERTIFICATE.

Army Form B108J

(If this CERTIFICATE is lost no duplicate can be obtained.)

1. Army No.	2. Surname
30044392	PLESZAK

3. First Names

MIKOŁAJ

4. Effective Date of Discharge	5. Corps from which Discharged	6. Rank on Discharge
21 NOV 1947	P.R.C.	PTE

7. Service with the Colours	8. Service on Class W(T) Reserve	9. Total Service
- Years 92 Days	- Years 242 Days	- Years 334 Days

10. Cause of Discharge K.R. 1940, para. 539(x). His services being no longer required for the purpose for which he enlisted.

11. Campaigns and Service Abroad

12. Medals	13. Military Conduct
	fair

Signature and Rank, Officer i/c Records.

780

Date 21 NOV 1947   Place Witley Camp

(S.11838) 250,000
Hw. 1/47 G.9939

POLISH RESETTLEMENT CORPS
RECORD OFFICE

15. Polish Resettlement Corps Discharge Certificate. (Pleszak family collection)

Right: 16. My father (extreme right) after his army exit medical. (My step-grandfather to be, Mikał Bucelewicz on the left). (Pleszak family collection)

Below: 17. Mikał Bucelewicz and Anne Elizabeth Chuwen. (Pleszak family collection)

(SD 11459)

Telephone:
Swinton 2271

NATIONAL COAL BOARD
NORTH WESTERN DIVISION

No. 1 (MANCHESTER) AREA

NO. 1 GROUP

OUR REF: JC/IE/AC.

YOUR REF:

Wheatsheaf Colliery,
Bolton Road,
PENDLEBURY.

8th August, 1960.

TO WHOM IT MAY CONCERN

Michael Pleszak, 5 Dale View, Haughton Green, Denton.

The above named was employed at Wheatsheaf Colliery
on three different occasions on underground work:-

13th September, 1950 to 9th June, 1954.   4 years.

7th July, 1954 to 27th July, 1954.   3 weeks.

1st April, 1957 to 15th July, 1960.   3 years.

He was employed at the coal face as a Packer and
Conveyor Mover respectively. During his periods of employment he proved himself to be a conscientious and reliable
workman, intelligent and disciplined. We have therefore
no hesitation in recommending him to you, with the knowledge
that if he is successful in his application for employment,
he will do his best to give satisfaction.

.... Evans ....

Training Officer.
WHEATSHEAF COLLIERY.

18. NCB letter of reference. (Pleszak family collection)

Above: 19. Dad, mum, and Michael (in the pushchair) with step-sons Robert (left), Ian, and my grandmother and 'Uncle Michael'. (Pleszak family collection)

Below: 20. My parents in 1974. (Pleszak family collection)

21. My dad with my son Henry, 1993. (Pleszak family collection)

22. Pleszaks at Monte Cassino, 17 May 2009. Lawrence, me, and my sons Henry and Oscar. (Pleszak family collection)

23. Anders' gravestone in the Polish cemetery looking up to the at Abbey of Monte Cassino. (Pleszak family collection)

Above: 24. The Polish cemetery at Abbey of Monte Cassino. (Pleszak family collection)

Below: 25. The funeral of Wincenty Pleszak, Kobylnik catholic cemetery, 1955 (Honorata, Walerian, and Aleksandra at the front with Maria behind). (Pleszak family collection)

26. My aunties Honorata and Maria (stood), grandmother Aleksandra, uncle Walerian, and grandfather Wincenty. Szwakszty, 1946. (Pleszak family collection)

Above: 27. Dad, mum, me, Lawrence, Krystyna, and Franciszek in Lyme Park near Stockport, 1965. (Pleszak family collection)

Below: 28. Me, Michelle (Michael's wife), Debi (Michael's daughter), Alison (my girlfriend, now wife), Michael, Jaqui (Michael's daughter), dad, uncle Franciszek, and Lawrence. Lachambre, France, 1981. (Pleszak family collection)

29. Brothers Mikołaj and Franciszek Pleszak. Lachambre, France, 1981. (Pleszak family collection)

30. My uncle, my dad's youngest brother Valera, whom he never met, with his wife Anya. (Pleszak family collection)

Above: 31. Lawrence, me, and Vileyka youth football team with their coach Ivan Sheblevski. (Pleszak family collection)

Below: 32. Owain at the side of Vileyka's cancer hospital and former NKVD prison. (Pleszak family collection)

Above: 33. The Pleszak family home, Szwakszty. (Pleszak family collection)

Right: 34. Three generations of Pleszak girls. My sister Christine, auntie Maria, and daughter Rose. (Pleszak family collection)

Above: 35. Oscar, Gena (the masseuse), Henry and Owain set off fishing on Lake Szwakszty. (Pleszak family collection)

Below: 36. Owain, Henry and Gena with the prize catch of the day. (Pleszak family collection)

37. Rose, Oscar, and Henry at the grave of their great-grandfather Wincenty, where their grandfather's (my father's) ashes were laid, Naroch. (Pleszak family collection)

38. Pleszak family at the Vileyka Forest partisan memorial. (Pleszak family collection)

39. Frank and Alison Pleszak at the Vileyka Forest partisan headquarters. (Pleszak family collection)

Arrangements for the infant army were immediately put in place. On 17 August General Michał Tokarzewski was given the task of establishing the Polish Army, starting with the embryonic Polish 6th Infantry Division, in the town of Totskoye (Тóцкое). Located about 1,000 km south-east of Moscow in the region of Orenburg in the southern Urals, the camp was huge. It covered an area of about 30 square km. It had originally been the Red Army's summer training camp, and although it had a firing range and some permanent buildings, consisting of administration units, living quarters for officers, power station, baths, washrooms, bakery, restaurants, shops, cafes, joint post office and hospital, they were all largely derelict and much of the site overgrown.

Soon additional army bases were established. The 5th Infantry Division at Tatishchevo, about 500 km from Totskoye on the River Volga near to the city of Saratov, and on 18 August Buzuluk, about 30 km north of Totskoye, became the headquarters of the new Polish Army. A place which many Poles, including Anders himself, held dear to their hearts for its part it played in the renaissance of the Poles exiled to Russia. In an attempt to assist the newly released Poles, Army collection centres and local relief offices were established throughout the Soviet Union, wherever there were large groups of Polish citizens. Though under great stress and harangued by constant difficulties these centres offered information and assistance, distributed food, and provided limited medical facilities.

On 22 August Anders issued his first orders in the role of General of the Polish Army in Russia. Despite the availability of permanent accommodation, hundreds of tents were erected to house the floods of recruits arriving from the places of incarceration, but even so, many of the new arrivees slept in the open until accommodation was made available to them.

In September the last remaining Russian soldiers departed the Polish bases and Anders made his first visit to his new army. Despite hardships in getting to Buzuluk the numbers arriving increased, with potential soldiers and large numbers of civilians. All without exception were in a wretched state of health, poorly clothed, and with dreadful physical appearance.

Stalin initially suggested that the Polish Army divisions created should be ready for deployment to the front lines by October. Anders knew that this was clearly unachievable, and with Sikorski's agreement argued that the Polish Army should be maintained as a separate army from the Red Army and given a specific military task. Anders also argued successfully with his own government that he would not exclude any Poles from his army, after it had been suggested that soldiers who had taken part in Piłsudski's coup and Jews should not be allowed to join his army.

Despite the lack of clothing, footwear and weapons, Anders presided over a moving parade of his ragged army, which he described in his book *An Army in Exile*. Despite their emaciated, poorly clothed forms, they were well shaved and retained their soldierly bearing.

In his address to the infant army, the most memorable moment for many present was when Anders once again referred to them as 'soldiers' and told them that 'the time had come to forget about the injustice and suffering they endured so far because their main goal would be to fight for a free Poland however long it takes.'

Eventually, more and more Poles were released from their camps. Some were to walk for months in search of an army that they were not even sure existed. Others departed their camps down rivers on rafts made of felled trees, many boarded trains with no tickets and no destination! Most had been released with nothing more than the clothes they wore, and few had been paid the allowance or given the free railway passes they had been promised. Thousands congregated at railway stations, waiting sometimes for weeks, and then fought to board a train heading south.

Information shows that most prisoners were released between 1 September and 15 October, but not my dad. Some of their journeys took weeks, and some even months to complete. Most journeys involved spending hungry and cold nights at isolated train stations, waiting for irregularly running trains. Many of these former prisoners, weakened by their labour camp existence, died from dysentery, typhus, exhaustion or starvation during their journeys. Many died soon after their arrival. Many memoirists describe trains stopping in the middle of nowhere to remove those who sadly had died from their ordeals. Most of whom never received proper burials, and were simply discarded at the side of the rail tracks!

As early as late August some of the Polish ex-prisoners of war that had been released were evacuated to England to bolster the Polish Navy and Air Force in Great Britain. As time went on it became more and more apparent to Anders that the numbers of officers arriving to join the Polish Army were much less than they had expected, but in spite of all hardships the army was beginning to evolve, the 5th Infantry Division in particular receiving some clothing and equipment from the Soviet authorities.

To the west, Germany was continuing its advance towards Moscow. Most of the diplomatic missions were relocated in September to Kuybyshev (Ку́йбышев – prior to 1935 and since 1990 called Samara (Сама́ра)), about 200 km north-west of Buzuluk on the Volga River. The Polish Army, unhindered by the lack of suitable clothing, equipment, and food, continued to prepare, often using hand-made wooden rifles and cannon.

By the middle of September the army was 27,000 soldiers strong and by the end of the month was over 20,000 soldiers in excess of the number agreed by Stalin. By the first week in November the army expanded, without Soviet authorisation, to nearly 50,000 soldiers, of which only one in four had shoes. Anders was ordered by the Soviets to reduce the army to 30,000 and send the surplus south to Tashkent to be used as labourers. Anders refused, despite the Russians supplying food only for the agreed numbers of the Polish Army. The Polish soldiers each gave up a day's ration each week to help support those in excess and feed the growing number of Polish civilians that had also arrived.

Conditions, though better than they had been and gradually improving, were still horrendous. But morale, in spite of everything, was gradually getting better and better. As the winter of 1941 approached temperatures in Buzuluk dropped to -50°c. Many, weakened by disease and their ordeals of the previous two years, lost their fight to survive, some freezing to death in their unsuitable tents during the long, cold nights. By December English supplies started to arrive via Murmansk, with much-needed supplies including army greatcoats and substantial boots.

The same month, December 1941, also brought the visit of General Sikorski, head of the Polish government-in-exile, to visit the emerging Polish Army. Prior to visiting the troops he had travelled to Moscow to discuss the Polish situation with Stalin. During these discussions Stalin agreed with Sikorski and Anders that the strength of the Polish Army should to be increased to around 100,000 men. Stalin also agreed that all Poles that were still detained in Soviet detention should be immediately released, and Anders suggested that the Polish Army should be moved to the better climes of the southern regions of the Soviet Union.

Sikorski took the opportunity and pressed Stalin on the question of the missing Polish Army officers captured in 1939. Stalin's reply was curt, suggesting they must have escaped from the Soviet Union – to Manchuria!

Slowly the Polish Army improved. Exercises, drills, and discipline together with slightly better food slowly metamorphosed the army into a fighting force. With equipment provided by the Russians and more equipment and clothing arriving from England, and in spite of the freezing weather, they started to look like a proper army.

Far away in Kolyma my father was still digging gold. Amnesty, Polish Army, rations, Buzuluk – these weren't the words that were going through my dad's mind. *Norms, paika,* gold, snow and ice were the things that were keeping him occupied.

February 1942, however, brought some changes. Stalin eventually agreed to allow the Polish Army move to the south of the Soviet Union. The headquarters were transferred from Buzuluk to Yangi-Yul (Jangi-Jul) near Tashkent in Uzbekistan. Columns of trains with the dreaded cattle trucks once more moved the Poles *en masse.* This time, though, it didn't seem so bad!

February 1942 also saw better news for my father. At one morning *poverka* his name was called out for transport to Magadan. Probably with a small group of other lucky Poles he trudged down the valley from Duskanya to find a lift that would hopefully take him on his first step to freedom. Tractors, bulldozers, and eventually trucks would have transported him through the deep snowy terrain and treacherous Kolyma roads to the port city of Magadan.

But even now, he still wasn't a free man, and he reported to the local transit prison again. Though no longer working in the gold-mines he still had to report for work with the gulag authorities.

City/town	Local name	Location	Approx. distance	Country
Magadan	Магада́н	400 km south-east of Duskanya	14,050 km	Russia (Росси́я)

Magadan is a port town on the Sea of Okhotsk. Though there has been a settlement at Magadan since the 1920s, as I have previously stated, it is generally considered to have been founded in 1933 by Eduard Berzin. It is very isolated; its nearest major city is Yakutsk, 2,000 km away along the Kolyma Highway, and though it has an international airport at Sokol just north of Magadan city centre it no longer has any regular international flights, only internal flights to Moscow, Vladivostok and several other large Russian cities.

The local economy is mainly based on gold-mining and fishing, but in recent years, gold production has declined. Overall conditions in Magadan have deteriorated since the 1970s and particularly since the collapse of the Soviet Union. Gold-mining no longer provides the high levels of investment and employment that it once did. Add to this the severe climate and poorly developed infrastructure, and it is not difficult to see why so many inhabitants have left the area.

The buildings in Magadan are mostly typical Soviet-era high-rise buildings, and many of the early Dalstroy buildings remain, renovated and still in use. The city now boasts the enormous new Orthodox Cathedral of the Holy Trinity, and the recently completed Roman Catholic church of the Nativity.

9

FINDING THE POLISH ARMY

Another Long Trek

My dad will have arrived in Magadan to find groups of Poles all in a similar predicament; they were no longer part of the harsh realities of the gulag gold-mines but were not yet truly free men. Stanislaw Kowalski, who had been released a short time earlier than my dad, arrived in the main Magadan transit camp to find 500 Poles waiting to get a passage on a boat away from the dreaded Kolyma.

Despite more and more new prisoners arriving at the port of Nagyevo on the dreaded 'slave ships', return passages were at a premium. Prisoners were only leaving Magadan for the 'mainland' in trickles. Those that remained, Kowalski being one of them, were subject to the same harsh rules and limited food rations and care that they had been used to in the gulags. Despite being free, and almost within sight of freedom, they continued to die, as Kowalski describes:

> I saw our ranks dwindling every day. I witnessed the increase of empty space on the bunks, I saw my colleagues turning into human shadows to disappear like a mist in emptiness of the eternal cold. One day, when assigned to the task of clearing snow off the road leading to cemetery, I saw a diabolic picture of humans exposing themselves, ahead of time, to still living phantoms working in the blowing snow. It was the burial procession of two drivers, two horses and a sleigh loaded with naked corpses. The stiff frozen bodies in the deadly embrace all too graphically epitomised the system's brutality, which promised to eventually consume the rest of us as well. By the end of the third month only 130 men of the original group of 500 still remained alive.

By the time my dad arrived in February 1942, conditions had, though imperceptibly, improved. Stalin, under intense pressure not least from Anders and Sikorski, together with the continued German advance towards Moscow, had relented. Polish prisoners were not only released in greater numbers, but at least in Magadan they were given better clothes and a slightly better food allowance. It seems that Stalin was worried by the stories they might tell once they were away from the clutches of the secretive NKVD.

Having said that, it wasn't all rosy for my dad in Magadan. Just like Kowalski had found some months earlier, departures for the Poles were strictly limited. Good news finally arrived on 17 February. My dad was summoned into the camp commandant's office and issued with his travel certificate (*udostoverenye* – Удостоверение) permitting him to travel across the Soviet Union to the city of Akmolinsk (previously called Tselinograd and now known as Astana) in the then Soviet Republic of Kazakhstan. Issued by the NKVD's north-eastern headquarters of correctional labour camps, it was numbered 1682 and valid for three months, after which it was supposed to be exchanged for a passport. With it he received a payment of 100 roubles and a stamp allowing him to use the Kolymsnab general store (Колымснаб, short for Колымскові Снабженй – Kolyma Supplies) in Magadan for a period of a week until 24 February. Particularly interesting for me was the photo of my dad on the front page. It was the earliest picture I have of him. At that time he would have been twenty-one, nearly twenty-two, and he bizarrely, though not surprisingly, bears an uncanny resemblance to my younger brother, not something we had previously noticed in later photos.

The authorities were clearly expecting him to have departed within a short time, but as his departure didn't materialise his Kolymsnab entitlement was extended for a total of four months until 17 June 1942. On 24 April he was awarded a further 100 roubles subsistence, and in May the validity on his *udostoverenye* was extended until 1 August 1942, and signed by none other than Colonel Drabkin (Драбкин) in red ink. While he was in Magadan, though essentially a free man, he would still have lived either in the transit camp or in prison accommodation, and he will have found any work he could to supplement his meagre existence. At times he worked as a night watchman at a small factory, and he will have surely again cleared roads of snow, laboured at the docks, and possibly even worked on one of the farms that surrounded Magadan.

During his 'freedom' in Magadan he associated with other Poles in the same predicament, but always under the watchful eye of at least one NKVD 'helper'. One of the Poles, Lucian Aksnowicz, also in Magadan at the same time (personal communication with his son Ron) worked as a waiter and general helper at a restaurant in Magadan. Lucian remarkably, and thankfully, used some of his earnings to purchase a camera, taking some excellent shots of his time in Magadan, including several in the restaurant, but one in particular was of a group of released Poles assembled in the Magadan cemetery. Lucian, who appears himself on the photo, arranged for their uncharacteristically helpful NKVD 'helper' to take the photo. The photo includes my father, together with the author and poet Anatol Krakowiecki, who included this picture in his 1959 book *Książka o Kołymie* (Book of Kolyma).

Interestingly Krakowiecki's *udostoverenye* (which also appears in his book) is numbered 1782 and dated 17 April 1942. This suggests that the photo is likely to have been taken after April. From the photo it's clear the men look much better fed and clothed; few are in their gulag quilted jackets, and some even wear ties!

My father told me that he spent as much time as he could hanging around the docks trying to get on a ship back to the 'mainland'. He was unsuccessful for so long I expect he must have been in a state of sheer desperation, but eventually he was able to secure his passage by bribing his way onto a ship bound for Vladivostok. I know my father was still in Magadan in May (his *udostoverenye* extension was dated May), which leads me to suspect that my father left in the group of 171 men that left on 8 July 1942, almost a year after the original amnesty (Anders, *An Army in Exile*).

So he left Kolyma in exactly the same way as he had arrived – on a dreaded 'slave ship'. This time, though, not as a prisoner but as a free man, and perhaps for the first time since his original arrest in Poland he had some sort of real hope for the future. Free man or not, he still travelled in the bowels of the ship, no comfortable cabin, just the converted hold of the ship, but I'm sure it was a voyage of joy and expectation, and not the terror as it was on the journey there. After a week re-crossing the Seas of Okhotsk and Japan his ship finally docked. This time it wasn't from his departure point of Nakhodka, but the Russian port city of Vladivostok.

City/town	Local name	Location	Approx. distance	Country
Vladivostok	Владивосто́к	3,200 km south-west of Magadan	17,250 km	Russia (Росси́я)

Vladivostok is Russia's largest port city on the Pacific Ocean. It is almost 9,300 km from Moscow, and its name means Ruler of the East. This cosmopolitan city is situated close to the borders of China and North Korea, and just across the Sea of Japan from Japan.

The city is located in the southern extremity of Muravyov–Amursky peninsula (полуостров Муравьёва-Амурского), which is about 30 km long and approximately 12 km wide. Its climate is warm summer continental and it has frequent summer torrential rainstorms.

Founded in 1860, its location means it has been a city of military importance ever since, so much so that during Soviet times it was closed to all foreigners and most Russians. It is one of Russia's most impressive cities, sitting across several peaks, peninsulas and islands. However, a recent survey revealed that two thirds of Vladivostok's suburbs are so polluted that living in them is classified as a health hazard.

It is the home port of the Russian Navy's Pacific fleet, and its military heritage has left it with a multitude of impressive fortifications, naval bases, and castles. Even today, at noon a huge cannon blasts out in celebration at the Vladivostok Fortress Museum.

It has a lively and bustling dock area where, in 1920 (the same year as my dad), the Hollywood actor Yul Brynner was born. He was born Yuliy Borisovich Brynner (Юлий Бори́сович Бри́ннер). His mother, Marusya Blagovidova, was the daughter of a Russian doctor and his father, Boris Brynner, was an engineer and inventor, who was of Swiss and Mongolian decent. He was named Yul after his paternal grandfather, Jules Brynner. Now a household name, he is most famous for his stage and screen portrayal of King Mongkut of Siam in *The King and I*.

My dad's long trek west in search of the Polish Army will have started at the magnificent Vladivostok train station. There may have been a Polish delegation to help with food and transport for the Poles, but with his *udostoverenye* he will almost have had a guaranteed passage at least to Akmolinsk. It was no assurance of any real Soviet help but it will have enabled him to get a daily food allowance along the way. I suppose in this respect he was fortunate; many of the Poles released from their places of incarceration in the *posioleks* received no such luxury and had to fend for themselves, struggling for transport, food and accommodation, requiring monumental amounts of inner strength to drive towards their goal of reaching the Polish collection centres and ultimately for the belief in a return to their homeland of Poland.

Many memoirists recall that their train journeys to freedom were comparable in horror and hardship to the train journeys that took them into their exile. Some descriptions even suggest that conditions on many of the journeys from captivity were even harder. Their weakened and emaciated bodies, which had struggled so hard to just stay alive for so long during their imprisonment, finally gave up just as they headed for their first taste of freedom and hope for their future. Trains were crammed with these poor souls travelling east and south, typically only stopping at isolated locations to brutally dump the dead from the train, often just leaving them lying at the side of the track with no burial or ceremony. There was no help from the Soviet authorities, often quite the opposite, with obstacles and further hardships being placed in their way. But as the news of the formation of the Polish Army grew, so too did the surge of hopefuls moving south, all clinging desperately to life in hopeful anticipation of salvation ahead.

Back in February, around the time my dad was being released from the gulag at Duskanya, Anders had finally got his wish, with Stalin agreeing to let the Polish Army relocate to the south of the Soviet Union. Anders' headquarters were relocated to Jangi-Jul near Tashkent in Uzbekistan where the climate was better, but contagious diseases were endemic.

The rapidly growing 'Polish Army in the USSR', as it was by then known, had expanded to five army divisions which were distributed widely throughout the region; the 5th Infantry Division at Dzalal-Abad in Kyrgyzstan, the 6th Infantry Division around Guzar and Shakhrisabz in Uzbekistan, the 7th Infantry Division at Kermine (now known as Navoiy) in Uzbekistan, the 8th Infantry Division at Czok-pak (near Chimkent) in Kazakhstan, the 9th Infantry Division at Margilan in Uzbekistan, and the 10th Infantry Division at Lugovoye in Kazakhstan.

The 5th Infantry Division, which had been partially supplied with clothing and equipment by the Soviet authorities, was up to strength but the Polish government refused to send them to fight alongside the Russian Army. They wanted the Polish soldiers to act as a single fighting force and not be scattered, almost inconspicuous within the Soviet Red Army. The decision wasn't taken lightly by Stalin, who in early March decreased the food allocation to the Polish Army to 26,000 rations despite the fact that the Polish Army had grown to around 70,000, not including the Polish civilians who sought refuge with the nascent Polish Army.

Anders appealed to Stalin directly, and on 18 March was summoned to a personal audience with him in Moscow. Despite the steadily worsening relationship between Poland and Russia, Stalin surprisingly, and perhaps uncharacteristically immediately agreed to 40,000 rations and eventually granted rations for 44,000 soldiers. The soldiers in excess of this were to be evacuated to Persia (now called Iran). The numbers arriving in Uzbekistan continued but, weakened by their ordeals and subject to the many endemic diseases like typhus, dysentery, and malaria, the death rates continued to be very high.

Many of these poor souls now rest in Polish cemeteries that remain in the remote desert areas of Kazakhstan, Kyrgyzstan, and Uzbekistan.

From 26 March to 10 April the 33,000 soldiers in excess of Stalin's stipulated army levels and over 10,000 civilians were transported by train west to the Turkmenistan port city of Krasnovodsk on the Caspian Sea. From there, on specially charted cargo boats, they were shipped across the Caspian Sea to the British-controlled Persian city of Pahlevi. It was to be the first of two such exoduses of Poles from Russian territory.

With his *udostoverenye* my dad will have been able to catch trains, albeit probably irregularly and infrequently, back west heading towards his destination of Akmolinsk. The trains carrying Poles were considered as military transport, but despite this they made slow progress and were often shunted into sidings while higher-prioirity Soviet military transport was given preference.

My dad's *udostoverenye* would also have allowed him claim a daily *paika* (bread), *kipiatok* (boiled water), and sometimes *balanda* (soup) allowance from the special kiosks at the stations he would have stopped at. This was usually undertaken by two men from each carriage delegated to collect the supplies and then equally distribute it to those who (like my dad) had a valid *udostoverenye*. Because the trains often left without warning, anybody not on the train would be left behind, so this was a task that nobody really wanted to do.

He may have been in contact with Polish military missions along the way, but as he slowly moved back west from Vladivostok, through Khabarovsk and Irkutsk, back to Krasnoyarsk he will have been joined by throngs of Poles all with the same unknown destination ahead of them. Brought together in a desperate struggle to find the Polish Army and hopefully, eventually a way home to Poland. While they were travelling together, it was survival of the fittest. Those that could, struggled on, but many simply were too weak or too ill to continue and sadly never left Siberia, and their burial places will never be known.

By the time my dad arrived in Krasnoyarsk in late July it had become clear that the Polish Army had moved to the south of the Soviet Union. At Novosibirsk he was able to change trains and continued on via Barnaul and Pavlodar to Akmolinsk (Astana). But instead of departing the train he was able to remain onboard. Rather than travel south he took a convoluted route towards the Soviet industrialised southern Urals and the city of Orsk in search of the Polish Army.

City/town	Local name	Location	Approx. distance	Country
Orsk	Орск	1,200 km south-west of Omsk	25,070 km	Russia (Россия)

The city of Orsk is situated in the southern Ural mountains, and straddles the Ural River. Since the river is generally considered a boundary between Europe and Asia, Orsk can be said to lie in two continents. Though it was founded in 1735 there is evidence of settlements back to the Bronze Age, and some artefacts discovered at the many archaeological sites in Orsk provide evidence to the hypothesis of Eastern European roots of Indo-European peoples. Today Orsk is the centre of the Orsk-Khalilovo industrial region, which has rich iron, copper, nickel, and coal deposits supporting metallurgical and chemical plants, machine works, and a major oil refinery.

From Orsk my father's route took him west to Orenburg and heading towards Buzuluk, now without the Polish Army and relegated (or perhaps even elevated) to the spiritual birthplace of the new Polish Army.

City/town	Local name	Location	Approx. distance	Country
Orenburg (Chkalov)	Оренбу́рг (Чка́лов)	250 km north-west of Orsk	25,320 km	Russia (Росси́я)

Orenburg like Orsk is a city on the Ural River. It is situated at the confluence of the Ural and the Or Rivers, and its Germanic name means 'fortress near the Or'. In the past it was an important military outpost on the frontier with the nomadic Kazakhs, and it later became the centre for the Orenburg Cossacks. Today several splendid bridges span the Ural at Orenburg.

From 1938 to 1957, the city was known as Chkalov in honour of the famous Russian test pilot Valery Chkalov who flew from the local air base. Valery Chkalov was renowned particularly for his endurance flights. In 1937 he made the famous sixty-three-hour (8,811 km) non-stop flight from Moscow, via the North Pole, to Pearson Airfield in Vancouver, Washington in a Tupolev ANT-25 aeroplane.

Another famous Russian aviator and former resident of Orenburg, and like Chkalov a 'Hero of the Soviet Union', was the Soviet cosmonaut Yuri Alexeyevich Gagarin (Ю́рий Алексе́евич Гага́рин). Gagarin initially qualified to fly MiG-15s at Orenburg Military Flying School, receiving his wings in 1955. He went on, famously, to become the first person in space and the first to orbit the Earth on 12 April 1961. Sadly he was to die in 1968 when the MiG-15 he was flying en route to Orenburg crashed.

Orenburg is also famous for its characteristic shawls and scarves, in fact these are considered by many to be as much of a symbol of Russia as are Matrioshka dolls and vodka! The shawls, often called wedding ring shawls, are finely knit and have been produced in the region for over 300 years. They are usually made from a blend of silk and indigenous goat fibre similar to cashmere or mohair.

City/town	Local name	Country
Buzuluk	Бузулу́к	Russia (Росси́я)

Though my father never actually went to Buzuluk, it's worth mentioning because of its significance in the history of the Polish Army and since my father at this point in his travels was so near. It is a city in Orenburg oblast (province) of the southern Ural mountains in west-central Russia. It is situated along the River Samara (a tributary of the River Volga), near its confluence with the River Buzuluk. It was founded in 1736 as a Russian fortress and was chartered in 1781. Local industries include the manufacture of heavy metallurgical and agricultural machinery.

It always retained its important military significance and was used for training of not only Russian soldiers, but pro-Russian foreign (i.e. Eastern Bloc) armies too. It is famous as being the base of the 1st Czechoslovakian Independent Field Battalion – the Czechoslovakian Army unit that fought alongside the Red Army during the Second World

War when Czechoslovakia was occupied by the Germans. The Czech Army connection though goes back even further; there was also a significant Czech presence in the First World War. Czech author Jaroslav Hašek, most famous for his humorous novel *Osudy Dobrého Vojáka Švejka za Svìtové Války* (The Good Soldier Švejk and his Fortunes in the World War), himself spent some time in Buzuluk, surviving a serious bout of typhoid while he was there.

After the war, Russian nuclear bombing tests were performed in Totskoye range during which some 45,000 people, Soviet soldiers and prisoners, were exposed to radiation from a bomb twice as powerful as the one dropped on Hiroshima nine years earlier. At 9.33 a.m. on 14 September 1954, a Soviet Tu-4 bomber (a Russian copy of the Boeing B-29 that dropped the first American atomic bomb) dropped a 40-kiloton atomic weapon from 8,000 m. The bomb exploded 350 m above Totskoye range, 13 km from the town of Totskoye. The commander in charge was none other than Georgy Konstantinovich Zhukov, who watched on from an underground nuclear bunker while about 5,000 Soviet military personnel staged a mock battle and about 40,000 troops were positioned about 8 miles away from the epicentre. The number of soldiers killed, injured or made infertile as a result of the explosion is unknown.

On arrival at Orenburg, the train turned sharply south heading away from the developed industrial heartland of Russia into the arid steppes of northern Kazakhstan. My father was now travelling along the very same train line that the Polish Army had travelled back in February, after leaving Buzuluk. At some point on the journey it became known to him, possibly through a Polish Army representative at one of the many stations they would have stopped at, or possibly from the omnipresent NKVD who still remained a significant part of everybody's daily life, that recruitment into the Polish Army would have to take place in the town of Guzar in Uzbekistan. He then knew for the first time since leaving Duskanya where he was heading. Things for the first time since September 1939 were looking better.

As the days went by my father moved ever further south, passing by the great cities of Aktyubinsk, Aralsk, Turkestan, Tashkent, and Anders' Army headquarters at Jangi-Jul. Shortly after passing Jangi-Jul the train turned sharply west and continued through Samarkand, Kermine (now called Navoiy after the Uzbek poet and politician Alisher Navoi) and arrived at the town of Bukhara, where he had to disembark and change trains for Guzar.

City/town	Local name	Location	Approx. distance	Country
Aktobe (Aktyubinsk)	Актюбинск	600 km south-east of Orenburg	25,920 km	Kazakhstan

Aktobe, known during Soviet times as Aktyubinsk, is a city on the Ilek River in Kazakhstan. It has a cosmopolitan mixed ethnic community, including Kazakhs, Russians, Ukrainians, Tatars, Uyghurs, Chechens, Armenians, Jews and Greeks.

Its name is derived from the location of the original nineteenth-century settlement of Aktobe – *Ak* (white) and *tobe* (hill) – and is a reference to the heights on which the original settlement was founded.

The area around Aktobe is mainly flat steppe, with low hills rising to the northeast and semi-desert to the south. Its climate is continental, with wide seasonal variations in temperature.

City/town	Local name	Location	Approx. distance	Country
Aralsk	Аральск	550 km south-east of Aktobe	26,470 km	Kazakhstan

My father passed through Aralsk on his way south to find the Polish Army in August 1942. If he had been able to, or was well enough to have noticed, he would have seen a prosperous port city at the northern end of the Aral Sea. He may even have been able to buy fish here as it is known that trains carrying Poles south did stop here (*Without Vodka*, Aleksander Topolski). But even then, large-scale canal networks diverting water away from the Aral Sea to irrigate the vast cotton fields of the Kara Kum and Kizyl Kum deserts were already under construction.

Once the world's fourth-largest lake, the mighty Aral Sea was from 1960 starved of its lifeblood waters from its two main rivers. The first is the Syr Darya, on which lies the town formally known as Leninsk but now better known to us as Baikonur (Байконур), the home to the famous Baikonur Cosmodrome. The second, flowing from the Pamir mountains, was known in ancient times as the Oxus but is now known as the Amu Darya. The sea that once lapped the very edge of the town itself has been shrinking ever since.

It has now receded more than 100 km and is no longer visible from the city. It has separated into two smaller, very salty, polluted lakes. What was previously the sea bottom is now just sand, salt and dust. Quayside hotels once busy and bustling are now crumbling into the sand that was once the seabed.

Attempts to create channels to the sea for the fishing fleets failed because the sea receded quicker than the channels could be built. The dry seabed has become a graveyard for the vast fishing fleet that once made a good living there.

The cost in ecological and socio-economic terms has been astronomical. Aralsk has become the town that time forgot. Dilapidated factories stand silent and crumbling. Rusty equipment looms over a bleak landscape littered with fragments of broken and abandoned machinery. The port, once the pride and joy of its residents, is dry, dusty, static and empty.

It is impossible to reach the edge of the sea by car except during the summer months, as the dried up seabed is boggy. But when possible Aralsk residents, particularly the older ones, make special trips 'to see the sea for one last time'.

City/town	Local name	Location	Approx. distance	Country
Hazrat-e Turkestan	Түркістан	700 km south-east of Aralsk	27,170 km	Kazakhstan

Hazrat-e Turkestan is considered to be the most historic city in Kazakhstan. It has recorded history dating back to before the fourth century, since when it has always been an important centre of trade. To the ancient Chinese it was known as Beitian, later changing its name first to Yasi and then Shavgar before being renamed in the sixteenth century to its current name, Hazrat-e Turkestan.

Its name means 'The Saint (or Blessed One) of Turkestan' and refers to Khwaja Ahmed Yasawi, the famous Turkic poet and sufi (Muslim mystic) who was buried in the city in 1166. Yasawi is credited with transforming the city into the most important seat of learning for all the people of the Kazakh steppe. After his death, Tamerlane, the conqueror of most of western and central Asia, who was born nearby, constructed a magnificent domed mazar (mausoleum) at his grave site. It is now a UNESCO World Heritage Site, regarded as the most significant architectural monument in Kazakhstan, and in some circles is even known as the Second Mecca.

City/town	Local name	Location	Approx. distance	Country
Samarkand	Самарканд	600 km south-east of Hazrat-e Turkestan	27,770 km	Uzbeksitan

Samarkand is situated in the valley of the River Zarafshan. It is the second-largest city of Uzbekistan and is about the same age as the city of Babylon. Majestic Samarkand sits in a region of outstanding architectural splendour and cultural diversity. It is on the Unesco World Heritage List. Despite its status as the second city of Uzbekistan, the majority of the city's inhabitants are Persian-speaking Tajiks.

So impressive it was (and still is) that an ancient poet wrote,

You can travel through the whole world, have a look at the pyramids and admire the smile of the Sphinx, you can listen to the soft singing of the wind at the Adriatic Sea, and kneel down reverently at the ruins of the Acropolis, be dazzled by Rome with its Forum and Coliseum, be charmed by Notre Dame in Paris or by old domes of Milan, but if you have seen buildings of Samarkanda, you will be enchanted by its magic forever.

Samarkand prospered from its location on the trade route between Europe and China (the Silk Road). At times it has been considered to have been the greatest city of Central Asia. It was, however, occupied during Alexander the Great's Arabic conquest, during the Genghis Khan conquest, and lastly by the local Tamerlane. Hence the culture of Samarkand has developed with a mixture of Iranian, Indian, Mongolian and bits of the Western and Eastern cultures.

The centre of Samarkand is the impressive Registan Square, which means 'sand place'. Its first madrassah (Muslim religious school) was built on the site of a dried-up river, and over the years two more madrassah were constructed, so now Registan Square impressively consists of Ulugbek Madrassah (fifteenth-century), Sher–Dor Madrassah (seventeenth-century), and the gold-covered Tilla-Kari Madrassah (seventeenth-century).

The local warlord Tamerlane is buried here in the Gur-i Amir ('Tomb of the Ruler'), and curiously on the night of 22 June 1941 the Russian scientist Gerasimov began the first ever exhumation of Tamerlane's remains just as Hitler's army began its onslaught on Russia.

Sadly, at the time my father passed through, most of these monuments were in a state of total disrepair. Badly damaged in an earthquake in the 1890s, they were further damaged by Soviet artillery in 1924 during local resistance to the Red Army. Coincidentally the

Soviet Army division responsible was commanded by the very same Marshall Budennyi who had been appointed by Stalin to defend the Soviet Union and very quickly dismissed as Germany marched on Moscow.

Happily, all these magnificent monuments have been restored to their former glory and Uzbekistan is renowned for having the most important historical sites and structures in the whole of the Middle East.

City/town	Local name	Location	Approx. distance	Country
Bukhara	Бухара	250 km west of Samarkand	28,020 km	Uzbekistan

Bukhara on the Silk Road has a very long history; the city itself was founded around 500 BC, but the area, around an oasis, had been inhabited even earlier. From 1920 to 1925 a Bukharan People's Soviet Republic existed before being integrated into the Uzbek Soviet Socialist Republic. Since its inception it has continued to be a centre of trade, scholarship, culture, and religion.

Bukhara's modern history starts as a colonial acquisition of the Russian Empire, and was significant during the 'Great Game', the strategic rivalry and conflict between the British Empire and the Russian Empire for supremacy in Central Asia.

In Sanskrit the word *bukhara* means monastery, and like the whole region Bukhara is bestowed with an outstanding wealth of historical structures. It has more than 140 architectural monuments, many of which are considered architectural masterpieces, so much so Bukhara is often referred to as a 'museum city'. Perhaps the most impressive building is the Ark Citadel, which dates back to the fifth century.

After his long journey my father must have thought he was nearly there, but Guzar was still some 200 km further away to the south. Trains were infrequent and he will probably have made his way to the park near to the station to bide his time, as had Roman Skulski (*In the Soviet Union Without Toilet Paper*) just a week or two before my dad.

It was a lovely park filled with numerous shady trees and soft, sun-dappled grass. Hundreds of civilians milled around, almost all were speaking Polish. Everyone was making enquiries about missing relatives and friends. They had been released from different gulags in Siberia and, like us, were going to Guzar to join the Polish Army.

Eventually my dad was able to get himself on a crowded train; Roman Skulski remembers that on his train some passengers even travelled on the roof. In the sweltering heat the train plodded through the desert landscape, and after about three hours it pulled into the station at Guzar. I've no idea what my dad's feelings and emotions were, but even for me, just writing this narrative, it has come as some sort of relief and respite after a long and tortuous journey.

The scene on arrival must have been chaotic. Hundreds of lost, desperate, and confused Poles. Civilians, women, children, and hopeful soldiers all frantically milling around the station not knowing what to do or where to go. Eventually, a Polish Army official will have arrived and took control of the situation, as described by Skulski.

Within minutes a Polish Warrant Officer appeared, dressed in a pre-war cavalry uniform. He wore riding boots, spurs, riding breaches, and a tunic displaying rows of medal ribbons above his left pocket. A sabre was held to his left hip, his handlebar moustache bristled defiantly and he wore a peaked cap with a Polish Eagle emblem on it. He appeared both ferocious and glorious at the same time. In his left hand he held a riding crop, and as he walked up and down the station platform he kept slapping his boot with the crop.

Everybody was soon organised; part of the group were to stay in Guzar, but many including my father were returned to the train to continue the journey to the Polish Army camp as Shakhrisabz, the garrison of the 6th Infantry Division.

City/town	Local name	Location	Approx. distance	Country
Shakhrisabz	Шахрисабз	250 km south-east of Bukhara	28,270 km	Uzbekistan

Shakhrisabz is located in a small fertile valley, surrounded by the foothills of the high, snow-capped Pamir mountains. It was originally called Kesh and is famous as the birthplace in 1336 of Tamerlane, or more correctly Amir Timur.

Tamerlane was one of the most influential Central Asian military leaders of the Middle Ages. Allegedly, he was a descendant of a granddaughter of Genghis Khan. His usual name, Tamerlane, is derived from Timur Lang, or Timur the Lame, because of a slight paralysis in his left side. Despite his physical disability and from humble beginnings as a sheep rustler, he had a long military career and was engaged in an almost constant state of warfare. At its peak his vast territory reached from the Mediterranean in the west to India in the south and Russia in the north.

Though he made Samarkand the capital of his empire he never forgot his roots and continued to strengthen and beautify Kesh. He built Ak Saray, the ruins of which still exist today, a magnificent white palace surrounded with high walls and a deep moat, and laid out green gardens which gave rise to its new name of Shakhrisabz (Tajik for 'Green City').

On arrival at Shakhrisabz they were formed into a long column outside Kitab railway station and then led away by a Polish Army official. The column of prospective army hopefuls were marched out of the town and after about an hour arrived at a large, tented military camp surrounded by a high barbed wire fence. Above the gate, guarded by Polish sentries flew the Eagle-emblazoned red-and-white flag of Poland. My father had at last found the Polish Army.

The column proceeded slowly up to the guards, each person showing their official Soviet release documentation before being allowed into the camp. My dad's *udostoverenye* was proof enough, and after having it checked by the guards, who registered his details, he was allowed into the camp and placed in a holding unit to await his medical examination. Civilians and those who had no documents or had lost theirs were turned away; they would sadly have to fend for themselves.

Inside the holding compound, the lucky newcomers were divided into groups of ten men and each group was allocated to a tent. Aleksander Topolski (*Without Vodka*) describes his induction.

The occupants of my tent were a motley bunch, ranging in age from teenagers to grizzlies. All had drawn faces, beards at least a month old and tattered togs. And all were thin and starved. After a few introductory grunts, we curled up on the ground awaiting the announcement of our first mealtime. It came none too soon. The line up to the kitchen where the soup was to be served and bread issued was long but orderly and patient.

The day after his arrival my dad, along with a large group of men, was summoned to a medical commission where they were presented naked in small groups to the medical examination board. It can only be imagined what a sight these men must have made; gaunt, emaciated, weak, dirty and undernourished. Not what you would expect from normal army recruits, but beneath their misleading exteriors beat the hearts of lions.

The medical examination began with completing of my father's details; name, age, date and place of birth, last address in Poland, previous occupation. He then had a quick but thorough medical, at the end of which the examining officer declared him 'Fit, Category A'. It was the first entry in his Polish Army records. He was in! The date was 10 August 1942, nearly three years after the German and Soviet Armies had trampled over the Polish border.

Two days later, he was assigned to the 18th Rifle Brigade of the 6th Infantry Division. He was sent to the quartermaster's store and allocated a British-supplied Polish Army uniform, blanket and kitbag containing a bowl and spoon. For the first time in years he could relax, eat properly, and talk freely to the other occupants of his tent, though some of the new soldiers were reluctant and found it hard to use their new equipment, preferring, presumably from old habits, to keep them concealed away for fear of theft.

My dad's stay in Shakhrisabz wasn't destined to be long; in fact he had only been conscripted into the army in the nick of time! On the very same day he'd been allocated to his first army unit, Tuesday 12 August, he received orders that the Polish Army was leaving the USSR and that they were moving camp the following day. Things were looking up.

Polish–Soviet relations, never good, were going from bad to worse and Stalin was under pressure as the German Army pressed on towards the great Russian cities of Moscow, Leningrad and now Stalingrad in the south. The Soviet authorities decided that it would be better to let the Polish Army, which it considered troublesome on Russian soil, relocate to Persia where they could be supplied directly by the British Army and when ready help protect the key oil fields in the Caucasus in the event of a German attack. On 5 July Molotov made the announcement that they were letting the Polish Army leave Soviet territory. Anders, however, didn't hear of the news until the 7th, and wasn't officially notified until the 8th when he received the following letter (from *An Army in Exile*):

From Moscow. Ref.2651/1224. Deliver immediately. Urgent. Official Yangi-Yul. Commander-in-Chief Polish Army in U.S.S.R., Lt-Gen Anders. The government of the U.S.S.R. agrees to the request of the Commander-in-Chief Polish Army in U.S.S.R., Lt-Gen Anders, concerning the evacuation of Polish units from U.S.S.R. to the Middle East and does not intend to put obstacles in the way of the immediate carrying out of that evacuation. Plenipotentiary of the Council of People's Commissars in U.S.S.R., for Polish Affaires. Seal. Major General of State Security, signed Zhukov.

It is considered by some that it was an intervention from Churchill himself that guaranteed this Russian change of heart, but whatever the reason Anders was firm in his demands that no minority group of Poland, including Byelorussians, Ukrainians and Jews, should be excluded from the evacuation. He went further, insisting that civilians too should also be allowed to leave.

The Russians were this time good to their word and under the command of General Georgii Sergeevich Zhukov, who Anders generally considered decent and helpful, arranged at short notice the diversion of trains south to provide the transport for the evacuation.

On the day my father was officially joining the Polish Army, 12 August, Anders was summoned to Moscow to meet with Stalin and Churchill. The final preparations for the evacuation were put in place, after which Anders returned for the last time to Jangi-Jul.

On 13 August the 6th Infantry Division with my dad had their final parade, packed up their belongings and took down their tents and marched to the waiting trains, heading back through Guzar and Bukhara before heading west to the Caspian Sea port of Kransovodsk, their embarkation point for the Persian port of Pahlevi.

It's believed that of the estimated 2.5 million Poles deported between 1939 and 1941, by that time only half still survived. Anders reported that of those sent to Kolyma, believed to be around 15–20,000, only 583 survived to join the Polish Army. I am indeed lucky that my dad was one of these.

For many their final resting place is the huge Polish Army cemetery at Guzar, which today, like several cemeteries in Uzbekistan, is still lovingly tended in respect of those poor Polish souls that never left.

10

EXODUS ACROSS THE CASPIAN SEA

Leaving the Soviet Union Forever

My father's train journey from Shakhrisabz took him via Guzar, and back to Bukhara before turning west and travelling along the northern border of Iran towards the Caspian Sea. The journey lasted for about five days, taking him via Ashgabat and through the hot and dry Kara-Kum desert. The Kara-Kum, which covers about 70 per cent of Turkmenistan, means 'black sands' in the local language, though most descriptions refer to it as having typical yellow sand. The train finally came to a stop at a large, barbed wire enclosed, tented Polish Army holding camp nestled between the Kara-Kum desert and the Caspian Sea just a few kilometres outside the Caspian Sea port city of Krasnovodsk.

City/town	Local name	Location	Approx. distance	Country
Ashgabat	Ашхабад	700 km south-west of Bukhara	29,220 km	Turkmenistan

Ashgabat is the capital and largest city of Turkmenistan. It lies just north of the Kopet-Dag mountain range, and just south of the Kara-Kum desert. It has an arid climate with hot and dry summers and mild and short winters. Rainfall is low, and it rarely experiences snow.

Though situated on the Silk Road, Ashgabat is a relatively new city, growing out of a village of the same name established by Russians in 1818. It featured in the 'Great Game', the struggle between the imperial expansionist giants of Russia and Great Britain. In 1917 Soviet Rule was established, only to be ceded to a coalition of British and White Russian forces in 1918. Soviet rule was then regained in 1919, when the city was renamed Poltoratsk (Полторацк) after a local revolutionary. It returned to its original and current name, Ashgabat, in 1927.

City/town	Local name	Location	Approx. distance	Country
Türkmenbaşy (Krasnovodsk)	Türkmenbaşy (Красноводск)	550 km north-west of Ashgabat	29,770 km	Turkmenistan

Türkmenbaşy, known as Krasnovodsk until 1993, is a port city in Turkmenistan, part of the Balkan Province, on the eastern shore of the Caspian Sea. The town itself lies in an area of the Kara-Kum desert that is below sea level. The climate is typical of that of a subtropical desert.

Although a fort had existed on the site since 1717, Krasnovodsk was founded as a town in 1869 when it was colonised by the Russian Army, who named it after the local name Kyzyl-Su (Red Water). Krasnovodsk was Tsarist Russia's base of operations against the Khiva and Bukhara nomadic Turkmen tribes. It fell to the Red Army in February 1920.

The town lacks a supply of fresh water, which must be imported or desalinised from the Caspian Sea. It is the centre of Turkmenistan's oil production industry.

Experiences of their journey to and of their stay in Krasnovodsk differ wildly between memoirists. Whilst nobody had an easy time of it, my father, now a soldier, was at least in a military transit camp and subject to the discipline and organisation that a military process can instil. For the thousands of civilians it was much harder, as one anonymous memoirist describes:

The journey from Kermine to Krasnovodsk lasted at least a week. For a long time one could see on the left side the range of mountains that divided the USSR from Persia. On the right: a sandy desert. Our transport was not in a hurry, the train moved at a snail's pace. For unknown reasons it would stop in the middle of the desert. It was the hottest time of the year and the temperature reached 120 degrees. The train was terribly crowded, the passengers – living ghosts. I am not sure whether in that whole train there was anyone who could have merited the term, 'healthy individual', in the normal sense of that word. People lay on the straw on the floor, some on the benches. The toilets were occupied the whole time. Yet dysentery was raging. The toilet spilled into the car. The results of the dysentery were to be seen everywhere.

The stay in Krasnovodsk seems to have been particularly hard for civilians; there was no adequate accommodation, food or sanitation. For most there wasn't even shade from the hot sun, and to make matters worse fresh drinking water was in very short supply since Krasnovodsk has no natural source for this much-needed commodity. Another anonymous description:

In Krasnovodsk – hell on earth. So hot that it was hard to breathe. We detrained at a bay, and onto an open area covered with pebbles roasted by the sun. One walked across it barefoot as if on glowing coals. We had to stay on those pebbles for a long time before being allowed to get under a roof held up by a few uprights. From the heat, the hunger, the physical exhaustion, I became too weak to stand. I sat down by one of the uprights and for a long time I could not move. That roof sheltered us from the rays of the sun which baked us unmercifully. In these conditions we waited two days for the ship. The water near the shore, at least in the areas accessible to us, was heavily contaminated with crude oil, so one could not refresh oneself or wash something. Further away from the port there may have been clean water, but no one had the strength to walk along the shore.

Commanding the Polish Army base at Krasnovodsk was Colonel Zygmunt Berling, who had been one of the first to visit Anders following his release. Anders wrote that he had always been sceptical of Berling, and Berling had in fact been banished to Krasnovodsk as punishment after crossing Anders. It turns out that Berling, though having fought alongside Piłsudski in 1914, was a communist sympathiser and eventually deserted the Polish Army to align himself closely with the Soviet authorities. In August 1943 he created the 'Polish I Corps in the Soviet Union', which was enlarged in 1944 to the 'Polish First Army in Russia', for which Stalin promoted him to a full general. His army, sometimes known as the 'Berling Army', fought alongside the Red Army in several important Soviet battles, including the liberation of Warsaw and ultimately the 'Battle of Berlin'. It can't be said that he was obstructive to the impending departure of the Polish Army under Anders, but as the senior officer at Krasnovodsk, he was reluctant to recruit those Poles that had been conscripted into the Soviet Army after September 1939, and then had fled in an effort to join emerging Polish Army. Roman Skulski was one such example:

When he came back he said that Colonel Berling will see us shortly. After a while we were asked to enter an office. Behind a desk was a colonel in Polish uniform, we saluted him and I introduced myself and my friends and stated that we wished to join the Polish Army. He asked me where we came from and when I briefly told him about our travels he asked me for the discharge papers from the Russian Army. I told him that we did not have any discharge papers, that we escaped from the Russians to join the Polish Army. Colonel Berling stood up, looked at us sternly and yelled at us that we were deserters, that we had no right to leave our unit without permission and told us to get out of his office before he called the NKVD. It was quite a shock to me, unbelievable disappointment and I suddenly had a sickly feeling in my stomach. How could he do this to us?

The Polish exodus from Russia was undertaken in three phases. The first phase had taken place at the end of March. Ships transported Polish refugees across the Caspian Sea from Krasnovodsk to Pahlevi in Persia (Iran). Initially housed in temporary camps on the beach, they had by 25 April moved on. Those in the Polish Army had moved to Iraq and Palestine, and the civilians had either been transferred to hospitals at Qazvin on the road to Tehran or to Tehran itself where the Ministry of Labour and Social Welfare had established a series of camps for civilians.

The second phase finally started on 10 August. The Polish government-in-exile again chartered a motley array of cargo ships including oil tankers and coal transporters. Most were totally unsuitable for the transport of passengers. All were inappropriate for the numbers of passengers they were to carry. Several of these aged ships were later to be used at the 'Battle of Stalingrad', sailing up the Volga to help supply the besieged city. Some, it is believed, are still extant, being used as port storehouses in Azerbaijan.

The day of my father's departure finally arrived. It was 25 August 1942 and the 12,600-ton 'Lenin class' oil tanker *Zhdanov* was moored ready in the harbour. My dad's unit were assembled and transported the short distance by train to the waiting vessel, patiently sitting on the beach waiting for their embarkation call.

Soldiers were given priority boarding, and everybody was ordered to leave excessive baggage and any Russian money in crates before they were allowed to proceed to the boats. Aleksander Topolski describes the scene as he boarded.

Next morning, while we stood in a long file waiting for hours under the sun for our turn to board the ship, we were told for the last time to put all our roubles in the large plywood boxes scattered along the waterfront. I dropped my pitiful hoard into a box that was already filled to the brim with the sturdy, well printed Soviet bills, among them wads of thirty-rouble notes tied with string.

Not everybody though was so willing to conform, and some individuals made better, or at least a different, use for their useless paper money, as described in an extract from the book *Providence Watching (Journeys from War-Torn Poland to the Canadian Prairies)* by Kazimierz Patalas. As they had been told they weren't to take the roubles out of Russia, they put the Soviet banknotes to good use in the latrines!

Eventually, my dad's unit was called for boarding and ordered in doubles up the steep makeshift gangplanks that clung scarily to the side of the ship. Everybody was desperate to get on, and everybody, without exception, feared being left behind to continue their incarceration in the Soviet Union. Roman Skulski describes an unfortunate incident as he was boarding the ship *Kaganovych* a few days before my dad on 19 August:

Slowly, the train entered the station. By then, however, people were refusing to wait for the train to even stop. They pushed towards it and some of them climbed on while the train was still moving. The fear of being left behind in the Soviet Union prompted irrational and paranoid behaviour from otherwise normal people. As the people forged ahead one of the women auxiliaries was pushed against the engine's steam piston, a moving shaft: the front wheel caught her left arm just at the elbow. Someone managed to grab her back and others put a tourniquet on her destroyed and bleeding arm. People were screaming for a medic and an ambulance. It was an unforgettable sight. At first the poor woman screamed from pain but as calls went out for an ambulance, the woman's cries turned to shouts. 'Please! No ambulance! Don't leave me behind, it doesn't hurt, it's nothing. Please don't let the Russians take me, I'm alright ... I can travel ... please don't leave me ... please ...' It was heartbreaking but there was no other choice and the Russian ambulance took the screaming and pleading woman away ...

A ship was there, moored and waiting for us. We climbed down from the boxcars and moved in doubles up the gangplank to board the Russian ship, *Kaganovych*. The ship was crowded beyond capacity and people were everywhere; on the deck, below the deck, in the steerage, on the stairs, and amongst all the passageways.

For bathroom facilities, the Russians had attached plywood boards to the main deck's railings, spaced about 10 m apart all around the ship. Between the ship's railings and the fixed plywood there was a space of approximately a half a metre that opened to the ocean below. Men and women had to squeeze between the ship railing and the plywood board to relieve themselves overboard.

Even though the crossing was short and the Poles lucky enough to be onboard were sailing into a more hopeful future, the crossing was still difficult and taxing. We can get an idea of how terrible the crossing was from some of the documented testimonies below:

Many of the people on the ship were ill and there were even a few deaths – mainly caused by serious illnesses like typhoid and dysentery. One main trouble was a lack of water – but far greater was the lack of toilets – this caused long queues and many people simply relieved themselves over the side. I felt desperately sorry for those who died on the very threshold of freedom.

Anonymous

The ship that was taking us to Iran was the large oil tanker *Kaganovich*, named after one of the original Bolsheviks who managed to survive Stalin's purges in the 1930s. The empty tanker was sitting high in the water. Soldiers and civilians, loaded with all their belongings, edged up and up the steep gangways. We had to balance between the ship's rusty hull and the long drop to the dock below, our steps carefully measured like those of mountain climbers. The flimsy rope handrail was of no use as we carried something in each hand and could not even wipe the sweat trickling into our eyes. Everything had to be taken on board at one go. There was no return from the ship. At the top of the gangway, the segments of the long khaki caterpillar of soldiers fell into the black opening of the entrance only to reappear from the hatches above on the slightly convex deck. By the time our unit started embarking, the ship already looked packed with people so tightly that the proverbial sardines in a tin could be considered travelling executive class. But soon we found ourselves on the hot deck being followed by yet more units. Only the danger of squeezing someone overboard stopped the loading.

All over the ship people were scrambling to find a place to lie down, to sit down, to stand up. Any place. Partnerships between total strangers began to form. 'If you stretch your leg a bit and put your haversack on top of my rucksack, then this lady could sit down here.' There were men and women, soldiers and civilians mixed every which way on this deck.

I found a place for myself on top of a solid cast-iron capstan and there I sat for the whole voyage. Whenever I mention it in my tales of crossing the Caspian Sea, I am confronted with incredulous stares and 'Ah, you're pulling my leg!' But it is true. I spent two days and a night sitting on top of that capstan. It was the size of a bar stool only far less comfortable and no barman to serve drinks. My rucksack was propped against the stem of the capstan, my haversack was resting on my lap. From my privileged but precarious perch I looked down on a human carpet of sweaty bodies covering the tanker's metal deck. I assessed my situation.

It did not look too good but at least nobody was leaning against me and in that heat this was already something. I was on the fore-deck so the fumes from the funnel would not suffocate me. There was a chance of getting temporary relief for my cramped muscles by planting my foot or even both feet on the deck and wedging them gently between the intertwined bodies sprawled below me while holding on to the capstan's head. Standing on my wobbly rucksack was of no use as I would have to lean forward or backward with my thighs against the edge of the capstan, a balancing act which I could not sustain for long.

Most of us had eaten the last bits of our rations in the morning. Now we learned that there would be no food and no water on this trip. This news was accepted with the equanimity befitting old lags of Soviet prisons and labour camps. We were so busy with nestling and re-arranging the positions of our legs, arms and chattels that we had not even noticed the hawsers being cast off, nor did we feel the *Kaganovich* giving the slip to Krasnovodsk and its moonscape to head for the open sea, leaving an oily Peacock-coloured wake behind it. The blaze of the fierce sun almost directly overhead was slowly turning the iron deck into a giant frying pan.

Then came the problem of how to cope with hundreds of people trying to answer the urgent calls of nature. The only way was through two gaps in the continuous deck-side railing. As three quarters of us passengers were suffering from chronic diarrhoea, that public show of private matters was going non-stop for the entire voyage. Our lot became worse next morning. We turned our canteens upside down and vigorously shook them. But they refused to yield another drop of liquid.

A few mugs of water filled by the crew in their quarters were passed from hand to hand across and along the ship to the neediest souls. Some died and their stiff bodies, held aloft by dozens of outstretched hands and given priority over those with stomach cramps, were passed overhead to the nearest opening in the ship's railing to be tossed overboard. There were no ceremonies and no formalities. Only the splash made by the falling body moved some people to cross themselves furtively.

Aleksander Topolski

When the ship left the Soviet shore, I began to believe that I would get out of the USSR. The breeze of fresh sea air revived us. People were lying so thickly on deck that one could not pass. Some become sea-sick as if there were not enough sickness to go around. The dysentery forced people to soil the deck. Some relieved themselves over the railings; people had become inured to shame. Everyone was hanging on with the rest of their strength, to make the further shore. It was, however, not everyone's destiny. Those dying were tossed overboard without any weights attached. Their bodies, pulled along by the ship's wake, followed the ship, some even to the Persian Port of Pahlevi which we reached on August 14, 1942. I had survived!

Anonymous

So my dad's turn came; the *Zhdanov*, packed to the brim with 3,214 soldiers together with 423 civilians, finally left Soviet territory. The ship sailed out of the sheltered bay of Krasnovodsk and proceeded south-west through the Caspian Sea towards Persia (Iran). I know I've outlined above the misery and squalor of this particular phase of the journey, but the underlying feeling of elation and impending expectation of salvation must have almost been tangible as they plied their way across the Caspian Sea on their last stage to freedom.

Caspian Sea (Каспийское море)

The Caspian Sea is the largest enclosed body of water on Earth by area. By some it is described as the world's largest lake and by others as a fully qualified sea. It is generally referred to as a sea because when the Romans first arrived, they tasted the water and found it to be salty. It has, however, a salinity of about one-third the salinity of most seawater.

It lies between the southern areas of the Russian Federation and northern Iran and is currently bordered by five countries and influenced by three others in its water catchment area. It was named after the ancient Caspians, who lived in the region.

It is fed from, among other rivers, the mighty Volga that flows through the western part of Russia and is widely regarded as the national river of Russia. So important has the Volga been that eleven out of the twenty largest cities of Russia, including its capital Moscow, are situated within the Volga basin.

On the eastern shore of the Caspian Sea and clearly visible in satellite photograghs is found the Garabogazköl, (or Kara-Bogaz-Gol) the 'Mighty Strait Lake'. This is a shallow inundated depression in the northwestern corner of Turkmenistan. It forms a bay of the Caspian Sea separated by a thin sandbar, having a narrow opening through which the Caspian waters flow, cascading down into Garabogazköl.

The Caspian Sea holds great numbers of sturgeon, whose roe can be processed into caviar. Though there are several species of sturgeon found in the Caspian Sea, it is most famous for the beluga sturgeon (*Huso huso*), which produces the world-famous Beluga Caviar. Interestingly though, the meat from these huge fish is not considered worth eating. This fish, which travels up the rivers to breed, can have a lifespan of up to 100 years and so is vulnerable to fishing pressure. Poor management, over-fishing, pollution and habitat destruction have contributed to severe population declines of this and other Caspian Sea sturgeon species, which has led to very high caviar prices.

The Caspian Sea is also famous for the indigenous Caspian seal (*Phoca caspica*) which, like the Baikal seal, is one of very few seal species living in inland waters.

Unlike Lake Baikal, the Caspian Sea definitely has its very own 'monster'. It was here during the mid-1960s at the height of the Cold War that American photoreconnaissance aircraft first spotted huge, strange machines which they dubbed the 'Caspian Sea Monster'.

On further investigation it turned out to be gigantic, 100 m-long aircraft with inexplicably short, square wings called the Ekranoplan (экраноплáн). It was initially thought that these were large but conventional seaplanes but it was discovered that they were water-hugging behemoths designed to use the ground effect to skim water at high speeds, undetected by radar. It is known now that these WIGE (Wing in Ground Effect) developments were to test the possibilities of the wing travelling close to the ground providing extra lift by the 'cushion' of air compressed under it – thereby enabling a combination of greater aircraft weight for less power and/or enhanced fuel economy.

Many weird but interesting designs were developed and tested, but sadly following the collapse of the Soviet Union restricted funding has seen further development of these incredible machines almost come to a halt. A modern, small utility version is currently under development but its commercial viability is doubtful.

Thankfully the voyage from Krasnovodsk to Pahlevi took just over a day. Most of the tankers with their precious Polish cargo arrived and moored at the small port, but some of the ships' captains anchored off shore, not risking the final difficult passage to Pahlevi port. Aleksander Topolski was on such a ship.

> Our impatience grew when we noticed the *Kaganovich* slowing down. Then she cut her engines and began to coast until the rumbling of her anchor chain confirmed the feeling of a complete standstill.
>
> Although our tanker was empty and riding high, the captain would not take the risk of running her aground at the harbour entrance between the two arching sand spits. Such a mishap could reduce the vital Baku oil supplies to the Soviet Army which at that time was being hard pressed by the Germans on all fronts. And for such a mistake there would be only one penalty for the guilty captain.
>
> A couple of jaunty tugboats were already approaching the tanker. They were to take us to the shore.

Another memoirist, Ryszard Tyrk, describes his arrival on the *Zhdanov* in Pahlevi two weeks before my dad (taken from *The Polish Deportees of World War II* by Tadeusz Piotrowski):

> On August 15, 1942 at 4:30 A.M., just after sunrise, we saw the Persian port at Pahlavi. We remained for a few hours on board ship while awaiting the barges which were to take us ashore. But before that happened a great consternation, a veritable panic, seized us all because of a rumour to the effect that the ship would soon sail back, that such orders had already arrived. Two people jumped ship intending to swim ashore; fortunately they were rescued. To restore order several shots were fired and that was that. At last the barges arrived.

So eventually my father will have disembarked, either directly from the *Zhdanov* or via a tugboat, and will have stepped foot on Persian soil. Though Persia was under British control, there was (since Operation Countenance) a joint occupation with Russia, so there was still a visible NKVD presence. Despite this, I suspect it will have been the first time since before his arrest that he could really relax, and feel that he was free from the shackles of the Soviet Union.

City/town	Local name	Location	Approx. distance	Country
Bandar-e Anzali (Pahlevi)	بندر انزلی	500 km south west of Türkmenbaşy	30,270 km	Iran (Persia)

Bandar-e Anzali is the most important Iranian seaport on the Caspian Sea. It is in the province of Gilan, close to the city of Rasht, and connected to Tehran by road. It consists of a main island of Mianposhteh and the surrounding lands. Bandar-e Anzali itself stands on both sides of the entrance to the huge Mordab Lagoon, though the port is mainly on the eastern side. The water level of the sea around Anzali is rising by 15 to 20 cm each year, and a peculiar sight of trees on the beach can be seen in the vicinity.

Before 1942 Bandar-e Anzali was known as 'Bandar (port) e Pahlavi' after the last Iranian dynasty, when Iran was then known as Persia. In fact, the last shah, Mohammed Reza Pahlavi, had a huge fondness for this port city and built huge palaces here. According to his wife's memoirs, *An Enduring Love* by Farah Pahlavi, this was the very place he departed from to get to his boarding school in Switzerland.

It has now, as it had when my dad was there, a cosmopolitan population including Iranians, Russians, Armenians, Caucasians and Turkmen, many of whom make their living in the huge, bustling, colourful and noisy markets around the town. The most famous market is every Saturday at the Shanbeh bazaar.

Anzali is the world-famous Iranian capital of caviar. The preparation and marketing of the precious sturgeon roe is a state monopoly, handled through 'the Iranian Fishing Company', which is a department of the Iranian Finance Ministry. The word caviar itself is derived from the Persian word *khaya* or egg.

Four days after my dad had disembarked from the *Zhdanov* and set foot on Persian soil, the *Zhadnov* again returned from Krasnovodsk and moored at Pahlevi. It was 30 October, and it was the last ever ship that would carry Poles to freedom across the Caspian Sea.

There was, however, to be a third, and much smaller phase of the exodus. On 20 September 1942 a small number of Polish soldiers and civilians were evacuated overland in army trucks. Their route took them from Ashgabat through the Kopet-Dag mountain range to the rail head at Mashhad in Persia. The civilians went on to to the refugee camps in Tehran and the soldiers to join up with the rest of the evacuated soldiers in Pahlevi. The estimated total numbers of Poles leaving the Soviet Union is shown in the table below.

Approximate numbers of Poles leaving the Soviet Union in 1942

	Dates	Army	Civilian	Total
Phase I	April 1942	33,000	11,000	44,000
Phase II	August 1942	44,000	30,000	74,000
Phase III	September 1942	1,000	2,000	3,000
Total		78,000	43,000	121,000

If we use a figure of 2 million Polish civilians, either taken prisoner of war or deported by the Soviet Union, then we can see the 120,000 (most reports actually use 115,000) lucky enough to have reached Persia was less than 10 per cent. I'm so privileged that my father was one of the fortunate few.

The British and Persian officials that had supervised the initial reception and watched the first ships arrive had no idea what to expect, and were clearly shocked by the condition of the evacuees. They witnessed the unsuitable and grossly overcrowded tankers disgorge their cargo of walking skeletons, many of whom were clothed in rags and infested with lice. They watched as many knelt and kissed the soil of Persia, whilst others sat down on the shoreline and prayed, or just wept for joy. Such was the reality of freedom, and the realisation of reaching a major step on their way to the Promised Land.

The Persian government had appointed their trusted General Esfandiari to work with British and Polish officials to oversee the evacuation. Under his auspices hundreds of Persian tents had been supplied and erected just outside of town, along a spit of beach separating the Caspian Sea from Mordab Lagoon. As the Poles disembarked they were met by friendly smiling residents of Pahlevi, offering gifts of dates, nuts, roasted peas with raisins and pomegranates. How different to the Soviet-controlled lands they had just left. The warmth and affection of the Persian people remained long in the memory of most memoirists.

All the evacuees were led from their ships, loaded onto trucks, and driven the short distance to their new transit camp on Pahlevi beach. They could now start to prepare in earnest, the soldiers to ready themselves for battle, and the civilians to start to rebuild their lives. There could now at last be some hope for the future.

11

RECUPERATION, TRAINING, BUT MORE TRAGEDY

Starting to Get Better

General Anders had finally departed the Soviet Union from Jangi-Jul on 19 August. He flew initially to his new headquarters in Tehran, but as early as the 22nd he was in Cairo meeting Churchill at the British Embassy. Though the meeting was wide ranging, the most significant outcome, and I suppose importantly for me, was that Anders agreed to place his soldiers under British control, which in real terms meant that the immediate destiny of the Poles was directly linked to that of the British Army.

Anders was subordinated to General Henry Maitland Wilson. Affectionately known as 'Jumbo', due to his massive physical presence, General Wilson had recently been appointed the commander of the newly created Persia and Iraq Command, 'Paiforce', and been given the task of protecting the oilfields of the southern Caucasus, if Germany, having conquered southern Russia, pressed on south into Persia. He was keen that Anders should prepare his army to assist. Anders left Cairo via General Wilson's HQ in Baghdad, and after inspecting the area allocated to the Polish Army at Quizil-Ribat in the desert of north-eastern Iraq returned overland to Tehran.

My dad finally set foot on Persian soil on 26 August 1942. Every account I've read tells not only of the feeling of immense relief of departing the Soviet Union, but especially of the kindness and generosity of the local inhabitants of Pahlevi and also from the Persian and British Army officials who were there to help them. All accounts speak of the awe of the Persian city with its wealth and abundance of food and amenities and the free and relaxed atmosphere – a stark contrast to their previous existence in Stalin's Russia.

My dad, along with 3,000 exhausted, hungry and mostly ill new army recruits made their way from the *Zhdanov* to the waiting army trucks. Along the way they were besieged by the warm and friendly Pahlevi residents who crowded around shouting words of welcome, and offering gifts of figs and dates, nuts, roasted peas, raisins, pomegranates and other delicacies they had not seen for such a long time, indeed if at all.

The short drive took them to the outskirts of Pahlevi and the edge of the Caspian Sea. Here a huge temporary complex of thousands of tents supplied by the Persian Army had been erected along the shoreline. The camp, with its neat lines of tents in military precision, marked with rows of white-painted stones, stretched for several miles along a beach. It contained, in rudimentary form, all the services needed to support an army with its associated civilian dependants. It had bathhouses, latrines, disinfection facilities, laundries, sleeping quarters, shops, post offices, bakeries and a hospital. However, despite its size it was still inadequate for all the people it was expected to support, so additional space was requisitioned within the city itself from empty houses to cinema halls.

The first port of call for all arrivals was the medical reception compound. There was one for the army recruits and a separate one for civilians. Manned by armed guards, each was divided into two separate areas by a barbed wire fence, one area called the 'infected', sometimes referred to as the 'dirty' area, and the other known as the 'clean' area. On arrival, anybody considered as having infectious diseases was quarantined in the closed 'dirty' section for four days. Those exhibiting chronic symptoms were sent directly to the camp hospital, where more than half of patients admitted were suffering from the fatal typhus. Sadly, for many of these Pahlevi was to be their final resting place.

My dad entered the 'clean' area and was channelled through a series of inspection tents where his recently acquired uniform, along with everybody else's, was presumed to be infected with typhus carrying lice and removed for burning. They were then showered, de-loused and shaved (all over) before being allocated new clothes and temporary living quarters.

For the first time in years food was available in abundance. Though no doubt enjoyable, to some of the starved, emaciated masses of Poles it became a problem in itself. Corned beef, fatty rich soup, lamb and rice distributed by the British soldiers, and boiled eggs, figs, dates and fruit sold by the Persian street vendors caused havoc with digestions accustomed only to small pieces of dry bread and watery soup. Stomach problems and in particular diarrhoea were a constant problem.

Romuald Lipinski in his autobiography, *My Story*, describes the scene:

Latrines were located at one end of the encampment, and if somebody's place was at the opposite end to the latrines he or she had a long distance to go. Diarrhoea that resulted from that was terrible. People were just so sick that they did not bother to go to their places but they laid on the sand by the latrines unable to move. Some of them unable to make it to the latrines on time relieved themselves wherever they could without any regard to privacy. The whole area stank.

Despite all the illness, continued hardship, and struggle things were definitely starting to look up. Everybody was being fed and housed and they could relax and start to enjoy their first taste of freedom. For the first time in years the pressure was off and everybody, soldiers and civilians alike, could enjoy their free time and simple pleasures. In those first few weeks of freedom bathing in the Caspian Sea was a great favourite for everybody.

Two days after arriving, my dad was privileged to witness the visit of his saviour to Pahlevi. General Anders had arrived on a special visit to the Polish Army and civilian camps. In his book *An Army in Exile*, he explains how heartening it was to see men, women and children arriving from Russia and expressing joy at being free again.

Unfortunately, the Polish–Russian relationship, always poor, was deteriorating rapidly. Despite the massive German offensive on the city of Stalingrad, Russia refused to allow any further soldiers to enlist in the Polish Army under Anders, and ordered those remaining officials still in the south of the Soviet Union to wind up their operations and leave immediately.

On arrival in Persia, Anders encouraged all those released from Russia to record their treatment by the Russians. This became known as the 'Documentation Office' in which handwritten statements were collected as evidence of the treatment of Poles by the Soviet Union. Most of these are now stored at the Hoover Institute at Stanford University in America, and some of the descriptions from my dad's story are taken directly from the Pleszak testimonies.

On 12 September General Sikorski formally announced that the Polish Army was to be known as the 'the Polish Army in the East'. Though the name was to change later to a more familiar and famous name, it will be forever endearingly known with great affection, and in honour, as 'Anders' Army'.

My dad was fortunate. He didn't succumb to malaria, typhus, yellow fever, dysentery or any of the multitude of illnesses that many of his compatriots had. Within two weeks of arriving in Pahlevi my dad was once again on the move. The temporary reception camps were being wound up and the soldiers were being transferred to the new Polish Army headquarters in Quizil-Ribat over the border in Iraq. The civilians were initially transferred to refugee camps in the Persian cities of Tehran and Isfahan. Now under British control, Anders could step up the development of his army. The temporary army base at Pahlevi, after playing a short but highly significant part in Polish history, was finally closed on 16 October 1942.

Long streams of covered army trucks departed Pahlevi every day carrying the new soldiers along the narrow, twisting roads initially south along the road towards Tehran. At the city and Polish Army camp at Qazvin they turned south-west, stopping at the army transit camp in the city of Hamadan.

It was along one of the narrow mountain roads between the towns of Hamadan and Kangavar that an earlier convoy of trucks came across a young Persian boy struggling with a bulky sack. It was found to contain a honey-coloured bear cub. The soldiers allegedly bartered some cans of meat in exchange for what turned out to be a very young Syrian brown bear, and the legend of Wojtek, the mascot of the 22 Kompania Zaopatrywania Artylerii (22nd Artillery Supply Company), was born.

From Kangavar the route took them to Kermanshah (now called Bakhtaran), through the highest mountains in Persia, the Zagros Mountains, and on to the Persia–Iraq border. Five days after leaving Pahlevi and less than 10 km after crossing into Iraq the trucks entered another huge, tented army camp. Situated in the desert about 140 km north-east of Baghdad in the Tigris River basin along the Alwand River, near to the town and oil refineries of Khanaqin, was the Mullah Azis army camp. It was home to Polish, British and Gurkha soldiers.

My dad's military training started immediately. Temperatures in the late summer were still reaching 50°c during the day, so training began early, leaving the afternoons for relaxing and getting back to full health. So my dad's induction into military life started in the hot deserts of Iraq. As the days and weeks went on his military education continued, and after General Maitland-Wilson relocated to his headquarters in Baghdad developments moved on rapidly. As Anders wrote in his book *An Army in Exile*, intensive training began, but there were many new methods to learn, new weapons to handle, and 20,000 drivers to be trained.

Shortly after arriving in Iraq the Polish Army in the East underwent a period of reorganisation. The first unit to be formed was the 3rd Carpathian Rifle Division (3 Dywizja Strzelcow Karpackich). This was created from the 9th and 10th Infantry units that had departed from the Soviet Union back in March, together with the Independent Carpathian Rifle Brigade which had been established from those Polish soldiers who had escaped to France in September 1939 and then on the fall of France moved on to British Palestine. They were already battle hardened, having fought together with the British Army at the Battle of Tobruk in Libya from August to December 1941. The other main formations created were (in recognition of the eastern borderland origins of the bulk of the soldiers) the 5th Kresy Infantry Division (5 Kresowa Dywizja Piechoty) and the 2nd Armoured Brigade (2 Brygudy Pancerna).

The last part of Anders' statement above was particularly important for my father. On 6 November he was assigned to his first proper army unit. It was the 5th Transport Squadron of the newly formed 2nd Armoured Brigade, and he was to train as one of the much-needed drivers in this new Polish mechanised army.

Despite the rapid military development of Anders' Army, Polish political developments were sadly regressing. The Soviet–Polish relationship was getting worse, and amid all the ongoing political machinations, rather ominously, concerns were being aired about Soviet representatives within Poland making preparations for a Soviet occupation rather than fighting the Germans. To add further insult to injury, in October 1942 a letter from the Soviet authorities refused any further enlistment into the Polish Army on the grounds that Anders had refused to send any Polish troops to the Soviet front.

By the beginning of 1943 the Soviet government had become tired of the Polish question, which had grown into a huge international political issue. It completely lost patience and withdrew all Polish aid and support. On 6 January 1943 Poland was told to close all 400 of its welfare agencies on Russian soil (including orphanages and hospitals), and on 16 January, in a note, Stalin affectively revoked the amnesty when his Soviet government officially informed the Polish government in London that all Poles remaining in the Soviet Union and originating from the provinces under Soviet occupation would be considered Soviet subjects.

My father was one of less than 200,000 Poles who were fortunate to have already escaped from Russia. The euphoria of the new-found freedom was already becoming tainted with a growing realisation of difficult times ahead.

But it wasn't all bad news; the British 8th Army (the famous Desert Rats) under the command of the General Bernard Montgomery had followed their success in the second Battle of El Alamein (Egypt) in early November with the successful capture of Tripoli (Libya) on 23 January. It probably wasn't appreciated at the time but these first major Allied successes of the war were quite probably decisive not only in the eventual outcome of the war, but as the first significant blow against Hitler's army some believe negatively influenced the fighting ability of the Germans at the Battle of Stalingrad and hence reduced the Soviet requirement for assistance from the Anders and his army, and with it any dependence Stalin had on Polish troops!

Though the training was tough and intensive, recuperation was rapid. Anders was able to review his troops with pride in a parade in Khanaqin on 31 January 1943. His parade was tinged with sadness and pride since he was having to release 3,500 of his troops to bolster the Polish forces in England. The parade was followed by an international football tournament involving the best of the Polish, British and Iraqi Armies. Legend has it the tournament was won by the British, but different accounts of the time from the different nationalities differ on the actual victors.

George Raynor

Interestingly for me as a fan of the 'beautiful game' (football), the Iraqi team was managed by an Englishman from Yorkshire called George Raynor. This colourful character is generally considered to be the second most successful English international football manager (after Sir Alf Ramsey), and is in the top-fifty list of most successful football managers ever. Yet few, even football scholars, have ever heard of him.

The son of a miner, he was born in Barnsley and had been a journeyman professional footballer during the 1930s, playing for five different clubs up to 1939. Playing for Aldershot when the war broke out, he was appointed by the British Ministry of Education as a PE teacher and football coach in the British protectorate of Iraq, where he went on to become the first foreign manager of the Iraqi national football team. His Iraqi team played several high-profile matches in Baghdad, most notably against the English Army team, complete with several professional footballers, and his team also beat the Polish Army team 4-2.

Raynor's achievements hadn't gone unnoticed. On returning to England after the war he was working as reserve team coach at his old club Aldershot when the secretary of the Football Association, Stanley Rous, who had received a very complimentary letter from the Prime Minister of Iraq, Nuri-al-Said, asked him in 1946 to assist the Swedish national squad. Although he had hoped to obtain a UK-based role, he accepted the offer.

Allegedly a strong-willed and single-minded character his talents worked well on the keen Swedish players who soon developed into a formidable footballing team. With Raynor at the helm, they gave an early account of their ambitions, giving England a scare before losing 4-2 at Arsenal's Highbury ground in 1947.

Under Raynor the early Swedish promise continued to develop, and at the London Summer Olympics of 1948 they beat Yugoslavia 3-1 in the final to claim the gold medal. With Raynor, the Swedish team went from strength to strength. In the 1950 World Cup in Brazil they were to finish third, only being narrowly beaten by the eventual champions, Uruguay, and were bronze medallists at the 1952 Olympic Games in Helsinki.

But Sweden's and Raynor's greatest footballing achievement came at the 1958 World Cup, which was held in Sweden. Early indications of their potential were clear in a 3-1 victory over the current world champions, West Germany. Battling their way to the final, they ended up losing 5-2 to the amazing Brazilian side, including arguably the greatest football player the world has seen, Edison Arantes do Nascimento, or to you and me simply Pelé. Sweden, on merit, were the top European footballing nation.

Raynor's success didn't stop there. The following year he managed the Swedish side to a 3-2 victory against England under the famous twin towers at the home of football, Wembley Stadium. They were only the second foreign side, after Hungary in 1953, to win at Wembley. Raynor also had spells in club management; AIK Stockholm, the great Italian teams of Lazio (Rome) and Juventus (Turin), and in England Coventry City, Doncaster Rovers and Skegness. Incredible.

Reports that the Red Army was getting the upper hand in Stalingrad were finally confirmed on 2 February with a victory for the Red Army in the bloodiest battle the world has ever seen. It was the first big defeat of Hitler's armies. The fate of the millions of Poles still in Russia had effectively been sealed.

In Iraq my dad's training continued and his health was regularly monitored. At Khanaqin on 15 February in a more rigorous medical his health was confirmed as category 'A' and his *zeszyt ewidencyjny* updated accordingly. A week later he was transferred to the 4th Transport Company of the 2nd Armoured Brigade to continue his training. It seems that his basic training was concluded on 11 April 1943 when he was given a lecture on army protocol, expectations, obligations and penalties for breaching them. His *zeszyt ewidencyjny* contains the entry signed by Captain Jacunski, the company commander for the Polish Army camp at Khanaqin.

Training continued apace and the development of Anders' Army surged forward. But two days after my dad's basic training had been completed, on 13 April, there was a radio announcement of such magnitude and importance it must have hit Poles all over the world like an earthquake. It was an event of such magnitude that it still hasn't been fully resolved to this day (May 2009 as I write this), and still raises highly charged emotions and accusations.

The Crime of Katyn

I have alluded several times in my story so far to a single event that was so massive and catastrophic but have not really given any substance to it. The first occasion was when I described those Polish soldiers that were able to escape through Romania to France as the lucky ones. The second time was when my dad was being deported, and the train that was transporting him passed through the city of Smolensk. The third time was when General Anders voiced concerns about smaller numbers than expected of Polish Army officers arriving to join his army when still in the Soviet Union.

(What happened at Katyn is well-documented elsewhere so I won't dwell on it in too much detail here other than to give a brief overview of my understanding of the events as relevant to my story.)

On 13 April an announcement on Radio Berlin was broadcast worldwide stating that they had received a report from Smolensk in which local inhabitants had mentioned to the German authorities the existence of a place where mass executions had been carried out by the Bolsheviks and where 10,000 Polish officers had been murdered by the Soviet Secret State Police. The announcement went on to say that German authorities had gone to the Russian health resort, known as the Hill of Goats, situated twelve kilometres west of Smolensk, where the gruesome discovery had been made.

The German claim of 10,000 was an exaggeration, but a final total of about 4,500 fully uniformed Polish officers were found buried, each with a single bullet-hole in the back of the head. Sadly, in light of the success of the Red Army and the ever-growing power of the Soviet Union, and since the announcement had been made by Germany's Josef Goebbels' Ministry of Propaganda, there was little Allied condemnation, even an almost acceptance of the Soviet counter-claim that the atrocity had been perpetrated by the German Army as they advanced east and not the Soviets.

There were many atrocities, both military and civilian, performed by the NKVD during their occupation of the Kresy lands. In the northern region, the civilians from the cities of Stara Wilejka (now Vileyka in modern-day Belarus), Brześć (Brest), Baranowicze (Baranavichy) and Pinsk were rounded up and murdered at Kuropaty near Minsk. In the southern region the same fate befell the citizens of Równe (now Rivne in modern-day Ukraine), Luck, Drohobycz, Tarnopol, Lwów (Lviv) and Stanisławów, who were deported to the Soviet Union and murdered at Bykovnia, Charkow and Cherson.

As horrific as these crimes are, it is the murder of the Polish Army officers that provokes much emotion and anger. Though Katyn is a single location, it specifically refers to the mass-murder of Polish officers at four separate locations.

When the German and Soviet armies had carved Poland between themselves in the September of 1939, many Polish soldiers had been taken prisoner. Those taken by the Germans were mainly conscripted into the German Army, some of whom would later desert and join Anders' Army. Of those taken prisoner by the Red Army, the low-ranking soldiers by October were being gradually released, some of whom were conscripted into the Red Army, though nearly 40,000 were retained as slave labour.

The Polish officers and senior NCOs, however, were deported to Russia and initially held in three main camps. Kozelsk, south-west of Moscow, 250 km east of Smolensk in Kaluga Oblast, Ostashkov, north-west of Moscow, 180 km west of Tver (formally known as Kalinin); and Starobelsk near the Ukrainian town of Kharkiv (Kharkov). Kozelsk also contained arrested Polish university lecturers, surgeons, physicians, barristers and lawyers. Ostashkov also held anybody from Poland who was considered to be 'bourgeois' from the pre-war Polish elite.

Recent investigations have discovered that a fourth Polish officers' camp existed at Bykovnia in Ukraine, and it's possible that further as yet undiscovered sites also existed.

What happened to these officers is normally, and quite correctly, referred to as a massacre. The details are best described by Piotr Kosicki in his case study, 'The Katyn Massacres of 1940'. Kozelsk held 4,750 Polish officers. At the beginning of April 1940 they were removed in groupds in small cars attached to regularly scheduled trains. They were transported to Gnezdovo station, where the NKVD loaded the prisoners on to transport buses, which carried them to a facility in the Katyń Forest. There, the

NKVD had dug eight mass graves. When the prisoners arrived, they were searched and their identification checked. Each man was then led to the edge of one of the eight ditches and shot in the back of the head. This continued until the whole camp had been liquidated by 12 May 1940. The Polish officers held at Starobelsk were taken in groups to the NKVD regional headquarters in Kharkiv. They too were shot in the back of the head on arrival, but not at the intended burial site. NKVD officers then used freight trucks to transport the bodies to a forest just outside Kharkiv. The NKVD filled in the graves on 12 May 1940. The Ostashkov prisoners were herded on foot over the frozen lake and then taken by train to Kalinin. They were briefly detained at NKVD headquarters, and by night an NKVD execution crew of thirty killed the prisoners with a shot to the back of the head. This continued until 19 May, and every night the bodies were transported by freight truck 32 km along the Moscow–Leningrad road to the town of Mednoye where they were buried.

Not all the officers were murdered. About 450 selected from the three main camps were sent initially to the prisoner of war camp at Pavlishchev Bor east of Smolensk, and then onto the camp at Griazowiec north of Moscow near to the town of Vologda, before being sent to the notorious Moscow prisons of Butyrki and Lubianka. Apparently, they had been selected for 'possible Soviet conversion', but of the 450 only thirteen were deemed suitable, and these were transferred to the 'Villa of Happiness' at Malakhova near Moscow. Of these thirteen only three were to remain with the Soviet authorities; one of these was none other than Colonel Zygmunt Berling! The remainder had escaped execution and were eventually released following the amnesty to join the forming Polish Army. As they had been removed prior to the massacres they were only able to provide limited information on the plight of their missing fellow officers.

As I have indicated earlier, there was, following the German radio broadcast, little international condemnation of the Soviet authorities. In fact on 15 April the British government publically stated via the BBC that the German explanation had been lies and that it accepted the Russian version of events. The Polish government-in-exile was incensed, and against the recommendations of Great Britain and the United States, in a communication on 17 April insisted on bringing the matter to the negotiation table. It went further, demanding a full and independent investigation by the International Red Cross.

Stalin wasted no time; his uneasy alliance with the Poles, always tenuous, was now effectively surplus to requirements. The Red Army had not only defeated the Germans at Stalingrad but was getting the better of the Germans throughout their western front, and since the Allies had almost routed the German armies in North Africa his dependence on the help of the Polish government-in-exile and its Army in the East had not only diminished, it had evaporated completely!

In a letter of 25 April, Stalin seized the opportunity and used the Polish government-in-exile's appeal to the Red Cross as a pretext for breaking diplomatic relations, accusing them of collaborating with Nazi Germany and taking a hostile stance against the Soviet Union. The Soviet powers went further and started a campaign to get the Western Allies to recognise the alternative Polish pro-Soviet government that had been established in Moscow and led by the famous Polish communist and novelist Wanda Wasilewska. Gradually Polish policy began to distance itself from the Polish government in London. Apparently the first conference between Sikorski and Churchill following the severing of ties was significantly low-key.

Despite the huge setback and obvious ramifications of the Soviet actions and of Allied international opinion towards the Poles, the training of the Polish Army continued. It was already developing into an efficient fighting force. In early May 1943 the Polish Army in the East once again relocated, moving about 300 km north-west further into Iraq. Stationed in the desert between the cities Kirkuk and Mosul, training continued unabated, and since the terrain was far more suitable for large-scale military exercises, the Polish Army moved nearer and nearer to battle readiness. The new location meant that they were also positioned to protect the oil wells in the area should the need arise.

City/town	Local name	Location	Approx. distance	Country
Mosul	لموصل	500 km north-west of Khanaqin	31,570 km	Iraq

Mosul is an impressive historical city in northern Iraq astride the Tigris River about 400 km north-west of Baghdad. It has five bridges linking the two sides.

The area around Mosul has been continuously inhabited for at least 8,000 years. Built on the site of an earlier Assyrian fortress, Mosul succeeded in importance the nearby ancient city of Nineveh, which was founded by the Assyrians. Mosul is rich in ancient buildings including mosques, castles, churches, monasteries and schools, most of which abound in architectural features and decorative works of major significance. The town centre is dominated by a maze of streets and attractive nineteenth-century houses. Some of the older houses are of majestic beauty, constructed around a central courtyard and with an impressive facade of the famous, locally produced Mosul marble.

The fabric muslin, which has long been manufactured here, derives its name from the city. The Mosul Museum contains many interesting artifacts from the nearby ancient sites of the old Assyrian capital cities Nineveh and Nimrud. Agatha Christie, the famous English novelist, lived for some time in Mosul while her second husband, the archaeologist Sir Max Mallowan, was involved in the excavation of Nimrud.

On 2 May my dad at last started his intensive military driving course. It must have been a completely new experience for him. Back in his home village of Szwakszty he had only ever been used to horse-and-carts, but the Polish Army was desperate for drivers, and my dad was about to become one of them.

I don't know much about his driver training other than that he received instruction on a range of military vehicles. While training I know that he continued to live in the same tents as he had since finding the Polish Army the previous August. One small morsel of information that he did tell me was that every time he went back to the tent, he checked all his belongings for scorpions and snakes; he had once pulled his bedroll back to find a snake curled up in his bed.

His driver training continued until 6 June when he passed his driving exams. His driving licence was awarded on 10 June allowing him to drive military motor cars, lorries, and tractors.

On 25 May, and despite concerns about his safety, General Sikorski departed London to visit his troops in Iraq. After stopping off in Gibraltar he was greeted in Cairo by General Anders on the 27th, to whom he said that in London he had received a message warning him not to visit the Polish Army in the east. He had been told that the army was undisciplined and an assassination attempt on his life was planned. Anders was able to reassure Sikorski about the state of the Polish Army, its commitment and about his safety while in the Middle East. By 2 June Sikorski had travelled to Kirkuk and had seen for himself the morale and the development that the army had made in such a short space of time. He was so impressed that he sent the following telegram to the Polish government-in-exile back in London. 'Kirkuk, June 2nd, 1943. Secret. For the President of the Polish Republic. After having carried out the first visits of inspection to the army I wish to inform you that to my great satisfaction I have found a spirit of most ardent patriotism amongst the soldiers, and also resolution to fight and a devotion to the Polish cause. Yours respectfully. Sikorski, Commander-in-Chief.'

My father was there on 8 June at Khanaqin to witness Sikorski inspecting his troops, and making the promise that they would soon see active service with the ultimate goal of restoring a sovereign Polish nation. Sikorski was then able to observe, no doubt with immense pride and pleasure, large-scale military exercises, before continuing on to Beirut where he was able to outline to his 'Chefs-du-Missions' and senior military commanders how grave the situation was beginning to look for the future of Poland, and quite possibly raising concerns about his diminishing faith in the British and US governments over their apparent lack of support over the Katyn affair. It was clear that Sikorski's uncompromising stance on that issue was beginning to create an unwanted rift between the Western Allies and the Soviet Union.

Around this time Sikorski approved the name-change of his army from the 'Polish Army in the East', to the better-known and internationally renowned 'Second Polish Corps', or in Polish 'Drugi Korpus Polski'. It adopted as its insignia a white design based on the coat of arms of Warsaw, the *syrenka* (little mermaid) on a red background, the national colours of Poland. The First Polish Corps had been formed in the United Kingdom from those soldiers who had escaped Poland to France in 1939 and been subsequently evacuated to England.

More Tragedy: the Death of a Great Leader

Anders presented to Sikorski a case for a European front to be made through the Balkans in an attempt to prevent the Red Army from liberating Poland before bidding farewell to Sikorski in Cairo and retuning to prepare his troops for battle readiness. (He was actually struck down by malaria and spent time convalescing in Lebanon so didn't return to Iraq immediately.) Sikorski left Cairo bound for London. His route took him back to Gibraltar, where on 3 July he visited Lieutenant-General Sir Frank Noel Mason-Macfarlane, the Governor of Gibraltar, and Lieutenant Ludwik Lubienski (father of the

British actress Rula Lenska, born Countess Roza-Marie Leopoldyna Lubienska), the chief of the Polish Military Mission in Gibraltar

The following day he inspected the Somerset Light Infantry, after which he met a group of ninety-five Polish soldiers evacuated from Spain awaiting transport to the United Kingdom. Later that day, General Sikorski, together with the British Minister of War, Sir Percy James Grigg, inspected the Gibraltar fortress. Sikorski arrived back at his apartment at about 6 p.m. and attended a cocktail party organised to celebrate the 167th anniversary of the Declaration of Independence of the USA.

At 11 p.m. General Sikorski's English Consolidated B-24 Liberator, registered AL523, took off on the easterly runway. Lieutenant Lubienski describes watching the aircraft climb slowly, then, while still quite low, level out and then begin slowly descending. The plane flew wings-level and apparently intact into the sea at an angle of about 10 degrees about a mile from the shore. With the exception of the Czech pilot, Edward Prchal, all on board, including the sixty-two-year-old general and his daughter Zofia Lenniowska, were killed. A British inquiry immediately after the crash concluded that it was caused by the plane's controls jamming.

The death of General Sikorski is considered by many to be one of the biggest mysteries of the Second World War, and not surprisingly many conspiracy theories abound regarding his death. While I'm clearly not privy to any new information, and it to this day is still shrouded in secrecy and mystery, all I can do is highlight some of the pertinent facts that I have come across in my research for this book.

By July 1943, not only had Stalin broken off diplomatic relations with Sikorski, but his once warm relationship with Churchill and the British authorities had noticeably cooled. His unwavering demand of Polish pre-war borders had become a formidable obstacle to any dialogue between London and Moscow, and his insistence on solving the Katyn massacre added further pressure to the bickering Allied coalition.

Sikorski had already survived two previous attempts on his life and had almost stubbornly ignored advice not to fly to the Middle East because of a fear of assassination. Many believe that the attempt on his life should have been on his outbound journey as the British Foreign Office in London received an anonymous call two weeks before his actual death, stating that Sikorski had been killed in an aeroplane accident at Gibraltar! What is clear is that parked near to Sikorski's Liberator on the day of the fateful crash was a Soviet plane carrying a delegation headed by Foreign Minister Ivan Maisky to Moscow.

Also stationed at Gibraltar at the time of the crash was the infamous British intelligence agent Harold Adrian Russell 'Kim' Philby, who notoriously defected to Russia in 1963. Additionally, the pilot, the sole survivor, choosing to wear a life vest for the take-off, something he would not normally have done, along with the facts that several of the passengers – including Silorski's daughter – were never found and that the aircraft spent an unusually long time running its engines at the western end of the runway before take-off add further spice to the suggestion of an assassination.

The conspiracy theorists variously implicate the British government, the Soviet authorities, the German secret service and even the Polish government, or combinations of the British and Russian or British and Polish. The implication of the Poles seems the most difficult to understand, but it is clear that by the time of his death some Poles were starting to consider Sikorski too weak a politician, one who would fail in safeguarding the nation's future.

Though none of the allegations have ever been proved it all seems highly suspicious to me. Even now much of the official documentation is sill classified as top-secret and not available for public consumption. Of the Polish veterans I have spoken to on this subject they are all unanimous in their belief that the Russians were solely responsible.

Whatever the reason for the accident, the death of the most prominent leader of the Polish exiles was a severe setback to the Polish cause. Sadly yet another nail had been firmly hammered into the coffin of the Polish people. The fate of those Poles remaining in Poland was unclear and for those like my dad, who were far away from their homes, the future was looking bleaker and bleaker.

Despite the tragedy of Sikorski's death the war continued apace, the Allies were making ground on all fronts and the Polish Army continued to work up towards battle readiness. Four days after Sikoski's death, his deputy, General Kazimierz Sosnkowski, was promoted to Commander-in-Chief of the Polish forces, and two days later on 10 July the Allies, following their success in North Africa, landed in Sicily. The battle for Europe had begun.

As more and more equipment became available the Polish 2nd Corps upped its training; massive infantry exercises and massive artillery firings honed an army so desperate to get involved. My dad's driving too was extended, driving supply and liaison missions between the various Polish Army bases in Iraq, and during this time he made at least one trip to the Iraqi capital of Baghdad.

Time and tide wait for no man, and on 21 July Anders received orders to move his army to Palestine for final training. The following day, as the American 7th Army under General George Patton captured Palermo in Sicily, General Maitland-Wilson informed Anders that he expected the Polish 2nd Corps to be ready for operational duties from 1 January 1944. The Polish Army was finally on its final countdown, and since the British Army was already in Italy, Anders and the men of the Polish 2nd Corps knew their destination. A few days later Benito Mussolini or 'Il Duce', the fascist dictator of Italy, and his Italian government failed; Mussolini was arrested and replaced by another fascist, Marshal Pietro Badoglio, who immediately entered into negotiations with the Allies.

The Polish Army training continued; the soldiers worked hard in difficult conditions, but it seems that they did find the time to let their hair down a little! My dad told me that during this time he was able to buy his first bottle of vodka, something that he hadn't tasted since well before the start of the war. He said that he and a friend got very drunk and when he eventually woke up he was lying on his camp bed, with his official documents under his back; apparently somebody had found him in a ditch and carried him back to his tent.

What he didn't tell me is that he was probably very abusive to the camp sentries on his return to camp. His *zeszyt ewidencyjny* carries an entry in the disciplinary section stating that from 21 to 30 August he was given a ten-day penalty of extra duty in relation to lack of subordination or tactless behaviour towards a non-commissioned officer fulfilling sentry duties! I suspect that he wasn't the only one to succumb to the powers of drink during his time in Iraq!

By September my dad was on the move again. The entire Polish 2nd Corps were on their way to Palestine. Initially their route took them south through the town of Tikrit, birthplace of the legendary Kurdish leader Saladin, but perhaps more famous for another despotic Stalinesque dictator, Saddam Hussein, who was born nearby in 1937. Perhaps as a young boy he witnessed the Polish troops passing through in their massive convoys.

Before long the convoy was travelling west along the well-surfaced Baghdad–Amman road, following the line of the Mosul-Hafa oil pipeline. Passing through the Iraqi towns of Ramadi, Toliahah and Rutbah, the huge convoys crossed into the territory of Transjordan of the British Mandate of Palestine (roughly the modern country of Jordan).

The convoy passed through a desolate desert landscape and through the town of Mafraq before skirting around north of the city of Amman, crossed the River Jordan into Palestine and then travelled south to the latest Polish Army headquarters at 'Kilo 89' near to Gaza. The journey took about a week and the army cooks always went ahead of the main body of the soldiers so that food and accommodation was always ready at each way-point when the soldiers arrived.

My dad continued his driving duties, making visits to most of the large, tented Polish Army camps from the HQ in Gaza to camps at Barbarah, Gedera and Rehovot, historical cities such as Nazareth and Jerusalem, and many of the holy places in the region. I remember my dad talking fondly of his time in Palestine, and the many accounts I have read of the time the Polish 2nd Corps spent there all tell of how the favourable climate, conditions and variety of food raised the soldiers' moods.

The war continued to develop rapidly and on 8 September the surrender of the Italian Army was announced, followed a day later by Allied landings at Salerno and Taranto on mainland Italy. On the 11th the German Army had occupied Rome and a day later in a daring raid, German paratroopers rescued Mussolini using a small Fieseler Fi 156 Storch aeroplane from a hotel in the ski resort of Campo Imperatore in the Gran Sasso d'Italia, high in the Apennine mountains of central Italy. On the 23rd Mussolini had re-established his fascist government in the German-controlled areas of Italy.

By 1 October the Allies had taken Naples and were slowly moving up through Italy towards Rome. Marshal Badoglio concluded his negotiations with the Allies and on the 13th, in a complete switch of allegiance, declared war on Germany.

Things were looking up for the Allies on their war with Germany, but for the Poles diplomacy seemed to be failing! Following the death of Sikorski, the Polish relationship with Russia was no better. In fact with Sosnkowski's absolute insistence on Polish sovereignty and the maintenance of pre-war Polish borders, they continued to deteriorate. Russia's hard stance continued and in meetings in Moscow between 19 and 30 October Anthony Eden, the British Foreign Minister, was told by Molotov in unequivocal terms that Russia considered Poland to have violated the 1941 treaty. Alarm bells were already ringing in the higher echelons of the Polish hierarchy, but there was little that could be done, so despite massive forebodings, the Polish build-up to their involvement in the war continued uninterrupted.

From 13 November my dad was able to take six days' leave. It was his first time of real relaxation for over four years. He was able to visit Jaffa and bought Polish newspapers, was able to listen to the radio in Polish, and was able to speak in Polish with the many Polish Jews who had settled there from Poland.

City/town	Local name	Location	Approx. distance	Country
Jaffa	آفاي	1,300 km south-west of Mosul	32,870 km	Israel (Palestine)

Jaffa is one of the most ancient port cities in the world; its natural harbour has been in constant use since the Bronze Age. It is located south of Tel Aviv on the Mediterranean Sea. Some believe that Jaffa was named after Japheth, one of the three sons of Noah.

While under British Occupation, the 1936–9 Arab Revolt in Palestine inflicted great economic and infrastructural damage on Jaffa. Urban warfare between the British forces and Arab resistance destroyed many of the city's historic narrow alleys and the British Army demolished many houses belonging to Arab resistance.

Despite its heritage, modern-day Jaffa is now mainly considered to be a suburb of Tel Aviv. Its superb location, and years of redevelopment means that Jaffa is now a much sought-after place to live.

It was here that the polish exile and Zionist leader Menachem Begin arrived after fleeing Russia with General Anders and the Polish 2nd Corps. He had been deported from Brest (Brześć) in Poland to Siberia. Upon arrival he deserted the Polish Army and joined the Jewish National Movement.

He soon became commander of the militant Irgun party that played a central role in Jewish military resistance to the British Mandate of Palestine. Eventually he was to become Prime Minister of Israel from 1977 to 1983, and will be remembered for his role in the Camp David Accord in 1978 which lead to the Israel–Egypt Peace Treaty with Egyptian President Anwar Sadat, for which they received the Nobel Peace Prize.

As I've indicated above, when the Polish 2nd Corps arrived in Palestine, many of the Jewish soldiers whom Anders had fought to include in the exodus from the Soviet Union deserted in what was called the 'Anders Aliyah' to join the many Polish Jewish settlements already established there. Some believe that Anders actually facilitated their release, including that of Corporal Begin, as he did not particularly want them in his army because there was a feeling in some areas that some Jews had been almost welcoming of the Soviet arrival in Poland in September 1939. Despite calls from British authorities, the Polish Army did not actively pursue the Jewish deserters, many of whom thanks to their military expertise, contributed to the defence of the Jewish settlement in Palestine, went on to play an important role in the founding of the state of Israel in 1948 and later fulfilled an important role in the creation of the Israel Defence Forces. In 2006 in recognition of his role a memorial to Anders' Army was erected on Mount Zion in Jerusalem.

Back from his break, my dad resumed his driving duties. His work was mainly supply, driving and transporting officers between the various Polish Army camps, firing ranges and locations where exercises and manoeuvres were being conducted.

General Sosnkowski, the Polish Commander-in-Chief, arrived in November to visit his troops. On the 26th he witnessed large-scale Army manoeuvres at a firing range near Be'er Sheva, and standing atop a Sherman tank together with General Anders he addressed the assembled crowd of soldiers, spectators and dignitaries, announcing that the Polish 2nd Corps would be travelling to Italy to finally take part in the war for Europe in the hope of returning to their homes in Poland.

At the same in Tehran, under the codename of Eureka, the first conference of 'The Big Three', Churchill, Roosevelt, and Stalin (the United Kingdom, the United States, and the Soviet Union) in which Stalin was present was convening. The conference, which started on 28 November, lasted four days and centred on Stalin's insistence on a second front in Europe which had originally been set for 1942. Eventually, after lengthy discussions the Allies committed to May 1944, and in return Stalin agreed the Soviets would assist the Allies against Japan once the war in Europe had been concluded.

However, 'in-camera', and in what many now see as the 'Western betrayal of Poland', the emotive issue of Poland's post-war borders was also discussed. In the absence of any Polish representation, Churchill and Roosevelt accepted the Soviet demand that Poland's eastern border should be roughly along the Curzon Line, with Poland receiving some of the German territory to the west and the north. Unfortunately, this bombshell was never communicated to the Polish government and although the destiny of the Poles had been dealt yet another severe blow, they were blissfully (or otherwise) unaware of it.

In total ignorance the training of the Polish Army continued unabated. But on Christmas Eve in the Holy Land, as General Anders attended a Polish Army Christmas mass in Bethlehem with thousands of Polish soldiers, my dad finally succumbed to malaria and was taken to Military Hospital Number 2 in Gaza. Ten days later he was back with his unit, who were already preparing for yet another move.

On the move yet again, the Polish 2nd Corps in huge convoys of trucks and trains travelled west across the border into to Egypt. Ironically, around about the same time in Europe the Red Army, with units of the Polish First Army, were crossing back into Polish territory and the Soviets were finally emerging triumphant following the Siege of Leningrad. The total lifting of the siege occurred on 27 January 1944; it was one of the longest and most destructive sieges of major cities in modern history, and after Stalingrad was the second most lethal. The Soviet government was on a high and wasted no time in increasing their propaganda campaign against the Polish government-in-exile, the Polish 2nd Corps and in particular Generals Anders and Sosnkowski. Sadly, the increasing strength of the Soviet beast and its growing influence over its western allies was being achieved at the expense of the free Poles and their hopes of a return to their homeland.

In early January 1944 most of the Polish 2nd Corps, including my dad, were encamped in the massive Army holding camp at Quassasin located between the Egyptian towns of Ismailiya and Zagazig just to the north-east of Cairo. There they continued with their exercises and training while waiting for their next orders. It was to be their last chance for rest before entering the war as a combat force.

Whilst at Quassasin Anders was visited in December by the famous American General Patton, to whom he apparently replied 'both' when asked who he would attack if surrounded by Germans and Russians, a quote usually attributed to Patton. During the visit they swapped Army formation shoulder patches.

On 30 January 1944 General Anders travelled to Algiers to discuss with General Maitland-Wilson the role of the 2nd Polish Corps. Fears that since Poland was occupied there would be no natural reserve of soldiers to draw from were allayed by Anders, who thought they would be able to supplement his Army with Polish deserters from the German Army who had been pressed into fighting for the Germans. Though Anders was unhappy at the dismissal of his idea of a front through the Balkans, giving his Army a chance to liberate Poland, he was anxious to assist and take on any role assigned to him by his British superiors.

General Maitland-Wilson duly placed the Polish 2nd Corps under General Montgomery's 8th Army, the famous Desert Rats who were already in Italy. Polish units started moving almost immediately, the 3rd Carpathian Rifle Division being the first unit to move to Italy.

My dad wasn't to move for a while and during his stay in Quassasin he was able to visit Cairo several times, both in role as an officer staff driver and also for recreation purposes. He told me that Cairo, and Giza in particular, was a popular destination and like most of his fellow soldiers and friends he visited the pyramids several times. He said that he had climbed the outside of the Great Pyramid of Khufu (Cheops) to get to the top and watch the sunrise. I know it's now not possible to even attempt this, but looking at the size of the blocks it looks extremely difficult and with my dad's fear of heights I'm not sure that I believe him, nice though it would have been.

City/town	Local name	Location	Approx. distance	Country
Cairo	ةرهاقلا	400 km south-west of Jaffa	33,270 km	Egypt

Cairo (al-Qāhirah), famous for the pyramids of Giza, is the administrative capital of Egypt and is one of the world's most populous metropolitan areas. It is located on the banks and islands of the River Nile in the north of Egypt and was founded just to the north of Memphis, the capital of Ancient Egypt.

The oldest parts of the city are to the east of the river where wide boulevards, public gardens and open spaces are loosely based on a model of Paris. The older quarters of the city have developed haphazardly over the centuries and are filled with ancient mosques, small bustling lanes and crowded tenements.

In stark contrast, to the west of the river modern Cairo is dominated by the government buildings, high-rise skyscrapers and modern architecture.

The magnificent splendour of Cairo with its continuous wealth of history covering all the periods of its history, from the Ancient Egyptians (3500–30 BC), the Romans (30 BC–AD 641), the Islamic Conquest (641–1168), Saladin and the Crusades (1168–1250), the Mamluks (1250–1517), the Ottoman Empire (1517–1798), Napoleon Bonaparte and French Expedition (1798–1801), the era of Muhammad Ali (generally considered to be the founder of modern Egypt) and his successors to the present day, together with the colour, customs and culture mean that Cairo is a truly premier city on the global map.

By early February, after nearly eighteen months since leaving the Soviet Union my dad's training was finally complete, and significantly a fleet of Allied ships had moored at the Mediterranean seaport of Alexandria. Once again he packed his few belongings and vacated his tent, his last temporary barracks in desert surroundings, and made the short journey north to Alexandria.

City/town	Local name	Location	Approx. distance	Country
Alexandria	هيردنكسا	200 km north-west of Cairo	33,470 km	Egypt

Alexandria, the Pearl of the Mediterranean, is the second-largest city in Egypt and its largest seaport. It extends for about 32 km along the coast of the Mediterranean Sea in northern central Egypt.

It was named after Alexander the Great, who founded it in about 330 BC, using his chief architect Dinocrates for the project. However, shortly after its foundation Alexander left Egypt for the East and never returned. Despite this the city grew in power and importance and became second only to Rome in size and wealth.

Alexandria is where the famous Egyptian Queen Cleopatra had love affairs with both Julius Caesar and notably Mark Anthony. She bore children to both, and one of the twins born to Mark Anthony was given the name Alexander, after this great city.

When Cairo was given precedence by Egypt's medieval Islamic rulers, Alexandria fell into decline. By the late Ottoman period it had become little more than a small fishing village. The city's revival was started in the mid-nineteenth century by Muhammad Ali, the Ottoman Governor of Egypt, as a part of his early industrialisation program. The current city is Egypt's leading port, a commercial and transportation centre and the heart of a major industrial area where refined petroleum, asphalt, cotton textiles, processed food, paper and plastics are produced.

It is also famous for the colossal lighthouse on the small island of Pharos, one of the Seven Wonders of the Ancient World. Built for the great Pharaoh Ptolemy Soter by Sostrates of Knidos in the third century BC, it is thought to have been up to 150 m high. Illuminated by the sun and mirrors during the day and by fires at night, it was one of the tallest man-made structures built. Sadly, unlike the nearby pyramids it no longer exists; it survived until the fourteenth century when it is believed to have been destroyed in earthquake subsidence. Some of the stonework was incorporated into the harbour fort of Qaitbey, but its most significant lasting legacy is that the word *pharos* is now used globally to describe lighthouse structures.

During his very short stay in Alexandria my dad was able to visit El Alamein, the location of the famous British 8th Army victory over Rommel's Afrika Corps in November 1942. When I was younger I thought that he had actually fought in the battle, but I now know that his time there was very brief, either on visit sightseeing or when driving on official Army business.

In any case, within days of arriving in Alexandria he had boarded one of the cargo ships leased by the British Army. The ship was possibly the *Takiva* or the famous Polish cruise liner the *Batory*.

Around about the time my dad was boarding so too was Wojtek, the Iranian brown bear, who by then had grown to almost 2 m tall and weighed over 200 kg. Initially, the British officers on the dockside refused to allow the bear to embark, citing strict instructions to allow no animals to board.

Wojtek, who had become more of a companion than a pet, was immediately enrolled into the 22nd Transport Division (Artillery Supply) of the Polish 2nd Army Corps, and with the correct paperwork in place was allowed access to board!

Once all the soldiers and equipment were aboard the fleet of ships moved out of the harbour at Alexandria, bound for Italy and direct involvement in the war at last. Protected by Polish cruisers and submarines the convoy sailed along the coast of North Africa and then plied their way in a north-westerly direction through the Mediterranean Sea destined for the southern Italian port of Taranto.

Mediterranean Sea

The Mediterranean Sea is a part of the Atlantic Ocean almost completely enclosed by the land of three continents; on the north by Europe, the south by Africa and on the east by Asia. Because of its near-total enclosure, like the Sea of Japan, it exhibits a minimal tidal flow.

It is made up of several smaller seas, each having its own name, and is only connected to the main body of the Atlantic by the Strait of Gibraltar, which at only 14 kilometres wide determines the limited tidal pattern. The Mediterranean Sea is characterised and immediately recognised by its imposing deep-blue colour, which is especially noticeable around the Greek islands.

The Mediterranean also has a characteristic water circulation, caused since evaporation greatly exceeds the effects of both precipitation and river runoff in the Mediterranean basin. Evaporation is especially high in its eastern half, causing the water level to decrease and salinity to increase eastward. This pressure gradient pushes relatively cool, low-salinity water from the Atlantic across the basin. It warms and becomes saltier as it travels east, then sinks in the region of the Levant (off the coast of Lebanon) and circulates westward, to return to the Atlantic through the Strait of Gibraltar. Thus, seawater flow is eastward in the Strait's surface waters but westward beneath.

The Mediterranean climate is generally one of wet winters and hot, dry summers. Crops of the region include olives, grapes, oranges, tangerines and cork.

It was the most important route for merchants and travellers in ancient times, allowing for trade and cultural exchange between emergent peoples of the region the Mesopotamian, Egyptian, Semitic, Persian, Phoenician, Carthaginian, Greek and Roman cultures.

12

INTO BATTLE AT LAST

Nearly Five Years Since the Invasion of Poland

After four uneventful days crossing the Mediterranean Sea my dad arrived at the seaport of a wet and miserable Taranto. He was at last back in Europe, getting ever nearer to his home country of Poland.

City/town	Location	Approximate distance	Country
Taranto	1,600 km north-west of Alexandria	35,070 km	Italy

Taranto is a fortified coastal city in the south of Italy. It is situated on a rocky islet in the region of Apulia. It is an important commercial port as well as the main Italian naval base. It also has well-developed steel and iron foundries, oil refineries, chemical works, some shipyards for building and maintaining warships, and food-processing factories.

The city lies at the base of the Salentine Peninsula on the northern inlet (Mare Grande) of the Gulf of Taranto. The old part of the city occupies a small island that lies between the Mare Grande and the inner harbour (Mare Piccolo). Newer areas of the city have developed along the adjacent mainland. It gets its name from Taras, the son of Neptune, god of the sea, whose image still adorns the Taranto coat of arms.

Taranto contains several interesting buildings, including a cathedral and castle. It is connected to the mainland by a six-arched bridge and an ancient aqueduct.

Taranto is also the origin of the name of the tarantula spider species, though the name tarantula was originally used for an unrelated species of European wolf spider. The locals, when bitten by these spiders, would frantically dance in order sweat out the poison. The dance was known as the tarantella and the spiders, not surprisingly, became known as tarantulas.

In his first few days in Italy my dad was billeted at the Santa Teresa camp just to the north of Taranto, but on 14 February he transferred units to the 9th Supply Company of the 2nd Armoured Brigade in readiness for his operational duties. He then spent some time honing his driving skills, acclimatising to Italian conditions and ferrying officers between the camps of Santa Teresa, Mottola and the nearby San Basilio on the Taranto to Bari road.

Before long my dad, with his unit, was on the move north to the front. By 17 February they had moved through the coastal city of Bari, along the Adriatic coastal road, and inland again past the war-damaged city of Foggia to the Polish Army camps at Vinchiaturo and Campobasso. On 23 February he was working in the Polish 2nd Corps sector on the River Sangro. Here they were under the command of the British 8th Army, commanded by Lieutenant-General Sir Oliver William Hargreaves Leese, who had replaced General Montgomery after 'Monty' had transferred to the UK on the last day of December 1943 to prepare for the Allied invasion of Normandy. Leese informed Anders that, subject to the result of the battles that were raging in the Cassino area of the River Liri valley, he would probably use the Polish 2nd Corps to assist in operations there.

Though my dad had at last reached the Polish 2nd Corps front line, which stretched for about 60 km along the headwaters of the River Rapido, the southern flank of the Parco Nazionale d'Abruzzo and the headwaters of the River Sangro, the Allies had pushed the Germans to the north and actual real military action was light. Despite this, the sound of distant combat was ever present, and the Polish Army were able to use the relative calm to their advantage for training their observers using a real enemy and also to provide practice for the gunners and computing centres.

During late February and March the weather was atrocious; snow still remained on most of the high ground and wet and muddy roads made transport and troop movement difficult. The Polish 2nd Corps were held in reserve for the British 8th Army and tasked with maintaining the continuity of the front line at Sangro, ensuring communications between the British 8th Army's 5th and 10th Corps. My dad continued driving officers and supplies to the various gun positions and observation posts, most of which were located high in the mountains where the final ascent to them could only be made on foot and sometimes with mules to carry the supplies.

During his time on the Sangro front, my father like many of the Polish 2nd Corps was billeted with Italian families. It was some real comfort for the first time in nearly five long years. The warmth and affection my dad held for Italians stayed with him for the rest of his life. What was less comfortable however was the outlook for Poland, which continued to look grim. The Soviet Union continued to grow in strength and influence. Fierce Soviet propaganda questioned and even ridiculed the Polish government-in-exile and in particular Anders and his army. Britain and America continued to distance themselves from the re-establishment of the pre-war Polish borders, but despite the continuing setbacks it was considered that the greatest possibility of success for the Poles would be if they continued the fight to defeat Hitler's German Army.

My dad was also during this time to make at least one trip to Naples, situated beneath the foreboding backdrop of Mount Vesuvius. The volcano, dormant since 1929, had burst into life on 6 January just as the Polish 2nd Corps was arriving in Italy. It was almost like a welcoming, or perhaps a warning, to the Polish and Allied troops. The massive explosions and dramatic lava flows (which, now solidified but glacier-like, can still be seen to this day), though significant, were small in comparison to those that devastated Pompeii in AD 79, causing havoc in the surrounding areas.

The main eruption was on 18 March after almost a month of relative inactivity. It lasted for about five days and one of the biggest casualties was the American Air Force's 340th Bombardment Group, who were stationed near to Pompeii at the Terzigno airbase.

Though no lives were lost, the volcano totally destroyed nearly ninety North American B-25 Mitchell medium bombers. The ash and tephra that rained down burned the fabric control surfaces, glazed, smashed, melted or cracked the Plexiglas, and even tipped some of the aircraft onto their tails.

Vesuvius has been quiescent since, and as the recorded inactive phases have varied from eighteen months to nearly eight years, the current lull in activity is the longest in nearly 500 years.

Around 23 March General Leese arrived at Anders' headquarters in Vinchiaturo and informed Anders that the British 8th Army had been ordered to breach the German 'Winter Line' in order to open the road to Rome. He went further to confirm that he would like the Polish 2nd Corps to be a key element of his plans and they would be tasked with capturing the German stronghold of Monte Cassino and the surrounding high ground.

I mentioned Monte Cassino right at the very beginning of this narrative and while I'm not going to give detailed descriptions of all the battles the Polish 2nd Corps were involved in, I feel I need to elaborate a little on the build-up to and the battle of Monte Cassino and its significance to the Polish people.

When the Allies landed in Sicily on 10 July, routed the German Army and then landed on the Italian mainland on 9 August, it was the first real sustained Allied offensive in Europe. In some quarters, and by Stalin in particular, this southern front was considered unnecessary and that a direct assault through Western Europe would have been more beneficial. Churchill argued that the operation in Italy would tie up essential German troops and equipment, effectively take Italy out of the war, and also give time for the preparation for the north-western front against Hitler.

Aided by the surrender of the Italian Army, the Allied forces advanced from Reggio at the very toe of Italy, Salerno (near Naples) and Taranto, pushing the German Army further and further north. But as they retreated they created, making maximum use of natural topographic features, a series of defensive lines of fortifications complete with gun pits, concrete bunkers, turreted machine-gun emplacements, barbed wire and minefields. These were collectively known as the 'Winter Line'.

Though there were three major lines, the primary line of fortification was the Gustav Line, which bisected Italy at its narrowest point. It ran from just north of the mouth of the River Garigliano in the Tyrrhenian Sea, through the Aurunci and Apennine Mountains to the mouth of the River Sangro on the Adriatic coast in the east. With the high Apennine Mountains running through the centre, the only route for the advancing Allied armies, intent on the capture of the 'trophy' city of Rome, was either via the unsuitable coastal road (Route 7) or along Route 6 (via Casillini) at the bottom of the River Liri valley, which ran between the Aurunci and Apennine Mountains.

Sitting at the southern entrance to the Liri Valley where the Gustav Line crossed Route 6 was the town of Cassino. This quaint historic market town with its own Roman amphitheatre, coliseum and medieval castle sat in the shadow of the impressive heights of Monastery Hill, with its ancient Benedictine abbey at its peak, which itself sat below the even higher peaks of Monte Castellone and Monte Caira.

German observation posts strategically positioned along high peaks commanded views of the whole of the Liri valley and its approaches. So convinced of its strategic military position behind the aptly named, fast-flowing River Rapido, the German Army considered their fortifications impregnable.

The German Army started to militarise Cassino in the autumn of 1943. They were commanded by the popular but skilful Field Marshal Albert Kesselring, who at the start of the war had commanded the Luftwaffe's Luftflotte 1, which had operated in support of General von Bock's Army Group North during the invasion of Poland in the September of 1939. As the German Army moved into Cassino most of the inhabitants fled. Some retired to the surrounding mountains in the hope of a quick passage of the Allies through the front, others were deported to the nearby communes of the upper province of Frosinone and afterwards transferred to other Italian regions, and some even sought refuge in the seventh-century abbey of Monte Cassino itself, believing that such an historic and religious icon would never be desecrated by the acts of war. Sadly, most of the refugees from Cassino were never to return home.

Kesselring, known as 'Uncle Albert' to his troops, and 'Smiling Albert' to the Allies, though a soldier through and through (his autobiography was entitled *Soldat Bis Zum Letzten Tag* – A Soldier to the Last Day), was also appreciative of culture and heritage. He strove to avoid the needless destruction of architecture and treasures; it is even reported that he had two German soldiers shot for looting at Monte Cassino. He agreed to neither fortify nor occupy the abbey itself in the hope that it wouldn't be targeted and, in foresight, agreed for the catholic Lt-Col Julius Schlegel to organise the removal to Castell St Angelo in Rome for safe storage the majority of the valuable book and art heritage of the monastery. Most of the abbey inhabitants were also persuaded to evacuate, but some remained together with those residents who had sought refuge there.

By mid-January 1944 the Allies, despite having been hindered by bad winter weather, difficult terrain and in particular efficient German defences, had reached to within striking distance of the Gustav Line. The last 11 km alone had taken a staggering six weeks to achieve!

On 17 January, in what is now called 'the First Battle of Monte Cassino', the British X Corps (56th and 5th Divisions) launched an attack across the River Garigliano near to the coast. Two days later the 46th Division attacked further up the river near the village of Sant Ambrogio. Though they met fierce opposition from the German 94th Infantry Division, their commander Generalleutnant Fridolin von Senger und Etterlin was so concerned that Kesselring ordered his 29th and 90th Panzer Grenadier Divisions from Rome as reinforcements to neutralise the British thrust.

On 20 January the American II Corps (141st and 143rd Regiments of the 36th Division) attempted to force a way up the Liri Valley around the town of St Angelo. The German 15th Panzer Grenadier Division was prepared; the river valley was strung with barbed wire and laced with minefields. From their concealed defensive positions they wreaked havoc, inflicing massive losses on the advancing American troops, so much so the Americans referred to the Rapido as the 'Blood River'.

Two days later, on the 22nd, with the two Gustav Line offensives failing, the American commander Mark Clarke under the codename 'Operation Shingle' launched an amphibious landing further up the coast at the city of Anzio. Using the American 3rd Infantry Division of the VI Corps and British 1st Infantry Divisions, he hoped to move rapidly inland to cut the German supply and communication lines south of Rome and hopefully draw German forces from the Cassino area.

Landing at three beachheads, the initial landings were relatively unopposed, with Luftwaffe fighters being the biggest cause for concern. However, the German Army was able to react quickly and the Anzio invasion force was penned into a pocket around Anzio and the nearby town of Nettuno and was unable to effect the breakout as planned.

The Germans made use of the Krupp K-5 rail-mounted Super Cannons which fired massive 255-kg, 280-mm artillery shells and were located over 40 km away. These beasts were stored in railway tunnels to avoid Allied aircraft and only moved into the open for firing. Two were used throughout the Battle of Anzio, they were known to the Allies as 'Anzio Annie', and 'Anzio Express'. They were later captured by US forces and shipped back to America, where one is displayed to this day at the United States Army Ordnance Museum in Maryland.

Back on the Gustav Line, on the 24th the American II Corps 34th Infantry Division launched an attack across the flooded Rapido just north of the town of Cassino in an attempt to gain a foothold in the mountains above Cassino. At the same time the French Expeditionary Corps moved into the mountains north of Monte Cassino.

German defence was carried out by 90th Panzer Grenadier Division, which had fought against Montgomery's British 8th Army in North Africa. It was reinforced by the paratroopers of the German 1st Parachute Division, who were reputedly the 'best division in the German Army'. Atrocious weather added to the difficulties; in particular heavy rain restricted armour to paths laid with steel matting, mud and flooded craters made all forms of transport difficult, but after eight days of bloody fighting across the Rapido valley they had only made good ground in the hills above Cassino. Unfortunately, the Germans were able to repel all attempts against the high ground of Monastery Hill and the significant vantage point of Monte Calvario (better known as Hill 593). After a final unsuccessful assault on Monastery Hill and Cassino town, the Americans were withdrawn on 11 February.

The French Expeditionary Corps had made good initial progress fighting in the mountains to the north against the German 5th Mountain Division. Moroccan and French forces captured positions on the slopes of Monte Cifalco and units of the 3rd Algerian Division had captured Monte Belvedere and Colle Abate. However, a request for reserves to maintain the momentum was refused and by 31 January the French assault had ground to a halt.

It seems that the Allies, who were battle weary (weary, though, doesn't seem to be a strong enough word), physically exhausted and having suffered huge numbers of casualties were tantalisingly close to achieving their objectives. The Germans were in fact also near to breaking point and the Allies were let down by the lack of adequate reserves and poor command decisions. Disagreements between the Allied commanders present since the landings in Sicily were becoming an obstacle to a co-ordinated effort; the American General Mark Clark in particular faced particular criticism. Despite Churchill having worries about the Americans withdrawing from the 'Southern Theatre' he criticised the lack of an Anzio breakout with the famous 'I thought we'd hurled a wild cat on to the shore, but we ended up with a stranded whale' speech, following which the American commander in charge at Anzio, General Lucas, was relieved of his duties.

Despite the setbacks and the continuing poor weather the Allies pressed forward with a renewed offensive. The second Battle of Monte Cassino, codenamed Operation Avenger began on 13 February. The 4th Indian Division continued the attack on Monastery Hill along the mountain ridges from the north while the 2nd New Zealand Division attacked along the railway track from the south-east.

Both assaults battled against heavy and determined defences, but the 4th Indian Division in particular struggled along the ridges and valleys north of Monte Cassino in terrain in full view of the German defenders and exposed to accurate artillery fire. So devastating were the German defences to the advancing Indian contingent that the last section of the valley between the rocky crests of Phantom Ridge and Snake's Head Ridge was appropriately named 'Death Valley', but even more significantly the acting commander of the 4th Indian Division, Brigadier Harry Dimoline, considered his task so hard that he requested fighter bombers to blast holes in the abbey walls to aid the advancing soldiers.

Like most controversial decisions made in war, truth is shrouded in rumour, conjecture and cover-up. The decision to bomb the abbey at Monte Cassino was no exception. It appears that most of the Allied commanders could not believe that the abbey had not been occupied by the Germans who were using it as an observation post for artillery spotting, but reports of German occupiers could not be categorically proved. What is clear is that Kesselring had an agreement not to enter the abbey while there were still monks living there, and as was known a small number remained together with some refugees from the town of Cassino. In addition Kesselring's most senior commander, the enigmatic Generalleutnant Fridolin von Senger und Etterlin, who had studied at Oxford University in England and bizarrely was a known anti-Nazi and anglophile, was also a lay member of the Benedictine order. It's inconceivable he would have risked the first and most famous of Saint Benedict's monasteries, which was one of Europe's most significant, spectacular and sacred religious sites.

What appears to have transpired was that there was a complex series of requests though Dimoline to the commander of the New Zealand Corps, Lt-Gen. Bernard Freyberg (who was convinced that the German defenders must be using the abbey), to General Mark Clark of the V Army and ultimately to Commander-in-Chief of Allied Armies in Italy, General Sir Harold Alexander. There may have been some misunderstanding and/or even misinterpretation of messages, and it seems that at first General Mark Clark refused the request, but eventually the bombing of the abbey was approved. On the 14th the American V Army, respectful of the remaining monks and Italian civilians still occupying the abbey, fired leaflets into the abbey warning of the impending armageddon.

In a curious twist of history Saint Benedict had predicted back in the sixth century that the abbey would be destroyed four times. In February 1944 the abbey had been destroyed three times previously; the last destruction had been at the hands of Napoleon in 1799!

During the morning of 15 February there was a relative lull in the fighting around the abbey. It was a beautiful, clear, sunny day. According to the German paratrooper Rudolf Valentin some of the German defenders on the high ground of Colle St Angelo overlooking the abbey were enjoying the break and taking in the sun, when wave after wave of American bombers darkened the sky.

At 9.45 a.m., not the fighter bombers requested, but 142 Boeing B-17 'Flying Fortress' four-engined heavy bombers of the 2nd Bombardment Group from the airbase at Foggia, forty-seven North American B-25 'Mitchell's and later forty Martin B-26 'Marauder' twin-engined medium bombers from the 319th Bombardment Group Decimomannu airbase on Sardinia unleashed 1,150 tons of high explosives and incendiary bombs onto the mountain-top abbey and the surrounding area.

Between bombing runs, the American II Corps artillery pounded the mountain-top and during the afternoon and the following day a further fifty-nine fighter bombers and continued artillery barrages turned the once-great abbey into a pile of rubble.

Despite the fact that media had been invited to witness the destruction and there had been frantic efforts through the previous night at the Vatican by Pope Pius XII to avoid the bombing of the abbey, the attack had been very poorly co-ordinated. Brigadier Dimoline, having initiated the request for the destruction of the abbey, tried desperately to get it delayed until such a time he could get his troops in a position to maximise the potential of the air raid, but the Allied troops positioned on the front line surrounding the abbey were taken as much by surprise as the German defenders. To make matters worse the inaccuracies of the high-altitude bombing wreaked havoc on the Allied and Axis soldiers alike, and the destruction of the abbey did not result in a single loss of life of a German soldier in the abbey itself. The only casualties, sadly, were Italian civilians who had sought refuge there.

With hindsight it seems that the destruction of the abbey provided no military value at all to the Allies. In fact the Germans, now removed from their obligation to preserve the abbey from the war, were able to swarm into the ready-made cover of the ruins and turn it into the fortress and observation post that the Allies had been trying to avoid.

The day after the bombing, though unprepared, elements of the 4th Indian Division pressed home an attack on the key point of Hill 593 along Snake's Head Ridge. Fierce resistance along the exposed ridge led to a massive loss of life and supply to the front lines using mules traversing up the steep goat tracks at night from the village of Caira were woefully inadequate, ensuring the attack failed. During the night of 17 February the 4th Indian Division made a further attempt on Hill 593 while at the same time elements of the Gurkha Rifles attempted a direct assault on the ruined monastery across the slopes and ravines of Monastery Hill. Despite brutal and often hand-to-hand fighting, there were additional heavy Allied casualties and the attacks once again failed. On 18 February Lt-Gen. Bernard Freyberg called a halt to the attacks on Monastery Hill.

Down at Cassino the 2nd New Zealand Division, using their 28th (Maori) Battalion, had succeeded in advancing along the narrow railway-line embankment and capturing Cassino railway station. But the continued torrential rain, compounded by the Germans having destroyed a dam and flood barriers on the River Rapido, causing extensive flooding, ensured that the isolated New Zealanders had no armoured support or any heavy artillery against the German counter-attack. After coming under counter-attack their forward position was clearly untenable, so during the afternoon of the 18th they too were withdrawn. After a mere three days the Second Battle of Monte Cassino had come to an end.

Bad weather delayed the Third Battle of Monte Cassino and many people consider that after 18 February there was a lull in the action, but I don't think those poor unfortunates, both Allied and Axis, still on the hills and slopes above Cassino thought there was much of a lull. Sporadic skirmishes, re-supplying, digging in, consolidating positions and removing the dead in atrocious weather continued unabated. Even those behind the Allied lines in terrible conditions in wet and muddy trenches, under constant observation from the heights of Monte Cassino and periodically harassed by mortar and artillery fire, were permanently kept on their toes.

Poor and in particular wet weather delayed the start of the third battle until 15 March when the forecast was for three days of dry weather. Under the code name of 'Bradman bats today' the battle began, starting with the New Zealand troops being withdrawn from the perimeter of Cassino town, then from 8.30 a.m., for nearly four hours, wave after wave of bombers reduced the historic and once beautiful town to a pile of rubble and dust.

After the bombers had departed artillery fire continued to pound the town and the New Zealand II Division advanced into the town behind a 'Creeping Barrage' of fire (coincidentally this technique had been first used by the German Army during the Battle of Lake Narocz in the spring of 1916 and known as the *feuerwalze* or 'fire roller'). The German defenders, having survived the bombing, were quick to reorganise their defences. As had happened after the bombing of the abbey, the bombing of the town had created as many opportunities for the defending Germans as it had for the attacking New Zealanders. Once again, just like along Snake's Head Ridge and the railway track, the Allied attack was forced down a narrow route, making an easy target. Route 6 from the south takes a sharp left turn in Cassino at the base of Castle Hill, where the German strongpoint of the Continental Hotel was located. Using a Sturmgeschütz III (StuG III) tracked assault gun the German paratroopers were able to wreak havoc on the attacking New Zealand soldiers.

Vicious fighting took place throughout the wrecked town. Advance was only made by fighting at close quarters, hand to hand, and from house to house; there were numerous instances of the same building being occupied by both sides at the same time! Despite the prediction of good weather for three days, torrential rain started again, filling the deep craters with water and severely restricting the advance of heavy armour, soaking the radio equipment, rendering it unserviceable and restricting vital communications. The rain also whipped up the large amounts of dust into a thick, sticky, gluey mess, making advancing on foot extremely difficult and laborious.

Despite the continuing difficulties and determined resistance, the New Zealand soldiers pressed on and were successful in capturing the significant vantage point of Castle Hill, and by 17 March a division of the Gurkha Rifles managed to take Hangman's Hill, which was just below and less than 300 m from the abbey itself.

Up on the hills above Cassino Indian and New Zealand engineers (under the cover of darkness) had extended the steep goat track leading from the village of Caira between Snake's Head and Phantom Ridges towards the abbey itself. Significantly widened and strengthened and by then known as Cavendish Road, it enabled on 19 February the New Zealand 20th Armoured Brigade to launch 'Operation Revenge', a surprise armoured assault on the abbey itself. Unfortunately, even as the tanks trundled up the steep slopes towards the abbey the Germans had mounted a successful counter attack and driven the Allied soldiers from both Hangman's and Castle Hills.

Poor Allied co-ordination and planning ensured a failure. The Allied units that had successfully taken Hangman's and Castle Hills were supposed to move on and support the tank attack on Monte Cassino; additionally Lt-Gen. Freyberg had not sent any additional infantry along Cavendish Road to support the tank attack either. The Germans were taken completely by surprise as the Sherman tanks burst from the north onto the relatively flat ground and viciously attacked the fortified farm at Albaneta (Masseria Albaneta). Though the tanks were initially able to get the better of the resistance without loss of life, the Germans defenders, in the absence of Allied infantry to support the tanks, were soon able to re-establish their defences at Albaneta and not only withstand the attack, but knock out all the attacking tanks by the afternoon. One Sherman, however, commanded by a Lieutenant Renall, passed Albaneta farm and beneath the strongpoint of Hill 593 to get within firing distance of the abbey itself before the tank was stopped and Renall sadly killed.

Once again the Allied hierarchy was in disarray. The New Zealand tank attack could, with proper coordination and planning, easily have launched a successful attack on the abbey itself and taken command of the high ground overlooking the Liri Valley. But it seems that in addition to the lack of supporting infantry and poor planning, there had been no re-supplies of ammunition or fuel and bizarrely no specific objectives given to the tank crews, leading to confusion and frustration.

Neither the 4th Indian Division on the slopes nor the 2nd New Zealand Division in the town of Cassino itself were faring any better. Heavy loss of life in difficult conditions prompted one German paratrooper, a veteran of France and the Eastern Front, to suggest the fighting was worse than at Stalingrad! By 23 March the Allies were so depleted and exhausted that Freyburg called off the attack and the Third Battle of Monte Cassino had ended once again in failure for the Allies.

The 'soft underbelly' predicted by Churchill was proving not to be the case; the failures at Monte Cassino couldn't continue. The Fourth Battle, codenamed Operation Diadem, would be conducted with planning and resources that had been lacking in the previous attempts. No longer would uncoordinated attacks take place on narrow fronts, time would be taken to ensure full use would be made of Allied infantry, air power and artillery. In order to achieve this, large Allied troop movements were required including the redeployment of the British 8th Army, and hence the Polish 2nd Corps from the Adriatic arena, which takes us back to the meeting between Leese and Anders at Vinchiaturo around about 23 March.

The Polish 2nd Corps started leaving for the Cassino area almost immediately, moving out in small units to maintain secrecy and surprise. My dad eventually departed the Sangro front on 23 April, leaving from the town of Cardito to Colli a Volturno, where the Polish Army had fought some of their first skirmishes on arriving in Italy, then on through the towns of Montaquila and finally Roccavindola. His new temporary base was at a holding area near the Bridge of Twenty-Five Arches over the Volturno River. The area had been hard won by the American 34th Division at the beginning of November when the Volturno had formed the first line of defence in the Winter Line. It wasn't the first historic battle that the Volturno had seen; it had previously been the site of fighting over eighty years before in 1860, during the famous wars for Italian unity when the revolutionary politician Giuseppe Garibaldi had defeated the Neapolitans there.

As the bulk of the soldiers continued to work up to battle readiness my dad continued his driving duties, making trips between the staging area at the Bridge of Twenty-Five Arches, the Polish Army base at Campobasso, and the large multinational Army base at Venafro. So much Allied traffic passed through this quaint mountain village, strategically located en route to Cassino, that it often became a vehicle bottleneck with long traffic jams.

Polish troops had started replacing British troops on the front line around 19 April and my dad soon began to transport supplies to support the front line. Before long he was driving along the narrow roads to the Allied forward supply depot at Acquafondata.

My dad was a driver throughout his entire career in the Polish 2nd Corps, he never used a weapon in either anger or defence (even the picture of my dad in the picture section with a rifle appears to be in an arcade or shooting gallery). While most military recognition goes to those that are quite rightly most deserving of it, especially the front-line infantry, the part played by the support services like drivers is often considered inglorious and goes unrecognised. But the work performed in the background often requires a massive effort and total devotion to duty, even though any reward or glory may be reflected from those at the front line. Without the devotion to task of the likes of the supply drivers, others wouldn't be able to carry out their duties.

So my dad, and I suspect most of the new Polish drivers, after the relative space and freedom of driving in the deserts, found Italy a nightmare. Driving skills developed in the unpressured environment of the deserts of the Middle East, in daylight on broad, empty and usually dry roads, were quickly put to the test in Italy. From landing at Taranto they had to adapt to negotiating the twisting, narrow, muddy and congested roads of the Italian winter. Even the short time he spent supporting the Sangro front line, though sometimes difficult, was nothing to what he was about to experience in the build-up to the Fourth Battle of Monte Cassino.

The main roads were usually not so bad if often busy, but they were few and far between. The bulk of the driving was on narrow heavily used tracks often damaged by war, sometimes in deep valleys and sometimes along narrow precipitous ridges, up and down steep and winding tracks, through small villages and usually in appalling weather. Delays were frequent; any attempt to make way by moving off the tracks would result in vehicles getting bogged down and if a vehicle broke down on a mountain track it would often be simply manhandled over the side. Much of the driving was done at night and roads that approached the front lines could only be negotiated at night and in total darkness. His driving experience could be described as total.

The most forward depot that could be approached in daylight was at Acquafondata, about 10 km north-east of Cassino. This small mountain village, hidden from the German observation posts in the mountains of the Gustav Line, following a fierce battle had become the main staging depot for supplying the Allied front-line troops. It was shared by the many nationalities of the Allied forces but particularly by the French, New Zealand, Indian and Polish Armies.

A problem soon discovered by the French Expeditionary Forces in January as they attacked near to the Rapido was that their supplies had to come along a single steep and narrow road from Acquafondata to Sant'Elia Fiumerapido. This road, in itself difficult to drive in the winter conditions with steep gradients and tight bends, was in full view of German observers on Monte Cassino, Monte Caira and to the north Monte Cifalco. German artillery constantly hampered supply convoys, causing not only loss of men, vehicles and supplies but causing secondary accidents and pile-ups. Transit was only possible only under the cover of darkness. The French immediately named the road 'la route de mort', the Road of Death. During a particularly fierce fight near the Rapido north of Cassino, a detachment of French forces were forced back into a valley near to the town of Portella. The steep sides protected them from both the German observation posts and their artillery and it was discovered that the valley ran back to near Acquafondata. French engineers quickly created a track, and within a short space of time trusty mules, which had played and were to continue to play such an important role in the Italian campaign, were being led down the steep track fully laden with supplies. So steep and difficult to negotiate was the track in parts, falling from nearly 1,000 m at Acquafondata to about 200 at Portella, it became known as the 'Ravin de l'Inferno'.

Development of the route continued to enable light transport, and when in April the New Zealand forces took over from the French in preparation for Operation Diadem they set about maintaining and extending the route for jeeps and trucks and renamed it to the Inferno Track. Significantly they also developed a huge forward supply depot for the storage of ammunition, fuel, food and fodder for the mules, out of sight of the German observers at the bottom of the track near to Portella, which they named Hove Dump.

By the time my dad arrived towards the end of April Acquafondata was heavily fortified and a busy hub of military activity. During the day columns of trucks laden for the forward depots and the front-line troops backed up for miles waiting for the cover of night. My dad was to take part of this period of intense activity, driving up and down the dangerous narrow track with its very steep gradients and tight turns often on roads blasted from the steep valley rock-face.

A complex traffic control network linked by telephone was established and operated by the New Zealanders to regulate the flow of traffic to Hove Dump by way of the Inferno Track, the Road of Death (by then known as the North Road) and a smaller, even more northerly road called the Ancina Track. Nobody could proceed without an appropriate pass and most of the time traffic could only proceed in one direction.

Driving the Inferno Track was considered difficult, and though I don't remember my dad as having been a particularly good driver, he must have been on top of his game during this period of his life. It appears that it wasn't so much as a drive down the Inferno Track as a crawl down; reports suggest that most of the time only the lowest gears could ever be used. Despite being mainly hidden from enemy observers with exposed areas protected with camouflage nets, driving, especially at night, had to be done with extreme care at all times. There are several reports of drivers misjudging sharp bends or ledges and driving over the edge. When the weather was bad driving was particularly taxing. If any vehicle broke down the instructions were simply to push it over the edge; nothing was going to be allowed to hold up the flow.

Despite the moon occasionally providing enough light for comparatively easy driving, at night and in the wet it was particularly challenging. With no lights, which were disconnected to remove the temptation of using them, often white tape along the roadside or white markings on the bumper of the vehicle in front were the only ways of following the track. On one occasion a convoy was particularly slow, and it was found that the inexperienced driver in the lead vehicle had placed a man out in front with a white towel around his head walking ahead. On another occasion a New Zealand supply convoy had covered three-quarters of the distance on a return journey when it came up against a stationary Polish convoy. The Polish drivers had decided it was too dark to drive any further, and were sound asleep and refused to budge until the New Zealanders brandished weapons and threatened to use them.

According to P. W. Bates in his *Official History of New Zealand in the Second World War 1939–45: Supply Company*, it seems that the New Zealanders weren't so impressed with the quality of the Polish driving. Maybe like my dad they were mostly relative novices; 'Perhaps the greatest danger, however, was that the North Road and Inferno Track were much used by Polish and Indian drivers who seemed to be in bitter competition for the title of World's Worst Driver.'

By the time convoys had reached Hove Dump, there was usually time for some sleep, as the return journey couldn't be made until all the downward convoys had arrived. So exhausted were some of the drivers when they arrived at Hove Dump (and similarly when they arrived back to Acquafondata) that on many occasion they were found fast asleep in their driving positions immediately after they had parked up.

In the beginning Hove Dump was concealed by the high sides of the valley from view of the German observers and the Allied stockpiling and distribution went on unseen and protected from shelling. However, as the Polish Army moved ever nearer to battle readiness their dump at the lower end of the valley, where the river bend took a turn to the south and towards the Cassino area, grew and began to protrude into the view of a German observation post. Disaster struck on 7 May following a night of shelling by heavy guns throughout the Sant'Elia Fiumerapido area. Hove Dump was busy in preparation for the night's convoys back to Acquafondata when a shell hit the dump late in the morning and started a fire which ignited a stockpile of ammunition. Once the German gunners realised they had hit an ammunition dump they opened up with a full artillery barrage. Hove Dump was completely destroyed, several soldiers were killed and many more were injured. Hove Dump was no longer suitable as a staging area and Acquafondata once again became the most forward supply depot. My dad then started supplying directly to the forward staging posts as advance units of the Polish 2nd Corps had been moving to their forward positions as early as 1 May.

After nearly two months of planning and preparation, D-Day for Operation Diadem, the Fourth Battle of Monte Cassino, was set for 11 May when better weather, less mud and dryer ground would enable a more effective use of heavy armour. Covert redeployment of troops in small units under cover of the night and decoy tanks positioned along the front north to the Adriatic ensured that Kesselring believed he was only facing six Allied Army divisions at Cassino when in fact thirteen were poised to attack on a front over 50 km long from the north of the town to the Tyrrhenian Sea. Additionally, misinformation led him to believe that another amphibious assault was about to take place north of Rome, tying up his reserves and preventing them from being used to help defend the Gustav Line.

The Polish Army was given the high ground above the abbey to attack. They were positioned between the 10th British Corps to their north and the 13th British Corps to the south and tasked with taking the hills around Monte Cassino, including the abbey itself, and then pushing on to link up with the 13th British Corps as they advanced up the Liri valley. Their task was far from easy; they were up against the German 1st Parachute Division (reputed to be the best regiment in the German Army), who were dug into fortified bunkers, excellent defensive positions all along the frontline.

The attitude of the Polish soldiers, who were fighting for the liberation of their homes, family and history was clear to the Allied comrades who in the main were fighting because their politicians had decided to go to war.

Polish sappers had, under cover of the night, been constructing, maintaining and preparing approach roads, gun positions, laying over 100 km of telephone lines, sorting thousands of rounds of ammunition and laying camouflage nets under conditions of unceasing harassing fire. The access route up to the high ground, Cavendish Road, was itself improved, enabling it to support the heavy equipment of the armoured units.

Polish artillery batteries were established in their firing positions, and infantry units started moving from their holding locations behind the front lines around the village of Portella to their mountain positions from the middle of April. The 5th Kresowa Infantry Division moved across the Rapido, through the village of Caira, up Cavendish Road (by then known to the Poles as Droga Polskich Saperow – Polish Sappers' Road), to their starting positions on the high ground around the northerly Phantom Ridge (Grzbiet Widmo or simply Widmo to the Poles), Colle Sant' Angelo and Hill 575.

The 3rd Carpathian Rifle Division crossed the Rapido near the ruined Carabinieri barracks at Villa, part-way between Cassino and Caira, before making their way to battle positions on and around Snake's Head Ridge (Głowa węża).

Veteran mortar crew soldier Romuald Lipinski (personal communication), originally from Brześć (now Brest in Belarus), of the 12th Podolski Lancers (3rd Carpathian Rifle Division) recalls his journey to and time at the front before the battle:

We came to the Cassino area on April 30, 1944. Our temporary camp was in an olive orchard, few kilometres from the Cassino town. It was about 4 o'clock in the afternoon, when I went to the edge of the orchard and took a look at the monastery. There was a valley in front of me, maybe 4 kilometres wide and at the other end of the valley there were rather steep mountains, about 500 feet high. To the left, I could see a powerful mountain, covered with smoke, and the ruins of once beautiful monastery.

We were told to deliver to the headquarters all papers that could identify us by name or by the regiment. All personal papers, letters to our families, documents etc., had to be collected and left with the regimental office. The only thing that we were allowed to retain were the dog tags, and the equipment that consisted of one blanket, mess kit, and of course, our side arms, in my case my rifle, and ammo.

We were given sneakers, or sometimes rubber boots and, I think it was 31 April, as soon as it became dark, we started our march towards the hills. We were told that any talk while marching is forbidden, because the enemy could hear it and that would bring on us artillery fire. Truck and carrier drivers and regimental administration remained with the headquarters.

The 3rd Division, 'Karpacka' went through the wooden bridge over the fast-flowing Rapido River in the area of the Barracks. That was on the night of May 1. There on a small square by the barracks, we waited for about forty-five minutes for the transport of mules to come down from the hills. The path was so narrow that the two columns could not be there at the same time. Climbing the hills outside of the foot path was impossible due to land mines scattered everywhere. We waited for the convoy on the small yard near the barracks, packed like sardines, for about half of an hour and then resumed our trip. When we climbed far enough that the last men from our regiment were leaving our waiting area by the barracks, a few artillery or mortar shells exploded right where our regiment was not long ago. If they did that a little earlier that would be a massacre because there were several hundred of us, shoulder to shoulder.

It was difficult to orient myself where we were at that time. On the basis of what I read about our movements during that period we must have been somewhere in the area of the Great Bowl (Wielka Miska). After two days we were moved, during night of course, to the left end of the Polish forces, to the hills almost overlooking the town of Cassino. Further to the left of us were some troops from the XIII British Corps.

We knew that there will be an offensive on the monastery, and that we will be playing a major role. Being in the mortar platoon we were not in the most advanced positions, but we were quite close to the enemy. Our shelter was camouflaged and could not be seen by Germans, but we had to walk with our heads down, otherwise there was an immediate fire. Our line platoons were so close to Germans that they could throw hand grenades at them. Sometimes, when our advanced positions required us to fire on Germans, some of our shells landed among our own troops due to vicinity to Germans. Yet, they did not allow us to fire further from them because, they claimed, our firing would be behind the enemy lines. There was always a shortage of food and water. Everything had to be brought by mules or in the final stage by men. Sometimes the mules were scattered around on the way up by German fire, got blown up on the mines, and only a fraction of the supplies arrived.

The area was a living testimony of what war is all about. There was not one tree that did have its branches green with leaves. There were only naked limbs, stumps, sticking out here and there. Grass has disappeared also. Bare rocks, covered with dust, unfriendly, were everywhere. Also, there was a testimony of what was there in the past – dead bodies. Some were half-decomposed, some half-covered with dust or whatever dirt could be scraped from the surface, in most cases, they were covered with lime. These were the reminders of the ferocious fighting that was going there for four months, since January, when the American 34th and 36th Divisions made the first assault, crossed the Rapido river just to be decimated by the Germans. Both of these fine divisions practically ceased to exist as a fighting force. The entire history of the battle could be read from these corpses. There were corpses of the Americans, Germans, Gurkhas, British soldiers, some with their faces half-eaten by insects, mice or other animals, darkened by time, empty eyes, with only teeth shining. Odor from these decomposing bodies was suffocating. They were all quiet now, resting in their eternal sleep after the dance of death a few months ago. Every time I looked at one of them a sad thought was going through my mind: when will I be like them? In this situation I realised that the odds are against me, that it is just a matter of time when my number will come up and sooner or later I will be looked at just the way I looked at these dead men, who at one time were young, vigorous, full of life and hopes for future. And look at them now.

And flies. They were big, fat, gorging themselves on the dead, decomposing bodies. Stink of death was everywhere. And there, down below was that beautiful valley full of red poppies. At times it was hard to realise the contrast: here an atmosphere of death and destruction and there beauty, peace and quiet. I thought: how these two worlds can coexist sided by side. But that is how it was.

My dad continued his supply and officer-driving duties, and initially remained behind the forward lines. His driving though was being tuned to the dryer conditions; as the tracks dried out he perfected techniques of cornering without creating clouds of tell-tale dust which could alert the German observers and bring down a barrage of artillery fire, a technique much appreciated by the officers as they were being driven close to the front line.

In the days leading up to the 11th, and particularly as the start time approached, pressure even for my dad, a so called non-combatant, increased and the tension was so intense it could be physically felt. Though he hadn't been in the town itself yet he'd arrived before the symbolic town of Cassino.

City/town	Location	Approximate distance	Country
Cassino	450 km north-west of Taranto	35,520 km	Italy

Cassino is located part-way between Rome and Naples at the foot of Monte Caira in the Apennine mountain range near the confluence of the Rivers Rapido, Gari and Liri. Today, Cassino is home to the University of Cassino, a huge FIAT motor car assembly plant and is a commercial and agricultural centre.

The modern town is on the site of the ancient town of Casinum of the ancient Volsci people, who inhabited the lower slopes of the mountain. Casinum passed into Roman control in 312 BC and developed into a prosperous and popular commune. Mark Anthony, the famed lover of Cleopatra, Roman politician and loyal friend of Gaius Julius Caesar, had a villa here, and the impressive, almost circular amphitheatre erected by Ummidia Quadratilla with five entrances still exists. Casinum was superseded by the medieval town of San Germano, whose name was officially reverted back to Cassino in 1863.

The abbey, which dominates the landscape and presides over the surrounding area, was founded by Saint Benedict in around AD 529 and was built on the remnants of a Roman fortification and pagan altar. Much is written about the history of Saint Benedict and the huge abbey, both of which play a crucial role in the development of Christianity globally. To this day the Rule of St Benedict is the most common and influential Rule used by monasteries and monks, nearly 1,500 years after its writing.

Cassino, once a quaint historic city with a castle, large villas, wide roads, a coliseum as well as an amphitheatre, was almost totally destroyed during the Allied advance on Rome. The sprawling new town with its unappealing, uniform, post-war concrete structures was rapidly rebuilt south-east of its original location.

13

MONTE CASSINO AND BEYOND

Success on the Battlefront But Continued Uncertainty on the Home Front

The attack began at 23.00 on 11 May with a massive Allied artillery barrage along the entire front. By all accounts it was an impressive display. Richard Flemington in his book *They Came to a Monastery – The Final Battle* describes the 'flashes from distant guns lighting the valley with lurid, dramatic beauty' while Romuald Lipinski from his position just below Widmo was clearly moved as he looked back towards the Polish artillery positions: 'I never saw anything like it. The entire area where the olive orchards were was in constant fireworks. I saw similar pictures of the artillery barrage in movies, about the battle of El Alamein, in Africa. One could hear the noise of artillery shells in the air.' Matthew Parker in his book *Monte Cassino – The Story of the Hardest-Fought Battle of World War Two* describes an artillery officer's account as 'the most exciting and exhilarating experience I have ever had. The roar of the guns is so deafening that you can shout at the man standing next to you and still not be heard.'

Polish guns pounded German artillery positions for forty minutes before targeting infantry positions. At first the Germans didn't respond, but after a while they replied with an equally savage barrage. By 00.30 the attack was in full motion in all Allied sectors. At 01.00 on 12 May infantry units of the 3rd Carpathian Rifle Division started to move south from their 'rejon Wyczekiwania' (waiting area) on Snake's Head Ridge towards Hills 593 and 569. After about half an hour they had reached the farm house just below Snake's Head Ridge that had been used as a Regimental Aid Post (RAP) for all Allied troops since the first attempt back in January. The house was known by all the Allied armies as the 'Doctor's House'; now returned to farm dwellings, it still remains known by its wartime name to this day. Amid appalling loss of life of First World War proportions, the Polish Army pressed on towards their key objectives of the high points of Hills 593 and 569.

The 5th Kresova Division simultaneously attacked along Phantom Ridge in an attempt to prevent the Germans units occupying it from providing flanking fire to the defenders of Snake's Head Ridge. Between the two ridges high hopes had been raised for the Polish tanks as they moved along Polish Sappers' Road, but as they reached the narrow gorge between the southerly ends of the two ridges, known to the Poles as Gardziel (Throat), they were severely hampered by anti-tank mines, laid after the shock New Zealand tank attack in March. Most of the Polish tanks very quickly succumbed to mines despite one Sherman of the Pulk 4 Pancerny (4th Armoured 'Skorpion' Regiment of the 2nd Armoured Brigade) getting to within firing distance of the dreaded Albaneta farm.

German defensive positions were superbly located on the high ground protecting, from multiple positions, every possible direction of approach. The description in *The Battle of Six Nations* compares the two rings of defences to Roman amphitheatres, where everyone in the audience could see everyone else. Each defence could take part in battle for any other position on the ring. It would require the capture of half the positions on the ring simultaneously to achieve success.

The Allied bombardment had, it seems, done little damage to the German defenders who had been protected in deep concrete-reinforced bunkers and caves. Once the Allied artillery bombardment had stopped they emerged and were able to wreak havoc on the Polish troops supported by their artillery teams using dreaded and destructive Nebelwerfers. These were essentially multi-barrelled smoke launchers converted to fire mortar shells six at a time. Their very distinctive whining noise earned them their nickname of 'moaning minnies' or to the Poles 'roaring cows'.

The fighting along Widmo was as ferocious as anywhere, but the 5th Kresova Division stubbornly struggled foreward in desperate, ruthless and often hand-to-hand combat. By 02.00 both Hills 593 and 569 were taken, but holding onto them was impossible as the German paratroopers counter-attacked again and again. Fighting went on through the day and both Hills changed hands several times, but the huge loss of life on both sides was clearly was unsustainable and by the evening of the 12th most Polish units were withdrawn to their starting positions while Anders reorganised his shattered force. Some unfortunate, isolated soldiers remained trapped in their forward locations unable to return. Tadeusz Matalski of the 3rd Carpathian Rifle Division (personal communication) described his terrifying ordeal where, without any supplies, he had to crawl on his back from his Sangar (rudimentary protection created from loose rocks) to collect wild berries while enemy bullets whizzed frighteningly around him.

To the south of the Polish attack the British XIII Corps (8th Army) in hard fighting had struggled to get across the Rapido. Tanks and infantry inched their way forward against determined German defenders. Towards the coast the American II Corps (5th Army) made little progress, but French Expeditionary Corps achieved their objectives and were fanning out in the Aurunci Mountains towards the British 8th Army to their right, rolling up the German positions between the two armies. Overall progress though was painfully slow; the Allied commanders must have despaired, fearing yet another costly failure at the Gustav Line. General Leese visited a disconsolate Anders and confirmed that despite the lack of material success by the Polish Army he considered that they had achieved their goal of tying up German defenders and in effect assisting the British XIII Corps in the valley below.

By the afternoon of 12 May the Rapido bridgeheads were moving forward despite ferocious counterattacks. Attrition along the coast as well as in the mountains continued to be high, but by 13 May the pressure was starting to tell on the German Army. Kesselring mobilised every available reserve in order to buy time to switch to his second prepared defensive position, the Hitler Line, about 15 km to the rear, running from Terracina on the coast through the fortified town of Piedimonte San Germano and joining the Gustav Line at Monte Caira.

The French Corps, continuing their successful start, moved on using their extensive mountain warfare experience, capturing Monte Maio to give supporting flank assistance to the British XIII Corps. On 14 May the Moroccan Goumiers (French Expeditionary Corps) rapidly traversed through the mountains parallel to the Liri Valley through ground which was considered inaccessible and left unprotected, outflanking German defences. The following day the British 78th Division moved forward into the XIII Corps line from reserve and executed a turning move to isolate Cassino from the Liri Valley.

A second Polish attack on the high ground was scheduled for the 17th to link in with the progress of the British XIII Corps along the Liri Valley. As the Poles prepared, their artillery in the Rapido valley, screened by 20,000 smoke generators, continued to hammer German positions around the abbey and during the night patrol parties in all parts of the sector made probing attacks, drawing enemy fire and locating the strongholds before returning to their shelters.

The second Polish offensive started with artillery fire at 06.00 followed at 07.00 by an infantry attack. Despite heavy fighting, steady progress was made. During the day Hill 593 was retaken and infantry and tank progress made through Gardziel and along Widmo. Depleted Polish troops were supplemented by all available cooks, drivers and an array of non-combatant personnel. My dad though was still behind the front lines, ferrying wounded soldiers on specially prepared racks on the back of his Willy's Jeep to medical aid posts and bringing forward supplies from the rear.

Fighting continued through the night and by the early hours of 18 May units of the 5th Kresova had linked up with the British 78th Division in the Liri Valley 3 km west of Cassino town. The tide had at last turned. The German defenders were completely exhausted and, fearing being isolated in the abbey, started to withdraw along a route that took them beneath the high points of Phantom Ridge, Hill 575, and Colle Sant' Angelo (Hill 601) to the hamlet of Villa Santa Lucia and eventually to the town of Piedimonte San Germano on the Hitler Line, which by then had been renamed the Senger Line, as the German High Command had previously decided by that the Hitler Line would never fall! As they pulled back the fighting around the abbey eased, but in a show of indignation the Germans, using loudspeakers, spewed insults and propaganda out over the smouldering terrain. The Poles replied with mortar fire.

Around 08.45 on 18 May, prompted by a lull in the hostilities, a reconnaissance group from Romuald Lipinski's Polish 12th Podolian Uhlans (12th Podolski Lancers) Regiment led by a Lieutenant Gurbiel were sent to assess the situation in the area of the abbey. They successfully crossed a minefield, passed through the outer walls and cautiously entered the abbey. As they patrolled through the crumbled ruins they confirmed that the Germans had indeed vacated the monastery during the night, leaving only nineteen terrified soldiers comprising of sixteen wounded soldiers and two medics under the command of a single officer cadet. These poor unfortunates were trembling in fear because it was widely believed that the Poles were out to wreak vengeance and murder any German soldiers captured. This certainly wasn't the case for the last defenders of the abbey, who were treated with care and respect, in fact one of them appeared on German radio in the 1970s to dispel some of the untruths about the ruthless accusations levelled at the Polish 2nd Corps during the Battle of Monte Cassino. Other prisoners taken by Polish forces also expressed the same fear, and several groups of Germans scrambled down towards the town of Cassino to surrender to British forces rather than risk being captured by Polish soldiers. It is also believed that some of the prolonged fighting at some of the isolated positions around Monte Cassino was because of the rumour that the Polish did not take prisoners.

At 09.30 at the Polish 2nd Corps headquarters, the young signals officer on duty received confirmation that the abbey was finally in Allied hands; the Polish Army had captured it without a single shot being fired. The glorious message was passed directly to the elated General Anders, still wearing his pyjamas, by the young signals officer himself. The bearer of the long-awaited news was Aleksander '*Without Vodka*' Topolski, who received a signed photograph of Anders to commemorate the historic event (Aleksander Topolski – personal communication).

Around 10.00 a hastily erected Polish regimental flag was flying over the highest point of the abbey and a solitary Polish bugler standing in the ruins of the once-mighty religious seat signalled the end of fighting for the abbey. Sporadic fighting continued in isolated areas throughout the day and Hill 575 saw some stiff resistance before being finally captured during the early morning of 19 May. Commendations came flooding into Anders from all the Allied commanders. The Polish 2nd Corps held an almost celebrity status among the Allies, hopes and expectations of a speedy return home were at the highest point since their homeland had first been invaded on 1 September 1939. Thousands had died to make the dream a reality; if only history was that straightforward!

Under Anders' instigation, the British Union Jack was soon flying alongside the Polish standard atop the ruins of the abbey and he was quick to arrive to see for himself the total devastation of both the abbey and his gallant Polish 2nd Corps, many of whom were scattered across the barren landscape of the battlefield.

As Polish soldiers scoured the ruins of the abbey clearing mines, the scale of the destruction of its once historic and religious splendour became clear. In stark contrast, those areas of the high ground that hadn't seen much of the fighting were resplendent with red poppies, which became the lasting symbol of the Polish involvement at the Battle of Monte Cassino.

There was no lull in action after the capture of Monte Cassino for the exhausted Polish troops. After the town of Cassino fell to the British 8th Army the Allies pressed hard their advantage. Polish infantry divisions fought up the steep slopes of Passo Corno and Monte Caira, and along Route 6 armoured divisions prepared for an assault on the strongly fortified hill fortress town of Piedimonte San Germano, the last bastion of the Senger Line.

However, the immediate follow-up assault on the Senger Line failed, causing the 8th Army to re-organise. Getting 20,000 vehicles and 2,000 tanks through the breached Gustav Line was a major logistical problem and took several days to prepare. One of the British drivers from Argyll and Sutherland Highlanders was a Jack Chuwen, the brother of my dad's wife-to-be, my uncle!

The final assault commenced on 23 May. The Polish Corps, using tanks, attacked Piedimonte in four consecutive assaults. In terrain clearly unsuited to heavy armour, the tenacity of the relentless assaults clearly took the Germans by surprise, preventing them from being able to defend Route 6, the road to Rome.

To the right of the Poles the 1st Canadian Infantry Division (fresh from being held in reserve) breached the line on 24 May, and together with the 5th Canadian Armoured Division poured through. On 25 May the Poles took Piedimonte, and the Senger Line collapsed. The way was clear for the advance northwards on to Rome and beyond. On the same day Polish Carpathian Lancers and the 15th Poznan Lancers finally overcame the difficult, steep, and rocky terrain to at last capture the high peaks of Passo Corno and Monte Caira. All the Polish 2nd Corps' objectives were complete, and they were able to take a hard-earned breather. Romauld Lipinski described his thoughts.

So, the battle of Monte Cassino came to an end. We left our positions on May 24. I will never forget, when we were leaving the Cassino area, we were passing close to the temporary cemetery. Long columns of bodies wrapped in blankets were laying waiting for burial. It had a chilling effect on me and on my buddies. We all realised that we were all very close to be among these less fortunate, who not long ago were young men, full of vigour and dreams about future, having somewhere somebody dear, who was praying for their safe return that will never come about.

After the battle our troops were very popular among the Allies. Wherever we appeared we were welcomed as heroes of Monte Cassino. Sometimes, when somebody was hitchhiking, a high-ranking officer be it a British, American or French, would stop, invite us to his car, offer something to drink, take us wherever we wanted to go.

One time we were drinking in a tavern, and at the neighbouring table were some American soldiers. When they heard that we are talking Polish, one of them approached us and asked: 'Polski? Polski?' When we said that we are Poles, they invited us to their table and we had a feast. Some of them were of Polish origin and they spoke some Polish, which helped us to communicate. From other tables came other American soldiers and we had to tell them about the battle, about our times in Siberia, how we got out from there, in other words the whole story. It impressed me then for the first time how little the world knows about the fact that close to 2 millions Poles were deported to Siberia. They thought that we ran away to Russia from Germans! Anyhow, we had a big time together, and our American friends brought us to our quarters at wee hours.

Though casualties had been high, morale was at the highest since leaving Russia. They had come through their first test with the German foe and were advancing north home towards Poland. As the Polish troops were stood down, they returned to the towns of Vinchiaturo, Riccia, Gambetesa, and Campobasso for much-needed rest and recuperation.

My father, like many of the drivers, had a much more gruesome task: having to clear the battlefields of the corpses of the many who had sadly died in action. The job was long and arduous, the smell apparently so awful that masks had to be worn for much of the time. So bad was it that some reports state that at times the mules refused to go into certain areas! Other areas, littered with mines, unexploded bombs and barbed wire, had to be made safe before the bodies were removed to a temporary cemetery.

So significant was the Polish victory at Monte Cassino that the Italian authorities immediately granted permission for a permanent Polish memorial cemetery to be constructed, located beneath Snake's Head Ridge in the shadows of the abbey. Anders for his part was awarded the Order of the Bath by the British government and other commendations followed from all the Allied nations. As a mark of respect General Leese granted soldiers of the Polish 2nd Corps the right to wear the British 8th Army Crusaders cross formation badge on their battle dress. This was thereafter worn with pride on the right arm of their uniforms. General Sosnkowski on behalf of the Polish government-in-exile awarded all participants of the battle their first medal of the war; the Monte Cassino Commemorative Cross.

Monte Cassino Commemorative Cross (*Krzyż Pamiątkowy Monte Cassino*) is a commemorative medal that was awarded to all soldiers of the Polish 2nd Corps who fought in the Battle of Monte Cassino. A consignment of 50,000 individually numbered crosses were ordered, of which 48,498 were issued in the field with an accompanying award certificate (*legitymacja*) to each soldier who took part in the battle. My dad's cross number is 31744. In 1992 the cross was promoted to the rank of a state decoration by the post-communist Polish government.

As the Poles attacked Piedimonte and Monte Cairo on 23 May to the north the American 6th Corps began their breakout from Anzio. Instead of moving east to cut off the German retreat from Cassino they inexplicably pressed on north towards Rome. The decision, surrounded in controversy, seems to stem from the egocentric General Mark Clark's ambition to gain the personal glory of the capture of the first Axis capital for himself. As the Allies pushed on through the Cesar Line just south of Rome, it is believed that Kesselring withdrew his forces from Rome to prevent the heritage of the city suffering any serious damage. On 4 June General Mark Clark and his 5th Army marched into the Italian capital. The ramifications of General Clark's decision were wide ranging and have been much debated and heavily criticised since. It is widely believed that had the German retreat been prevented much of the subsequent heavy fighting in Italy could have been avoided and the actual end of the war may have been brought significantly forward. My dad remembered seeing General Clark on several occasions while in Italy.

On 6 June 1944, a mere two days after General Clark entered Rome, the main Allied offensive on mainland Europe began. D-Day or Operation Overlord had commenced, and the fighting in Italy, as significant as it was, became largely overshadowed by the drive to Berlin through France.

The news changed very little for the Poles, whose rest period didn't last very long. By the beginning of June General Anders had been appointed commander of the Adriatic sector and his Polish 2nd Corps were swelled (after screening) by Polish deserters who had been forced into the German Army, some British regiments, and the Italian Liberation Corps (*Corpo Italiano di Liberazione*). After much debate and several changes of plans they were tasked with securing the strategic Adriatic seaport of Ancona.

My dad finally left the shattered town of Cassino on 1 June to resume his officer-driving duties with the 2nd Warsaw Armoured Brigade. By 17 June the Polish 2nd Corps had passed Pescara and was rapidly advancing along the undulating coastal Route 16 in the wake of the retreating but organised German Army. Enemy engagement was light but progress was hindered by destroyed bridges and heavily mined roads and river crossings.

Polish troops were back in action on 21 June fighting across the Potenza River, with some units pushing inland to the town of Macerata and then on to the town of Loreto just south of Ancona.

The Battle of Loreto started on 2 July; its success was key to the taking of Ancona. Fierce fighting hampered by long and difficult supply lines and stubborn defending by the German Army delayed its capture until 9 July. Detailed plans were drawn up and during the morning of the 17th the assault on Ancona began. Once again fierce German resistance and heavy losses to both sides characterised the battle, but by the afternoon of the 18th the German defenders had withdrawn and units of the Carpathian Lancers entered the town.

Having secured Ancona, the Allies could now move supplies via the sea, reducing supply lines and enabling detailed preparations to be made for the attack on the German last line of defence in Italy, the Gothic Line.

As the port was being prepared my dad was once again given the onerous task of removing the dead from the battlefield, taking them to a temporary cemetery from where they would eventually be buried at a massive Polish memorial cemetery at Loreto. He also spent time driving officers around the war-shattered town and he commented several times in later years on how much he had liked Ancona.

City/town	Location	Approx. distance	Country
Ancona	300 km north-west of Cassino	35,820 km	Italy

Ancona is a provincial capital of the Marche region in the north-east of Italy and an important port city on the edge of the Adriatic Sea. Its harbour was originally protected only by an elbow-shaped promontory from which the city takes its name (Greek *angkon*, 'elbow').

The older parts of Ancona are high above the port on a spur of rock, and though it has been continually inhabited for more than 3,000 years and was a significant Roman settlement, comparatively little evidence now remains. The notable exception, located in the port itself, is the marble Arch of Trajan constructed at the beginning of the second century AD, which is considered by some to be the finest Roman monument in the Marche region. Ancona is home, however, to one of the best museums in Italy for pre-Roman archaeology.

Outside the town of Ancona the coast is characterised by sandy beaches to the north and rocky and shingly beaches to the south. Apart from the flourishing tourism and port industries, towns in the vicinity prosper from fishing and those inland from the production of fruit and vegetables from farms, orchards, vineyards and olive-groves.

More commendations came flooding in to the officers and soldiers of the Polish 2nd Corps. Anders was presented to King George VI at Perugia on 26 July and on 1 August he was awarded the American Legion of Merit (by General Devers of the American VI Army) at a ceremony in Rome.

Following the months of intense activity and success on the battlefield, there was a lull in fighting after Ancona. The Poles were able to reassess and take stock of the political situation, and it didn't look good. Alarm bells were set ringing as news came through that the Soviet Red Army had crossed the emotive Curzon Line and was advancing into territory that it hadn't planned on incorporating into the Soviet Union. The extent of the Tehran meeting back in November 1943 was only just becoming clear when on 21 July the Soviet authorities established the Polish Committee of National Liberation (Polski Komitet Wyzwolenia Narodowego, PKWN). It was essentially an interim pro-Soviet Polish government controlled from Russia who proclaimed they were 'the only legitimate Polish government', and thus formally rejected the Polish government-in-exile! On the 25th Lublin was declared the temporary capital of Poland.

The stark reality was that the Allies had two diametrically opposed Polish governments and were forced to choose between supporting the Polish government-in-exile in London or recognising the Polish government in Lublin. Though the Allies had been appeasing Stalin for some time, the Soviet declaration on 26 July that administration in the liberated areas of Poland had been handed over to the PKWN essentially sealed the coffin lid on a free Poland; there would be no way the Allies would jeopardise the Soviet contribution to the war. Sad, very sad.

In Poland itself the Polish Home Army (*Armia Krajowa* –AK), which was under direct control of the Polish government-in-exile and commanded by General Tadeusz Bór-Komorowski, had grown to almost 400,000 of which about 40,000 were in Warsaw. Their task was of continual resistance and to rise up at a time when it was deemed to be most effective and appropriate.

By the end of July 1944, as Soviet forces advanced into central Poland, the Polish government-in-exile in London instructed Bór-Komorowski to prepare the armed uprising in Warsaw. Despite all the political setbacks there was an overriding desire to return to a capital city liberated by Poles and not one seized by the Soviets and to prevent a communist take-over of Poland which had clearly been set in motion.

On 1 August amid confusing messages and uncertain orders the Warsaw Uprising began. The *Armia Krajowa*, comprising women and children together with soldiers, started well, seizing large areas of the historic capital city. Much is written about the Warsaw Uprising and I'm not going to dwell on it here, but it is significant in the context of my father's journey so it is worth highlighting some of the issues.

From the outset it was clear that an uprising would have little hope of success without the assistance of Allied forces. The Red Army, less than 40 km away, would have been the best hope, but the icy political relationship between the Polish government-in-exile and Stalin precluded this. In fact the Red Army were actively disarming and arresting members of the AK as they moved west through Poland. Limited assistance from Britain and America using aircraft proved costly and, despite desperate pleading by both Anders and Sosnkowski with all the leading Allied politicians and military leaders, it couldn't be increased. To make matters worse, a request to stage American aircraft out of Russian territory to support the uprising went unanswered for three weeks before finally being rejected. The Polish position looked more and more hopeless; god knows what my father and his fellow soldiers praying for a return home must have thought!

Despite the gloom and concern about the future, units of the Polish 2nd Corps were all too quickly back in action. In mid-July the British 8th and the American 5th Armies had continued their push north through Italy and were approaching Kesselring's last major line of defence, the heavily fortified Gothic Line that ran from just north of Pisa in the west to Pesaro on the Adriatic Sea. Anders was given the task of breaking the Gothic Line where it reached the Adriatic near to Pesaro.

The attack commenced on 19 August. Bad weather turned roads to mud and prevented air support, but the sheer willpower and determination drove the Polish 2nd Corps forwards. Amid some of the heaviest fighting in the Adriatic sector they crossed the River Cesano and by the 22nd were fighting to cross the Metauro River just south of the Adriatic city of Fano. The 2nd Warsaw Armoured Brigade was heavily involved and my dad was still performing his driving duties, ferrying officers in his Willy's Jeep to command posts along the front and ferrying casualties to Regimental Aid Posts and sadly to temporary mortuaries behind the forward lines. Anders moved his headquarters to Mondolfo, just south-east of Fano, as the final push on Pesaro started on the 25th. The German defenders were none other than the 1st Parachute Division (1st Fallschirmjäger), their fearsome adversaries from Monte Cassino, and just as at Monte Cassino they proved no match for the rampant Polish 2nd Corps. By 29 August the town of Foglia had been captured and the Poles were fighting in Pesaro itself.

By 2 September the Poles had taken Pesaro and advanced to the town of Cattolica north of Pesaro and linked up with Canadian troops. They had breached the Gothic Line and achieved all their objectives in the Adriatic sector.

A few days earlier, as the Polish 2nd Corps began their final push on Pesaro, the Prime Minister of England Winston Churchill arrived at Mondolfo for meetings with Anders. I suspect that amid much political talk, the text of which can be found in Anders' book *An Army on Exile*, and despite Churchill's repeated claims that Britain would not abandon the Poles, there was in reality no real reassurance to the growing despair that was felt by all the Poles fighting to return home.

After the capture of Pesaro the Polish Army was withdrawn back to Ancona for a much-deserved rest. My father left the front line on 4 September but continued his officer-driving duties. As the Polish Army rested, General Anders, because of his prominent position and standing with not only the Polish citizens and soldiers and the higher echelons of the Allied forces in Europe but also the main political statesmen, was thrust into a period of intense political activity.

After a week of meetings with all the Allied commanders in Italy he was recalled to Britain on 19 September for discussions with his government-in-exile. Sadly the outlook was worse than ever. Not only was the government-in-exile itself in turmoil, but it was clear that Churchill was increasingly bowing to Soviet demands, particularly over the question of the post-war Polish border demarcation.

The relationship between the Polish Prime Minister in exile Stanisław Mikołajczyk and the Commander-in-Chief General Sosnkowski was the biggest cause for concern. They had rarely seen eye-to-eye, and because of Sosnkowski's open criticism of the Allies for failure to adequately support the Warsaw Uprising and for their growing abandonment of Poland to the Soviets, there were repeated calls for his dismissal.

Anders returned to Italy on 29 September to be informed that General Leese was being replaced by the recently knighted former commander of the British 10th Army Corps General Richard McCreery. The political maelstrom continued and the following day, in what is widely believed to be a concession to the Soviets, but in reality because of his fierce and vocal anti-Soviet and pro-Polish rhetoric, General Sosnkowski was relieved of all his command.

In Italy Anders was occupied with military matters and preparations for the Polish 2nd Corps' next task when on 2 October the Warsaw Uprising, after sixty-three days, finally came to an end. 15,000 insurgents including General Bór-Komorowski were taken away and into captivity. The same day the Polish government announced General Tadeusz Bór-Komorowski as successor to General Sosnkowski as (honorary) Commander-in-Chief of Polish forces.

For the Poles the war was difficult to rationalise; they were increasingly fighting a war for which they knew there would be no final conclusion. The victory, which for the Allies would surely come, didn't include the liberation of the homeland of most of the fighting Poles. It seemed that they were now just fighting somebody else's war, a war where the combatants were fighting for a political end, whereas the Poles they were literally fighting for their lives.

From the very top to the lowly drivers they questioned their involvement. But fight on they must, and their next task was to move inland and provide support to the British 8th Army fighting up the Adriatic coast. My dad was on the move by 10 October, driving in a huge convoy firstly south-westerly towards Perugia then north through the war-devastated Umbertide and on towards Cesena before moving into the beautiful and congested narrow roads around the town of Bibiena.

Before long the roads turned north through deep valleys onto what were little more than mountain tracks. The tanks and trucks passed through the spectacular Mandrioli Pass in what is now (since 1993) the Parco Nazionale delle Foreste Casentinesi Monte Falterona Campigna, heading for their next objective: Santa Sofia.

The attack began during the evening of 17 October and though being taken by surprise the German defenders put up a solid resistance. As in their previous battles the Polish onslaught was dogged, but even then and unbeknownst to them, far away in Moscow, Polish Prime Minister Mikołajczyk had arrived for discussions with Churchill (who had arrived several days previously) and Stalin. The fate of the Poles outside of Poland was becoming evermore depressing.

In ignorance of the Moscow meetings and despite appalling autumn weather that turned the roads into rivers of mud, the Poles pressed on through Santa Sofia to take Monte Grosso on the 22nd. Two days later my dad was transferred from the 9th Supply Company to HQ of the 2nd Armoured Brigade. His duties were largely the same as before but he spent more time driving junior officers and less on supply and evacuation driving.

By the 26th the Polish Army had advanced rapidly through difficult territory in terrible weather and captured Monte Colombo, Monte Mirabello, bypassed Mussolini's birthplace (and later place of burial) at Predappio and were advancing on the high ground around the Castle Rocca delle Caminate in order to open a way through Meldola for the British 8th Army as they advanced towards Forli on Route 9 towards Bologna. On the Polish eastern flank Dovadola was taken on 8 November and Castrocaro and Bagnola on the 12th.

As they continued their slow but steady advance towards Faenza, news came through of continuing turmoil within the Polish government-in-exile in London. In a shock decision, no doubt prompted by the intransigence of the Allies and in particular Churchill to the Polish cause, Prime Minister Mikołajczyk had resigned on 24 November to take part in the proposed Provisional Government of National Unity. While the reasons were highly complicated and beyond the scope of this description, what appears to have happened in simple terms, was that because of the western Allies' increasing acceptance of Stalin's demands for a post-war partition of Poland based on the Curzon Line, recognition of the Soviet-supported new communist Polish government, and at the same time distancing themselves from the Polish government-in-exile in London, Mikołajczyk believed the needs of the Poles abroad could be best served from within the Soviet-installed Polish government. It wasn't, however, a view shared by the majority of the Poles fighting in Italy!

Despite being floored yet again, the Polish troops pressed on towards the River Senio. On 16 December the city of Faenza on Route 9 was liberated by the New Zealand Army and the Polish 2nd Corps advanced to start consolidating their positions along the River Senio just south of Route 9. As the harsh winter of December 1944 moved into 1945, plans were made to expand the 2nd Armoured Brigade by the addition of the 16th Pomorska Infantry Brigade (16 Pomorska Brygada Piechoty) and renaming it the 2nd Warsaw Armoured Division.

My dad arrived for duties in the Senio sector on 2 January and during the lull in front-line action the Polish Army dug in and prepared for the spring offensive. For a while they were battling more with the miserable winter conditions than German soldiers. The outlook seemed a little brighter during early February when a proposal to the British high command to unite all Polish land forces, i.e. the 2nd Polish Corps in Italy and the Polish 1st Corps fighting in France, seemed favourable.

The idea of a single Polish Army all fighting in the same theatre of war was well received by the troops and a noticeable positive mood-swing was clearly apparent. But even at that moment, far away on the Crimean Peninsula, in more political machinations their future was formally being sealed.

From 4 to 11 February, codenamed the 'Argonaut Conference', the second wartime meeting of the 'Big Three' was held at Livadiya Palace (Ливадийский дворец), the summer retreat of Nicholas II, the last Russian Tsar, at Livadiya on the Black Sea coast just south of Yalta. Each of the 'Three' came with their own agenda and despite previously having decided that Germany would be divided into occupied zones administered by American, British, French, and Soviet forces, the structure of post-war Europe was key to the talks.

Roosevelt was there because of his desire to create a United Nations before the Second World War ended. Churchill feared the growing power of the Soviet Union in a devastated post-war Europe. Stalin was intent on protecting the Soviet Union against another German invasion. Of the major issues facing the three leaders, which included what to do about Germany, Soviet entry into the war against Japan, and the United Nations, the question of Poland was high on the agenda.

Basically, in what is widely known as the 'Western Betrayal', the Allies, in spite of having promoted democracy and self-determination in the East, signing pacts and forming military alliances prior and during the Second World War, were perceived to have betrayed their Central European allies by abandoning these pacts. In what is key to my story, the agreement that had been outlined at Tehran on the Polish question, i.e. the Soviet demands regarding post-war Polish borders and the construction of a Polish government, was effectively rubber-stamped at Yalta. Stalin had got his way.

What effect this had in reality was that the Allies (and the finger of history points at Churchill in particular) had agreed that tens of thousands of Polish troops under British command and their dependants exiled during the Soviet invasion on 17 September 1939, fighting and expecting to return to an independent and democratic Poland at the end of the war, would lose their Kresy homes, lifestyle, properties and even families to the Soviet Union.

To the likes of my dad and the soldiers of the Polish 2nd Corps there was at first a shocked disbelief, which was followed by anger and resentment as Anders describes in his book *An Army in Exile* – they felt numb for a few days but there was then a violent reaction as they realised the injustice. They had all believed they would be able to return home at the end of their ordeal, but that was no longer true.

It has been reported that at least thirty officers and men from the 2nd Corps were so distressed by the prospect that they committed suicide, and even for those who didn't react so desperately it was a bitter pill to swallow. For many the bad taste remains to this day.

Anders was clearly incensed, and despite the Polish government-in-exile making a public protest, on 13 February he telegrammed his president and at the same time in a written letter to General McCreery formally gave his intention to withdraw all Polish 2nd Corps troops from the frontline because 'I cannot in conscience demand at present any sacrifice of the soldiers' blood'. Anders then had a series of high-level meetings with General McCreery on the 15th, General Clarke on the 16th and finally General Alexander on 17 February. The Allied requirement was simple; they could not afford the loss of the Polish contingent from the front lines, they simply had no reserves to replace them with. Anders' reaction was swift; he agreed to carry on, assuring the Allies of the Polish 2nd Corps' continuing devotion to duty.

By 20 February Anders was back in London for discussions with his equally shocked government-in-exile, and a day later was being admonished by Churchill who, contradicting his officers at the front, angrily informed Anders that he didn't need his Polish troops in Italy! Despite Churchill's outburst the Polish government-in-exile formally announced on the 25th its intention for the Polish 2nd Corps to keep fighting in Italy.

On 26 February the president of the Polish government-in-exile appointed Anders the acting Commander-in-Chief. Because of Anders' strongly felt feelings and outspoken opposition of Russia, the appointment wasn't greatly welcomed by the British government, who for a time distanced themselves from him, cancelling meetings and trying to get the news of the appointment hushed up. But you can't keep a good man down and Anders, to me the 'man of the match' so far for the Polish cause, made his first order the same day, with extracts being published in the press on 27 February.

But even then, on the very same day, at the start of a three-day parliamentary debate in the House of Commons Churchill confirmed the acceptance of the new Polish borders as proposed by Stalin; a day later the British Foreign Secretary Anthony Eden made a declaration in which he outlined the recognition of the creation of a new Polish government as proposed by the Soviet Union. The Poles' worst fears had been announced to the world. During the debate, many MPs openly criticised Churchill and passionately voiced loyalty to Britain's Polish allies and expressed deep reservations about Yalta. Churchill attempted to defend his actions but the debate ended in a vote of confidence. Twenty-five MPs risked their careers to draft an amendment protesting against Britain's tacit acceptance of Poland's domination by the Soviet Union. The amendment sadly failed but one MP, Henry Strauss, 1st Baron Conesford, the Member of Parliament for Norwich, resigned his seat in protest at the British treatment of Poland.

The western Allies continued to distance themselves from the Polish government-in-exile, and on 5 March it was learned through the press that the US had issued forty-one invitations to a conference in San Francisco to draw up the charter of the United Nations. Poland was not on the list.

Anders had given his word to continue fighting and despite the political trauma he was back in Italy by 11 March. Command of the Polish 2nd Corps had been handed to General Zygmunt Bohusz-Szyszko and during March and early April the Polish 2nd Corps' front line extended north along the River Senio across Route 9 to San Severo.

The spring offensive began on 9 April starting with a large aerial bombardment by American B-17 Flying Fortresses. Unfortunately, one of the aircraft released its bombs too early which fell on the forward line of Polish troops. This friendly fire killed over 200 troops but a swift reorganisation meant that there was no delay in the start of the offensive. My dad's involvement started with infantry support, advancing behind the front lines of the 5th Kresy Division from south of Faenza. On the 10th he had crossed the River Senio and was moving towards the River Santerno and on towards the town of Imola.

By the 11th elements of the 3rd Carpathian Rifle Division advancing along Route 9 had already crossed the River Santerno and by the 14th, despite heavy fighting, they had captured Imola. At the same time slightly further north my dad had crossed to the north of Route 9 and was advancing behind the 5th Kresy Division as they approached the River Silaro. By the 17th the Silaro had been crossed and in merciless fighting along the Gaino and Idice Rivers around the village of Zambonini for the third time they were pitted against their arch-nemesis from Monte Cassino and Pesaro, the crack German 1st Parachute Division. At the same time the 3rd Carpathian Rifle Division had taken Castel San Pietro and was within striking distance of Bologna itself.

The German position was hopeless, Bologna was surrounded. General Mark Clark's American II Corps were advancing from the south, the 3rd Carpathian Rifle Division was rapidly approaching along Route 9 from the east, and the 5th Kresy together with my dad and the 2nd Warsaw Armoured Brigade were moving in from the north. With no other options available the 1st Parachute Division withdrew from Bologna during the night of 20 April.

General Clark gave the honour of liberating the city to Anders and the Polish 2nd Corps. The victorious Polish soldiers entered the city to a rapturous heroes' welcome; only small pockets of German resistance remained and fortunately a large-scale bombardment of the historic city was averted. By 06.15 the Poles had secured the city, hoisting Polish flags from the town hall and the highest tower and symbol of the city, the Torre Asinelli. It was the last combat action of the war in which the Polish 2nd Corps were ever involved.

City/town	Location	Approx. distance	Country
Bologna	225 km north-west of Ancona	36,045 km	Italy

Bologna is the capital city of the Emilia-Romagna region in northern Italy. It lies surrounded by hills in the fertile lands between the River Po and the Apennine mountain range.

It was founded by the Etruscans with the name of Felsina in about 534 BC and grew like much of Italy around a sanctuary built on a hill. By the thirteenth century Bologna was a sprawling metropolis with nearly 200 spectacular towers built by the local leading families, notable public edifices, churches and abbeys.

Many remain to this day, including the famous Two Towers, both of them leaning, which are the symbol of the city. They are located at the intersection of the roads that lead to the five gates of the old ring wall (*mura dei torresotti*). The taller one is called the Asinelli while the smaller but more leaning tower is called the Garisenda. Both tower into the Bologna skyline above beautiful, dusky, red-coloured buildings, wide piazzas and arched porticoes with floors laid with marble.

Until the late nineteenth century, when large-scale urban reconstruction was undertaken, Bologna remained one of the best-preserved medieval cities in the whole of Europe. It remains to this day unique in its historic value despite some destruction during the last war. Bologna's historic centre, Europe's second-largest (after Venice), contains a wealth of important medieval, Renaissance, and Baroque artistic monuments.

Bologna is renowned for its culinary tradition and some regard it as the food capital of Italy. It has a rich local cuisine which depends heavily on meats and cheeses, and has given its name to Bolognese sauce, a meat-based pasta sauce called in Italy *ragù alla Bolognese*.

Like most of his comments about Italy my dad only had nice words about Bologna, in fact I got the impression that it was his favourite place there, but I never got to know why this was so. Following the success in capturing Bologna the Polish 2nd Corps were stood down and on 22 April started pulling back from the front line. My dad, however, remained driving officers around, helping with the moving casualties and performing general driving duties.

Once again the Poles could reflect on the gross injustice that had befallen them. I'm sure that at times the atmosphere was fraught, but away from the Polish dilemma the world events continued on towards the impending climax of the war.

On 27 April Mussolini and his mistress Claretta Petacci were captured near Lake Como by Italian partisans while trying to escape to Spain via Switzerland. Despite allegedly carrying incriminating letters from Churchill, the following day they, together with their entourage, were summarily shot and their bodies taken to Milan where they were famously hung by their feet on meat hooks at an Esso petrol station, coincidentally in the Piazza Loreto, while an angry crowd publicly vented their anger on the corpses.

The next day General Heinrich von Vietinghoff, one of the senior commanders from Monte Cassino, who had replaced Kesselring as Commander-in-Chief of German forces in Italy, signed the surrender document for the German forces in Italy. Further north the Red Army were fighting in the streets of central Berlin and on 30 April Adolf Hitler finally conceded defeat and commited suicide using a pistol and cyanide tablet in the Führerbunker located beneath his Reich Chancellery.

On 2 May, my dad completed his work in Bologna and rejoined the HQ of the 2nd Warsaw Armoured Brigade at Loreto just to the south of Ancona. The very same day the lasts shots in anger were fired in Italy. Less than a week later, on 7 May Germany signed an unconditional surrender of all its forces.

The eighth day of May was designated Victory in Europe (V-E) day. The war against Nazi Germany had come to an end, but for the Poles nothing had changed; in fact, it was worse. Poland was in Allied hands but it hadn't been liberated, the Polish 2nd Corps were now an army without a nation, and since the Allies were getting further and further into bed with the Soviet Union, they were also becoming a political embarrassment. The world celebrated victory in Europe; for the Poles it was a hollow victory, and like the Germans they wallowed in defeat.

The mood was at an all-time low. Some units even considered driving north with the intention of liberating Poland themselves. Officers used all their diplomacy to ensure that frustration and anger didn't develop into anything worse. The British continued to fund the Polish Army, but at the same time encouraged its soldiers to return home to Poland. For most, like my father their homes were no longer Poland but part of the Soviet Union, and life under Stalin was not an option most could stomach. Of the 112,000 soldiers in the 2nd Polish Corps at the end of 1945, such was the fear of the Soviet tyranny that only about 14,000 applied for repatriation of which 8,700 were those that had joined after the end of fighting and were probably from the west of Poland and not from the Kresy region. Those that applied to return to Poland were sent to a repatriation camp at Cervinara near Naples until they could be returned to Poland. Sadly, but probably not surprisingly, reports say some that did return were treated as traitors and were even sent to Siberia!

In May General Bór-Komorowski was released from his prison in Germany and arrived in London. Anders returned to his role as General of the 2nd Polish Corps, which was growing with Poles that had been released from camps across Europe. He pressed the British high command to have the Polish 2nd Corps moved to Germany where they could be used as occupation forces, but it was decided that politically it was impracticable. The Polish government-in-exile, and in particular Anders, were becoming less and less powerful on the world stage in the rapidly evolving new Europe. Anders in particular, once invincible, was becoming a thorn in the British side as they moved ever closer to a union with the Soviet Union and communist-led emerging new Polish government.

I wouldn't say he had become a pariah but his influence was clearly being eroded, especially when a tirade of abuse and almost libellous propaganda against Anders and the soldiers of the Polish 2nd Corps was being broadcast daily from radio stations in Russia and communist Poland. Bad relationships got dramatically worse when in May it was announced that sixteen Polish political delegates from the government-in-exile, including several senior officers, who had gone missing in February when summoned to meetings in Poland, had been arrested for anti-Red Army activities. In a farcical trial most were found guilty. In what is remembered as the 'Trial of Sixteen' (in Polish as 'Proces Szesnastu'), they were sentenced to varying prison terms. The most prominent was Anders' personal friend and his Chief of Staff from the days when the 2nd Corps were still in Russia, Leopold Okulicki.

Okulicki had replaced Bór-Komorowski as the Commander-in-Chief of the *Armia Krajowa* and like Anders was a fervent anti-communist. He was sentenced to ten years in prison but died, believed to have been murdered, on 24 December 1946 at the Butyrka prison in Moscow.

No longer fighting, my dad and all the Polish 2nd Corps had time to reflect and no doubt debate their plight. They did, however, have some time, like Anders, to enjoy and relax along the deserted beaches along the Adriatic coastline, though most reports I have read say that they couldn't really fully enjoy that time because of the uncertainty of their position.

The 2nd Corps, though, were not left idle. Some units were used to police the resurgent communist activities around Bologna. Other units were stationed in the north-eastern region around Trieste to ensure there were no insurgents from Yugoslavia.

Many soldiers attended the universities in Rome, Turin, Padua and Bologna. Poles in Italy were joined by Polish refugees from Poland, Germany and France, and Anders explains that camps were set up to provide vocational training in a number of different trades.

My dad, though, continued his driving duties, based with the HQ of the 2nd Armoured Brigade, and on 7 June 1945 they were officially made up to divisional strength and became known as the 2nd Warsaw Armoured Division.

One of the few stories that my dad did tell me and my brothers was that he regularly drove his officers to specific, usually well-presented houses on the outskirts of Ancona, where he would wait outside for his officer(s) to complete their business. This was a regular event, and he was initially not so curious (so he said) about his officers' business. He was a very shy individual who came from a very poor rural farming community and was single before his arrest; in fact he had never had a girlfriend. He (allegedly) had no idea what they were doing and since he was a frequent visitor he became curious. He explained that he eventually plucked up enough courage and ventured inside to be met with the 'lady employees'. When he eventually came out, he was a little more worldly wise but lighter by all the money he had on him together with all his 'valuable items' like cigarettes, cigarette case, belt, and (I'm not sure I believe this) his boot laces. He didn't say how many times he went back!

World events continued to develop; on 26 June, in a further snub to the Polish people the United Nations Charter was signed in San Francisco by fifty governments but without the Polish having been invited. This was followed on 28 June by the formal establishment of the Polish Provisional Government of National Unity (Tymczasowy Rząd Jedności Narodowej or TRJN) with mostly members imposed by Russia! It got worse, on 6 July the Allies officially recognised the TRJN and by doing so effectively discarded the Polish government-in-exile and all the Poles abroad. Anders was incensed and issued an honest and forthright order to his troops in which he tried to reassure them but clearly outline the difficult issues that lay ahead. It was an order for which he was later to be admonished in no uncertain terms by General Alexander for what was considered by the Allies to be inflammatory.

By 17 July 'The Big Three' were once again in conference. This time they were held at Schloss Cecilienhof in Potsdam on the southern outskirts of Berlin. The make-up of the leaders was slightly different than on previous occasions; America was represented by President Harry S. Truman, successor to Roosevelt, who had died of a cerebral haemorrhage on 12 April; Britain was represented not only by Churchill, but also by the leader of the opposition Labour party Clement Attlee. Britain had just held a general election and Churchill's strong Conservative government favoured during the war was thought to be less likely to win a post-war election than the socialist Labour party, who were considered to give the best option for reconstructing a war-depleted Britain; the Soviet Union was represented by the rock that was Stalin.

Part-way through the conference the Labour party were indeed returned triumphant in the election, Churchill was deposed as arguably the greatest Prime Minister Britain has ever had, and Attlee as the new Prime Minister represented Britain alone from 24 July, though his win wasn't formally confirmed until the 26th.

The conference lasted until 2 August. The topics discussed were far-reaching, including the Allied control of defeated Germany, how to administer punishment to defeated Nazi Germany, the management of post-war world order, peace treaty issues, countering the effects of war, and Russia joining the war in the Far East. Significantly for the Poles it included establishment of the Oder/Neisse Line as the new western border of Poland, an agreement to give all Poles returning to communist Poland the same rights as all Polish citizens, to enable free elections in Poland as soon as possible and the conference also rubber-stamped the Polish eastern border roughly along the Curzon Line.

Anders' worst fears (but by then expectations) had been realised. Most Poles considered themselves and their nation betrayed. Many like my father, who had already suffered Soviet repressions, felt unable to return to Poland. The Trial of the Sixteen, and other arrests and executions of pro-democracy Poles, particularly the former members of the *Armia Krajowa*, only served to strengthen their resolve not to return.

Anders was summoned to London on 8 August for crisis meetings with all senior Polish commanding officers to be informed officially that the British government had ceased to recognise the Polish government-in-exile and its Commander-in-Chief of armed forces. An already uncertain future looked evermore so, but the Polish 2nd Corps were still subordinated to the British Army so still had to continue as before while a decision on what to do next was decided.

On 14 August, following the horrific destruction of the Japanese cities of Hiroshima and Nagasaki using the world's first atomic bombs, Japan agreed to an unconditional surrender, bringing about the end of the Second World War. While most of the world could rejoice, for most of the Poles and especially of those outside of Poland there could be no celebrations. The war in which they were the first to fight and in whose name it had been declared had left Poland devastated, fragmented, and worst of all under total control of its worst nemesis – Russia.

14

POST-WAR: WHAT NEXT?

No Home to Go to!

Polish Armed Forces Day is celebrated on 15 August to commemorate the 'Miracle at the Vistula' (Cud nad Wisłą), the Battle of Warsaw (Bitwa Warszawska) in which Józef Piłsudski against all odds recorded a famous victory over Russian troops near to Warsaw. The 1945 Armed Forces Day was to be the last ever for the Polish 2nd Corps and was held on the airfield at Loreto. My father attended the huge parade which featured the massed equipment of the 2nd Warsaw Armoured Division displayed triumphantly for the gathered dignitaries including General Anders and the departing Commander-in-Chief of Allied forces in Italy, Field Marshall Harold Alexander.

Two weeks later on 2 September 1945 the Japanese government formally signed a surrender document; the Second World War that had started for the British on 3 September 1939, the Russians (but known as the Great Patriotic War) on 20 June 1941 and the Americans on 8 December 1941 was officially declared over. It had lasted very nearly six years. Most of the major powers of Europe were involved, battles had been on every continent of the globe, and over 45 million people had been killed. It was the most devastating war in history.

The soldiers, citizens and politicians of all the Allied nations could now start to think about returning home and rebuilding their lives. But for the Poles, the war which had started before any of these on 1 September 1939 hadn't really resolved anything. While the world rejoiced the Poles finally resolved themselves to 'defeat in victory'. As they fought north from the very foot of Italy they lived in anticipation that they could keep on going, eventually all the way to liberate their homeland. It wasn't to be, the Red Army had 'liberated' and now occupied Poland. The road they had been fighting along leading back to Warsaw and their homes across Poland was now left shattered and firmly blocked.

The United Nations was officially born on 24 October 1945 following the ratification of the charter by the five permanent members of the Security Council (France, the Republic of China, the Soviet Union, the United Kingdom, and the United States) and by a majority of the other forty-six signatories. But the desperate plight of the Poles away from Poland remained unaltered. Their continuing existence as an almost separate Polish nation was becoming less and less tenable, and with increasing uncertainty it continued to be so as 1945 moved into 1946.

As the Provisional Government of National Unity (TRJN), together with the Polish and Soviet communist administrative, military, and security organs began to exert an increasingly powerful control over the land and population, it also began to flex its muscles abroad. As it did so, the power of the Poles in the west continued to diminish and became increasingly unco-ordinated and ineffective. They continued undeterred to fight hard for a Poland independent of Russia, so much so that the free elections promised in Poland were delayed by the TRJN until they were sure they could subdue all opposition.

On 14 February the TRJN heaped further pressure on the British government and the Polish forces in exile by announcing to the British government that it no longer recognised any Polish Army outside Poland. The continued existence of the Polish 2nd Corps was now a real concern to the Allies. Anders was summoned to London and the British Foreign Secretary, Ernest Bevin, made clear the British position that the 2nd Corps should be demobilised and return to Poland where they could take part in the forthcoming elections in which their votes could count in the attainment of Polish freedom! For Anders and his men, including my dad, it came as a surprise as it had been assumed, if not agreed, that the 2nd Corps would not return until after the elections. The British decision changed nothing; the Poles were only too aware of Soviet promises, having suffered too many times in the past to believe anything the Soviet authorities ever promised.

The British Labour government, though preferring that the Polish forces be demobilised and repatriated to Poland, were clear that many would not and so began to make provisions for the majority that were clearly going to stay in the west. Ernest Bevin in a statement to the House of Commons on 20 March confirmed that he had reached an agreement with the TRJN for the terms of repatriation, and that he would send a document outlining the terms to every member of the Polish 2nd Corps.

My dad along with the whole 2nd Corps received their personal letter, which had been translated rather hastily into poor Polish, with complete bewilderment. Apparently soldiers just stood around dazed and disconsolate after taking it in. Anders, once again, had to use his best leadership qualities to ensure the anger and frustration didn't develop into something more. It was perhaps due to the personal esteem in which he was held by his subordinates and soldiers that he was able to prevent something of a mutiny. But it mattered not; the fate of the Poles was again out of their own hands. On 12 May Anders received orders to transfer the Polish 2nd Corps as quickly as possible to Britain for demobilisation. There would be no option to form part of the garrison policing Germany. The short-lived Polish 2nd Corps would cease to exist and the hope of returning to a free Poland was lost forever while a communist-controlled government presided over Poland.

For those not willing to return to Poland the British government did offer sanctuary and announced the establishment of the Polish Resettlement Corps (Polski Korpus Przysposobienia i Rozmieszczenia) in order to ease the transition from a Polish military environment to British civilian life, offering support and accommodation until they were able to find work and housing.

Army life in Italy continued in the meantime but my dad was able to take six days' leave from 20 April. I'm not sure what he did, but his future must have weighed heavily on his mind. He was back at Loreto on 29 April to witness Anders inspect the troops, and on 18 May he was at Monte Cassino for the anniversary of the their famous victory the year before. The Polish cemetery beneath Snake's Head Ridge was well under construction and bodies were already being moved from the temporary cemetery at Acquafondata.

At the same time he was able to attend an opening ceremony of a polish memorial created from the destroyed Sherman tank on Cavendish Road. The tank from the 4 Pancerny (4th Armoured 'Skorpion' Regiment of the 2nd Armoured Brigade) had been taken out of action by mines in the first Polish assault on 12 May 1945. Polish engineers had created a huge cross welded from tank tracks and adorned the memorial with commemorative plaques supported by two huge and impressive cast-steel scorpions.

At that time the devastated abbey was still out of bounds for all except senior clerics, but even then preparations were in place for its reconstruction. Notices positioned clearly requested that fragments of the abbey were not to be taken as souvenirs. A dispensation for access must have been allowed though, as the Polish troops present were able to attend a makeshift mass within the ruins.

Similarly the town of Cassino, almost completely obliterated during the long siege, still had large unsafe areas but was starting to function again. Though most of the pre-war inhabitants had moved away, never to return, small numbers had returned to eke out a meagre living while the more enterprising were salvaging the discarded remnants of war to make money from scrap.

Back in England preparations were being made to celebrate the victory of the previous year. 8 June 1946 was designated for VE (Victory in Europe) Day and a massive celebration and triumphal victory parade of the Allied armed forces was planned for London.

In sharp contrast to the end of the First World War when the Allies had stood up for a free and independent post-war Poland, this time was just the opposite. In a final act of injustice, adding insult to injury, the socialist British Labour government under Attlee, who were keen to avoid offending Stalin, invited the Read Army and communist Poland to participate and barred the hundreds of thousands of Poles who had fought under British command from attending. Though the RAF insisted that a contingent of Polish airmen be included and the government relented, the Polish airmen declined the invitation in protest to the exclusion of their Army and Navy compatriots. Not one Pole marched in the parade, and ironically the Soviet Union and the Polish provisional government in Warsaw refused to send delegations for the parade.

It was another snub to the free Poland, the thousands of its citizens who remained homeless, and its soldiers who had taken part in the major battles during six long years of fighting. It was particularly cruel to the Polish soldiers whose numbers had made up the fourth-largest combatant force fighting the Germans, yet not one was present during that victory parade of 8 June 1946. There were heated debates in the House of Commons following the exclusion but like so many of the 'Polish issues' it was swept quickly and permanently under the carpet.

On 15 June Anders celebrated the last Soldiers' Day of the Polish 2nd Corps at a massed gathering near Ancona. It was a solemn event during which each unit was read a vow signed by Anders to continue the struggle, however hard and from wherever they would ultimately end up, for the liberty of Poland. Though well received by the massed soldiers it was less so by the British authorities, who once again chastised Anders, making it clear in no uncertain terms that they wouldn't tolerate this type of political interfering and that if it continued he could be relieved of his command!

I suspect the threat meant very little as plans for transfer to Britain and demobilisation were by then well underway. During this time my dad was still driving officers around the Ancona region bases of Loreto, Potenza Picena and Civitanova Marche. There were some small-scale field exercises at Civitanova on 4 July but on the 10th all vehicles and equipment returned to British control. Some units stationed in the north moved their equipment, vehicles, armour and infrastructure to a depot just south of Milan where they were crushed and reduced to scrap. It was an emotional experience for those involved; soldiers hardened by war and exile wept openly as they saw their history, present and future wiped away before their very eyes.

The 2nd Warsaw Armoured Division stationed around Loreto moved their heavy equipment the short distance to the rail depot at Civitanova Marche, where they were loaded onto flatbed rail cars for delivery back to the Allied forces.

Four days later, my father was leaving from the very same train station. This time the passenger coaches were loaded with the men and officers of the 2nd Armoured Division and was destined for the southern Italian port city of Naples and their transport to the UK.

City/town	Local name	Location	Approx. distance	Country
Naples	Napoli	550 km south-east of Bologna	36,595 km	Italy

The city of Naples was founded nearly 3,000 years ago as Partenope by Turkish and Greek merchants. The original settlement was further developed by the Greeks into Palepolis (Old City) and by 475 BC was known as Neapolis (New City). The city expanded and grew into the capital of the most important of the pre-unification Italian states, the Kingdom of the Two Sicilies, whose rulers the Bourbons constructed a magnificent palace in nearby Caserta in which the Allied command were located following the invasion of Italy in late 1943. Naples has seen many civilisations come and go, each leaving its unique mark, and now the historic city centre is listed by UNESCO as a World Heritage Site.

Its metropolitan area is the second-most populated in Italy and one of the largest in Europe. It is located halfway between the volcano Vesuvius to the east and an equally active and unpredictable area of volcanic activity, the Campi Flegrei, to the west. Its geographical location is spectacular with impressive views over the gulf of Naples and the beautiful islands of Capri, Ischia and Procida in the Tyrrhenian Sea.

It has over 1 million inhabitants, making it the third-largest city in Italy and though some tourist guides, albeit accurately, describe it as a polluted, violent and dangerous city it is in reality a sunny, truly vibrant and cosmopolitan city known for its rich history, art, culture, architecture, music and food. To some, and I'd have to include myself in this, it is 'simply unforgettable'.

My father had a few days' transit break while in Naples, so like many of the Polish 2nd Corps took the opportunity for some sightseeing. He no doubt visited the fantastic sights of Naples and he definitely visited the historic ruins of Pompeii, something I was able to do a mere sixty-three years later.

Back in Britain the War Office had drawn up plans for the dispersal of the nearly 121,000 2nd Polish Corps soldiers throughout Britain. The various units were to be distributed in accordance with the various British Army commands as below.

Dispersal of the Polish 2nd Corps in Great Britain

Scottish Command (HQ Artillery Group, Base Troops)

Berwickshire	1,930	
Roxburghshire	1,880	
Wigtownshire	830	Total: 4,640

Northern Command (2nd Warsaw Armoured Division)

Derbyshire	580	
Lincolnshire	5,730	
Northumberland	5,080	
Yorkshire	4,780	Total: 16,170

Southern Command (5th Kresowa Infantry Division)

Berkshire	1,200	
Gloucestershire	4,720	
Oxfordshire	3,530	
Wiltshire	6,540	Total: 15,990

Eastern Command (3rd Carpathian Rifle Division & 14th Armoured Brigade)

Buckinghamshire	4,970	
Hertfordshire	860	
Huntingdonshire	200	
Norfolk	12,850	
Suffolk	650	
Sussex	3,760	Total: 23,290

Western Command (HQ & Base Troops)

Anglesey	3,560
Brecon	1,450
Cheshire	1,330

Cumberland	26,850	
Derby	840	
Glamorgan	1,850	
Hereford	7,260	
Lancashire	6,790	
Merioneth	490	
Montgomeryshire	1,730	
Pembroke	2,060	
Shropshire	1,240	
Stafford	5,100	
Yorkshire	170	Total: 60,720

So my father's destination was clear; it was going to be to Northern Command and the north of England. On 21 July he was called to the port for embarkation.

The ship which had been requisitioned by the Polish government-in-exile was the SS *Duchess of Bedford*. This pre-war cruise liner already had quite a colourful history; she was built by John Brown & Co. Ltd of Glasgow in 1928 for the transatlantic routes of Canadian Pacific SS Ltd. Having a length of 183 m, a beam of 23 m and at 20,445 gross tonnes she had two funnels, two masts, twin screws and a speed of 18 knots. She was designed with her sister ships the *Duchess of York*, and the *Duchess of Atholl* with flatter keels for travelling up the St Lawrence River to Montreal. This design, however, gave a tendency for the ships to roll, for which they were lovingly dubbed 'the drunken duchesses'!

Impressed into military service, the *Duchess of Bedford* had been used in the evacuation of Singapore in January 1942 and for the Salerno landings in 1943. By the time my dad climbed the access steps she was known as 'the most bombed ship still afloat'! She had sunk a U-boat, damaged another, was shot at and bombed on a number of occasions and had once even struck an iceberg without sustaining damage.

After the war she was refitted and in 1948 renamed the *Empress of France II*. She returned to her north Atlantic crossings and finally arrived at Liverpool after her very last crossing on 19 December 1960, from where she made her final voyage to the breakers John Cashmore of Newport in South Wales.

So with mixed emotions my dad, together with 3,081 comrades, boarded the *Duchess of Bedford* bound for England and the northern seaport city of Liverpool. The seven-day trip was thankfully uneventful. Throughout his life my dad enjoyed being on ships. This was the first voyage he was able to relax and enjoy (the others previously were the 'slave ships', the exodus across the Caspian Sea, and the voyage into battle across the Mediterranean from Egypt to Italy), but despite this he was sailing into an uncertain future. One story he did tell me was that while at sea many of his fellow travellers were very seasick and since he never suffered from this was able to help them. I can't imagine that this was any of his other 'cruises' so I feel it must have been the voyage to England, especially considering the ship's reputation as one of the 'the drunken duchesses'.

City/town	Location	Approx. distance	Country
Liverpool	4,400 km north-west of Naples	40,995 km	England

Liverpool is located on the north-eastern coast of England, running along the River Mersey Estuary. It is the nearest seaport to the Irish Sea and has historically gained most of its wealth via this connection, not least of all through the slave trade.

It is built across a ridge of hills rising up to a height of around 70 m above sea level at Everton Hill and looks across the River Mersey to Wallasey and Birkenhead. It supports two impressive cathedrals and an impressive dock area.

Inhabitants of Liverpool are referred to as Liverpudlians and generally nicknamed 'Scousers', which is in reference to a local meal known as 'scouse', a form of stew.

Liverpool is a beautiful city, full of culture and history. It was here that Adolf Hitler allegedly stayed with his half-brother Alois for five months from December 1912 until April 1913 on his only ever visit to England.

My dad's stay in Liverpool wasn't to be very long; following some administrative procedures he was back on a train heading into Yorkshire. At some point most, if not all, the Poles arriving were warned not to speak about their time in the Soviet Union. It seems that British authorities didn't want to besmirch the 'good name' of their 'friend' Stalin! It is likely that the warning came as he arrived in England. It was a warning he heeded well as he rarely even mentioned it.

As indicated previously, where the newly arrived Poles were garrisoned and to some extent ultimately settled was dependant on which Army unit they belonged to. For most new arivees their first accommodation in the UK was in empty barracks (often American, Canadian or even sometimes prisoner of war) that at that time were still scattered around the British countryside. My dad's first stop was at a substantial but temporary tented camp (now completely gone) at the side of the world-famous racecourse in the Yorkshire capital city of York.

City/town	Location	Approx. distance	Country
York	150 km north-east of Liverpool	41,145 km	England

York is a city in the north of England in the county of Yorkshire. It is located at the confluence of the Rivers Ouse and Foss. It was one of England's main cities throughout the Middle Ages and in fact was the capital city of the country before London. It remained a key city, only declining in importance with the Industrial Revolution. Today it is an historic, vibrant and thriving city.

It lies within the Vale of York, a flat area of arable land bordered by the Pennines, North York Moors and Yorkshire Wolds. It is steeped in history, with the famous York Minster, the largest Gothic cathedral in Northern Europe, standing in the city's centre.

York was originally founded by the Romans and has been fortified several times. Even now its centre is enclosed by about 3 miles of medieval walls. Clifford's Tower, a medieval castle, stands in the centre of these walls. It has numerous other historic features including a strong Viking heritage, the Vikings having sailed up the Ouse from the North Sea to colonise the city in 877.

Guy Fawkes, famous in England for his attempt to blow up the Houses of Parliament, was born here in April 1570. So significant in English history were his efforts that he is still today celebrated throughout the country in spectacular fashion with huge bonfires and incredible firework displays on 5 November every single year.

I don't have much information about this period of my dad's time, but by 22 September he had been transferred to a demobilisation centre and had moved to the more permanent camp at Sand Hutton about 15 km north-east of York. I remember that he once said he was driving an officer somewhere in the countryside during heavy snowfall. He said that they got hopelessly lost but a friendly farmer put them up for the night.

Sadly, not everybody in Britain was so sympathetic to the plight of the Poles. The huge influx of mainly able-bodied men put pressure on an already stretched indigenous workforce, and in some instances Poles were considered second-class citizens. Months of sensitive negotiations with the left-wing trade unions, some of whom who were openly pro-Soviet and opposed to what they considered 'Fascist Poles', eventually led to an agreement that the Poles could be used in the much-needed farming and mining jobs.

Despite having arrived in England, the Polish forces continued to be subjected to a tirade of anti-Polish diatribes and public propaganda from the Soviet Union clearly aimed at discrediting and smearing those that had chose not to return to Poland. Stalin even went as far as revoking Anders' Polish citizenship and this may have been extended to my father and many others. He told me that he had a lifetime ban and would never be allowed to return to Poland.

Like many of the new immigrants my dad spoke no or very little English and as a prerequisite to integrating into British society he spent many hours trying to master the language. I'm not sure he was such a good student as my mum said when she met him his English was still very poor. As his English improved, he never managed to rid himself of his thick Polish accent, which remained with him throughout his life.

The numbers of Poles continued to increase as the civilians that had been transferred to refugee camps around the world arrived to seek their loved ones and fellow exiles. Many moved into large Displaced Persons (DP) camps, which again tended to be ex-military buildings, where they established close-knit Polish communities which continued well into the 1950s when the residents became completely integrated into British society or moved on to Australia, Canada or America.

By December 1946 my dad's demobilisation was almost complete. He entered the Polish Resettlement Corps with a pay scale equivalent to that of a private just before Christmas and so transferred from a military to a civilian life. During this time he was awarded the Polish Army Medal for the war to go with his Monte Cassino cross, ironically inscribed on the reverse with 'POLSKA SWEMU OBROŃCY' – 'FROM POLAND FOR HER DEFENDER'.

The British government also awarded him the 1939–45 Star, the Italy Star, the Defence Medal and the 1939–45 War Medal. However, for some reason he chose not to collect them. This seems quite common for those exiled Poles who hadn't returned home. Maybe it was a protest against the British government's stance on Poland, maybe apathy over his plight or maybe he just didn't want any more reminders of what he had just endured for nearly eight years.

The manpower requirement in the north of England was for the mining and heavy industries, and despite originally coming from a farming community in pre-war Poland and having trained as a tailor he was by virtue of his location in northern England destined for one of these. My mum said that his poor spoken English at an exit interview ensured that when asked what he had done before the war the employment staff confused his pronunciation of the word 'farmer' with 'miner'. I suspect this wasn't the case. It may have been the fact he had worked in gold-mines in exile in Siberia and was considered therefore to have mining experience. I don't think it was that either, it was more than likely the only employment option available to him and an opportunity not to be missed.

Whatever the reason, by 24 March 1947 he completed his Army exit medical at Sand Hutton, was issued with an Alien Identity Certificate and National Registration Identity Card, exited the PRC (but was placed in reserve) and was sent on his way to new life in 'civvy street' as a trainee miner with his new employer, the National Coal Board (NCB).

So off in his brand-new 'demob' civvy clothes he went to his job as a trainee miner at the NCB Askern training colliery just north of the North Yorkshire town of Doncaster. This colliery first started to deliver coal in 1911 and was used for coal production until the late 1980s. Sadly the last of the buildings were demolished in 1992 and the site has since been redeveloped.

Michael Short was one of the young 'Bevin Boys' who were conscripted to work in the coal mines during the later period of the war and just after. His experience of arriving at Askern will have been much the same as my dad's. Upon arriving at the Miners Hostel he was registered and allocated somewhere to sleep in a dormitory that held twenty. Each bed had a bedside table and cupboard. After depositing his belongings, he had his evening meal in the dining hall and relaxed with a cup of tea and a bun afterwards. In the morning, a bus took they were taken by bus to the Askern training colliery. There was an introductory talk and each person was issued with a helmet and boots. They were taught how to shackle pit tubs onto a moving steel hawser – a particularly difficult job in the cold. There were then more talks on all aspects of mining from safety to geology to various Acts of Parliament. Michael Short describes the lecturers as very 'Yorkshire' and consequently difficult to understand. I can imagine my dad experiencing the same problem. After a week, they went down the pit for the first time. The training underground was similar to that on the surface, but this way they got used to going down in the cage and being enclosed in the pit.

Just over three weeks later my father's initial training had been successfully completed and on 24 April he was transferred a short distance to his new permanent accommodation at the Broadway Miners' Hostel on Moorlands Road in Barnsley.

City/town	Location	Approx. distance	Country
Barnsley	60 km south-west of York	41,205 km	England

Barnsley is a large town in South Yorkshire. It was referred to as Berneslai in the famous Domesday Book (land census) of 1086 and has a long history both as a market and mining town. Though most famous for coal mining, most of the pits were actually in the surrounding villages, rather than in the town itself. Sadly all the mines are now closed, Goldthorpe Colliery being the last to close in 1994.

Wire, linen, and glass-making were also major industries, but only glass-making remains. Barnsley also has a proud tradition of brass bands, originally created as social clubs for the mining communities. Many of these brass bands continue to this day with several famous bands resident in Barnsley.

So my dad was now out of the Polish Army and although not a British citizen he was no longer under Polish control. He lived in cramped impersonal lodgings which he never really liked and he looked forward to the day he would eventually move out. Over the next twenty months or so he worked in a variety of the coal pits local to Barnsley such as the Monckton Main Colliery at nearby Royston and the Yorkshire Main Colliery on the road east towards Doncaster. During this period, on 21 of November 1947 he received his discharge from the PRC; he was now officially integrated into English civilian life at last. It wasn't the Poland he longed for but at least he was free.

While living and working in Barnsley he didn't really take part in any Polish communities, and the war had severely dented his religious resolve, so much so that he considered his attempt to take part in the British Catholic Church a let-down and he more or less permanently turned his back on the Church and his Catholic faith.

He did have lots of friends, many of whom had endured a similar epic to his own, but as the months and years moved on they drifted away, starting their own lives afresh. He did however make two special friends. The first was Bronislaw (Bruno) Gordianiek, who uncannily came from the same small village of Szwakszty as my father, although he was a few years older and they hadn't known each other before the war. They became very close. Bruno eventually moved to Stoke in the Midlands but they remained in contact for the rest of their lives.

The second close friend of my father's was Mikał Bucelewicz, whom he had first met at Sand Hutton. Again he was slightly older than my father and originated from Warsaw. Mikał had struck up a relationship with a widow called Anne Elizabeth Chuwen (*née* Heaney) after a chance meeting in Stockport near Manchester. Anne, who lived in Manchester, was of Irish descent. She was born in Warwick near Birmingham and had lost her first husband Isaac Chuwen, a Jewish Pole from Lwów, in 1937.

Anne had five adult children. Four men, Harold, Maurice, Sammy, Jack (mentioned earlier; a driver attached to the British 8th Army at the Battle of Monte Cassino), and a single daughter, Clara (my mother), who was born in Salford in 1924. I'm not going to go into the very colourful past of the family Chuwen, it's far too complicated and would be the subject of another book (possibly even several books) but to cut a long story short, my father accompanied Mikał Bucelewicz on at least one visit the short distance over the Pennines to Manchester. Despite having Ian Keen and Robert Holland from previous relationships, my mother and my father became friendly, so much so that he was invited to spend the New Year celebrations of 1948 with the Chuwen family.

It must have been a memorable time; within a month Clara had become Mrs Pleszak at the Manchester registry office, my father transferred to the Wheatsheaf Colliery at Pendlebury in north-west Manchester and he had moved into the Chuwen household in Hamilton Road in the Manchester suburb of Longsite. Shortly afterwards my grandmother married Mikał Bucelewicz, whom we always referred to as 'Uncle Michael'.

City/town	Location	Approx. distance	Country
Manchester	50 km south-west of Barnsley	41,255 km	England

Manchester is a fantastic, friendly and cosmopolitan city. It has recently undergone a massive transformation and regeneration into a modern, classy international city. It is now far removed from the industrial hub it was when my father arrived but still retains its traditional roots borne out of its leading role in the Industrial Revolution. The docks area, with the historic Manchester Ship Canal built to link Manchester with Irish Sea near Liverpool, once provided the lifeblood of communication and trade. The area bombed during the Second World War in 1940 and left derelict and neglected for years is now the heart of the modern Manchester. Fittingly and coincidentally, Manchester is a sister town to Saint Petersburg (Leningrad) in Russia, where my dad was born.

I was born in Manchester. It is my hometown. I love Manchester and am proud to be a Mancunian (or a Manc as we are sometimes 'affectionately' known). I still live near to Manchester in the foothills of the Pennines to the east, from where on clear days the metropolis that is Manchester can be seen sprawling below and away into the distance.

Complementing its world-famous arts, theatre and music scenes Manchester has a massive sporting heritage; football, cricket, athletics, rugby, cycling, swimming, tennis (Fred Perry, the last English tennis champion, was born in Stockport), ice hockey, and basketball to name but a few.

Though I have described some fantastic and magical places along my dad's journey to get to Manchester, there's only one place I want to be on a Saturday afternoon at 3 o'clock, and that's at Manchester's 'Theatre of Dreams', better known to most as Old Trafford, the home of the world-famous Manchester United football club.

Manchester has an undeserved reputation as England's wettest city. Well it's not, statistically Plymouth has the highest rainfall in England, while Swansea (in Wales) has highest rainfall in the UK. However, there is no denying that Manchester does seem to get more than its fair share of rain, but despite that it's a great place to live and to visit with lots of interesting aspects. Apart from the city centre itself with its galleries, theatres and museums it is located just below and to the west of the beautiful Pennines (a row of hills that runs north to south like the backbone of England), and has the English Lake District and the Yorkshire Dales to the north, the Midlands to the south, and the Cheshire Plain leading to the hills and valleys of Wales and the Irish Sea to the west.

The city is steeped in history. It is the birthplace of the Industrial Revolution and was significant in the creation of the Labour Party. Mr Rolls met Mr Royce in Manchester and they started their first car business here; the company they founded went on to make some of the most prestigious cars in the world. They also developed some of the most famous aero engines, which like their cars are still being produced to this day. Sadly, Mr Rolls, or more correctly Charles Stewart Rolls, was killed in 1910 at the age of thirty-two while flying a Wright Flyer aeroplane at an airfield in the south of England, giving him the dubious distinction of being the first Briton to be killed in an aviation accident.

Karl Marx, the Prussian philosopher and founder of modern communism, spent some time here in the 1840s with fellow German and social reformer Friedrich Engels, who shared Marx's idealism and essentially bankrolled him. Engels had been sent to Manchester to work in the family textile business by his father in order that he might reconsider his radical political tendencies. Apparently, it was in Manchester that Engels became concerned by the plight of the English working classes. He was so appalled by the conditions of the low-paid labour force and particularly by the use of child labour that he described parts of Manchester as 'Hell on Earth'! It may have been then, but I prefer to quote, and am in agreement with, Sir Matt Busby, celebrated manager of Manchester United, who stated 'Manchester is my Heaven'.

Another notable development from Manchester was the world's first computer. The device on which we all now depend so much was created here in 1948. Known as 'Baby' or 'the Small Scale Experimental Machine', the valve-driven monster had the equivalent processing power of a low-end mobile phone but filled an entire room with technical apparatus and cables. A replica is on display within the Manchester Museum of Science and Industry, and in 1965 the University of Manchester was the first in the country to open a Computer Science degree course.

Though of Polish decent the Chuwen family were a staunch Jewish household and spoke no Polish. Sadly, my dad became further removed from not only the Polish communities that had developed in Manchester but also from his Catholic beliefs. As he established himself in post-war England his family life flourished and on 29 October 1949 his first son, my eldest brother Michael, was born.

Throughout the remainder of the 1940s and all the way through the 1950s my dad worked in his new vocation as a coal miner, labouring deep underground at several of the now long-gone pits in the Manchester area, including Bradford Colliery east of Manchester city centre, Ashton Moss (the Snipe) Colliery in Ashton-under-Lyne (east Manchester) and the Wheatsheaf Colliery at Pendlebury (north-west Manchester). Until his death he proudly displayed the marks of his years of work down the pits, very distinctive blue scars on his back and arms formed from scratches and cuts filling with coal dust, to me almost as interesting as tattoos, a sort of catalogue of his years of hard work at the coalface.

Despite becoming more and more distant from his Polish Catholic roots, he did maintain his friendship with several Polish friends he met after the war and his close friendship with Bruno Gordianiek never diminished. Neither did his longing for his homeland and contact with his family, from whom he was dragged away in late 1939.

Though moving further and further away from his natural roots he remained proud to be Polish. He, like General Anders and thousands of Poles who remained in exile, never sought British citizenship and never became a naturalised British citizen. When travelling abroad on holidays, he was not recognised by the new Poland and they certainly would not issue a passport to him; he had to use a British-issued Travel Document, which clearly stated its validity for all countries except Poland.

In fact, there was less and less likelihood of him returning home because of the public propaganda, anti-communist accusations and smears attempting to discredit Anders and those Poles who hadn't returned to the new Poland after the war. Sadly most accepted the inevitable and began their new lives in permanent exile. Many like my dad stayed in England, but others moved on to America, Canada, Australia, New Zealand, Argentina and beyond.

My dad's longing for his home and contact with his family never waned. He tried establishing contact via the Red Cross, but it seems he was told in no uncertain terms that he should not persist and if he was to do so it could be detrimental to his family now living in the Byelorussian Soviet Socialist Republic! It was another hard pill to swallow, and he was never to have contact with his parents or family, in what to him had been Poland, ever again!

Life went on. His priorities were his new family, he continued labouring at the coalface and on 12 July 1950 my parents together with children Ian, Robert and Michael moved into their first, albeit rented, home of their own. It was located in the southern suburb of Manchester in Wythenshawe close to the former wartime airfield of RAF Ringway, which has since been extensively developed into the modern Manchester International Airport, England's north-west gateway to the world.

They lived in Wythenshawe for about a year. My mum was too far from her friends and family and commuting to north Manchester wasn't so easy for my dad who had to use public transport. They eventually secured a house swap and on 28 July 1951 moved back to central Manchester. Their house was on the famous Upper Brook Street close to the Manchester Royal Infirmary and Manchester University, or to give it its full and correct name, the Victoria University of Manchester.

My parents' second child together, my sister Christine Victoria-Anne, was born on 1 June 1953, and in July of the following year my dad transferred pits to the massive Bradford Colliery, just 1½ miles east of Manchester city centre. By 1955 my parents' house had been compulsorily purchased to make way for hospital developments. As they were in a position to take out a mortgage they moved to their first owned property, 5 Dale View in Haughton Green, a district of Denton in what was then a rural suburb of east Manchester.

City/town	Location	Approx. distance	Country
Denton	10 km east of Manchester	41,265 km	England

Denton sits at a crossroads whose centre is known as Crown Point. Roads radiate west to Manchester, north towards Lancashire, east towards Derbyshire and south into Cheshire.

It was famous for its hat industry, which was mainly located north of the crossroads, sadly now completely gone. Thomas and William Bowler, the world-famous hat makers and felt producers after whose surname the distinctive hat was named, were born here. Denton's hat-making heritage now only lives on in Denton's coat of arms, which contains an image of a beaver, the symbol of the hat industry.

Denton also had a long history of coal mining and in its heyday had many coal pits. All were closed by the start of the 1930s, so my father was never to work in any of them. Even though mining in Denton, like the hat industry, is no more, if you look carefully some remnants of this fascinating industrial archaeology can be clearly seen to this day. The most prominent is the original colliery office buildings for the main pit, Denton Colliery (originally called Ellis Pit), which is still in use today as residential dwellings and a monumental stonemasons. Nearby can also be seen traces of colliery retaining walls and the route of the former colliery tramway (known as the 'Bogie Track'). A little further away in Hulme's Wood, close to the River Tame (a subsidiary of the River Mersey that flows to Liverpool), can still be seen the foundations, slag heaps, reservoir, drainage soughs and other mine workings of several small pits including Hulme's Pit. Denton Colliery and Hulme's Pit were the last two of Denton's coal mines; both suffered through lack of maintenance during the crippling 1926 miners' strike and the Great Depression that followed. Both became flooded and were deemed economically unviable. They were never again mined. Both closed in 1929.

By the time my parents moved to Haughton Green, the national coal industry was already well into decline. The remaining extant pits around Manchester were suffering the same fate as those nationally. My dad's future in the coal industry looked bleak, and in addition he was becoming disillusioned with some of the working practices and heavy machinery he was having to use at the coal face.

He persevered, but the days were numbered for Bradford Colliery and on 1 April 1957 he returned once again to work at the Wheatsheaf Colliery in Pendelbury. Bradford Colliery itself struggled on for a while before finally closing for good in 1968. The site was redeveloped several times. The latest development was a memorial stadium for the Commonwealth Games in 2002 and is currently the home of Manchester City, the other great football team of Manchester.

Even with well-organised public transport, the long daily journey from Haughton Green to Pendlebury was a considerable burden on my dad, but despite this my parents managed to have their third child; me. I was born at home in Dale View on 29 December 1957. Although christened Francis Christopher, I have always been known as Frank. I presumed I'd been named after my uncle Frank (Franek), my dad's younger brother whom he had last seen in Szwakszty nearly twenty years before. It wasn't the case, my mother told me I was named after Frankie Vaughan, a 1950s English pop star and actor (famous for his song 'Give Me the Moonlight, Give Me the Girl' and for wearing a top hat, bow tie, tails and carrying a cane) who was very popular at that time. The Christopher I'm led to believe was because I was born around Christmas!

Dad worked for a further three years as a miner. He eventually found a new job in the large Sunblest Bakery (part of the massive Allied Bakeries group) in Bredbury, just a few miles from our home in Haughton Green. His final day as a coal miner was on 15 July 1960. He departed from the Coal Board's employment with a good letter of reference and the distinctive blue scars on his arms and body as his legacy of his time as a coal miner.

My dad was finally settled in his work and within a year his fourth and final child was born. Lawrence, like myself, was born at home in Dale View, Haughton Green on 2 May 1961.

As the family grew the house in Dale View became too small, so in May 1964 we transferred to a large council house in Lees Avenue in Denton, still within easy walking distance of the Sunblest Bakery in Bredbury. I used to play in the nearby fields which, I didn't realise then, were the site of the old Denton Colliery. In fact, I used to walk along a track to school which had originally been the main access route for miners living in Denton to Denton Colliery. The track also went alongside of the remains of the main pit shaft in which we often played; it was at the top of a small hill enclosed by a huge wooden palisade. I remember stories from boys slightly older than myself of when the shaft was still open and they used to throw things down it.

The shaft was finally capped and the palisade removed in 1974. It was the same year that, as only myself and Lawrence remained at home, we transferred to a smaller council house less than a mile away on the Yew Tree estate, which had been constructed on the site of the old Denton Colliery.

My dad worked at the Sunblest Bakery until the late 1970s when he moved to a smaller bakery in central Manchester behind what was then the Manchester Polytechnic (now Manchester Metropolitan University). He continued to work there until the bakery closed in 1982. He then worked as a labourer in a small engineering company in Heyrod near to Stalybridge until he retired in 1985.

After his retirement he spent much of his time working on his allotment, in which he grew mainly vegetables and pulses. He had always been a smoker, and though I now realise he didn't have a healthy diet and I suppose he didn't do much real exercise, I didn't consider him as having a health risk.

Well, I was wrong. Not long after his seventieth birthday in 1990, he suffered a severe heart attack while at home. Fortunately, my mother was there at the time and immediately rang the emergency services. The ambulance service arrived within half an hour and rushed him to the former Victorian Workhouse Tameside General Hospital in Ashton-under-Lyne. The prognosis wasn't good; the cardiac unit gave him less than a 50/50 chance of surviving the night.

Thankfully, their predictions were wrong. He gradually started to recover and though having a severely damaged heart he was, with a multitude of medications, soon able to return home. He was able to enjoy his home life but his health was clearly affected and it continued to slowly deteriorate, necessitating several spells back in the cardiac unit of Tameside General Hospital.

In late 1993 after a period of prolonged ill health spent in Tameside Hospital, it became clear that his condition was becoming critical. Rather than send him home, just before Christmas he was transferred to the hospice at Shire Hill Hospital in Glossop.

City/town	Location	Approx. distance	Country
Glossop	12 km east of Denton	41,277 km	England

Glossop is about 15 miles east of Manchester in the county of Derbyshire. It is a busy, bustling former mill town and the largest settlement in the north-western corner of the Peak District, though it lies just outside the Peak District National Park boundary.

Glossop, though a small but interesting town, is best known for it proximity to the world-renowned Peak District National Park, known as such because of its numerous small peaks and valleys. It was Britain's first national park, established in April 1951, and is the world's second-most visited national park. About 50,000 people live in the park and visitors from all over the world come to visit for peace and tranquillity and to enjoy the outdoor activities of the area. Some of England's finest climbing, caving, walking, cycling, horse riding, shooting and cycling are to be found there.

The National Park itself covers 1,438 square km with over 2,500 km of public rights of way and has in excess of 900 listed buildings, about 110 conservation areas, nearly 80,000 hectares of Environmentally Sensitive Areas (ESA), 10,000 km of dry stone walls and over 50,000 hectares of moorland. Its main economic activities are tourism, manufacturing, farming and quarrying. Despite the fact that the weather can at times be a little unpredictable and very changeable it is a beautiful and spectacular place to visit at any time of the year.

Shire Hill Hospital, a former workhouse like Ashton General Hospital, sits beneath the beautiful rolling moorland on the edge of the Peak District. My dad was to spend his final weeks here. It was the last place I was to see him alive. It was neither his homeland nor the place of his birth but nevertheless it was a pleasant place to spend his final days.

He died on 21 February 1994 of complications caused by his heart attack and was cremated in the crematorium in Dukinfield Cemetery near to Ashton-under-Lyne. It seemed only appropriate that some of his ashes were spread around his beloved allotment in Denton, his passion in the last years of his life.

Despite spending most of his life in Manchester, in fact almost two thirds of it, he like so many of his fellow deportees never became a British citizen; his official status remained 'Alien'. He was passionately Polish, longing for a Poland that would never return. Even now, though Poland is free from the constraints of the Soviet Union and was fully integrated into the European Union in May 2004, it isn't the Poland he would have wanted. His Poland is now part of Belarus, a nation that had never existed during his lifetime.

Since his death the British Ministry of Defence (APC Polish Enquiries) have kindly sent me his complete Army records and also supplied me with the four British medals that he never claimed, and the Memorial Society in Moscow provided details of his arrest and prison sentence.

The Polish government-in-exile continued from their headquarters in London until the Soviet Union dissolved in 1989, after which the symbols of the Polish Republic (the presidential banner, the presidential and state seals, the presidential sashes and the original text of the 1935 Constitution) were passed over to Lech Wałęsa, the first post-communist president of Poland. The government-in-exile passed into history, its memory now honoured by the 'the Polish Institute and Sikorski Museum', still located in the same building in London.

After years of slanderous accusation and denial of the exiled Poles, following the establishment of the post-communist Polish government they once again became accepted and acknowledged in their own country. Their exploits and notable personalities, like General Anders for example, removed from official history during Soviet times, became once again celebrated and honoured.

In 1992 the Monte Cassino Cross was elevated to an official Polish decoration (as opposed to decoration of the government-in-exile) and several other awards made available to the ex-veterans still in exile, including the 'Cross for Action in the West' (Krzyż Czynu Bojowego na Zachodzie) and the 'Deported to Siberia Cross' (Krzyż Zesłańców Sybiru).

As with his British-awarded medals, my dad never claimed these. Fortunately, I was able to receive his British medals from the MOD and I was able to obtain copies of the 'Cross for Action in the West' and the 'Deported to Siberia Cross' via the internet.

15

WHAT BECAME OF ... ?

I set out at the start of this epic to explain why I, the son of a poor Polish farmer, came to be raised in the affluent western city of Manchester. I achieved this by describing my father's enforced journey from a peasant village in eastern Poland. Though his story is long, convoluted, interesting and captivating he was but one of millions, all with similar tragic tales. So in a way it's the end of the story.

However, throughout my narration I have mentioned various other people and places and I think in order to complete the story it would be interesting to briefly highlight the fate of a few of them since their interaction with my father's story.

Poland

The Second World War totally devastated Poland. It lost over a 500,000 soldiers and 6 million civilians, nearly 20 per cent of its pre-war population. In addition, it lost 38 per cent of its national assets and as I have described earlier its borders were moved west, in the process losing 77,500 square km (about 20 per cent) of its pre-war territory.

Post-war Poland became a significant ally to the Soviet Union, so much so that for many it was intrinsic element of the Eastern Bloc. But as the influence of communism waned throughout the 1980s, Poland's long-suppressed independence began to emerge. The labour turmoil of 1980 led to the creation of the independent trade union ('Solidarity'), which rapidly developed into a true political force. It's co-founder and leader of the celebrated strike at the Lenin Shipyards in Gdansk, Lech Wałęsa, eventually became the first president of the post-communist Poland in 1990.

As the Soviet Union continued to implode, the revolutions of 1989 saw communist rule overthrown throughout Eastern Europe. It's not surprising that Poland became the first to denounce communism, and in a relatively bloodless upheaval Poland moved into what is constitutionally known as the 'Third Polish Republic'. Throughout the 1990s Poland aligned itself more and more with the West, joining the North Atlantic Treaty Organization (NATO) in 1999 and finally becoming a full member of the European Union on 1 May 2004.

Kresy Wschodnie

Sadly the eastern borderlands annexed by the Red Army in 1939 were never to rejoin Poland, and it seems that the Polish government does not put forward any claims for fear of losing its good relationship with its neighbours. The northern area became part of Lithuania, the area known as western Belarus joined with the Belarusian SSR and the southern part was incorporated into the Ukrainian SSR.

Lithuania, Belarus, and Ukraine all became independent in 1991 following the breakup of the Soviet Union, with Lithuania and Ukraine, like Poland, firmly aligning themselves along the lines of western democracy. Belarus retains its Soviet principles and has maintained closer political and economic ties to Russia than any of the other former Soviet republics, so much so that it remains isolated in modern Europe.

Szwakszty

The small village of my dad's birth remains largely the same to this day. The twentieth, let alone the twenty-first century, has largely passed it by. Most of the pretty wooden-built houses that were there when my dad lived there still remain. Few have any modern facilities, many still don't have electricity and all obtain their water from wells.

Kobylnik

Like Szwakszty, Kobylnik has changed little. It remains the centre of the local rural economy, but since 1964 has been called Naroch (Нарочь) after the nearby lake, even though there is a small village of Naroch along the shore of the lake.

Before the war about 375 Jews lived in Kobylnik. 320 were brutally killed during the German occupation. The remainder escaped to join the partisan groups in the surrounding dense forests. After the war the few remaining Jews resettled in Israel, America, Canada, Germany, Sweden, Poland and some in Russia itself.

Along the shores of Lake Naroch are many hotels, campsites and centres for recreation. The locally known Naroch Sanatorium, once a place solely of repost for Soviet Party members, has now become the Naroch Tourist Centre and includes two hotel buildings and provides a vast array of outdoor activities such as hiking, water-skiing, sailing, bicycle tours and other recreational activities.

Vileyka

Vileyka was totally devastated during the war and little of the old town now remains. After the war the town was rebuilt and became a regional centre of Soviet industry. Unfortunately, the town's fortunes have followed the demise of the Soviet Union so that now the huge factories don't employ the large numbers of workers they once did and there is high unemployment and a migration of the young to the larger Belarusian cites.

Just to the west of the town of Vileyka, clearly visible on aerial photographs, is a very large, polygon-shaped enclosure. Bizarrely for this land-locked country, it is the site of the 43rd Russian Navy's communication centre, codenamed 'Antey'. This VLF (Very Low Frequency) transmitter is still used for communicating with Russian submarines around the world. It comprises eighteen radio towers, incredibly tall and thin (each about 305 m), holding a net of steel cords which functions as a giant antenna.

Soviet Union

Emerging from the Tsarist Empire, the Russian-dominated idealistic union of socialist republics lasted nearly seventy-five years until its dissolution in 1991, following which Russia resumed her dominant global position. From the end of the Second World War until its dissolution it was generally antagonistic to the American-dominated West in a period known as the Cold War.

Adolf Hitler

The Austrian-born architect and initiator of the Second World War fundamental to this piece of work came to power in 1933. He died at his own hand in his underground bunker (the Führerbunker) in Berlin on 30 April 1945, just over a week after the Polish 2nd Corps had captured the Italian city of Bologna.

Josef Stalin

Following the war Stalin continued his reign of terror over his vastly increased empire. The American use of the atomic bomb to end the war with Japan also succeeded in preventing further Soviet gains in the east. Having installed communist governments in most of Eastern Europe, forming the Eastern Bloc, behind what Churchill referred to as the 'Iron Curtain' Stalin continued his isolation from western democracies until his death aged seventy-four on 5 March 1953. He died four days after suffering a huge stroke, or as some suspect from being poisoned. His body was initially preserved in Lenin's mausoleum, but was removed and buried next to the Kremlin walls in October 1961 during a period of de-Stalinisation.

The death of Stalin also heralded the demise of the dreaded gulag infrastructure. Within a short time of his death an amnesty for non-political prisoners and for political prisoners sentenced to not more than five years was followed by the widespread release of political prisoners in 1954. After Nikita Khrushchev came to power his mass rehabilitations signalled its end, but even so harsh punitive sentencing continued to exist in the Soviet Union and possibly still does to the present day.

Lavrentiy Beria

Beria had 'played by the Soviet book', rising to power in the wake of his fellow Georgian Stalin. After the death of Stalin, in which he was variously implicated by senior members of the Politburo, he made a play for supreme power. His dubious past had made him many enemies, and after Khrushchev came to power in the June of 1953 he was arrested, tried and executed.

Nakhodka

A small fishing village when my dad passed through, it grew from the days of the gulag slave ship trade and today is a modern fishing and commercial port city. During the communist era it gained prominence for its foreign trade as the nearby port and naval base of Vladivostok was closed to all westerners.

The sea route that my father travelled from Nakhodka to Magadan and back to Vladivostok now has much less traffic, but the Cape Aniva Lighthouse guarding the eastern entrance to the La Pérouse Strait can still be seen. It is no longer used, and though derelict it remains impressive, standing majestic and defiant against some of the worst coastal conditions that nature can conjure.

Kolyma

Magadan and indeed some of the other Kolyma towns are slightly more developed than they were in the 1940s, and gold is now extensively and commercially mined but in reality Kolyma is still cold, isolated and remains largely the same as it was when it was a prison to my dad.

The dreaded gulags have now long gone, but a huge monument commemorating the many prisoners who suffered within them was unveiled on 12 June 1996. Known as the 'Mask of Sorrow' (Маска скорби), its stands 15 m high on top of hill overlooking Magadan. It was designed by the Russian sculptor Ernst Neizvestny, famous for his *Lotus Flower* sculpture at the Aswan Dam in Egypt. It comprises a face with tears pouring from the left eye in the form of small masks while the right eye is in the form of a barred gulag window. At the rear there is small sculpture of a weeping young woman and a headless man on a cross, and inside there is a representation of a typical Stalin-era prison cell.

Duskanya, the camp complex where my dad was imprisoned, was used right up to the end of Stalin's reign. I'm not sure when it finally closed down but I know that it was still in use as a gulag in the August of 1953, and gold is still mined there to the present day. Scattered through the interior of Kolyma can still be found relics of those terrible days of Stalin. Isolated remains of the gulag camps, mine workings and even wooden gold-mining structures can still be seen. Though hiding a morbid past, they for me have the appeal of modern archaeology, now derelict and overgrown but still powerful and full of thought-provoking imagery.

Georgy Konstantinovich Zhukov

Following his successful and highly celebrated capture of Berlin he returned to Russia as a national hero. Hailed as 'Our Saint George' by the Muscovites, a poignant fact in that Saint George is the patron saint of Moscow, he led the Victory Parade through Red Square on a rainy 24 June 1945 on a beautiful white stallion. Apparently, Stalin himself planned to lead the parade but the stallion bolted because of his lack of riding skills and he grudgingly consented to Zhukov taking pride of place.

Following the war, he assumed the role of supreme military commander of the Soviet Occupation Zone in Germany. Within less than a year his enormous public acclaim was, not surprisingly, perceived by Stalin as a direct threat to his rule. This was intolerable to Stalin and Zhukov was posted to command the relatively insignificant Odessa Military District, where at times he was kept under virtual house arrest.

He survived further discrediting accusations and the Stalinist purges of 1949 and was recalled to Moscow after Stalin's death in 1953, first becoming Deputy Defence Minister in 1953 and then Defence Minister in 1955, for which he was involved in the invasion of Hungary in October 1956. By 1957 he was a full member of the Central Committee of the Communist Party but in 1960 after a disagreement with Khrushchev about the reduction in size of the Red Army he was stripped of his ministry, expelled from the Central Committee and confined to his Moscow apartment.

After Khrushchev was deposed in 1964 Zhukov was rehabilitated, but never returned to any position of political power. He spent the remainder of his days in retirement writing his memoirs – *Reminiscences and Reflections* (Vospominaniia i Razmyshleniia – Воспоминания и размышления).

He died on 18 June 1974 and millions people paid their respects as his body lay in state prior to his funeral. He was fittingly buried with full military honours in Red Square at the Kremlin Wall. Of the many monuments in his memory perhaps the most impressive is the equestrian statue in Manege Square (Манежная площадь – Manezhnaya ploshchad), sculpted by Vyacheslav Klykov.

Georgii Sergeevich Zhukov

Nowhere near as famous as his more senior namesake, this General Zhukov, seen as liberal if not helpful to the newly amnestied Poles in 1941 and 1942, rose through the ranks of the NKVD to reach the position of chief of 2nd Section, 4th Directorate, Ministry of Internal Affairs MVD by 1954. The very same year, like many of his contemporaries, he was stripped of his rank, ejected from the service and consigned to spend the rest of life in ignominy.

Władysław Anders

Clearly the leading figure in the salvation of the Poles throughout and following the war, he was for me without doubt 'the man of the match'. Despite his personal distress, frustration and no doubt bitter disillusionment, his unerring loyalty and resolution remained unaffected. He never faltered, he stood strong in his belief with dignity and compassion and under his firm leadership the Polish Corps fought with distinction until the very end of the war.

After the war he suffered what we would now consider libellous, slanderous accusations of crimes against Poland from the provisional government in Warsaw, who went on to revoke his Polish citizenship. In post-war communist Poland he didn't officially exist and the successes of the Polish 2nd Corps were never discussed, let alone celebrated. He never gave up fighting for his vision of a free Poland and devoted himself to the care of his old comrades of all ranks and to preserving by every possible means the memories and the hopes of the country that disappeared on the first day of the war in September 1939. He continued to play an important role in the government-in-exile which remained in London, and was a founder member of 'the Council of Three' (Rada Trzech) formed in 1954 when differences began to appear in the unity of the government-in-exile.

He remained prominent and active in the affairs of the Poles who remained in exile until his death in London on 12 May 1970, almost twenty-six years after his great victory at Monte Cassino. He lay in state at the church of Andrzej Bobola in London before, in accordance with his wishes, being buried alongside his soldiers in the Polish cemetery at Monte Cassino.

Today he is finally recognised and celebrated by the government of Poland as a national hero. Many streets and schools are now named after him, and 2007 was the first ever year of Anders. Respect and recognition at last.

Varlam Shalamov

Varlam Tikhonovich Shalamov (Варлáм Тѝхонович Шалáмов) was born in 1907 in Vologda. By 1929 he had been arrested and imprisoned in the Butyrka prison for being a member of a Trotskyist group. After his release in 1931 he worked on the construction of a chemical plant in Perm Oblast before returning to Moscow a year later as a writer and journalist.

At the beginning of the Great Terror of 1937 he was again arrested for 'counter-revolutionary Trotskyist activities' and sentenced to five years in Kolyma. Like many others his sentence was repeatedly extended and by 1946 the harsh rigours of Kolyma had taken their toll; he was thin, wasted and near to death – a real *dokhodyaga*. Miraculously, he was saved by a fellow inmate who worked as a doctor who managed to secure Shalamov work as a camp hospital attendant. His health gradually improved and he was able to begin writing poems and short stories.

He was eventually released in 1951, but wasn't permitted to return to Moscow until after he had been officially rehabilitated in 1956. The following year he became a correspondent for the literary journal *Moskva*, after which his poetry began to be published. He is most famous for his work, a series of excellent and informative short stories, written between 1953 and 1971 and collectively published as *Kolyma Tales*, which at first had limited visibility particularly in the West.

He died in 1982 and is now regarded as a literary hero, some believe on a level with Solzhenitsyn. His life has been immortalised by the Shalamov Society and a museum based in his original family home in Vologda.

Janusz Bardach

Janusz Bardach was born in Odessa in 1919, but moved to Poland when he was less than a year old. After the invasion of Poland, he joined the Red Army and became a tank driver, but following an unfortunate accident with his tank in 1941 he was sentenced to ten years' hard labour and sent to Kolyma.

Having obtained various positions as a *feldsher* (camp medical assistant), he secured himself some immunity from the brutality of the gulag structure and began to learn about the medical profession. He was eventually released in 1946, and made his way to Moscow where he studied medicine, before returning to Poland to specialise in plastic surgery.

Following a spate of anti-Semitism he emigrated to the United States in 1972 where he continued his pioneering work on plastic and reconstructive surgery and developed a surgical procedure for patients with congenital cleft palate. Following his retirement in 1991 he published the account of his time in the camps of Kolyma (*Man Is Wolf to Man: Surviving Stalin's Gulag*). He died in Iowa in 2002.

Vladimir Petrov

An enigmatic character, Petrov, a nineteen-year-old Russian, was studying in Leningrad when Sergey Kirov was assassinated in December 1934. He was arrested during the mass purges that followed and after several brutal months in prison he was sentenced to six years' hard labour in the goldfields of Kolyma. His experiences in Kolyma ranged from times of near-freedom to times of the sheer brutality we normally associate with the gulag regime.

He was released shortly after the Poles started arriving in Kolyma, and made his way back to his home town near Leningrad. He avoided Soviet mobilisation and after his home town was captured by the German Army he managed to work his way across Europe through Germany and into Italy, where it's believed he had some involvement with the operations of General Vlasov, the ex-Soviet officer who had defected to the German side and was attempting to create a Russian Liberation Army (POA – Русская Освободительная Армия) with the intention of overthrowing Stalin!

By 1947 Petrov he had arrived in America, where he became an academic and taught at such eminent seats of education as Yale University and the George Washington University. His first book *Soviet Gold*, which I have to say, I thought was magnificent – informative, descriptive and enthralling – was published in 1949 and was apparently the first memoir of a gulag prisoner to be seen in the West. Petrov died in 1999 at his home in Kensington, Maryland.

Roman Skulski

Born in the Polish town of Stryj, now the Ukrainian town of Stryi, he was conscripted into the Red Army and was marching to the defence of Stalingrad when he fled to join the Polish Army. Crossing the Caspian Sea to Krasnovodsk, he almost fell foul of a furious Colonel Berling who at that time was still an officer in the Polish Army. Avoiding arrest, he made his way to Guzar and was able to join General Anders' Polish Army.

After being evacuated to Iran, he volunteered for service in the Polish Air Force and was transferred to the UK via India and South Africa. Air sickness cut short his flying career and after the war he settled for a short time in England before emigrating to Canada in 1949, where he became a chartered accountant. His often amusing book *In The Soviet Union Without Toilet Paper* describes his struggles, and I exchanged many emails with him about his experiences. Sadly, Roman passed away in 2008.

Stanislaw 'Stanley' Kowalski

Not the fictional character in Tennessee Williams' play *A Streetcar Named Desire*, Stanley Kowalski is a Pole from the town of Jazlowiec (now in Ukraine), who like my father spent time in Kolyma and then fought in vain for the freedom of his country. He survived the war and eventually settled in Canada, where he still lives to this day. His enlightening unpublished works about his arrest and time in Kolyma have recently been revised and published as *No Place to Call Home: The Memories of a Polish Survivor of the Soviet Gulag.*

Aleksander Topolski

Aleks was just sixteen years old when he started his military service in late August 1939. His early childhood was in Pruzana (now in Belarus), but he spent most of his youth in Horodenka (now in Ukraine). After the Russian invasion he tried to leave Russian-occupied Poland for nearby Romania.

Captured at the border he spent two years as the 'guest' of the NKVD. Educated and artistic, his lively account of his time in the Soviet penal system, *Without Vodka*, is fascinating and, surprisingly, at times humorous. Of the many books I read during my research I found this one of the most enthralling.

After being amnestied, he served with the Polish 2nd Corps. He, like my father, arrived in England, and eventually graduated from Manchester University as an architect. His work took him around North America and the Caribbean, but he settled in Canada. He still lives in Quebec and is finalising the English of his second book *Without A Roof: WAR!* In 2012 it was published in Polish as *Bez Dachu*. Aleks has been a regular visitor to Monte Cassino where I had the great pleasure of meeting him during the sixty-fifth anniversary celebrations.

Nikolai Getman

Nikolai Getman was born in 1917 in Kharkiv, Ukraine where he studied art. He served in the Red Army during the war, but shortly afterwards he was arrested for participating in anti-Soviet propaganda and spent seven years in forced labour camps in Siberia and Kolyma, and survived as a result of his ability to sketch for the propaganda requirements of the authorities.

After his release he started to paint in secret, documenting the harsh realities of the brutal regime from memory. In 1997, with the support of the Jamestown Foundation his paintings were eventually brought to the West. He died at his home in Orel, Russia in 2004.

Romuald Lipinski

Originally from Brześć nad Bugiem (now Brest in Belarus), he was deported to Siberia in June 1940. After the 'Amnesty' he joined Anders' Army and fought in Italy. After the war he had a short spell in the UK before leaving for America in 1953.

A fantastic chronicler of life under Soviet occupation, the realties of his time in exile and in particular his first-hand accounts of the Battle of Monte Cassino, Romuald is still alive and well and active in researching, remembering and recognising the Polish citizens deported, enslaved and killed by the Soviet Union during the Second World War.

Zygmunt Berling

After deserting Anders at Krasnovodsk, Berling totally embraced the Soviet ideal, for which he was rewarded with the command of the 1st Polish Army in the Soviet Union. Having fought his way west towards Warsaw he was ordered to stop at the River Vistula. Alledgedly without authorisation from his Soviet superiors he issued orders to engage the German enemy and assist the Polish resistance. Though noble, this action was futile without full Soviet support, and Berling was soon relieved of his command.

He was transferred to the War Academy in Moscow, where he remained until returning to Poland in 1947. He organised and directed the Academy of General Staff (Akademia Sztabu Generalnego) until his retirement from the army in 1953. He then served in various communist Polish ministries until 1970. He died in July 1980.

Kazimierz Sosnkowski

Following his dismissal in 1944, General Sosnkowski emigrated to Canada and though not having any real position of state continued to fight the Polish cause. He died in Arundel (Quebec) in 1969, and following the independence of Poland in 1989 his ashes were returned to Warsaw and symbolically buried beneath St John's Cathedral (Katedra św. Jana).

Wojtek the Bear

The Syrian brown bear found in Iran accompanied the 22nd Artillery Supply Company throughout its Italian campaign. There are many stories, indeed books, about the adventures of this incredible animal. Wojtek enjoyed wrestling with the soldiers and legend has it that he not only liked to drink beer and smoke cigarettes, but during battles actually helped by carrying heavy supplies. In recognition of the bear's popularity a representation of a bear holding an artillery shell was approved as the official emblem of the 22nd Artillery Supply Company.

At the end of the war Wojtek was transported with the 22nd Artillery Supply Company to the village of Hutton, near Duns in Berwickshire, Scotland. Initially, he stayed with the unit but in late 1947 as they disbanded and dispersed into civilian life the bear was given over to the Edinburgh Zoo where it was to spend the rest of its life.

Though it was clearly unhappy in its captivity it was frequently visited by former Polish soldiers and journalists. It is said the visitors would often throw him cigarettes, and in some instances would climb into his pen to wrestle with him. Wojtek died in December 1963, at the age of twenty-two, but he will never be forgotten. A full-size sculpture can be found in the Polish Institute and Sikorski Museum in London as well as commemorative plaques in Edinburgh Zoo, the Imperial War Museum in London and the Canadian War Museum in Ottawa. Even as recently as 2008 plans for a memorial were being finalised for Edinburgh and for a full-size sculpture for the village of Hutton.

Polish Government-in-Exile

With the emergence of communist Poland and its growing world-wide recognition, the government-in-exile became largely symbolic of continued resistance to the Soviet occupation of Poland. It did, however, command the loyalty of around 150,000 Polish veterans and their descendants living in Britain and maintained important archives from pre-war Poland. Though exerting no political power it continued its existence in London until Soviet rule over Poland came to an end in 1989.

When Lech Wałęsa became the first post-communist president of Poland in December 1990, the last president of the government-in-exile, Ryszard Kaczorowski, transferred the symbols of the Polish Republic (the presidential banner, the presidential and state seals, the presidential sashes and the original text of the 1935 Constitution) back to Poland and in so doing formally dissolved the Polish government-in-exile and thus 'closed the curtain' on a particularly sad chapter in Polish history.

Monte Cassino

The Battle of Monte Cassino is even now a sensitive subject and I have clearly generalised and simplified many of the complex issues in my narrative. For the Allies it was a costly failure, a public relations 'shot in the foot'. With hindsight the savage battles and near-total destruction of the historic abbey could have been avoided if, as had been suggested in some quarters in early 1944, the Allies simply bypassed the Cassino area and encircled the German forces, which was in actual fact what happened to enable the Poles to make the final assault.

Hindsight, as we all know, is a wonderful thing. It took four separate fierce battles to capture the area, after which the abbey lay in ruins. German experts still deny occupying the abbey and despite thorough investigations there is still no firm evidence that the Germans were using the abbey before it was bombed. Though there had been fierce fighting for almost six months, the actual capture took place without any real fighting at all; the German Army had withdrawn and the Polish Lancers simply walked in. The Polish flag that was hastily hoisted over the ruins to mark the end of the battle is now proudly displayed at the Polish Institute and Sikorski Museum in London.

While the Battle of Monte Cassino is seen by the Poles as their finest military achievement, it was in reality to the Allies a costly blunder, almost an embarrassment. It was, however, and still is regarded by the Germans as one of their finest military achievements. It is considered by them, and particularly the surviving veterans and their descendants, as a matter of national pride. Not only was it a rare interlude of pure military success which highlighted the efficiency of their soldiers, who fought long and hard in a war which for them had so many failures and ended ultimately in embarrassing defeat, but also the battles were fought on strictly military levels; there were no Nazi atrocities or wrongdoings associated with any stage of the battles or the build-up to them. These facts, coupled with the care, amid all the destruction, of removing for safekeeping all the treasures that were housed within the abbey, give Monte Cassino true esteem in the eyes of the German people.

After the war the careful restoration and redecoration of the abbey was started in earnest. The work took over ten years to complete and was financed solely by the Italian state. America apparently had offered to support the restoration but in the end provided no funds. The abbey, with all its treasures returned, was finally re-consecrated by Pope Paul VI in 1964 and is once again, as it quite rightly should be, a place of pilgrimage.

The Polish war cemetery at Monte Cassino has always been a shrine to the 'free' Poles and has scores of visitors coming to pay their respects at the graves of their fallen Polish brethren. Sadly, during communist times it suffered from a lack of upkeep and was poorly maintained. The communist Polish Government who disregarded Anders and those Poles in exile who would not accept Stalin were, it seems, not prepared to maintain an icon of their greatest achievement. Thankfully with dissolution of the Soviet Union and the welcoming of the Polish 2nd Corps into the revised Polish history, the cemetery has once again returned to its former greatness. It has been honoured by visits from both the Polish-born Pope John Paul II in 1979 on the occasion of the thirty-fifth anniversary of the battle, and recently, on the sixty-fifth anniversary by the former German soldier and current Bishop of Rome, Pope Benedict XVI.

So significant in the history of all the nations that took part, the Battles of Monte Cassino are still celebrated every May, though sadly each year drawing fewer and fewer veterans who were there all those years ago. The sixty-fifth anniversary celebration took place on 18 May 2009. It was conducted on a glorious sunny day by the current Polish President Lech Kaczynski and I was privileged, with my brother and two sons, to be in the huge crowd among veterans and well-wishers of all nations to witness the event.

The scars of battle have now mostly healed; however, apart from the large memorials that adorn Hills 593, 505 and others, testimonies of those awful months of battle can still be found to remind us of the epic struggle that went on on those beautiful Italian hilltops. Rummaging around the now-wooded hillsides will soon turn up fragments of metal and the remains of sangars, and other decaying reminders of the events sixty-five years ago.

Albaneta Farm (Massa Albaneta) was a large farm complex between and below Hills 593 and 505. It was at the top of Cavendish Road on the 'back-door' route to the abbey of Monte Cassino. Occupied by German troops early in the fighting, it was the scene of heavy fighting on 19 March 1944 when the New Zealand 20th Armoured Regiment attacked up through Cavendish Road. German paratroopers dug in around it were taken by surprise by the armoured thrust but nevertheless thwarted the tank attack. It was again attacked in the armoured Polish assault on 17 May and eventually taken by units of the 3rd Carpathian Rifle Division, who pressed on towards Hill 505. The farm has never been restored and remains derelict and overgrown with trees; a sad tombstone, it bears silent witness to the fierce battles that it was once party to.

To the north of Albaneta Farm, a short way up Cavendish Road can be found a Polish tank memorial. The tank of the 4th Armoured 'Skorpion' Regiment foundered on mines on 17 May 1944 during the final Polish armoured thrust on the abbey. The following year, tank tracks in the shape of a cross and huge cast scorpions holding memorial placards were welded to its top. This lasting memorial can be seen to this day, pretty much as it was when it was first destroyed, but somebody has tried to steal the beautiful scorpions, sadly leaving just one of the claws in place for posterity.

Cavendish Road or the Polish Sappers' Road, the goat track that was developed into a main highway to the abbey, is still there. Though overgrown in places it has almost returned to the goat track it once was, but with care it can still be walked today. The views are spectacular and it is a testimony to those drivers who magnificently manoeuvred their vehicles up this steep, winding path clinging to the edge of a precipice.

Hill 593, the highest point on Snake's Head Ridge, saw some of the heaviest loss of life during the whole campaign. The once barren, rocky landscape is now lush with trees and shrubs. A memorial to the Poles who gave their lives proudly perches on the highest point.

The 'Doctor's House', the Regimental Aid Post sitting just below Snake's Head Ridge which saw so much of the action during the long months of the battle, has been restored to its former status as a farm. The family who occupied it before the war amazingly still occupy it today and it is visited annually by veterans of all the nations who used its sanctuary in the Battles of Monte Cassino.

It's interesting that the names of the key points used during the battles over sixty-five years ago have remained in peoples' minds and are still used to this day. Though little used as a road now, the name Cavendish Road remains in use as do points 593, 569, Phantom Ridge, Snake's Head Ridge and the 'Doctors House'. One name that hasn't is the Inferno Track, and the track itself, which saw such intense activity for a very brief period of time, was abandoned once it ceased to be used by advancing armies, and was very quickly reclaimed by nature. An almost impenetrable path does exist, and whilst it can be walked with care it would now be impossible to drive.

Albert Kesselring

A veteran of the First World War, he left the army in 1933 to become head of the Department of Administration at the Reich Commissariat for Aviation, which was basically developing the foundations for the Luftwaffe.

During the Second World War he was involved in campaigns in Poland and France, the Battle of Britain and the invasion of Russia. But he is most remembered as the smiling Commander-in-Chief South, the overall German commander in the Mediterranean theatre, which included the operations in North Africa and Italy. It is said, and I don't know how much truth there is in it, that he often had meals with his Allied counterparts while in North Africa, but what appears to be a fact is that he rewarded one captured Allied soldier with freedom after he had had led some of Kesselring's soldiers safely across an Allied minefield back to their lines.

He was one of only twenty-seven German officers to be awarded the Knight's Cross of the Iron Cross with Oak Leaves, Swords and Diamonds. It is, however, his stubborn defensive campaign against the Allied forces in Italy for which he is most famous, and while compassionate and respected by his Allied counterparts he was also ruthless. After the war he was implicated in massacres committed by troops under his command in Italy and sentenced to death. The sentence was subsequently commuted to life imprisonment. He was released in 1952 on medical grounds following a political and media campaign. He died at the age of seventy-four in 1960.

Fridolin von Senger und Etterlin

Aristocratic, educated and enigmatic, Frido von Senger und Etterlin, like Kesselring, was a veteran of the First World War. He had distinguished himself in battle and when his younger brother Johann-Gustav, who served as a fighter pilot in Jagdstaffel (Fighter Squadron) 12 and attached to Fridolin's Army group, was killed in 1917, Fridolin went out of his way to find the mass grave where his brother was buried and, in the midst of the Battle of Cambrai, removed his body for a more dignified burial.

Though a devout catholic and an anglophile (he had studied in Oxford) he was also a master military scholar and tactician. He strongly opposed the principles of Nazism, but was never implicated in any plot against Hitler and probably survived Hitler's purges because he was such a dedicated and efficient soldier. During the war he commanded Army brigades in France, was part of the German commission for the French–Italian Armistice of 1940, commander of the 17th Panzer Division in Southern Russia and organised the safe evacuation of German forces from Sicily, Sardinia and Corsica as the Allied armies pressed forward.

As overall commander of the Gustav Line he masterminded the successful defence around Monte Cassino, and though he was away in Germany when the final assault took place in May 1944, he was soon back at the front line organising and cajoling his troops. According to his biography, his last night before withdrawing from his HQ near to Monte Cassino he spent drinking tea with a British pilot who had been shot down!

He remained one of the key commanders in Italy as the German forces were pushed ever further back towards Germany. When the war in Italy ended he became the chief negotiator of the surrender of German forces in Italy to General Mark W. Clark, by then the commander of all Allied forces in Italy.

After being held in several prisoner of war (POW) camps in Italy and Germany he was eventually transferred to London for interrogation, after which he remained at Special Camp 11 at Bridgend, South Wales until his repatriation to Germany in May 1948. He remained active working in higher education establishments and on specialist military commissions until his death in 1963.

Polish Civilians

For those unfortunate not to be evacuated to Persia, it is a sad story. Some of the adults joined Berling in the communist Polish 1st Army, small numbers were eventually able to make their way back to Poland, but for many others there are no records.

Of the civilians that were lucky enough to be evacuated to Iran (Persia at the time), most were eventually transported to refugee camps in India, South and East Africa, Australia, New Zealand and Mexico. After the war many were 'repatriated' to England to rejoin their families that had served under Anders. Living for many years in Displaced Persons (DP) camps, they eventually moved on throughout the globe, becoming part of what we now know as the Polish Diaspora.

16

RETURN HOME

No Longer Poland!

So that's almost the end of my book. Even for me, just researching and writing it has been an epic journey. I have recounted an incredible set of circumstances which led my father to spend the majority of his life in Manchester. He and his fellow Poles forced into exile and now dispersed around the globe have left lasting memories in all of the many places they passed through; memorials and cemeteries in Russia, Siberia, Kazakhstan, Uzbekistan, Turkmenistan, Iran, Iraq, Israel, Egypt, Italy and here in my native England remind the passers-by of the ordeal that millions of Poles went through not so long ago.

I have been amazed at many of the places and peoples that my dad must have come into contact with; some of the places I would never even have heard of had it not have been for their connection with this convoluted tale. And while I've only followed in his footsteps to a few of the places he passed through, I never followed in his footsteps professionally. Being brought up in the absolute comfort and safety of England I was able to benefit from a higher education structure and find employment in the relative security of the white-collar sector.

Many things have struck me in writing this book, but I suppose the biggest two are the unfairness meted out to the Poles from the day Germany invaded on 1 September 1939 pretty well until the present day, and secondly how lucky I am to be here at all. Several other less invidious observations are also worth a mention and while I could write about many, I don't propose to do so. However, I think its worth mentioning a few of my lingering thoughts.

I have almost blithely described mass deportations, families and individuals sent into exile, and even executions without attempting to describe the feelings and emotions of those involved. Whole families and communities torn apart and then thrust into a long and bloody war, whose suffering, anguish and mental torment is unimaginable. For those like me who never experienced it, it would be impossible let alone difficult to even attempt to describe, even though I have experienced some personal tragedy during the course of writing this book when my eldest son Owain died suddenly of meningitis.

What is clear, however, is the resilience of people, to suffer what they did and still carry on overcoming each and every hurdle that was thrust in their way. I'm amazed at their ability to cope, and when I read that my dad was working in winter conditions of down to -50°c with inappropriate clothing, underfed, tired and often ill, it astounds me. I have hiked in moderately extreme conditions, well fed and with proper clothing, and still found it tough. It's not surprising so many died in Kolyma, I think what is more amazing is that any survived at all!

I have depended heavily on the writings of others to whom I am eternally grateful. Some of these memoirists were clearly eloquent and educated and not surprisingly they often found favour with uneducated *urka* types because of their story-reading and tale-telling abilities. Others with artistic abilities found similar favour with the lower Soviet classes for their ability to create tattoos.

I found many of the descriptions of the *urkas* disturbing and frightening, but at the same time I found this low social anthropological class not only intriguing but interesting and extremely complex. I even found some of the descriptions amusing, as they cowered and cried when having to have simple injection and then would without a second thought subject themselves to crude tattooing and violence. The fact that they existed in a complex micro-environment with clear but unwritten rules where supply, demand and bartering were the accepted rules of life is bizarre on many levels but not least of all as it was contrary to the ideals of communism. In a similar way homosexuality, completely outlawed under communism outside of the prison environment, was not only accepted in the world of the Soviet prison structure but considered as a normal state of affairs.

I also found some of the written descriptions of the brutality that existed right from the start of the story right through to the end of the war almost dispassionate and removed from the facts they were describing. But I suppose they were so awful that it would be impossible to remain attached and involved and maintain any semblance of sanity. I sort of witnessed this myself when working on a project in Africa with a helicopter company that employed Vietnam veteran pilots. I was surprised by their stories too, which also showed an indifference, if not acceptance, to the death, horror and suffering of the stories they were describing.

So that is almost that, and in summary it took a long journey, an incredible set of events and an awful lot of luck for me to be born and raised in Manchester. My dad suffered the excesses of the Soviet penal system, arrest, brutal prisons, deportation, harsh and unforgiving labour camps, long journeys, illness and war before getting to Manchester. In doing so he was lucky not to have been executed, lucky to reach the Polish Army as it was evacuating from the Soviet Union and fortunate to survive the hideous, bloody battles in Italy.

It has taken me nearly fifty years to realise it, but I am very, very fortunate. In addition I have, bizarrely, also discovered that my father's Christian name wasn't what I thought it was. All of my life, together with my siblings I knew my father as Michael or Mick, which I in my ignorance presumed to have been an Anglicised version of his Polish name, Mikołaj. However, on several documents I have received in Cyrillic his name (transliterated) is shown as Nikolai or in English Nicholas. At first I assumed this to be a typing error but I discovered that he was known by his sister as Kolya, which is a diminutive of Nikolai, so the Russian documents were correct. As he spoke no English when he arrived in Liverpool it must have been the initial interpretation of his Polish name Mikołaj that led to him being called Michael, and it stuck. So not only did I not know very much about my dad, I, embarrassingly, didn't even know his correct Christian name!

So that's the end...

Well it is, apart from that so far I haven't mentioned what became of my dad's family he left behind. It is not surprising I suppose, since he wasn't allowed to have any contact, but I can now add the last two pieces of this very complicated jigsaw into place.

I mentioned that his two younger brothers, Bolesław and Franciszek, had been taken from their village of Szwakszty by the German Army when they occupied the Kobylnik region. They were both used for forced labour across Germany and by the end of the war both had wound up in the dreaded Dachau concentration camp about 20 km north-west of Munich.

Miraculously both survived and were liberated on 29 April 1945 by the US 7th Army's 45th 'Thunderbird' Division (who had been part of the Anzio landings) and the 42nd Rainbow Division. Little consolation I know, but they were less than 1,000 km from their older brother in Bologna, the nearest they had been for nearly six years.

After their release, they had a long period of recuperation and stayed for a while in a Displaced Persons camp in Bavaria before moving to temporary camps in western Germany. They both eventually found work on farms around the German town of Saarbrücken, which at that time was under French administration. Bolek married a French girl and settled in the village of Folschviller near to the border town of St Avold in the Lorraine region of north-eastern France. Franciszek married his long-time Polish partner Krystyna, bought a piece of land and built a home in the village of Lachambre, also near to St Avold.

As they settled into their new life they wondered what had happened to their older brother, whom they had not heard from since his arrest by the NKVD. They had no knowledge of whether my dad was dead or alive, but Franciszek contacted the Red Cross tracing services to see if they had any information on what had happened to my father. It took a long time, during which I'm sure they must have almost given up hope of any news, but in 1964 the Red Cross did indeed reply with my dad's details in England.

Letters were exchanged and in the summer of 1965 my uncle Franciszek and auntie Krystyna came to visit us in Denton. I can't remember how their first meeting went but I'm sure it was very emotional.

My dad stayed in contact with his brothers and my first-ever trip abroad was in the summer of 1970 when we spent two weeks in Lachambre. We made regular trips back to France and I have very fond memories of those times and especially of my auntie Krystyna, who was a wonderful, warm and friendly lady.

Sadly she died in 1978; it was a great loss to the family, but my dad and his brothers remained close. It's a shame that they were so far away as they enjoyed each other's company a great deal; they obviously had much reminiscing to make up.

My dad's last trip to France was in the summer of 1981, he had travelled there by train with my brother Lawrence. I was at university at the time and hitch-hiking around Europe, but I managed to get to Lachambre where my elder brother Michael had also arrived with his family. It was a huge family get-together.

I remember my dad being particularly emotional when he came to depart; it wasn't something I'd seen much before in my dad. Perhaps he knew something!

Sadly it was the last time he was to see either of his brothers; both died in 1982. My dad was very fortunate to have those few years of contact with his brothers again, he must surely never have expected it as he spent his years in exile.

I have said that my dad was never allowed to attempt to make contact with his family in Szwakszty, but despite the loss of the three sons their life did carry on. I mentioned very early on that despite having neighbours that were deported in 1940 by the NKVD, my grandfather's family miraculously escaped it, and after the war they returned to the subsistence farming lifestyle they had known before the war, but minus three sons.

I also mentioned that when my dad was deported his mother was pregnant. In 1940 my grandmother gave birth to my dad's youngest brother Walerian. In his first few years he was to experience Soviet, German and then more Soviet occupation. Raised in a Soviet-dominated environment, he grew up to be known as Valera. Growing up in a Soviet culture he never learned – or more specifically was not allowed to learn – Polish, even though my grandfather Wincenty remained staunchly Polish. Shortly after the war Wincenty even applied for permission to move to Poland. Amazingly, this seems to have been granted, but with his health failing my grandfather decided to stay in Szwakszty and the life he had always known. Life continued for them in pretty much the same harsh way it had before the war, but as citizens of the Belarussian SSR rather than as Poles.

Wincenty died at the age of sixty-five in 1955 and was buried at the Catholic cemetery in Kobylnik. Aleksandra, my grandmother, struggled on for a while but she eventually returned with the young Walerian to her family home near to Radviliškis in Lithuania to live with her sister. Maria, her eldest daughter, had married a local man and lived in the Pleszak family home in Szwakszty, and Honorata after getting married moved into the home of her husband.

Aleksandra died in 1970 by which time Walerian, who had never known Polish culture and who spoke no Polish, was serving as a driver in the Soviet Army. When he demobbed he moved back to the family home in Szwakszty for a while before eventually moving to work at the Zenith Camera factory in Vileyka. Maria continued to live in the family house almost to her death in 2005. Honorata moved to Saratov in Russia to live with her daughter Varya, who had married a Russian soldier. Honorata also died in 2005.

So that is the end of my story, except...

Shortly before my dad died he was visiting his old friend Bruno Gordianiek in Stoke. Both were old and frail. The anti-communist revolution had taken place a few years before, the Soviet Union no longer existed, and their home village of Szwakszty was a part of the newly independent Republic of Belarus. Bruno had been able to make contact with his family in Szwakszty and was planning a visit to his former home. During his correspondence he was able to confirm that my dad's sister Maria was still alive and living in the village. Sadly my dad was to die before he could make any communication, but my brother Lawrence wrote in English and miraculously he received a very brief letter of reply from Maria, also in English.

It was decided that the remainder of my dad's ashes should be returned to his home village, so Lawrence, together with my sister Christine, brother Michael and his wife chelle, together with my mother drove via Germany and Poland to Belarus where they managed to find the village of Szwakszty, where Maria and Valera came running down the lane to greet them. Sadly I wasn't able to make the trip as my wife Alison had just given birth to our fourth child, but my dad's ashes completed the final stage of his long journey and were spread on the grave of his father in the Catholic cemetery on the road between his village, Szwakszty, and the town of Naroch (Kobylnik) near to the Catholic Andreevsky church. It was the same church that my dad attended as a child; it had avoided destruction in two world wars and been ever present since 1463.

By the summer of 2004 the twentieth century had started to make communications slightly easier, even for Belarus, and as my family were old enough we made the necessary arrangements to travel to Belarus. Independent of the Soviet Union and with no real ties to the West, it was still very bureaucratic; letters of invitation and special health certificates were required before a visa was issued.

We flew to the Lithuanian capital of Vilnius, the city my dad had known as Wilno, and then took the Vilnius–Minsk train across the border to Molodechno. Even though the town had been ravaged by war and had largely been rebuilt, the train station had changed little since the 1940s. Interestingly and coincidentally, it was the very same station that my dad was deported from and the last place he would have stood on Polish soil in the first stage of his journey into exile, while for me it was the first place I arrived on my journey into his past, though it was now Belarus and not Poland.

We were collected by family and driven the short distance to Vileyka, where my uncle Valera still lives. He never knew my father, and despite being a generation removed from my dad he did spookily have some very similar mannerisms. Even though he spoke no English (only Russian), his voice was amazingly similar to my dads.

Vileyka was largely rebuilt after the war but the court house where my dad was initially tried and sentenced is still there. It is now a police station and community sports hall, where I had to register with the local police as was the requirement of my visa. I was also invited with my brother Lawrence and son Owain to play football with a group of local boys. I don't think they or the adult bystanders could quite believe such fat old men running around kicking a ball!

As a memorial to this great sporting event of international football, pre-dating the English national football team's successful 2010 World Cup qualifying campaign against Belarus by several years, we were honoured with a certificate of commemoration.

Adjacent to the police station on 1 May Street is Vileyka's specialist cancer hospital. This featureless, old, grey building is also a survivor of the devastation of the Second World War. Formerly it had been the dreaded Vileyka Tiurma, the NKVD's prison, the location of brutal murders and repressive prisoner subjugation. It is where my dad was held between his arrest and his deportation. Sadly, I wasn't allowed inside but even now it is a frighteningly austere and macabre building which does nothing to belie its gruesome past.

Maria, my father's sister, still lived near to Naroch, the town previously known as Kobylnik. She had lived in the Pleszak family home for nearly all her life; she was there when my dad was taken away and there when her two younger brothers were taken. I was privileged and honoured that my long-lost family were still there to greet me and my family and make us so welcome.

The house itself had changed little since my dad lived there. It still had no runnin water and a rather unreliable electricity supply; the only concession to the twenty-firs century was a telephone (but it didn't work). The inside was almost as it had been sixty years before. There was a kitchen area and a food store and the rest of the house was a single large room separated by rugs hung from the ceiling. Outside there was a small vegetable plot, a well and a toilet.

Valera knew nothing about my dad, and Maria, always tearful, gave us a few insights into his early life, but couldn't answer the question as to why he was ever taken away by the NKVD; she just didn't know.

While there we were able to experience the pleasure of the *banya*. I now know the Russian expression 'As happy as if just coming from the banya' is surely true. My kids, like myself, growing up in the west are used to hot baths and showers; occasionally when on holiday we use a sauna, but a traditional Russian *banya* was an experience so far denied us. We used the communal village *banya* (Баня). It was a primitive affair in a small wooden building towards the edge of the village. The wood fire was stoked up and first to go were the men: myself, my brother Lawrence, sons Owain, Oscar, and Henry and our driver Henardzi (Gena) Tsikhonchanka. We undressed in the small *predbannik* (предбанник) and hung our clothes before making our way into the small, dimly lit and smoky washing room. The heat was intense. I, presumably because I was the most senior member of the party, was invited by Gena to lie on my back on the top wooden bunk. Gena gave me a rather grubby cloth cap that looked like a crocheted tea cosy, which appeared to serve no other purpose than to make me, otherwise completely naked, look utterly ridiculous.

Anyway, I lay there, cap in place, with my bemused sons looking on, while Gena produced a series of dried birch switches and began to flagellate me from my neck down. I have to say it felt rather pleasant, and as he moved within striking distance of my nether regions, he gently cupped his hand over my family jewels, and in very poor English said, 'Is ok?' What could I do? As he continued with his hand firmly in place, one of my startled sons exclaimed, 'He's holding his knob!'

After a while I attempted humour in my very poor Russian; 'лучше чем моя жена' (better than my wife), at which Gena burst into hysterical laughter, so much so that in the oppressive atmosphere he started gasping violently for breath and we, completely naked, had to carry him outside to get some cooler air. After a while he was composed enough to resume. I felt great for the beating and made way for my eldest son Owain, who as he climbed up into position to lay on his back stated indignantly, 'I'll hold my own knob thanks.' I didn't need to attempt to translate that.

After we had all taken turns on the top bunk, with my sons using I suspect a little too much vigour in the beating of their brothers, we finished with a thorough wash from a barrel of scalding-hot water heated from the fire. When we had finished, Alison, my daughter Rose, who was ten years old at the time, my sister Christine, and our translator Elena took their turn. Rose looked on concerned as Elena whacked her mother with what looked like an old stick. When it came to her turn she politely refused until Elena stepped out of the *banya* then said to Alison, 'OK, do me.'

was a magical experience and walking back from the *banya* we did indeed feel happy exhilarated. The old expression was true. However, the story of our *banya* is now ost fabled in my house; it seems to get brought up at any gathering that includes any ember of our family and I am made the object of ridicule. I don't care; I wouldn't have issed it for the world.

The cap, though, did confuse me; I wasn't sure why I needed to wear it. I looked it up on the internet, and apparently a woollen or felt cap is a recommendation, particularly to those not experienced in the *banya*, to keep the head from overheating!

Near to my dad's village was (the larger) Lake Szwakszty, where he told me he used to go fishing as a boy. His stories of the quantity and size of the fish in the clear lake were legendary. My Belarusian family members and their friends confirmed that the lake was abundant in many types of edible fish and because it was so isolated it wasn't ever overfished. We accepted an invite to go fishing, and Lawrence and Owain as keen anglers led the party. Off they went in two boats that looked like they hadn't been used since my dad had lived there. After bailing them out they quickly disappeared out of sight around a headland. Not being a fisher myself, I stayed behind.

Despite it being late summer, the weather was extremely wet and cold. For three hours they were out of sight. Alison and myself were paranoid, our mobile phones had no signal and we feared the worst. They eventually reappeared, wet and bedraggled, complete with a huge haul of fish. Well, actually one tiny tiddler.

So that is practically that; except for a document I recently received from the Memorial Foundation in Moscow. They had obtained information on my father from the Central Archive of the KGB in Belarus. It contained all the information about my father's arrest and amnesty I had previously seen, except for the short last paragraph, which simply read,

the conclusion of Office of Public Prosecutor of the Belarusian SSR on the 11th of October 1989 for M. W. Pleszak is to refuse a pardon (rehabilitation).

Perhaps this occurred on the fiftieth anniversary of his arrest, and while many of his contemporaries did receive a pardon, my father's crime must have been considered too serious. So maybe he had been involved in 'counter-revolutionary activities' after all.

Whilst I have discovered so much about my father during the writing of this book, I will sadly never know the answer.

The End

THE CHANGING FACE OF MIKOŁAJ PLESZAK

DISTANCES TRAVELLED AND CITIES PASSED THROUGH

City/Town	Local Name	Approx. distance	Distance travelled	Country
Szwakszty				Poland (Polska)
Kobylnik (Naroch)	Нароч	5 km south east of Szwakszty		Poland (Polska)
Stara Wilejka (Vileyka)	Вилейка	50 km south of Kobylnik	55 km	Poland (Polska)
Maladzyechna (Molodechno)	Молодéчно	25 km south of Stara Wilejka	80 km	Poland (Polska)
Minsk	Минск	60 km south of Aaladzyechna		Russia (Россúя)
Smolensk	Смоленск	350 km north-east of Minsk	495 km	Russia (Россúя)
Moscow	Смоленск	350 km north-east of Smolensk	495 km	Russia (Россúя)
Nizhny Novgorod	Нúжний Нóвгород (Гóрький)	550 km north-east of Moscow	1,395 km	Russia (Россúя)
Kazan	Казáнь	450 km south-east of Nizhny Novgorod	1,845 km	Tatarstan (Татарстан)
Yekaterinburg (Sverdlovsk)	Екатеринбýрг (Свердловск)	800 km north-east of Kazan	2,645 km	Russia (Россúя)
Omsk	Омск	800 km south-east of Yekaterinburg	3,445 km	Russia (Россúя)
Novosibirsk	Новосибúрск	700 km east of Omsk	4,145 km	Russia (Россúя)
Krasnoyarsk	Красноярск	800 km north-east of Novosibirsk	4,945 km	Russia (Россúя)
Irkutsk	Иркýтск	1,100 km south-east of Krasnoyarsk	6,045 km	Russia (Россúя)
Skovorodino	Сковородино	2,150 km north-east of Irkutsk	8,195 km	Russia (Россúя)

arovsk	Хабáровск	1,200 km south-east of Skovorodino	9,395 km	Russia (Россия)
odka	Нахóдка	750 km south-west of Khabarovsk	10,145 km	Russia (Россия)
agayevo	Нагаево	3,100 km north-east of Nakhodka	13,245 km	Russia (Россия)
Duskanya	Дусканья	405 km north-west of Nagayevo	13,650 km	Russia (Россия)
Magadan	Магадáн	400 km south-east of Duskanya	14,050 km	Russia (Россия)
Vladivostok	Владивостóк	3,200 km south-west of Magadan	17,250km	Russia (Россия)
Omsk	Омск	6,620 km north-west of Vladivostok	23,870 km	Russia (Россия)
Orsk	Орск	1,200 km south-west of Omsk	25,070 km	Russia (Россия)
Orenburg (Chkalov)	Оренбýрг (Чкáлов)	250 km north-west of Orsk	25,320 km	Russia (Россия)
Buzuluk	Бузулýк			Russia (Россия)
Aktobe (Aktyubinsk)	Актюбинск	600 km south-east of Orenburg	25,920 km	Kazakhstan
Aralsk	Аральск	550km south-east of Aktobe	26,470 km	Kazakhstan
Hazrat-e Turkestan	Туркістан	700 km south-east of Aralsk	27,170 km	Kazakhstan
Samarkand	Самарканд	600 km south-east of Hazrat-e-Turkestan	27,770 km	Uzbekistan
Bukhara	Бухара	250 km west of Samarkand	28,020 km	Uzbekistan
Shakhrisabz	Шахрисабз	250 km south-east of Bukhara	28,270 km	Uzbekistan
Bukhara	Бухара	250 km north-west of Shakhrisabz	28,520 km	Uzbekistan
Ashgabat	Ашхабад	700 km south-west of Bukhara	29,220 km	Turkmenistan
Türkmenbaşy (Krasnovodsk)	Türkmenbaşy (Красноводск)	550 km north-west of Ashgabat	29,770 km	Turkmenistan
Bandar-e Anzali	بندر انزلی	500 km south west of Türkmenbaşy	30,270 km	Iran (Persia)
Khanaqin	خانقين	800 km south-west of Bandar-e Anzali	31,070 km	Iraq

Mosul	لصوملا	500 km north-west of Khanaqin	31,570 km	Iraq
Jaffa	أفآي	1,300 km south-west of Mosul	32,870 km	Israel (Palestine)
Cairo	ةرهاقل	400 km south-west of Jaffa	33,270 km	Egypt
Alexandria	هيردنكس	200 km north-west of Cairo	33,470 km	Egypt
Taranto		1,600 km north-west of Alexandria	35,070 km	Italy
Cassino		450 km north-west of Taranto	35,520 km	Italy
Ancona		300 km north-west of Cassino	35,820 km	Italy
Bologna		225 km north-west of Ancona	36,045 km	Italy
Naples	Napoli	550 km south-east of Bologna	36,595 km	Italy
Liverpool		4,400 km north-west of Naples	40,995 km	Italy
York		150 km north-east of Liverpool	41,145 km	England
Barnsley		60 km south-west of York	42,205 km	England
Manchester		50 km south-west of Barnsley	41,225 km	England
Denton		10 km east of Manchester	41,265 km	England
Glossop		12 km east of Denton	41,227 km	England
Szwatszky		2,000 km north-east of Glossop	43,227 km	Belarus

GULAG GLOSSARY

Article 58	Soviet criminal code used as the 'legal' basis for much of their political repression.
Balanda	Watery soup supplied to prisoners.
Banya	(баня) A traditional Russian steam bath.
Bolshevik	'Majority' and most powerful faction of the Marxist Russian Revolutionary Party that led the Revolution of 1917 to form the Soviet Union.
Bushlat	A long-sleeved jacket made of wadding.
Cheka	ЧК – чрезвычайная комиссия was the first of a succession of Soviet state security organisations. Formed by Lenin in 1917.
Ch-te-zed	Rudimentary shoes made from old rubber tyres. Named after the Chelyabinsk Tractor Zavod (Chelyabinsk Tractor Factory).
Collectivisation	Soviet policy under Stalin between 1928 and 1940 to consolidate individual land and labour into collective forms known as *kolkhoz*.
Concentration Camp	Camps used for the 'concentration' of large numbers of prisoners, now usually used to refer to the Nazi camps used to collect prisoners for execution.
Conveyor	Nights of repeated interrogation used to force a confession.
Dalstroy	(Дальстрой) The organisation originally set up to manage road construction, mining and all projects involving forced labour in the Soviet Far East. Its full name was the 'State Trust for Road and Industrial Construction it the Upper Kolyma Area' (Государственный трест по дорожному и промышленному строительству в районе Верхней Колымы – Дальстрой).
Decembrist	Russian aristocrat who staged an anti-Tsarist rebellion in 1825.
Dokhodilovka	A hard labour camp where the mortality rate was high.
Dokhodyaga	A prisoner who was about to die. A goner.
Etap	A general term used for the transport or movement of prisoners.
Feldsher	Camp medical assistant.
FSB	Federal Security Service (ФСБ, Федеральная служба безопасности – Federalnaya Sluzhba Bezopasnosti). The domestic state security agency of the Russian Federation created from the KGB on the dissolution of the Soviet Union.
Fufakaya	Warm, quilted coat.

GPU	Gosudarstvennoye Politicheskoye Upravlenie (ГПУ Государство Политическое Управление). Secret police of the Soviet Union. Fc from the Cheka in 1922.
Grashdanin	(Гражданин) Really means citizen. Soviet term for the general pu who were not members of the Communist Party.
Great Terror	Stalinist purges of the late 1930s.
Gulag	(ГУЛАГ) Acronym for the name of the Soviet government agency responsible for managing and administering the labour camps – the NKVD's Главное Управление Исправительно-Трудовых Лагерей и колоний (or transliterated into English, Glavnoye Upravleniye Ispravitel'no-Trudovykh Lagerey i Koloniy – the Chief Administration of Corrective Labour Camps and Colonies). Widely used to describe any camp used in the Soviet repressive system.
Isolator	(изолятор) Solitary confinement punishment cells.
Kasha	Porridge.
KGB	КГБ Комитéт Госудáрственной Безопáсности). Committee for State Security. Formed from the MGB in 1953. Generally regarded as the supreme Soviet state security organisation.
Khvoya	A foul-tasting drink made from the extract of pine needles. Supposed to combat scurvy.
Kipiatok	Warm or hot water.
Kolkhoz	(колхóз) Collective farm.
Kotelok	Literally a kettle but was actually used for any can, bowl or pot that could be used for soup or drinks.
Kulak	Rich peasants.
Laptys	Hand-made shoes from any available material.
Makhorka	Low-quality tobacco favoured by prisoners.
Mastirka	Self-inflicted infection.
MGB	Ministerstvo Gosudarstvennoi Bezopasnosti (Мгб Министерство государственной безопасности). The Ministry of State Security and Soviet secret police agency. Created from the NKVD in 1946.
Menshevik	'Minority' faction of the Marxist Russian Revolutionary Party made illegal and persecuted after 1921.
NKVD	Narodny Komissariat Vnutrennikh Del (НКВД, Народный комиссариат внутренних дел). The People's Commissariat for Internal Affairs was the leading secret police organisation of the Soviet Union. Created in 1934 from the OGPU. Sometimes known as the Organy or simply 'The Organ'.
Norm	A food ration allocated for work tasks completed.
OGPU	Joint State Political Directorate – Ob'edinennoe Gosudarstvennoe Politicheskoe Upravlenie (ОГПУ – Объединённое государственное политическое управление) created in 1923 from the GPU. Responsible for the creation of the gulag system and persecution of the Russian Orthodox Church and other religious organisations.

(пайка)	Bread ration (usually low-quality).
⁣n	Ringleader of a group of *urkas*.
⁣ha	Crude toilet facility for prisoners, usually nothing more than a barrel.
⁣gra	Nasty skin disorder brought on by the lack of vitamins, typically niacin (vitamin B3).
⁣erekur	A prison camp smoke break.
Politruk	Political officer of the Red Army.
Ponyatoy	A civilian who assisted the NKVD.
Posiolek	Work camps or settlements for families.
Poverka	Head count – roll call.
Predurok	High-ranking prisoner who worked for the administration systems.
Scurvy	Potentially fatal disease caused by a lack of vitamin C.
Shizo	шизо (штрафа изолятор) Penalty isolator (see isolator).
Shtetl	A small town with a large Jewish population in pre-Second World War Europe.
Shock worker	Exceptional workers, also known as Stakhanovites after Aleksei Stakhanov.
Shmon	Thorough personal search.
Stakhanovite	See shock worker.
Starosta	Camp elder or leader.
Stolypin	A converted train carriage for transporting prisoners. Slightly better than cattle trucks.
Stukach	An informer.
Taiga	Ecosystem characterised by dense confierous forests and harsh, changeable climates. Winters are very cold with only snowfall. Summers are warm, rainy and humid. The taiga is also known as the Boreal Forest Biome. Geographically just south of the Arctic tundra.
TFT	(Tyazoly fezichesky trud) The term for hard, physical work assigned to healthy prisoners on inspection for work.
Tovarisch	(товарищ) Comrade. Salutation to a member of the Communist Party.
Troika	A three-man committee.
Trotskyite	A follower of Trotsky.
Tufta	Cheating or fabricating information about work carried out to get more food allowance.
Tuftach	A prisoner who falsified his work, i.e. somebody who used *tufta*.
Tundra	Northernmost and coldest of all the ecosystems. Has frost-moulded landscapes, extremely low temperatures, little precipitation, poor nutrients and short growing seasons.
Urka	(Урка) Criminal prisoner.
Valenki	Boots made from felt.
Zek	Prisoner. (заключённый -zakloochnie) abbreviated to 'з/к' or Zek.
Zone/Zona	An outside area of a prison camp.

BIBLIOGRAPHY

Amis, Martin, *House of Meetings* (2006).

Anders, Władysław, *An Army in Exile* (1949).

Applebaum, Anne, *GULAG – A History of the Soviet Camps* (2003).

Association of the Families of the Borderland Settlers, *Stalin's Ethnic Cleansing in Eastern Poland: Tales of the Deported, 1940–1946* (2000).

Baghirov, Ayyub, *Kolyma – Off to the Unknown: Stalin's Notorious Prison Camps in Siberia* (2006).

Baldaev, Danzig, *Russian Criminal Tattoo* (3 vols) (2006).

Baldaev, Danzig, *Drawings from the Gulag* (2010).

Bardach, J. and K. Gleeson, *Man is Wolf to Man: Surviving Stalin's Gulag* (1998).

Bates, P. W., *Official History of New Zealand in the Second World War, 1939–45: Supply Company* (1955).

Bloch, Herbert, *The Bombardment of Monte Cassino* (1979).

Bollinger, Martin, *Stalin's Slave Ships* (2003).

Brodecki, B., Wawer, Z. and T. Kondracki, *The Poles on the Battlefronts of the Second World War* (2005).

Bron, Barwa I., *Wojsko Polskie 1939–1945* (1984).

Crosby, Ron, *Albaneta: Lost Opportunity at Cassino* (2007).

Conquest, Robert, *Kolyma: The Arctic Death Camps* (1978).

Conquest, Robert, *The Great Terror: A Reassessment* (2008).

Dziennika, Zolnierzow, *Monte Cassino: Battle of Six Nations* (1946).

Flemington, Richard, *Monte Cassino: They Came to a Monastery – The Final Battle* (1998).

Genocide and Research Centre of Lithuania, *Siberia: Mass Deportations from Lithuania to the USSR* (2004).

Ginzburg, Evgenia, *Into the Whirlwind* (1967).

Ginzburg, Evgenia, *Within the Whirlwind* (1979).

Gross, Jan, *Revolution from Abroad* (1988).

Hapgood, D. and D. Richardson, *Monte Cassino: The True Story of the Most Controversial Battle of the Second World War* (1984).

Jonkajtys-Luba, Grażyna, *Opowieść 02 Korpusie Polskim Generała Władysława Andersa* (2004).

Kizny, Tomasz, *GULAG: Life and Death Inside the Soviet Concentration Camps* (2004).

Komornicki (*et al.*), *Wojsko Polsie* (1984).

Kosicki, Piotr, *The Katyn Massacres of 1940* (2008).

Kowalski, Ludwik, *Hell on Earth: Brutality and Violence Under the Stalinist Regime* (2008).

Kowalski, Stanislaw, *Autobiography of Stanislaw J. Kowalski* (unpub.).

Kowalski, Stanislaw, *Kolyma: The Land of Gold and Death* (unpub.).

Kowalski, Stanislaw, *No Place to Call Home: The Memories of a Polish Survivor of the Soviet Gulag* (2009).

Kowalski, Stanislaw, *White Auschwitz of Kolyma* (unpub.).

Krakowiecki, Anatol, *Książka o Kołymie* (1950).

Krupa, Michael, *Shallow Graves in Siberia* (1995).

ki, Romuald, *My Story* (unpub.).

icz, Mieczyslaw and Ann Maitland-Chuwen (trans.), *Chronicles of Lake Narocz* (1945).

ński, Mieczysław, *Dzieje 2GO Korpusu* (1994).

lany, Fred, *Cassino: Portrait of a Battle* (1957).

,an, G. and W. A. Lasocki, *Soldier Bear* (1970).

Gregor, E. and C. Boorman, *Long Way Round: Chasing Shadows Across the World* (2005).

:urgrabia, Jerzy, *Symbole Wojskowe Polskich Sił Zbrojnych Na Zachodzie (1939–46)* (1990).

Murphy, *Official History of New Zealand in the Second World War, 1939–45: 2nd New Zealand Divisional Artillery* (1966).

Norlander, David, *Magadan and the Evolution of the Dal'stroi Bosses in the 1930s* (2001).

Parker, Matthew, *Monte Cassino: The Story of the Hardest-Fought Battle of World War Two* (2003).

Petrov, Vladimir and Mirra Ginsburg (trans.), *Soviet Gold: My Life as a Slave Labourer in the Siberian Mines* (1949).

Pleszak, Frank, 'Battle of the Mud – 1916': *The Unknown Battle of Lake Narocz* (in preparation).

Raynor, George, *Football Ambassador at Large* (1960).

Rybakov, Anatoli, *Children of the Arbat* (1987).

Shalamov, Varlam and John Glad (trans.), *Kolyma Tales* (1994).

Shifrin, Avraham, *The First Guidebook to Prisons and Concentration Camps of the Soviet Union* (1980).

Short, Michael, 'BBC People's War (An Archive of WWII Memories) – The Bevin Boy' (online). http://www.bbc.co.uk/ww2peopleswar/stories/40/a7735340.shtml.

Siemiński, Janusz, *Moja Kołyma* (1995).

Skulski, Roman Vladimir, *In the Soviet Union without Toilet Paper* (2007).

Solzhenitsyn, Alexander and Gillon Aitken (trans.), *One Day in the Life of Ivan Denisovich* (1971).

Szmagier, Krzysztof, *Generał Anders I Jego żołnierze* (1993).

Thubron, Colin, *In Siberia* (1999).

Topolski, Aleksander, *Without Vodka: Adventures in Wartime Russia* (2001).

Von Senger und Etterlin, Frido, *Neither Fear nor Hope: The Wartime Memoirs of the German Defender of Cassino* (1963).

Wańkowicz, Melchior, *Bitwa o Monte Cassino* (3 vols) (1945).

Waver, Zbigniew, *From Buzuluk to Monte Cassino* (2009).

Wenig, Larry, *From Nazi Inferno to Soviet Hell* (2000).

Zarod, Kazimierz, *Inside Stalin's Gulag* (1990).